A Prayer of John Calvin

"Heavenly Father, in your son, Jesus Christ, are hidden all the treasures of wisdom and knowledge. Enlighten our minds by your Holy Spirit and grant us that reverence and humility without which no one can understand your truth. Through the same Jesus Christ our Lord, Amen."

Christian Faith and Practice in the Modern World

Theology from an Evangelical Point of View

Edited by

Mark A. Noll *and* David F. Wells

WILLIAM B. EERDMANS PUBLISHING COMPANY
GRAND RAPIDS, MICHIGAN

To
Carl F. H. Henry

Copyright © 1988 by Wm. B. Eerdmans Publishing Co.
255 Jefferson Ave. S.E., Grand Rapids, Mich. 49503

Library of Congress Cataloging-in-Publication Data

Christian faith and practice in the modern world.

Includes bibliographies
1. Evangelicalism. 2. Theology, Doctrinal.
I. Noll, Mark A., 1946– . II. Wells, David F.
BR1640.C48   1988   230'.044   88-3635

ISBN 0-8028-0279-6

Contents

CONTENTS

PART III: CREATION AND ITS RESTORATION

Contributors

Donald Bloesch is professor of theology, University of Dubuque Theological Seminary, and author of the two-volume *Essentials of Evangelical Theology*, as well as of *The Future of Evangelical Christianity* and many other books. His Ph.D. is from the University of Chicago.

Klaus Bockmuehl, who studied in several German universities as well as the London School of Economics, completed the Th.D. from the University of Basel. He is professor of theology and ethics, Regent College, Vancouver, the author of *The Challenge of Marxism, Evangelicals and Social Ethics,* as well as a number of books in German.

C. Stephen Evans (Ph.D. Yale) is professor of philosophy and curator of the Hong Kierkegaard Library at St. Olaf College. He has written *Kierkegaard's Fragments and Postscripts: The Religious Philosophy of Johannes Climacus, Preserving the Person: A Look at the Human Sciences,* and many other essays in philosophy and psychology.

Gabriel Fackre is Abbot Professor of Christian Theology at Andover Newton Theological School. He is the author of *The Christian Story, The Promise of Reinhold Niebuhr,* and *The Religious Right and Christian Faith.* His Ph.D. is from the University of Chicago.

David Livingstone is Research Officer in Geography at the Queen's University of Belfast, where he did his doctoral work. He is the editor of the *Journal of the Irish Christian Study Centre* and author of *Nathaniel Southgate Shaler and the Culture of American Science* and *Darwin's Forgotten Defenders: The Encounter between Evangelical Theology and Evolutionary Thought.*

Paul Marshall is vice-president and senior member in political theory at the Institute for Christian Studies in Toronto. His academic training was in the United Kingdom and Canada (Ph.D. York). He is the author of *Human Rights Theories in Christian Perspective* and *Thine is the Kingdom: A Biblical Perspective on the Nature of Politics and Government Today.*

Thomas V. Morris, who did his doctoral work at Yale in religion and philosophy, is the author of *Understanding Identity Statements* and *The Logic of God Incarnate.* He teaches philosophy at the University of Notre Dame.

Richard Mouw was trained in Canada and the United States and completed doctoral studies at the University of Chicago. He has been a member of the National Council of Churches' commission on Faith and Order. He teaches theological ethics at Fuller Theological Seminary and is the author of *Called to Worldly Holiness, When Kings Come Marching In: Isaiah and the New Jerusalem,* and *Politics and the Biblical Drama.*

Mark Noll teaches history at Wheaton College. He completed the Ph.D. at Vanderbilt University, has written *Between Faith and Criticism: Evangelical Biblical Study in the United States since 1880,* and edited *The Bible in America.*

J. I. Packer (D.Phil. Oxford) is professor of historical and systematic theology at Regent College, Vancouver. He is the author of *"Fundamentalism" and the Word of God, Knowing God, Beyond the Battle for the Bible,* and many other works on theology and the religious life.

Clark Pinnock did his Ph.D. at the University of Manchester in England. He is the author of *The Scripture Principle* and editor of *Grace Unlimited.* He is the founder of the North American Theological Students Fellowship and teaches theology at McMaster Divinity College, Ontario.

Cornelius Plantinga, Jr., is associate professor of systematic theology at Calvin Theological Seminary. He has written *A Place to Stand: A Reformed Study of Creeds and Confessions* and *Beyond Doubt: A Devotional Response to Questions of Faith.* His Ph.D. is from Princeton Theological Seminary.

John Stott (M.A. Cambridge, D.D. Oxford) is rector emeritus of All Souls Church, London, and president of the London Institute for Contemporary Christianity. He is a widely traveled biblical expositor who has written *Your Mind Matters, Between Two Worlds: The Art of*

Preaching in the Twentieth Century, Basic Christianity, and many other books.

Anthony Thiselton was reader in New Testament at Sheffield University in England, where he received his Ph.D., until recently becoming the principal of St. John's College, Durham. He is the author of *The Two Horizons: New Testament Hermeneutics and Philosophical Description,* as well as of other works in the theory and practice of textual interpretation.

David Wells (Ph.D. University of Manchester, England) is the Andrew Mutch Professor of Historical and Systematic Theology at Gordon-Conwell Theological Seminary. He has written *The Person of Christ* and *The Search for Salvation* and was coordinating editor of *Eerdmans Handbook to Christianity in America.*

Acknowledgments

The chapters of this book were first presented at a conference on "Christian Theology in a Post-Christian World," held March 20-22, 1985, at the Billy Graham Center of Wheaton College. The editors would like to thank all who attended this meeting, especially those who prepared comments our authors have used in the revision of their work for publication: William Barker, Stephen Board, William Dyrness, John Frame, Stephen Franklin, Stan Gaede, Vernon Grounds, Arthur Holmes, Kenneth Kantzer, George Marsden, Ronald Nash, Vern Poythress, Kenneth Shipps, James Sire, and Mary Stewart Van Leeuwen.

The editors also wish to express their gratitude to the Lilly Endowment of Indianapolis for its financial support of the conference sponsor, Wheaton's Institute for the Study of American Evangelicals, and to Dr. Robert Lynn of the Lilly Endowment for his many-faceted encouragement of this Institute.

Thanks are due as well to Nathan Hatch and J. I. Packer for assistance in planning the conference and this book; to Joel Carpenter for expert management in his capacity as coordinator of the Institute for the Study of American Evangelicals; to John Stackhouse for stenographic service during the conference; to Brenda Buchweitz and Larry Snyder for efficient handling of many details; to Mrs. Buchweitz, Ronald Frank, and Beatrice Horne for typing the manuscript; and to Jane Wells and Maggie Noll for cheerful persistence in good works.

Introduction: Modern Evangelicalism

Mark A. Noll and David F. Wells

Events of recent decades have made it increasingly clear that the process of "modernization" and the practice of religion are not automatically antithetical. While organized religion languishes in some of the most developed parts of the world, it also flourishes in other places where, following a secular model of modernization, one might least expect to find it. Religious practice in the United States, for example, seems every bit as vigorous as fifty years ago, in spite of unprecedented economic growth, rampant consumerism, high-order rationalization of sociopolitical life, and extraordinary legal protection for those who want to insulate themselves from religion.[1] At least some Marxist countries find themselves in the embarrassing position of devoting more attention to resurgent Christianity and other religions than to promoting the new socialist person. And in developing countries, heightened aspirations for economic growth and social reorganization are as likely to be accompanied by the renewal of religion as by its decline.[2]

The enduring vitality of religious practice, in other words, is making a greater impression upon political pundits, social planners, and the other soothsayers of our age. Not as clear, however, is the status of religious reflection. Religious practices often seem so otherworldly, bizarre, fanatical, or irrational—especially to denizens of Western universities where a fiction of moral neutrality, if not an outright hostility to inherited faith, has prevailed for over a century—that it is hard to imagine such behavior reflecting a coherent intellectual pattern. Religious believers, furthermore, often seem so unconcerned about the major interpreters of modern consciousness—Kant, Marx, Darwin, Weber, Freud, Durkheim, Einstein, Sartre, Foucault, and many more—that they in effect rule themselves out of active participation in the established marketplace of ideas. Thus, while even the universities no longer ignore the persistence of traditional religious behavior, the place of traditional religious thought is less certain.

The situation for religion generally is very much the situation for Christianity in particular, especially its evangelical manifestations. In the United States only someone who has slept through the last several presidential elections, turned a deaf ear to the national debate on abortion, and overlooked the host of controversies concerning religion in the public schools could miss the imposing presence of theologically conservative Christians. Activities by like-minded believers in Canada, Britain, and the continent have not been noticed as widely, but are by no means absent.[3] Once again, however, this activity raises questions about the character of thought, of coherent reflection. What do such religious conservatives believe? How do they relate their beliefs to movements of modern thought as well as to the vicissitudes of modern life? Can they sustain meaningful interaction with both the contemporary world and the traditions of their faith? Is such thinking true? Useful? Intellectually responsible?

The purpose of this book is to offer answers for these questions from one segment of theologically conservative Protestantism. Its authors are "evangelicals." They affirm that traditional Christian teachings about the Trinity, the Bible, and the Christian life are relevant in the modern world, as they have been relevant throughout all of human history. At the same time, these authors are neither obscurantists nor anti-intellectuals. They believe that Christian scholars need to be heard in the modern world even as they have sought to recognize that the experiences of modernity, its triumphs and its tragedies, must ever be on the mind of the church.

In short, this is a book about Christian faith and modern life. It is predicated on the conviction that "conservative" Christians need to take seriously the contemporary forms of the great questions—about existence, the nature of the person, and human destiny. At the same time, however, its authors believe that God has revealed himself uniquely through Christ and through the work of the Holy Spirit, who produced the written Scriptures, and that such revelation deserves attention, respect, and obedience. The essays that make up this book are therefore intended as contributions both to the discipline of theology and to the ongoing dialogue between Christianity and modern thought.

THE PROBLEM OF DEFINITION

Such an effort must of necessity begin by defining *evangelical,* a plastic term put to use in several legitimate ways. We can summarize the most important of these as follows:

1. *Evangelical* may designate the Protestant Reformation generally, or, more particularly, the Lutheran churches that emerged from the sixteenth-century upheavals. Luther and his earliest followers preferred the label "evangelical" to any partisan designation because it expressed the centrality of "the gospel of Christ" for their activity.[4] These early "evangelicals" also insisted that the Scriptures provided the normative statement of the gospel, and that top-heavy ecclesiastical structures often deprived ordinary believers of their due rights and responsibilities as servants of Christ.

2. In English-speaking lands *evangelical* is often linked with the revival movements of the eighteenth century. Thus, John Wesley in Great Britain, Jonathan Edwards in America, George Whitefield who preached on both sides of the Atlantic, as well as the Pietists of Germany, all led movements that stressed conversion, piety of life, energetic witness-bearing, and reform of social evil. In America these movements inspired a revival tradition that, despite many internal adjustments, has remained identifiable to this day. The line of popular evangelists stretching from Edwards in the eighteenth century, through Charles Grandison Finney and Dwight L. Moody in the nineteenth, to Billy Graham in the twentieth represents not so much an undeviating set of practices and beliefs as a continuing evangelical tradition.

In Great Britain, the eighteenth-century revivals led to a distinctly evangelical, or low-church, party within the Church of England and to the renewal of several dissenting, or nonconformist, denominations outside of the established church. Together these heirs of the evangelical revival emphasized lay initiative, active social involvement, evangelistic preaching, and strenuous piety. In large measure they were responsible for the anomalies as well as the accomplishments of Britain's Victorian morality.[5]

3. In more recent decades some have used the term *evangelical* as a catchall for theologically conservative Protestants of whatever heritage. In this usage the term is open also to Roman Catholics, especially those stressing the extraordinary gifts of the Holy Spirit. The Johns Hopkins historian Timothy L. Smith has used two apt phrases to describe these groups—they are an evangelical "mosaic" or even "kaleidescope" because of the diverse cultural, social, and political tendencies found among believers in a relatively common faith.[6] That faith shares a common commitment to the Bible, a belief in salvation by faith in Christ, a desire for holiness of life, and some form of concern for righteousness in the world more largely. Its adherents may be found in many different groups: Lutherans, Pente-

costals, Baptists of all shades and opinions, Presbyterians in several denominations, Wesleyan Methodists, Holiness denominations, independents rural and urban, black and white, Churches of Christ, Mennonites, Brethren, and many more.

4. Finally, it is also possible to use the term narrowly to describe what historian George Marsden has recently called an "evangelical denomination."[7] In this usage, evangelicals are those who use this label to identify themselves in preference to any other denominational or traditional designation. In North America this more narrowly defined group is joined together through a common network of theological seminaries (e.g., Gordon-Conwell near Boston, Trinity near Chicago, Asbury in Kentucky, Regent College in Vancouver, or Fuller in Pasadena), publications (like *Christianity Today*), and ad hoc evangelicalistic and social agencies (e.g., the Billy Graham Evangelistic Association or World Vision). Postfundamentalists, individuals who have moved beyond the confrontational style of revivalistic Protestantism to more civil forms of theological conservatism, have been the most active participants in this group. Yet the boundaries between this identifiable evangelical network and the larger worlds of theologically conservative Protestantism are fluid enough to permit a great deal of interchange.

The authors of this book sustain some connection with each of these various senses of the term *evangelical*. They value the heritage of the Reformation. Most come from ecclesiastical bodies that are the heirs of the eighteenth-century revivals. Many are part of "the evangelical denomination" through vocational, educational, or personal connections. And all fit easily within the umbrella of the more generic evangelicalism.

THE STANDPOINT OF THIS BOOK

More specifically, however, the essays that make up this book reflect a distinct intellectual emphasis and a distinct history. They come from authors who share a particular concern for Christian thinking in modern life and who are the product of an identifiable series of historical developments. In turn, this common concern and the shared history give the volume its cohesion.

The conceptual unity of the book arises from its authors' vision of the Christian intellectual task. This is a vision, first of all, that is shaped by the Ecumenical Creeds and by classical Protestantism, but it is also one influenced self-consciously by a determination to engage the modern world. The formative creeds of the early church provide the foundation for the Christian reflection presented here. The authors believe in the Trinitarian faith of the Apostles' Creed. They believe, in terms set out in the Nicene Creed (325/381 A.D.) and the Definition of Chalcedon (451), that Jesus Christ, fully human and fully divine, is the redeemer of the lost. In these regards the evangelical Protestants of this book differ hardly at all from traditional Roman Catholic and Eastern Orthodox believers who also embrace these foundational expressions of Christian faith.

The book's authors, however, appropriate these basic Christian teachings in a Protestant shape. For them, the Bible offers unique and ultimate authority. They may be uneasy with the popular slogan, "the Bible alone," just as the Reformers were, for they recognize the religious value of ecclesiastical tradition, the exercise of reason, and the experience of individual spirituality. Yet such authorities are always secondary influences, always under the correcting presence of Scripture. The authors would likewise reserve an important place for church authority, but affirm as Protestants that God's grace in Christ is accessible to every person through a variety of means: preaching, prayer, private Bible reading, Christian fellowship, and the sacraments or ordinances. Church authorities exist as servants of these gifts, not as their masters. Many of the authors of this book would even consider the great Protestant confessions—whether the Thirty-Nine Articles of the Church of England, the Heidelberg Catechism of the German and Dutch Reformed Churches, or the Westminster Confession of the Presbyterians—to be compelling summaries of the Christian faith still useful today as secondary norms after Scripture itself.

Since the book's authors come mostly from Reformed, Anglican, and Baptist communions their Protestantism is somewhat different from that of other evangelical bodies—for example, Lutheran, Pentecostal, Wesleyan, Anabaptist, or Restorationist. These too are legitimate expressions of evangelical faith, and the book would accomplish one of its goals if it encouraged other such evangelical groups to undertake similar enterprises of a cooperative nature.

Yet more is at stake in these pages than a mere recitation of themes from one variety of classical Protestantism. The contributors intend their essays also to be statements about the modern world, and that in two senses. On the one hand, they value the contributions of modern thought. On the other hand, they are self-consciously anti-modernist.

5

The modernity of these pieces resides in their frank, and sometimes fulsome, employment of contemporary thought. Several of the essays, in fact, are premised upon the usefulness of "secular" thinking for Christian reflection. Thus, Anthony Thiselton's assessment of interpretive theory, Tom Morris's attempt to judge the rationality of the Christian claim to revelation, David Livingstone's evaluation of the relationship between science and religion, and David Wells's consideration of the future all draw explicitly on the insights of nonbelievers to construct a Christian stance on a particular issue. Most of the other essays do the same, if in less obvious ways. We hope that the result is a presentation of the Christian faith that is worldly-wise without being worldly. Christians of all types have long held doctrines of "common grace" or "general revelation" that acknowledge the abilities of humanity in general, and not just Christians, to understand important truths about the world. In spite of these affirmations, theologically conservative Protestants in recent decades have not been quick to act on this belief. These essays seek to correct that sectarian failing.

At the same time, however, the essays are also self-consciously antimodernist. Their authors are committed to the fundamentally ancient propositions that the universe is "open" and that a loving and all-powerful God exists and has made himself known. Dominant assumptions of the modern age, like materialism or naturalism, are to them intellectual scandals. In addition, they are "realists" in believing that the world enjoys an existence apart from its perception by humans, that essence precedes existence, and that mind is capable of perceiving reality beyond itself with at least some accuracy. As much as they have benefited from the work of recent savants, they do not believe that mind is the determining element of ontology or ethics, that history writing is thoroughly relative to the perspective of the historian, that scientific knowledge depends entirely upon social structure, that modern consciousness has rendered obsolete the perceptions and judgments of bygone centuries, that class-identity defines moral judgment, or that psychological accounts provide ultimate explanations for human actions or existence.

The distinctive thing about the antimodernism of these essays is its self-consciousness. These are not merely intuitive judgments, but conclusions derived carefully, step-by-step, as implications of Christian commitment. This book is not primarily an apology for Christian faith, nor is it concerned with a triumphalist proclamation of Christianity. It is rather a patient effort to think through major questions of

6

Christian belief in relation to significant theories and compelling practical needs of the modern world, and to do so with as few intellectual shortcuts as possible. We hope, in other words, to play the game with no stacked deck, no phony deals, and no tricks up our sleeves.

As creedal Christians and confessional Protestants seeking meaningful engagement with the twentieth century, we are attempting what others—like the German Lutheran Helmut Thielicke, the Swiss Reformed Karl Barth, or the French jurist Jacques Ellul—have attempted much more comprehensively. Our efforts resemble theirs in certain theological particulars and differ in others, as will be clear from the individual essays. The clearest way to show the specific provenance of this book, however, is not in cataloging theological debts and differences, but in tracing the history that has resulted in the conjunction of interests represented in its pages.

AN AMERICAN-BRITISH-CONFESSIONAL COALITION

The authors of these essays are members of a loose coalition made up of American postfundamentalists, British evangelicals, and European-American confessionalists. While the United States has been the primary mixing pot for these interests, the coalition itself has had widespread influence in Canada and Great Britain, as well as some significance for the continent and the rest of the world. Four parallel developments in the 1930s and 1940s lay behind the emergence of this coalition. Although the individual stories are different, in each case the movement was toward greater balance between active piety and intellectual sophistication. And each story manifests growing concern for a common evangelicalism, less for sectarian distinctives.

The first and most dramatic story was the emergence within American fundamentalism of younger leaders seeking an intellectually responsible expression of the Christian faith. During the 1920s a series of reversals had seemed to signal the end of evangelical intellectual vitality in the United States.[8] Baptists and Presbyterians in the North reorganized their denominations to diminish the influence of theological conservatives. The Scopes Trial of 1925, where William Jennings Bryan and Clarence Darrow dueled over evolution and the Bible, lent support to an equation of conservative Protestantism with cultural backwardness, intellectual naiveté, and religious provincialism. The failure of prohibition and the eventual collapse of the American economy in the 1930s created further uncertainties among the nation's moral conservatives. As a consequence it became all too easy for fundamentalists to forsake public life, and the life of the mind, in order to tend their own separated vineyards.[9] Before too long, however, ambitious young fundamentalists were finding sectarianism and separation an obstruction to Christian faith and practice. Harold John Ockenga (1905–1985), at various times the president of Fuller and Gordon-Conwell seminaries, called for a "new evangelicalism" that could value scholarship and take an active interest in society while maintaining traditional Protestant orthodoxy. Edward John Carnell (1919–1967) was only one of many who sought training at the nation's best graduate schools. After attending evangelical institutions, he completed doctorates at both Harvard and Boston University before entering into a career of writing and teaching at the new Fuller Theological Seminary in California. Carl F. H. Henry (b. 1913), who expressed his concern for an intellectually responsible evangelicalism through teaching at Fuller and as the founding editor of *Christianity Today* (1956), called fundamentalists to a new engagement with American society and a new concern for theological reflection. Together these and like-minded leaders soon spoke for a significant number of theological conservatives who valued responsible education and an intellectually responsible expression of the faith.[10]

The second story concerns theological conservatives who never became fundamentalists. The major American denominations always contained individuals who valued the traditional confessions and sought to exert a leavening restraint on the drift toward theological modernism that has characterized many groups in the twentieth century. For these individuals the significant development was finding "fundamentalists" who, like themselves, possessed confidence in a traditional understanding of Scripture, but who also valued well-considered theological argumentation. As tumult from the fundamentalist-modernist wars receded into the historical background, it became easier for these theological conservatives to reestablish lines of contact with evangelicals outside of their denominations.

The third story was one of assimilation. By the early twentieth century, European Protestants with strong attachment to confessions from the Reformation era had established significant communities in America. The largest of these were Lutheran. In spite of efforts by leaders like Carl Henry, however, connections between America's "new evangelicals" and the Lutherans have always remained somewhat tenuous.[11] The situation was different with a smaller group of European confessionalists, the Dutch Reformed. During the 1930s and 1940s, members of the Christian Reformed Church, the denomination representing the most recent immigration from Holland, continued the process of Americanization that had started in earnest during World War I. Evangelicals offered these Dutch Reformed an important reference point as they moved closer to American ways. The Dutch, like the American evangelicals, confessed reliance in the Scriptures and greatly valued practical spirituality. Although their standards of piety bore the impress of Europe (drinking and smoking were never automatically sinful as they were for many American evangelicals), they could appreciate the spirituality of American pietists. As they grew closer to evangelical networks, the Dutch Reformed offered their American counterparts a heritage of serious academic work and experienced philosophical reasoning. In their native Holland, these Dutch Reformed had founded a major center of higher education at the end of the nineteenth century, the Free University of Amsterdam; they had made significant contributions to political theory and practice (their leader, Abraham Kuyper, was prime minister of the Netherlands from 1900 to 1905); and they took for granted a full Christian participation in artistic and cultural life.[12]

The most obvious link between these Dutch Reformed and American evangelicals came through their publishers. By the late 1940s, several firms in Grand Rapids, Michigan, a center of Dutch immigration, were publishing the books of Carl Henry, E. J. Carnell, and other American evangelicals. Especially the William B. Eerdmans Publishing Company was aggressively seeking new authors and markets from the world of American evangelicals.

Eerdmans also played an important part in drawing a fourth strand of evangelical renewal into the American picture. Beginning in the 1930s, a number of British evangelicals—from the Church of England as well as from dissenting denominations—united in efforts to extend an evangelical influence in the universities. The cradle for this effort was the British Inter-Varsity Fellowship (IVF); its nursemaids were graduate students and young professors convinced of the intellectual integrity of evangelical faith. Led by preachers like Martyn Lloyd-Jones, scholars like F. F. Bruce and David Wenham, and organizers like Douglas Johnson, these British evangelicals made significant progress in a relatively short time. Forceful yet dignified preaching missions to Oxford, Cambridge, and other universities established an evangelical presence and led to the conversion of under-graduates. By the end of the 1940s, the Theological Students Fellowship of IVF established Tyndale House in Cambridge to encourage evangelical study of the Scriptures, and soon thereafter evangelicals began to gain research positions in major British universities. The British Inter-Varsity Press published many products of this renewed evangelicalism, often with Eerdmans as a cosponsor or the American distributor. The printed word thus served as a medium linking British evangelicals to Americans of several varieties—postfundamentalists, mainline conservatives, and Americanizing confessionalists. In addition, by the 1950s, American evangelicals were regularly going across the Atlantic to pursue graduate work with scholars either holding a similar faith or open to its emphases at the British universities.[13]

This British connection served also as a conduit for establishing relations between Americans and evangelicals further afield. British evangelicals reached out to confessional Protestants on the continent, to the Commonwealth, and to mission efforts in Africa and Asia. Through these connections American evangelicals were drawn into even wider orbits.

The glue uniting these different strands of evangelical renewal came in many forms. Besides educational exchange carried on by private parties, notable individuals, projects, and institutions also made a contribution. The American evangelist, Billy Graham, was a contact point of nearly universal recognition. What he did on a large scale through popular evangelism to establish networks of evangelical interest, the work of British "missioners" to the universities, like Martin Lloyd-Jones or John Stott, accomplished among more strictly academic groups. Cooperative publishing ventures, like the *New Bible Commentary* and the *New Bible Dictionary* from British Inter-Varsity, Carl Henry's work at *Christianity Today*,[14] and several different projects at Eerdmans, drew evangelical scholars from both sides of the Atlantic into common labor. Eventually, other institutions, like the American InterVarsity Christian Fellowship, or the Lausanne Committee for World Evangelization, became arenas that strengthened cross-cultural evangelical ties.

The result has been the establishment of an evangelical network with certain well-fixed reference points in the United States, Great Britain, and Canada, as well as other parts of the world. The extended connections of British Inter-Varsity, the insights of Dutch Reformed confessionalists, the common valuing of the classical Protestant heritage, and an ingrained respect for an even broader range of historic

Christian expressions have all shaped the coalition represented by the essays of this book. In addition, many of its members share both an indebtedness to the convictions of fundamentalism and an awareness of its limitations. The brief biographical sketches of the authors can suggest only the most superficial of a dense network of these interconnections.

No one should conclude that common points of reference constitute a uniform theological perspective; the merest survey of the following pages will easily dispel that notion. Nor do they establish a formal institutional structure. Rather, they make for a shared perspective, a point of view that appropriates with similar respect the inheritance of the Reformation and the Trinitarian orthodoxy that the Reformers presupposed. And since that point of view has developed through a connected series of parallel histories, it has greater cohesion than one might otherwise expect from a disparate group of evangelicals.

THEOLOGY AS BRIDGE BUILDING:
THE WORD AND THE WORLD

To say that evangelical theology is awakening from its methodological slumbers would be going too far. There is, nevertheless, an unmistakable stirring in these essays of something different. The difference is not in the set of convictions that govern evangelical theology so much as in the self-conscious way they are being related to the contemporary world.

In much of the post-Reformation period, and until relatively recently, the task of the evangelical theologian was easily defined. Theologians were to study the biblical text, crystallize doctrines from its pages, explore their relationships, sharpen their cutting edges, proclaim their truth, and confound those who disagreed or disbelieved. This set of activities was predicated on the assumption that biblical doctrine once explained was not only readily comprehensible to reasonable people, but also self-evident in its application to daily life. These assumptions, however, are now in ruins. The theological task no longer can be limited simply to the reception, refinement, repristination, and promulgation of the received orthodoxy; it must now concern itself with understanding what that faith means in a world whose cognitive horizons are so vastly different from the biblical and whose life poses questions the biblical authors did not foresee nor answer directly.

11

In the West evangelical theology must now function cross-culturally. Theologians, by circumstance if not by desire, are missionaries; there is no longer a home base to which they can retreat. For four centuries they had enjoyed such a home base in the broad Christian assumptions on which Western culture was predicated and by which it has been nourished. In the presence of those assumptions, even where they suffered cultural dilution, biblical doctrine had made ready sense. Moreover, the work of theologians had been accorded cultural legitimacy even by those who neither understood theology nor trusted its conclusions. Today, however, those assumptions have not merely been diluted; they have dissipated. Without them, biblical doctrine has lost its cultural coordinates and the professional guardians of that doctrine have been deprived of their legitimacy. They have become disinherited strangers in their own world, wanderers whose message strikes no chords and creates no resonance in a naturalistic, technological age. They are cognitive hermits.

Perhaps the power of Enlightenment ideas in Western culture has been exaggerated, both by admirers who promote their wisdom and opponents who fear their consequences. And perhaps modern secularism is neither as irreversible as its practitioners suppose nor as invincible as its opponents fear. Yet it can hardly be doubted that the forces responsible for the dissolution of Christian understanding are advancing with all that is most characteristic of the modern world. Technology not only renders the world rational but envelops its users and beneficiaries in a relentless naturalism whose only ethic is efficiency. Urbanization, now a world phenomenon, and relativism go hand-in-hand, for cosmopolitan cities create environments where competing worldviews coexist peacefully because each tacitly surrenders its claim to absolute truth. Television, largely the preserve of an unholy alliance between show business and big business, fosters a shallow, unreflective response to life in which the only consistent value is self-gratification, whether through violence, drugs, or sex. These powerful vehicles have reinforced secular interests. Theologians who work in isolation from these developments are surely living in Alice's Wonderland.

As a matter of fact, there can be no forceful, meaningful evangelical theology that does not seek to communicate between the in-group, the church, and the out-group, the world. This communication, moreover, requires that the world be understood with sensitivity and clarity so that the church states the meaning of faith in terms germane to the world. This necessity calls evangelicals to hard and sympathetic attention to this world and conditions them to accept help from all who advance comprehension of its inner workings. A Christian theology that uses only the resources from the in-group is a paltry thing, both because it talks mostly with itself and because it is deprived of the insights of the out-group. The evangelicals who have contributed to this book believe that understanding of the world may come as readily from nonbelievers as from believers. They affirm that non-Christians may enable Christians to see more clearly the implications of the gospel. And nearly all the essays bear witness to a wide indebtedness of knowledge the authors have happily incurred.

This new sense of the evangelical task in theology is certainly a product of the declining status of Christian thinking in the West. But it also arises from changes among evangelicals themselves, two of which deserve attention.

First, evangelicals have been steadily reclaiming the importance of worldviews, and this has had its inevitable impact in enlarging theological purview. In point of fact, significant segments of the evangelical world had never lost their sense of worldview, even if the functional importance of thinking on such a level had been diminished by ethnic parochialism and denominational sectarianism. The evangelical streams that came through, rather than around, fundamentalism, however, have had much to unlearn.

In the 1930s and 1940s, fundamentalism offered a textbook case of a wounded, threatened cognitive minority tenaciously insulating itself from the world. It created a world within the world, surrounding itself with high walls. Within these walls it remade life closer to the heart's desire. Fundamentalism developed new denominations, its own comprehensive Christian educational systems, its own radio, music, and eventually television, its own books and journals, its own yellow pages, and its own conceptuality and language. It also developed highly sensitive warning systems to sound the alert whenever the modern world hove into sight. Within this tight enclave, Christian faith was preserved—but at the deliberate cost of dislocation from the wider culture.[15]

More recent evangelicals, however, have not been content to live within this self-imposed exile. They have recognized the irony in this unhappy cultural arrangement, as fundamentalists could not (until the extraordinary emergence of Jerry Falwell). Fundamentalists were partly responsible for the virtually uncontested passage secularism enjoyed: the separatistic means they chose for self-preservation also removed a major deterrent to the spread of secular values. They could comfort themselves by railing loudly at the modern world from behind their psychological stockade, but their cries were audible only within the citadel.

It was this fallen banner, this surrendered responsibility for the world beyond the barricade, that evangelicals began to assume in the 1950s. At first only a few lonely voices could be heard, Carl Henry's being the most important.[16] But slowly a consensus began to emerge: Christian faith would cease to be Christian if it were deprived of the gospel, but Christian faith is not simply proclamation of the gospel. The evangelistic message is the entrance to faith, not its whole substance; it is the beginning of the pilgrimage, not the journey itself. Since social responsibility is the context, accompaniment, and result of the gospel, these evangelicals began to ask how a wider understanding of the world could lead to a more responsible proclamation of God's saving love in Christ and how they were to authenticate that message through loving service to all humanity. What does it mean in the twentieth century to think God's thoughts after him? What view of the world is implied by the greatest of all divine acts, the incarnation of the divine Word?

These considerations ran parallel to a second major internal change among evangelicals, a growing consciousness of the globe. World-awareness is a powerful ingredient in human perception. Indeed, without a self-conscious Christian framework, an awareness of the planet as a whole, with all its strains and strife, has the potential to make life unbearable.

Television, of course, has greatly shrunk our world and enabled all of us to witness major triumphs and tragedies of the human spirit. Television certainly enhances global consciousness. Among evangelicals, however, other dramatic developments have also lifted the horizon for quite different reasons and in quite different ways.

This change in outlook was anticipated by the explosion after World War II of evangelical missions organizations.[17] It was then given a sharply focused impetus by the Berlin Congress on World Evangelization (1966), jointly sponsored by the Billy Graham Evangelistic Association and *Christianity Today.* Some twelve hundred evangelical leaders from over 100 countries gathered for reflection on the nature of the gospel and to lay plans for its worldwide proclamation. Berlin spawned numerous regional gatherings that constituted a link to the next major milestone, the International Congress on World Evangelization in Lausanne, Switzerland (1974). This meeting was attended by twenty-seven hundred leaders from over 150 nations, fully one-half of them from the Third World. This Congress set in motion a worldwide process of consultation and cooperation among evangelicals. And there have been further regional gatherings: Hong Kong (1976), India (1977), Singapore (1978), North America (1981), South America (1982), and the Caribbean (1984). In 1980, the Consultation on World Evangelization brought together 650 delegates from 87 countries.[18]

The significance of this formidable, worldwide movement for the shape and interests of evangelical theology has been at least fourfold. First, it has continued to keep the proclamation of the gospel at the heart of evangelical thinking.

Second, while these meetings have concerned themselves with spreading the Christian message, they have explored the subject not in isolation from the whole framework of Christian understanding but in self-conscious relation to it. The world is being interpreted within a broad intellectual perspective growing out of reflection on the life, death, and resurrection of Christ.

Third, the resurgence in thinking about evangelism has been paralleled by a deliberate reemphasis on social witness and service. For example, World Vision, the evangelical service agency that was created to channel relief to places in the world beset by natural or social disasters, today has a budget substantially larger than that of the entire World Council of Churches. Year by year evangelicals are doing more to cement the alliance between evangelistic proclamation and practical aid for the stricken neighbor. From that bond has grown the sense that a theology that does not deal with the conditions of life as they actually are cannot be fully or consistently evangelical.

Fourth, the live contacts across national, cultural, and intellectual barriers these congresses afforded—at least for the leaders involved—have demolished safe nationalistic assumptions, exploded smug securities, provoked numerous questions, sparked fresh ideas, and opened up new vistas. They have pushed evangelicals to think in terms large enough to encompass the world and deep enough to fathom the whole human story.

The new agenda, then, requires evangelicals to trace the trajectory of divine revelation from its point of origination to its point of arrival, from the biblical word to the contemporary world, from what is fixed, unchanging, and infallible to what is shifting, changing, and relative. There can be no question, however, that this interpretive journey from word to world is fraught with peril even as it is ripe with potential. Bridges built between God's word and our world are susceptible of carrying traffic in both directions. In the wider context of contemporary theology, where the need for this bridge building has long been accepted, most of the traffic has been moving in the wrong direction. Twentieth-century people have allowed the cognitive constraints and the psychological conventions of our own day to limit what the Bible may say. This reverses the proper situation. It is the Bible that deserves to prescribe the cognitive horizon for the twentieth century, just as it has for every century. Much more than the Bible, it is the twentieth century that needs to be demythologized. But the very fact that such an argument needs to be made is a warning to evangelicals of the dangers implicit in the process of building bridges.

In addition, the effort to forge an interpretive relationship between word and world raises the question as to what the proper stance is to be between the Christian and the culture of this world. Evangelical theologians have agreed that in this relationship there are elements of both antithesis (what we have described as the antimodernist bias of evangelicals) and identity (in which God's general work in creation receives its full due). For any given problem, however, elements of antithesis and identity intermingle, and so evangelicals have often called for a strategy to purify, reform, or transform culture on the basis of Christian conviction. As it happens, however, evangelical theologians often develop special affinities for one or another of these particular tendencies. The Anabaptists (as antimodern separatists) accentuate antithesis, many Anglicans (confident in a general revelation from God) stress identity, and Reformed spokespersons (who read Scripture as a blueprint for cultural renewal) favor reformation or transformation. This means, almost certainly, that some readers will be surprised by the absence of antithesis in some essays, and some by its presence in other pieces. Some essays may appear naively blind to the distortions modernisms can work in Christian faith, while others may sound too strident, too unyielding.

It is important to remember, therefore, that both authors and readers search for the knowledge of God within the frailty of fallen human nature. The doing of theology requires an acknowledgment of fallibility and inherent waywardness. These essays, therefore, are not offered on a take-it-or-leave-it basis. They are serious proposals that invite serious responses, for it is from many such "counsellors" that wisdom emerges.[19]

THE SHAPE OF THE BOOK

The diversity of this book arises from an effort to reflect the bridge-building that must be done in communicating a Christian message in an increasingly complex world. As evangelicals, first of all, we place supreme value in the significance of Scripture for the believer and for the church. The Bible is the source of divinely given knowledge about God, his actions and his will, and about ourselves. Yet to live out the truth of the Bible we must know both the world of Scripture and the world in which we live. Naive biblicism short-circuits that understanding and deprives theology of its proper weight. One of the contributors to this volume, Anthony Thiselton, has written at length about the "two horizons"—of scriptural perspective and contemporary understanding—that must come into play for a full and meaningful understanding of the Bible. Another, John Stott, has used the bridge-building metaphor to describe fruitfully the preacher's task.[20] Both accent the fact that while the Bible's authority is absolute for evangelicals, that authority should function in context; it must be interpreted. The more self-conscious that process of interpretation, the more confidence we may have that we are not confusing the conventions of a particular time with the God-ordained norms of Scripture.

This book testifies to the evangelical confidence in Scripture by beginning each of its major sections with a biblical meditation. Their presence is not an icon for mere pious display, but a confession that unless we first hear the word of God, all our words will be of little value.

One other specifically Christian mediation plays a determinative role in what follows. In spite of some evangelical affirmations to the contrary, it simply is not the case that each generation of Christians rediscovers the faith for itself. The history of the church, in other words, has a large and well-appreciated place for the evangelicals who write here. Believers who make much of Christian fellowship often underestimate the value of that fellowship over time. But the communion of the saints includes Tertullian, Augustine, Anselm, Aquinas, Luther, Calvin, Pascal, Wesley, Edwards, and many, many more who have compelling significance for contemporary theological reflection. None of the problems of our day are entirely new; all of our theological insights into those problems will have been anticipated in some fashion before. One of the characteristics of the evangelical coalition from which this book arises is a due regard for history. As a consequence, the essays often include a serious consideration of the insight mediated to the present by the worthies of the past.

Bridge-building between Scripture and the community of faith, between the church's past and its present, is only the first of several important interactions that constitute the theological task. Forceful, meaningful theology must communicate between the church and the world outside the church. Thus, as we have said, it is a Christian duty to understand the world. And here is the place where common grace plays such an important role.

Bridge-building between the world and the church is, however, a more complicated thing than it first appears, especially for heirs of the Reformation. Luther's classic description of the Christian was of someone *simul justus et peccator,* a person who was both justified and a sinner. This insight means that the Christian theologian is never merely a spokesperson for God. To do theology is to realize the depths of one's own need as well as to proclaim the provision of God for others. By its nature, therefore, evangelical theology is a theology of humility. The word of God may be clear and sharp, but the one who passes on that word can never confuse the theologian with the source of theology. Theologians who attempt to interpret God's word for our world must first hear that word themselves.

Finally, theological reflection properly needs to perceive the conjunctions in the world in which it speaks. Practice shapes theory while theory influences practice. Religious observance orients, even as it embodies, theology. The psychological, social, economic, political, and artistic environments of our lives are not discrete entities unrelated to each other or to the message of Scripture. They are rather parts of a whole; each in its turn has a contribution to make to the theological task; each can be enlightened by theological reflection.

The essays below are efforts to grasp aspects of the way in which God has ordained the word to relate to the world. None treats every relationship, and this is by design. The project as a whole does, nonetheless, deal with most of the significant interconnections from which theology grows and to which it is addressed. The biblical meditations by John Stott are an indication of the primary place we reserve for the written word of God. The essays by J. I. Packer (God as image-maker), Cornelius Plantinga (humanity as made in that image), Gabriel Fackre (on the nature of revelation), and Donald Bloesch (on God as civilizer) reflect engagement with the great traditions of Western theology. Clark Pinnock's discussion of the finality of Jesus Christ illustrates the importance of positioning Christianity in relationship to other faiths. Stephen Evans draws on both historical and contemporary considerations to interpret the character of human nature. Tom Morris, Anthony Thiselton, and David Livingstone examine and use the wisdom of the world in their discussions of, respectively, the logic of the Christian view of revelation, the perils and possibilities of responsible hermeneutics, and the potential for rapprochement between science and faith. Possibilities without number exist for Christian reflection on the practical concerns of the day. The book's efforts in this area—Richard Mouw on the poor, Paul Marshall on work and rest, David Wells on the meaning of an uncertain human future—suggest what great rewards await Christians who reflect theologically on the practicalities of existence. And Klaus Bockmuehl's programmatic piece on secularism and secularization considers seriously both the phenomenon of de-Christianization and possible Christian responses to that phenomenon.

Each essay is able to stand by itself as a self-contained argument. Together they speak more comprehensively to the needs, as well as to the rewards, of meaningful theological reflection in the modern world.

The arrangement of the papers is also designed to make a specifically evangelical statement. First comes God and his nature, and the implications of the divine nature for those who have been made in his image. Next is a consideration of how God has made himself known, and of some of the issues involved in the human reception of that revelation. Last come papers treating the restoration of creation, a restoration involving both a theoretical dimension and several practical problems.

Within each major section chapters are grouped in the same pattern. First in each section is a positive statement of Christian belief that is sensitive to twentieth-century concerns, but positions itself also in the broader stream of historic Christian reflection. Then follow the chapters considering individual aspects of the general subject, with special attention to the human circumstances that now characterize the reception of divine activity or the understanding of God's will.

Evangelicals make no claims for extraordinary insights into God or the world. They do believe that, by grace, they have been allowed to catch something of the meaning of divine revelation, and that this revelation makes possible meaningful reflection on God, his creatures, and his ways with the world. Such is the reflection to which we now turn.

Part I

THE IMAGE OF GOD

Evangelicals believe in humanity because they believe in God. Modern discussions of the person, no less than renewed focus by theologians on the humanity of God, require Christians to speak carefully, yet forthrightly, about what it means to be made in the image of God. This question properly requires, however, an understanding of what God is like, before attempting to understand how he shares his character with those who bear his image.

Our discussion of this theme begins with humbling words from the Book of Job on the nature of true wisdom. A chapter on "theology proper," the being of God, then addresses modern concerns about God's character and activity. It also serves to introduce two full considerations of the way in which evangelicals take advantage of modern theological and psychological discussions to formulate a conception of the person consistent with historic Christian reflection. The first of these concentrates on the early chapters of Genesis and on the Trinitarian implications of the Gospel of John to illuminate the nature of the imago dei *that humans bear. The second finds resources in ancient Christian traditions for addressing the modern vacillation between viewing humans as akin to divinity and seeing them as merely another form of materiality.*

2

Biblical Meditation: True Wisdom

John R. W. Stott

It may be appropriate to begin with a meditation on the topic of wisdom. All of us would like to be considered wise. Wisdom is also a prominent theme in the Bible, particularly in the five books of wisdom literature in the Old Testament, as these consider how suffering, evil, injustice, and love relate to our humanness. The twenty-eighth chapter of Job contains these words about wisdom:

> Where can wisdom be found? Where does understanding dwell? Man does not comprehend its worth; it cannot be found in the land of the living. The deep says, "It is not in me"; the sea says, "It is not with me." It cannot be bought with the finest gold, nor can its price be weighed in silver. It cannot be bought with the gold of Ophir, with precious onyx or sapphires. Neither gold nor crystal can compare with it, nor can it be had for jewels of gold. Coral and jasper are not worthy of mention; the price of wisdom is beyond rubies. The topaz of Cush cannot compare with it; it cannot be bought with pure gold. Where then does wisdom come from? Where does understanding dwell? It is hidden from the eyes of every living thing, concealed even from the birds of the air. Destruction and Death say, "Only a rumor of it has reached our ears." God understands the way to it and he alone knows where it dwells, for he views the ends of the earth and sees everything under the heavens. When he established the force of the wind and measured out the waters, when he made a decree for the rain and a path for the thunderstorm, then he looked at wisdom and appraised it; he confirmed it and tested it. And he said to man, "The fear of the Lord—that is wisdom, and to shun evil is understanding." (Vv. 12-28, NIV)

Here in verse 28 are two realities of human experience: God and evil. Of course, they are not equal realities. Christians are not dualists. Evil had a beginning and, thank God, evil will have an end. Only God is eternal, from everlasting to everlasting. Nevertheless, in the long history of humankind, God and evil have dominated the scene.

The one, God, brings human fulfillment and even ecstasy; the other, evil, brings human alienation and even despair.

This passage and others in the wisdom literature tell us that wisdom consists in adopting a right attitude toward both. On the one hand, wise people fear God. Not that they live in terror of him or fawn upon him obsequiously, as if his moods were unpredictable or his favor could be purchased. But wise people acknowledge as the ultimate reality the greatness and sovereignty of the living God. To fear God is to worship him with humility, love, and reverence. For these are the chief ingredients of the fear of the Lord.

But on the other hand, wise people shun evil. We refuse to give it a spurious homage as if it had any rights to be respected. We despise evil as it deserves to be despised; we hate it as it deserves to be hated, for the affront that it is to God and the pain that it has brought to human beings. We turn resolutely away from it. We know that in order to be wise it is necessary to be good; and that without goodness, there is no wisdom.

Moreover, these two basic attitudes of wisdom, fearing God and shunning evil, belong inescapably together, as the Hebrew parallelism indicates. There are some people who claim to know God who do not turn from evil. Their claim is bogus and must be rejected. Mystical experience without moral commitment is false religion. For "God is light; in him there is no darkness at all. If we claim to have fellowship with him yet walk in darkness, we lie and do not live by the truth" (1 John 1:5-6).

Others try to turn from evil without having come to know God. And some achieve a modicum of success. Not every atheist is a blackguard; some are quite decent and honest people. Yet the impressive testimony of the saints down the ages is that there is no stronger incentive to holiness than the fear of God. Paul wrote of "perfecting holiness out of reverence for God" (2 Cor. 7:1). It is when we live close to him and practice his presence that we grasp the incompatibility of God and evil. The real presence of the one occasions the real absence of the other—for God and evil, light and darkness, cannot coexist.

The fact that wisdom consists in fearing God and shunning evil is traced in Christian theology to our creation. Religion and ethics, or godliness and goodness, are essential to wisdom because they are essential to our God-created humanness. For man—male and female, made in the image of God—is both a spiritual being capable of knowing and loving him and a moral being capable of ethical choice. These things still distinguish man and woman from the beasts and constitute our chief claim to nobility.

Hence the tragedy of the spiritual and moral vacuum created by modern secularism. It is destructive of authentic humanness because it is inherently reductionist, reducing human beings to less than their full God-given potential.

The ultimate in dehumanization is the denial of transcendence and the loss of moral absolutes. And yet, these two things are common in the secular world around us. Marxism, or at least Euro-Marxism, may be pronounced a failure because of its gross materialism. It began by offering an ideological substitute for outworn religious beliefs. But it is no more a substitute for true religion than husks are a substitute for bread. Marxism leaves the spiritual vacuum unfilled. Hence the continuing resilience of Christianity in the Soviet Union and Eastern Europe.

But Western secularism has proved an equal failure, as Theodore Roszak, for example, makes plain in *Where the Wasteland Ends*. He castigates science for its debunking spirit and for what he calls its "undoing of the mysteries," and adds, "Without transcendence, the person shrivels." The proliferation of mindless cults today is, alas, a quest for transcendence in the wrong place. As an editorial writer put it in Britain's *Economist*, when reporting the Jonestown tragedy in Guyana, in young people's search for God, "it is all too easy to blunder into the arms of Satan instead."

The loss of the transcendent leads naturally to the loss of moral absolutes. We all know that our generation is faced with grave moral dilemmas: the nuclear threat, the population explosion, North/South economic inequality, problems of bio- ethics, and the rest. There is no slick solution to these complex problems. Yet their solution is made even harder by the loss of moral absolutes today.

So then an urgent need exists to reverse these contemporary trends and to recover true wisdom, which is the fear of God and the hatred of evil. Without these, human life becomes brutish and human society sick, or, in the words of Ecclesiastes, "meaningless, meaningless, utterly meaningless" (NIV).

In conclusion, note how Job depicts wisdom as our preeminent concern. The Bible not only gives us a definition of wisdom; it also insists heavily on its priceless value. As Job puts it earlier in this same chapter, men mine for silver and gold; they extract iron from the bowels of the earth; they smelt copper from ore; they open underground shafts and overturn mountains; they dam rivers and cut channels in the rock, all for mineral treasure. But the price of wisdom is above rubies, it cannot be measured in gold. So should we not seek it with even greater diligence than those who seek for mineral treasure? I end with the reminder that true wisdom is found in Jesus Christ. In our search for wisdom we cannot stay in the Old Testament, or even in the wisdom literature. We have to move on to its fulfillment in Jesus Christ. For he is made unto us wisdom, and in him all the treasures of wisdom and knowledge are to be found. Especially the cross, which is foolishness to the proud, is the wisdom and the power of God. For the two chief blessings of Jesus' death and resurrection are the knowledge of God and deliverance from evil. And so we are back where we started: the fear of the Lord, that is wisdom; and to depart from evil is understanding.

2A

God the Image-Maker

J. I. Packer

THE STUDY OF THEOLOGY

What is theology? In the broadest sense, any speech or writing about God is theology, even if its burden is only a denial of someone else's assertion that God exists. In this broad sense, theology can be theistic, deistic, pantheistic, panentheistic, dualistic, agnostic, or atheistic; indeed, theologies of all sorts exist today, and one does not have to leave the United States in order to find them. Every form of religion and antireligion (which is itself a religion of a kind) has a theology in this sense. But our concern is with religion, not antireligion, and with Christian religion specifically; so our opening question should be restated as: what is *Christian* theology? And here, I take it, our interest is in finding a normative account, a prescriptive, persuasive, and ideal definition, rather than in seeking an inclusive formula of a sociological, phenomenological, and in the last analysis external and uncommitted type. We want to know not only what Christian theology has been and is, but also what it ought to be. Nonnormative descriptive definitions of Christian theology as thought and speech about God that is shaped in some way by some sort of commitment to some conception or other of Jesus of Nazareth are fashionable in some circles; they are not, however, sufficient for our purpose. We want an account of theology that is confessional and functional, relating theology to the revelation that must control it and the religion that it must in turn control. Nothing less will satisfy us, either in our present deliberations or at any other time.

Why is this? Because our own redemption from sin has been divinely revealed to us. The mediation of Jesus Christ, "the God incarnate, man divine," sin-bearer, intercessor, risen and returning Lord, whom Paul calls our life and our hope (Col. 3:4; 1 Tim. 1:1), has made this redemption the supreme existential reality for us, from which our present identity, experience, and expectations all derive.

27

Evangelicals should be resolved always to theologize out of this redemption, whatever others may do. We should see ourselves as having been brought from darkness to light, from paths of error to the place of truth, from the power of Satan to the kingdom of God. Evangelicals do not worship the Bible, as we are sometimes accused of doing, but the God and the Christ of the Bible; nonetheless, we revere the Bible as the God-given means whereby the Holy Spirit has made known to us God's amazing grace and his unspeakable gift of eternal life. Rejecting the idea that our certainties are sectarian eccentricities, we see them, rather, as belonging to the historic and biblically mapped mainstream of catholic Christianity; eccentricity develops not when they are affirmed but when they are distorted, diminished, or denied. We believe that in principle, even if not always in expression, evangelical religion, thus conceived, is the Christian norm, and that the God-intended purpose of theology is to explain, nourish, and commend this norm. Thus, we look for an account of theology that does justice to our sense of being taught by God the Spirit about God the Son from the God-breathed Scriptures, and of being led by the same Spirit into responsive faith, worship, and obedience: in other words, into devotion, doxology, and delighting in God.

Evangelicals who have learned to value education as the inculcating of habits of clear thought, fruitful questioning, and judgment according to evidence rationally weighed will rightly require, as do others, that theology be pursued with academic rigor, and will regard the "popular piety" that is not informed by rigorous theological thought as to that extent defective, however great its zeal and impressive its vitality. But evangelicals who have a grip on their own Christian identity will not forget that rigorous theological thought is never to be pursued merely as a pastime or a professional skill, even if as a teacher one is paid to instill habits of theological rigor into others. Against such "academicism" evangelicals will set their face. Remembering that truth is for obedience, their goal always will be to reduce theology to practice, as the Puritans used to put it—that is, to discern what effect each revealed verity is meant to have on themselves and others in terms of both outward action and inward spirituality. Where, therefore, evangelicals fail to study moral, devotional, and missiological theology with a thoroughness equal to their labours in the systematic and apologetic fields, their faith must be judged to be already out of shape.

The appropriate perspective, in this or any age, for the study of theology—"the science of living blessedly forever," as Perkins the

Puritan defined it—now becomes evident. It is true that theology consists of a clutch of disciplines—exegesis, biblical theology, historical theology and church history, systematic and philosophical theology, ethics, apologetics, liturgy, spirituality, missiology, and pastoral theology, sometimes called poimenics—any of which could occupy a person for a lifetime. It is true that theologians, like other professional groups, have their own associations for pooling knowledge and stimulating thought, and that these tend to be exclusively academic in focus. It is true that theologians who labor in preaching or pastoring are often thought of as among the wonders of the world, that seminary teaching is not usually expected to have any practical thrust, and that congregations rarely require their preachers and pastors to keep themselves theologically informed. In other words, it is a fact that theological labor and the practicalities of godliness and ministry are widely (and unhealthily) viewed as separate compartments of life. Thus, much in the current situation conspires to make us forget the importance of studying theology in the light of its God-intended practical purpose. But this is something that we must not allow ourselves to forget. For theology, the study of biblical truth in application and apprehension, is the theory of religion in the same way that form, harmony, and instrumentation are the theory of music. As music theory is studied with a view to making music, so theology should be studied with a view to furthering Christian life and ministry, to developing faith, worship, and obedience, both individual and corporate; fruitful biblical interpretation in the pulpit and the class meeting; and overall competence in catechesis, apologetics, and the injecting of Christian contributions into the contemporary marketplace of jostling ideas. This leads me to my next observation.

THE "POST-CHRISTIAN" CHALLENGE
TO THEOLOGY

We need to ask ourselves what we mean when we speak of the world in which we Christians now theologize as "post-Christian." We have in view the Western world, which continues to reel before the chilly blasts of Enlightenment rationalism and technologically inspired materialism; "post-Christian" would make little sense as an adjective describing, say, Africa. With this designation, nonetheless, we show our awareness that in the West the majority of those who see themselves as the intelligentsia and who do most to shape public opinion have detached themselves from the Western Christian heritage in order to identify with some latter-day viewpoint that is either reacting against or consciously moving beyond Christianity. Such viewpoints include Marxism in its many mutations, plus nontheistic humanism with its confidence that evolution and science together can build heaven on earth, plus a variety of pessimistic blends of reductionism, relativism, irrationalism, and nihilism. Those who embrace these positions either oppose Christianity as false and damaging or ignore it as a patent absurdity, not worth bothering about. When we call our milieu "post-Christian" we are saying that the intellectual challenges of adverse attitudes must now be dealt with at every turn of the theological road, that Christian truth is neither a referent nor an assumption in the culture. Perhaps these cold winds blowing in our faces will prove bracing. Perhaps their provocation will lead to major theological achievements, as similar cultural dynamics and secular challenges did in the patristic period. Perhaps the magisterial work of such systematic thinkers as the Baptist Carl Henry, the Presbyterian T. F. Torrance, and the Anglican E. L. Mascall will prove to be the firstfruits of such achievements.[1] We shall see. Meantime, we are undoubtedly wise to be taking soundings, in order to get some idea of the magnitude of the task.

Against the background of these general comments I now turn to the doctrine of God.

THE DOCTRINE OF GOD

The first point I would make is that though starting a survey of Christian theology with the doctrine of God is natural and logical, and indeed one would not choose to begin anywhere else, it is nevertheless in one way awkward. The awkwardness springs from the fact that theology is a uniquely organic study, in which everything to some extent presupposes everything else. In Protestant textbooks since the seventeenth century the usual sequence of topics has been: (1) revelation and method (commonly classified as prolegomenon or introduction, rather than as primary doctrine); (2) the character and triunity of God, and his work in creation and providence; (3) man and sin; (4) Christology and mediation; (5) redemption applied to the individual; (6) ecclesiology; (7) the future (last things).[2] None of these matters can be studied properly, however, without bringing in the others. Theology is not like a mathematical system in which everything is deduced in order from basic definitions and axioms, and we go astray when at any point we allow ourselves to proceed as if it is. Deduction belongs in theology only in the drawing out of analytic entailments (e.g., biblical inerrancy from the fact of divine inspiration) and in applying universal truths to particular cases, and this I take to be all that the Westminster Confession means when it says that the whole counsel of God "is either expressly set down in Scripture, or by good and necessary consequence may be deduced from Scripture" (I.vi). Otherwise, it is not at all from our rational deduction, but entirely from God's rational revelation, that we must draw our knowledge of the living, personal, creative Lord whom we serve. And as our knowledge of other persons needs to be comprehensive and inclusive, so it is with him: we cannot be sure that we understand any of his behavior without some understanding of all of it. Therefore theology, which is essentially our proclamation of God and his behavior, his works, will, and ways, is of necessity like a circle: wherever you break into it, you have to go right around it before you have adequate knowledge of where you are, or full understanding of the point from which you started. (In one sense, of course, we never in this world have full understanding of any matter of theology, for there is always more to God and his work than we have grasped yet. In glory we may hope for knowledge as clear and full as is God's present knowledge of us [1 Cor. 13:12], though even that, one imagines, will be knowledge of many things rather than of everything, and will not match God's omniscience. In this world, however, we must face the fact that all our knowledge of God and his works, though true as far as it goes and adequate for our faith-relationship with him, remains inadequate to the reality. This is the truth that we are signaling when we speak of the *mystery* of God, and call him *incomprehensible*. But what I have in mind when speaking of "full" understanding is relative, not absolute fullness.) Now the doctrine of God is a prime example of the need to go around the circle before you can understand.

The content of the doctrine of God comes from the total presentation of God's words and works that forms the content of all the other doctrines in the sequence given above. Those doctrines state the specifics of what God did, and does, and will do, while the doctrine of God focuses on the Doer himself, as his words and works have made him known. Ideally, therefore, it might seem that the doctrine of God should come last in the sequence rather than first: we should approach the study of who and what God is via our survey of his various actions. But then, how could that survey be adequate, how could we hope to see clearly what we are looking at in the scriptural narrative and testimony, if we had no mental grid for God through which to view it? There is awkwardness either way, and we cannot wonder that the traditional order of exposition remains as it is.

But the status of the doctrine of God as a distillation from what we are told about the doings of God seems rarely to be perceived. Why is that? It is partly (I guess) because in catechisms and courses on systematic theology it is regularly dealt with first, as we have noted, before God's acts come up for treatment; partly, too, because so much of it is couched in historic Latinized terms (aseity, omniscience, omnipresence, eternity, immensity, simplicity, transcendence, immanence, infinity, immutability, impassibility, invisibility, spirituality, coequality, coinherence) that do not obviously link up with the statements and speech-style of Scripture; partly, also, because the custom is to expound it as traditional ecclesiastical lore rather than display it as the constant implication of the Bible's own narrative; and partly, I am sure, because so many have for so long followed Justin, Clement, Augustine, and Thomas Aquinas in thinking of the foundations of the doctrine as laid by natural theology rather than by biblical exegesis. In truth, however, the doctrine of God stands on exactly the same footing as any other doctrine: it is as biblical teaching, and therefore as God's own testimony to himself, that we are to receive it, irrespective of any support that rational argument and traditional status might give it. Though their support could confirm it once Scripture has established it, their support could never establish it in the absence of Scripture confirming it. So, at least, I maintain, and this conviction is basic to the rest of what I have to say.

At the present time, the doctrine of God is a confused area in Protestant theology. Each of its three departments, the divine attributes, the Trinity, and God's relation to the world he made and rules, is disputed territory. This confusion results from a lack of agreement as to how the doctrine should be constructed and defended. Different intellectual methods for doing this naturally produce different theological results. The Western heritage of postbiblical theism is a hybrid that grew out of the apologetic theology of the early centuries in which much was made of the thought that Greco-Roman philosophy (mainly Platonic and Stoic, for Aristotle's day was to come later) was a providential preparation for the gospel, just as the Old Testament revelation was from the Jews. This theism, which found its statement when Thomas Aquinas formulated it in terms of the Aristotelian potency-act dialectic, is part of the common heritage of both Roman Catholicism and Protestantism, though the Thomist element in its ancestry is something that since the seventeenth century most Protestants have not wanted to know. Western Christian theism as generally received today is a blend of philosophical and exegetical reasoning, the former appearing to constitute the frame into which the latter has to fit. During the seventeenth, eighteenth, and nineteenth centuries, when Protestant natural theology was having its field day, though deistic and pantheistic thinking did in fact erode much of the theistic outlook, the concept of God, as such, was not a matter of widespread theological debate. But since the Kuyperian, Barthian, and neo-Lutheran renewal, in their different ways, of Luther's and Calvin's polemic against natural theology, theism in its traditional form has become widely suspect among Protestant theologians, both for its method and to some extent for its content, too. This means that when facing challenges to theism from post-Christian and anti-Christian sources Protestant theologians have not always known what to say, and consequently have been tempted sometimes to take up with panicky and defeatist slogans like that fathered on to the late John Robinson, "Our Image of God must Go."[3] It may be, however, that *aggiornamento* rather than abandonment of traditional theism is what our situation calls for: perhaps the argument of this present chapter will help to crystallize a point of view on that question.

THE ANATOMY OF THEISM

It will now help us forward if we review the ingredients that make up mainstream Christian theism. Expositors differ on the details, but here is a checklist of the usual items, expressed in as simple a way as the thoughts themselves allow.

1. God is personal and triune. Tritheism and Sabellianism (modalism) are both untrue, and God is as truly three personal centers in a sustained relationship of mutual love and harmony as he is a single personal deity. The three persons of the Godhead are individuated in relation to each other without ever being separated from each other; they are consciously three while yet ontologically as well as cooperatively one.

2. God is self-existent and self-sufficient. In Thomist terms, his existence (being) is identical with his essence (nature), and is necessary in the sense that he does not have it in him, either in purpose or in power, to stop existing. God exists necessarily, inasmuch as he cannot not-be. The answer to the child's question, Who made God? is that God did not need to be made, since he was always there. This

quality of God is called aseity, which means that he draws his existence, his life and vitality, *a se* (from himself). He depends on nothing outside himself, but is at every point self-sustaining.

3. God is simple, perfect, and immutable. That is, he is wholly and totally involved in everything that he is and does, and his nature, goals, plans, and ways of acting do not change, either for the better (for, being perfect, he cannot become better than he is) or for the worse (for it is not in his nature to become worse). Simplicity, perfection, and immutability together are the basis of that glorious divine integrity, fidelity, and constancy that Scripture sees as being worthy of endless praise.

4. God is infinite, incorporeal, immense ("measureless," as the hymn puts it), omnipresent, omniscient, and eternal. This means that he is not bound by any of the limitations of space or time that apply to us, his creatures, in our body-anchored existence. Instead, he is always present everywhere, really though invisibly and imperceptibly, and is at every moment cognizant of everything that ever was, or shall be, or now is.

5. God is purposeful and omnipotent. He has a plan for the history of the universe he made, and in executing it he governs and controls all created realities. Without violating the nature of things or, under ordinary circumstances, the ongoing of natural processes, and without at any stage infringing upon the self-determined, spontaneous, creative, and morally responsible quality of human behavior (the things we do "of our own free will," as we phrase it), God acts in, with, and through his creatures to do everything that he wishes to do exactly as he wishes to do it, and by this sovereign action he achieves his goals.

6. God is both transcendent over and immanent in his world. On the one hand he is distinct from the world, does not need it, and exceeds the grasp of any created intelligence found in it, yet on the other hand he permeates it in sustaining and new-creating power, shaping and steering it in a way that keeps it on its planned course in a steady and stable state.

7. God is impassible. This means that no one can inflict suffering, pain, or any sort of distress upon him. Insofar as God enters into experience of that kind, it is by empathy for his creatures and according to his own deliberate decision, not as his creatures' victim. The words "of that kind" are important, for this impassibility has never been taken by the main Christian tradition to mean that God is a stranger to joy and delight; it has, rather, been construed as an asser-

tion of the permanence of God's joy, which no pain clouds. How the formula applies to the atoning sufferings of the incarnate Son is a special and open question, on which different views have been, and are, maintained.

8. God is love. That is, giving out of goodwill, for the recipient's benefit, is the abiding quality both of ongoing relationships within the Godhead and of God's primary outgoings in creation and to his creatures. This love is qualified by holiness (purity), a further facet of God's character that finds expression in his abhorrence and rejection of moral evil; toward resolute nonworshipers and wrongdoers God shows the hostility of righteous retributive judgment. Nonetheless, both we and they must acknowledge that their creation, as such, was an act of love, and it is basically the spurning of that love in thankless unconcern that brings them under the judgment whereby God rejects them. This rejection is, in fact, precisely an endorsing and ratifying of their rejection of him.

9. God's ways with humankind, as set forth in Scripture, show him to be both awesome and adorable by reason of his truthfulness, faithfulness, grace, mercy, patience, constancy, wisdom, justice, goodness, and generosity. For these glorious qualities God is eternally worthy of our praise, loyalty, and love. The ultimate purpose of human life is to render to him that multiform worship and service in which both he and we find our fullness of joy.

10. God uses his gift to humankind of language to tell us things directly in and through the words of his spokesmen—prophets, apostles, the incarnate Son, the writers of holy Scripture, and those who preach the Bible. God's messages all come to us as good news of grace, whatever they may contain by way of particular commands, prohibitions, threats, or warnings, for the fact that God addresses us at all is an expression of his goodwill and an invitation to fellowship. And the central message of Scripture, the hub of the wheel whose spokes are the various truths about God that the Bible teaches, is and always will be God's free gift of salvation, freely offered to us in and by Jesus Christ.

Such, in outline, are the elements of mainstream Christian theism. Facile and sentimental as its verbal form may be, Frederick W. Faber's hymn could hardly be bettered as an expression of the Christian theist's view of his God.

> My God, how wonderful thou art!
> Thy majesty how bright!

How beautiful thy mercy-seat
  In depths of burning light!

How dread are thine eternal years,
  O everlasting Lord,
By prostrate spirits day and night
  Incessantly adored!

How beautiful, how beautiful
  The sight of thee must be;
Thine endless wisdom, boundless power,
  And awful purity!

O how I fear thee, living God,
  With deepest, tenderest fears,
And worship thee with trembling hope
  And penitential tears!

Yet I may love thee too, O Lord,
  Almighty as thou art,
For thou hast stooped to ask of me
  The love of my poor heart.

No earthly father loves like thee;
  No mother, e'er so mild,
Bears and forbears as thou hast done
  With me, thy sinful child.

Father of Jesus, love's reward,
  What rapture will it be
Prostrate before thy throne to lie
  And gaze, and gaze, on thee!

The fact that Faber was a Roman Catholic reminds us that whatever differences Christian theists may have about the church, the gospel, and specific moral questions, their doctrine, devotion, and doxology as theists have given them a wide expanse of common ground. In face of any resurgence of Gnostic and Manichean dualism, Arian and Socinian unitarianism, or any thoughts of God as finite, or impotent, or remote, or subpersonal, or amoral, or inconstant, or dumb, Protestant and Roman Catholic theists have usually closed ranks in order to present a united front, as indeed they still do. At present, only the "panentheism" of process theology and its offshoots offers any serious challenge to theism within the Western churches. (Tillich's much-publicized rejection of the idea of God found in "ordinary theism" as "a holy, perfect person who resides above the world and mankind," and his replacement of it by a nonpersonal "God beyond God" has proved over a generation to be not a rallying-point but a grotesque and barren freak from which Christian teachers of all schools of thought now take care to dissociate themselves.)[4] Nonetheless, the church doctrine of God is currently in some trouble due to uncertainties about its source, status, and the method of determining it. To these questions we must now attend.

Traditionally, Christian theism has embraced five topics: the reality of God (could such a being exist?); God's attributes, also referred to as his perfections, virtues, name, and character; the Trinity; creation; and providence. Historically, the consensus has been that Scripture tells us almost, if not quite, all that it is given to us to know about the Trinity, creation, providence, and God's moral nature; but the Platonist-Augustinian-Thomist tradition of Christian philosophical thought has persistently held that knowledge of God's reality and of certain basic facts about him may be gleaned by rational analysis of experience apart from either the Bible or the church's witness. This is where the uncertainty centers. In Karl Barth's powerful Bible-based restatement of Trinitarian theism in *Church Dogmatics* I/1 and II/1, he spurned the help, condemned the products, and kicked away the foundations of this kind of rational theology (natural theology, as it has traditionally been called); this did more than any other twentieth-century contribution to produce a pendulum-swing against attempts to wed theology to philosophy in a way that gives natural theology the job of establishing and delimiting the intellectual frame within which revealed theology may operate. Barth himself would use philosophical concepts heuristically, as tools to help investigate biblical teaching, but not dogmatically, as grids setting limits in advance to what God is free to say to us through Scripture. Many have wheeled into line, more or less, behind Barth at this point, and in many quarters natural theology has been redefined as philosophical theology, whose task is not to lay foundations for faith, but to make faith appear reasonable by anchoring the verities of revelation in our knowledge of the natural order and explicating them in their relation to natural realities as these are empirically discerned. But the pendulum still swings between Thomist and Barthian extremes, and shows no sign of coming to rest.

KARL BARTH'S THEISM

Barth's contribution paves the way for some clarifications of the doctrine of God that the present age badly needs. We may move toward these through some evaluations of what Barth himself wrote. To start with, his attack on the basis of natural theology, that is, the *analogia entis* (analogy of being), the recognition that our existence and God's, however qualitatively distinct, nonetheless have something in common, was certainly overdone; and if he believed, as he seemed on occasion to do, that "being" was conceived by Thomists as a metaphysical category superior to both God and humanity, he was wrong. Nonetheless, his polemic against the claim of natural theology, whether based on idealism (as generally among Protestants) or on realism (as generally among Roman Catholics), to establish foundation-truths about God as a kind of runway for revelation, now appears as a largely justified attack on nineteenth-century attempts to domesticate God—icebergs of which the audacities of natural theology were the tip. And Barth's insistence that all our doctrine of God must come from the Bible was healthy and right. Yet it is not the case that all his own exegesis of the biblical witness to God is convincing; the revelational positivism that allowed him to duck the discipline of commending, defending, and justifying the faith rationally, and the supralapsarian Christocentrism that made him see redemption as creation crowned rather than restored, distorts Barth's reading of Scripture on key points.

One, for instance, is the general (universal and inescapable) self-revelation of the Creator and his claims that is given to human creatures through created things as such. Barth, pursuing his axiom that revelation means Christ and Christ only, tried in vain to evade the natural sense of Paul's words in Romans 1:18-32 and 2:9-16.[5] In 1934, partly for political reasons (it was the time of the Barmen Declaration in protest against Hitler's "German Christianity"), Barth tried to slaughter Emil Brunner for wanting to take seriously the natural theology to which general revelation gives rise. But although Barth affirmed that Calvin and the Bible were with him in negating general revelation and dismissing natural theology as nonsensical fantasy, Brunner was in fact much closer to both.[6]

Another oddity, relevant to our present discussions, is Barth's appeal to Christology as the hermeneutical key for understanding the divine attributes, in the sense, not simply that God is declared to be "Jesuslike" (that would be unexceptionable) but that a mapping of what the attributes signify in connection with the incarnation exhausts their meaning throughout the Scriptures. For all the luminous brilliance with which Barth expounds grace and holiness, mercy and righteousness, patience and wisdom, as "the perfections of the divine loving," and unity and omnipresence, constancy and omnipotence, eternity and glory, as "the perfections of the divine freedom," systematically viewing each perfection in terms of transcendence (freedom) expressed in condescendence (love), we can still ask whether the method itself, however fruitful within its limits, does not by its limits keep Barth and those who follow him from achieving a full account of what the Bible discloses about God.[7]

However, Barth's purpose of being rigorously, radically, and ruthlessly biblical, and his demand for interpretation that is theologically coherent, is surely exemplary for evangelicals as we attempt to spruce up historic Christian theism in meeting post-Christian challenges. It will not be enough to dismiss Barth as eccentric while slumping back into traditional postures and parrotings. If Barth with his type of biblicism did not do well enough, we must try with ours to do better. To that end I now venture some programmatic comments on the doctrine of God as today's evangelicals have received it.

THE DOCTRINE OF GOD'S NATURE

I look first at the doctrine of the divine attributes. Here there are three respects, it seems to me, in which inherited methods of formulation need overhauling.

Elements of natural theology need to be purged out.

Why do I say this? Not for Barthian reasons! Against Barth I affirm that general revelation is a fact, and its impact will again and again produce thoughts about God that, so far as they go, are right—like those of Epimenides and Aratus that Paul cites in Acts 17:28, and the insights into God's law that C. S. Lewis called the Tao (see *The Abolition of Man*) and that tell Gentiles practicing depravities that "those who do such things deserve to die" (Rom. 1:32). Many are confident that rational apologetics (a form of natural theology) can under God trigger and crystallize such thoughts and insights, and unlike Barth I see no reason to query their confidence.

Yet I have reasons of my own for wanting to see natural theology purged out of our attempts at theological construction. There are five of them, as follows.

First, we do not need natural theology for information. Everything that natural theology, operating upon general revelation, can discern about the Creator, his laws, his providence, and his final judgment, is republished for us in those very Scriptures that refer to the general revelation of these things (see Ps. 19; Acts 14:17; 17:28; Rom. 1:18-32; 2:9-16). And Scripture, which we rightly receive on the grounds that it is God's own word of testimony and *torah,* and God speaks only the truth, is a better source of knowledge about God than natural theology can ever be.

Second, we do not strengthen our position by invoking natural theology. On the contrary, the Thomist and idealist habit of claiming to lay by means of philosophy foundations on which biblical truths may rest can only give the impression that the biblical message about God redeeming is no more certain than is the prior assertion of God's reality that, in this scenario, reason must labor unaided to establish.

Third, all arguments for God's existence, all expositions of the analogy of being, of proportionality and of attribution, as means of intelligibly conceptualizing God, and all attempts to show the naturalness of theism, are logically loose. They state no more than possibilities (for probabilities are only one kind of possibilities) and can all be argued against indefinitely. They cannot be made watertight, and if offered as such they can be shown not to be watertight by anyone who knows any logic. This will damage the credit of any theology that appears to be building and relying on these arguments.

Fourth, the speculative method for building up a theology is inappropriate. Writes Louis Berkhof:

> The Scholastics in their attempt to construct a system of natural theology posited three ways in which to determine the attributes of God. . . . By the *way of causality* we rise from the effects which we see in the world round about us to the idea of a first Cause. . . . By *way of negation* we remove from our idea of God all the imperfections seen in His creatures . . . and ascribe to him the opposite perfection. . . . By *way of eminence* we ascribe to God *in the most eminent manner* the relative perfections which we discover in man, according to the principle that what exists in an effect, pre-exists in its cause. . . . This method . . . takes its startingpoint in man, and concludes from what it finds in man to what is found in God. And in so far as it does this it makes man the measure of God. This is certainly not a theological method of procedure. . . . It does not fit in a theology of revelation.[8]

Fifth, there is always a risk that the foundations that natural theology lays will prove too narrow to build all the emphases of Scripture upon. Thus, for instance, in Thomas Aquinas's *Summa Theologica,* 1a, 1-26, natural theology purports to establish that there is one God, perfect, infinite, incorporeal, simple, and good, who exists necessarily, eternally, and incomprehensibly and is the first cause of everything. But nothing is said here about the personal aspects of God's being, the fact that he is "thou" to our "I" just as each of us is "thou" to his "I." This personal dimension is central to the biblical revelation of God, setting it in stark contrast with (for instance) Plotinus's One, Spinoza's *deus sive natura,* and the divine principle in Hindu thought. But Thomas's natural theology says nothing about it, and thereby encourages the theologian to downplay it, to treat God as an impersonal object rather than a personal subject and to see himself as standing over God to study him rather than under God to obey him. God will then be treated, deistically or pantheistically, as a static principle rather than as a personal agent, and theology will become spiritually deadening rather than enlivening. Surely these are consequences that we are better without, and that it is worth making some effort to avoid. The appropriate effort in this case is to limit our use of natural theology to the realm of apologetics (showing biblical faith to be reasonable), and not to give it any place in our attempts to state what the biblical faith actually is.

Let it be noted, however, that in pouring cold water on the Thomist appeal to ontological analogies as a hinge on which speculations in natural theology may turn I have not in any way queried the epistemological principle that biblical language about God, the living, personal Creator, "the Father, from whom every family, whether spiritual or natural, takes its name" (Eph. 3:14, Jerusalem Bible), "works" (communicates its meaning) by analogy. What this means is that the human, dictionary significance of the verbs, nouns, adjectives, and adverbs that Scripture applies to God are to be qualified (diminished, augmented, refocused) both by each other and by the things that Scripture says about the difference between God's life, acts, and attitudes and those of his human creatures. Ian Crombie's description of biblical theological language as "balanced parables," Ian Ramsey's characterization of it as "qualified models," and Carl Henry's insistence that there is a univocal core when terms used of humans are applied to God[9] are all ways of affirming this principle, while the appropriate cognitive procedure in biblical exegesis and theological construction is well stated by Basil Mitchell as follows:

A word should be presumed to carry with it as many of the original entailments as the new context allows, and this is determined by their compatibility with the other descriptions which . . . also apply to God. That God is incorporeal dictates that "father" does not mean "physical progenitor," but the word continues to bear the connotation of tender protective care. Similarly God's "wisdom" is qualified by the totality of other descriptions which are applicable to him; it does not, for example, have to be learned, since he is omniscient and eternal.[10]

The procedure Mitchell describes will involve following, under the Bible's own guidance, the "ways" (procedures) of negation and eminence, referred to above. As speculative tools these "ways" must be rejected, for the reasons I gave, but as pointers to what Scripture leads us to do when we talk about God they are entirely right, and in this frame of reference we should affirm them emphatically.

Elements of mystification need to be purged out.

By "mystification" I mean the idea that some biblical statements about God mislead as they stand, and ought to be explained away. Surely any such idea must prove an Achilles' heel hermeneutically, and an albatross in terms of apologetics, to any contemporary account of God that claims to be biblically based. To be specific, a persistent tendency in orthodox theism has been to overlook the legitimate and necessary distinction between God in himself *(apud se)* and God in relation to us precisely where in Scripture God is said sometimes to change his mind, to feel regret and pain, and to make new decisions as he reacts to human doings. But God in himself does not suffer these reactive experiences, for he is eternally immutable and impassible. So we ought to take these anthropomorphisms and anthropopathisms to be "as-if" statements, accommodated to nonfactual ideas of God formed by analogical projection from our knowledge of ourselves, and we should recognize that, as Louis Berkhof puts it, *"in reality* the change is not in God, but in man and man's relations to God."[11] But to say that is to say that some things Scripture affirms about God do not mean what they seem to mean, and do mean what they do not seem to mean, and thus to provoke the question: How can these statements be part of the *revelation* of God when they actually *misrepresent* and so *conceal* God? Or rather, formulating the problem from the other end, as biblical evangelicals surely must: What do we need to do to traditional theism to enable us to treat the revelational status of these statements as seriously as we do the rest of the Bible's statements about God? In other words, how may we explain these statements about God's grief and repentance without seeming to explain them away? Surely we must accept Barth's insistence that at every point in his self-disclosure God reveals what he essentially is, with no gestures that mystify, and surely we must reject as intolerable any suggestion that God *in reality* is different at any point from what Scripture makes him appear to be. Scripture was not written to mystify, and therefore we need to ask how to dispel the contrary impression that this time-honored line of explanation leaves.

Three things seem to me to be necessary as means to this end. First, we need *exegetical restraint* in handling the anthropomorphisms of Scripture. They are there not to invite us to imagine God's state of mind and feelings in the manner of idealist historians (Dilthey, say, or Collingwood) empathizing with characters in human history, but simply to show us what reasons God had for acting as he did in the biblical story, and how therefore he might act toward us in our own personal stories. Anthropomorphism is characteristic of the entire biblical presentation of God, not because God bears man's image but because man bears God's, and hence is capable of understanding God's testimony to the reasons for his actions and the scale of values by which he operates. But nothing that is said about God's wrath, hatred, vengeance, displeasure, and other negative reactions, any more than what is said about what he delights to see in his human creatures, is meant to put us in a position where we can tell what it feels like to be God. The logic of biblical anthropomorphisms is consistent, and these particular anthropomorphisms must be exegeted as informing us about God's purposes, intentions, attitudes, and actions manward, just as all other biblical anthropomorphisms do.

Second, we need to guard against misunderstanding God's *immutability*. We must understand the divine changelessness of which Scripture speaks not as an eternally frozen pose but as the Creator's moral constancy and consistency, his uniform and unwavering faithfulness and dependability in respect of his goals, values, purposes, and promises throughout all his sovereign, preplanned activity. Louis Berkhof was correct when he wrote:

> The divine immutability should not be understood as implying *immobility,* as if there were no movement in God. It is even customary in theology to speak of God as *actus purus,* a God who is always in action. The Bible teaches us that God enters into manifold relations with man and, as it were, lives their life with them. There is change round about Him, change in the relations of men to Him, but there is no

change in His Being, His attributes, His purpose, His motives of action, or His promises.[12]

So the immutability of God is a matter of moral fixity expressed in endless activity—which is why Scripture shows him dealing variously with one and another according to their own moral and spiritual attitudes, treating different people differently at the same time and the same people differently at different times. "Faithful are you with the faithful, blameless with the blameless, pure with the one who is pure, but crafty with the devious, you save a people that is humble and humiliate eyes that are haughty" (Ps. 18:25-27, Jerusalem Bible). When one conceives of God's immutability in this biblical way, as a moral quality that is expressed whenever God changes his way of dealing with people for moral reasons, the biblical references to such change will cease to mystify.

Third, we need to rethink God's *impassibility,* as indeed Anglican and Roman Catholic theologians have been trying to do since the First World War. The thought of God as *apathetos,* free from all *pathos,* characterized always by *apatheia,* represents no single biblical term, but was introduced into Christian theology in the second century. What was it supposed to mean? Historically it did not mean impassivity, unconcern, and impersonal detachment in face of the creation, nor insensitivity and indifference to the distresses of a fallen world, nor inability or unwillingness to empathize with human pain and grief, but simply that God's experiences do not come upon him as ours come upon us, for his are foreknown, willed and chosen by himself, and are not involuntary surprises forced on him from outside, apart from his own decision, in the way that ours regularly are. In other words, he is never in reality the victim whom man makes to suffer: even the Son on his cross, where "a victim led, thy blood was shed," was suffering by his and the Father's conscious foreknowledge and choice, and those who made him suffer, however free and guilty their action, were tools of divine wisdom and agents of the divine plan (cf. Acts 2:23; 1 Pet. 1:20). As G. L. Prestige, expounding the patristic concept, put it: "It is clear that impassibility means not that God is inactive or uninterested, not that he surveys existence with Epicurean impassivity from the shelter of a metaphysical insulation, but that His will is determined from within instead of being swayed from without. It safeguards the truth that the impulse alike in providential order and in redemption and sanctification comes from the will of God."[13] This, and only this, is what the affirmation of impassibility is intended to signify.

Thus, as we ought to see God's change of ways toward those whose ways toward him change as being the expression of his immutability, so we should see the chosenness of God's grief and distress as the expression of his impassibility—and then, having seen this, we may permit ourselves to reflect on the fact that both words are apt to mislead, as also are words like "incomprehensible" as applied to God, "total" in "total depravity," "irresistible" in "irresistible grace," and many more. These words are infelicities of our inherited ecclesiastical vocabulary and the theologoumena that have grown up around them. The mystification that they consequently bring about ought not at any point to be read back into the Bible itself. From a consistent biblical-theological account of anthropomorphism and immutability and impassibility, no mystification will arise at all; for we shall then have no reason to doubt that the relevant texts are telling it like it is— or rather, telling us about God as he is, in his gracious self-presentation to us for our knowledge of him through faith. That last phrase leads us into the third revision that our conventional doctrine of God's nature seems to need.

Elements of rationalism must be purged out.

With vigor equal to that with which we must oppose the thought of mystification and self-concealment in God's revelation, we must affirm the condescension and accommodation in that revelation. Just as the two-year-old son of a man with a brain like Einstein's could not understand all that was going on in his father's mind if his father told him, so (we may be sure) it would be beyond us under any circumstances to understand all that goes on in the omniscient, all-wise, and not in any way time-bound mind of God. But, just as the genius who loves his boy will take care that in talking to him he speaks in such a way that all he says can be understood, even though that means reducing everything nearly to baby talk, so God does when he opens his mind and heart in the written Scriptures, which are in truth his love-letter to the human race. As Paul could say of the cross: "he loved me, and gave himself for me" (Gal. 2:20), so everyone who reads and hears Scripture may say of it: he loved me, and had this book written for me. The child, though in general terms aware that his father knows far more than his present words express, may yet learn— indeed, is intended to learn—from these words all that as a child he needs to know for as full and happy a relationship with his father as a two-year-old is capable of; similarly, we may learn from "God's Word written" (Anglican Article 20)—from Scripture, that is, viewed as *torah*, God's fatherly law, proceeding as Calvin put it from God's own holy mouth[14]—all that we need to know for faith and godliness. But we must never forget that we are in the little boy's position in my parable. At no point dare we imagine, therefore, that the thoughts about God that Scripture teaches us take the full measure of his reality. The fact that God condescends and accommodates himself to us in his revelation certainly makes possible clarity and certainty of understanding, so far as our understanding goes; equally certainly, however, it involves limitation in the revelation itself. The fact that through Scripture we know everything we need to know for living with God in faith, hope, love, and joy does not mean that through Scripture we know everything about God that he knows about himself.

But we forget this, or so it seems, and it is this apparent non-awareness of God's incomprehensibility that constitutes the rationalism of which I am speaking. It is more, I think, a temper than a tenet, but it produces a style of speech that is at odds with the substance of what we have to say, and therefore needs correcting. It is sometimes described as putting God in a box: that is, thinking and talking about him in a way that appears to scale him down to the measure of our minds, to make him seem transparent to us by diminishing his transcendence over us, and to lose sight of the revealed fact that he dwells in thick darkness and unapproachable light (1 Kings 8:12; 1 Tim. 6:16; two opposite figures making the same point about intrinsic intellectual inaccessibility). In our proper zeal to stress, as against the sleep of reason in the world and the zaniness of subjectivism in the church, that scriptural revelation is rational, we forget that even thoroughgoing Bible-believers are sometimes required, like Job, to go on adoring God when we do not specifically understand what he is doing and why he is doing it.

Epistemologically, the point here is that all the analogies for conceiving God that Scripture teaches us must be treated as open-ended and open-sided, true as far as they take us but at every point incomplete as declarations of God's being and activity. Certainly they reveal his essence, but we may be sure that there is more to his essence than they reveal. While they are all God's teaching, they are the teaching of a God who stoops to speak to us, and who, we may be sure, limits the scope of what he says precisely in order that it may be clear, and clearly understood. Religiously, the point is that in our worship of God for what we know of him, and our witness to him in terms of that knowledge, we ought to be humble and modest, remembering that there is certainly a great deal in his mind that he has not told us. We should avoid like the plague any talk that suggests that we have enlisted him on our side and now have him in our pockets, that he has kept no secrets from us, and that what we are now saying about him is the last and fullest word on the subject that anyone will ever be able to speak. Confidence in the teaching of God's written word is to be maintained at all times, but this stance of theological triumphalism and finality is something quite different and is to be avoided. No doubt it is our necessary polemical stance, both in our confused and divided churches and in our aggressive neopagan world, that betrays us into embracing this triumphalist style and mentality; but the fact is that by doing so we abuse our minds, exchange humility for pride and sometimes wisdom for folly, and so spoil our service of the God we love. Apologetically, the point is that if we claim to know everything about God we overreach ourselves, and destroy both our own credibility as witnesses and the credibility of our testimony itself. In this sense, therefore, our penchant for rationalism in proclaiming God needs to be rigorously purged out.

THE DOCTRINE OF THE TRINITY

I should mention here one subject of discussion on which, as it appears to me, conservative theists sometimes tend to display rationalist naiveté: the doctrine of the Trinity. Acknowledgment of the triunity of God is forced upon us both by gospel facts (Jesus, effectively claiming deity, explicitly distinguished himself from the Father and the Spirit) and by New Testament thinking about those facts (Father, Son, and Spirit work together in a fixed relational pattern to save us). But the Trinity is a divine mystery without parallel, and the certainty of its reality does not entail clarity as to what sort of a reality it can be. How then are we to testify to it? Despite all difficulties felt about the unscriptural word *person,* we need to continue to use it, not because we fully know what it means to be a divine person in relation to two other divine persons, but because, as Augustine said, the alternative is to say nothing, and, as evangelicals know, only those who conceive the Father, Son, and Spirit as personal on the analogy of our own personhood will ever enter into the "I-thou" relationship of trust in the Father through the Son that is true biblical faith. Against the current tendency to fight shy of the concept of multiple personhood within the Godhead, and to substitute for it a trinity of manifestation within a unitarian or modalist frame, we ought to set our face, on the ground that this view really does deny that at this point the revelation of God in Scripture is a revelation of what he essentially is. We should certainly be insisting that, so far from the Three being less personal than we are, they must be conceived as *more* personal—more integrated, more sensitive and responsive to all that is not themselves, and more individually self-aware—than we fallen and mixed-up creatures are. We should undoubtedly be saying that the distinct, transcendent personhood of Father, Son, and Spirit is the inescapable presupposition of all that Scripture tells us about their cooperation in the plan of salvation. We ought most definitely to recognize that, purely in terms of New Testament thought forms, there is far more to be said in favor of Leonard Hodgson's "social" than of Karl Barth's "model" image of the divine Triunity. We ought beyond question to stress that the Lord Yahweh in the Old Testament is in fact the Three-in-One, even though he was not yet known as such, and to expound the Old Testament witness to God in Trinitarian terms. (And we should never, never speak of the Three as "members" or "parts" of the Trinity, as if the Godhead were some sort of club, or physical organism; nor should we confuse or identify the three persons in our prayers.) But the dimension of mystery in relation to the personhood and unity of the Three will not be dispelled.

GOD THE IMAGE-MAKER

By this time my readers may suspect that I have quite lost sight of the title under which this paper is written. But the suspicion is untrue. What is true is that, before I could say anything about the idea of God as image-maker that would not be misunderstood, I needed to deploy the whole line of thought pursued up to this point. Having now, however, specified what I take to be the nonnegotiable content of theism, and set up my roadblocks both against the corrupting influence of natural theology in cognizing and explaining them, and also against the rationalistic triumphalism of our long-embattled way of expounding them, I can now at last introduce and discuss "God the Image-maker" with what the old tract called safety, certainty, and enjoyment. I wish as I conclude to commend this phrase, within the methodological frame that I have tried to establish, as both a convenient tag whereby to summarize and a fine launching-pad from which to spell out Christian theism as it needs to be stated for today and tomorrow.

What this phrase does is to bind together three main emphases in the theistic position that our world needs to face. Say "maker," and at once you are pointing to the fundamental relationship between God and this world, and ourselves as part of it: that is, the relationship of ontological dependence out of which, as the first verse of Genesis, the first chapter of Calvin's *Institutio,* and philosophical analysis of our situation combine to tell us, all true relational knowledge of God must grow, and which is itself the first element in that knowledge. Say "Image-Maker," and at once you are pointing to the basis and presupposition of our knowledge of God, namely, the fact that we bear his image, of which rationality, relationality, and the capacity for that righteousness which consists of receiving and responding to God's revelation are the basic formal elements. We are able to know God because as thinking, feeling, relating, loving beings we are to that extent like him. Carl Henry keeps this thought running like a Wagnerian *leitmotiv* through his massive *God, Revelation and Authority,* and surely he is right to do so. Finally, say "God," and at once you are pointing to the unique nature and character of the Triune Creator whom, as creatures made in his image, we truly know through the truth of his revelation. The phrase is thus not to be treated as inviting us to reconceive God, or take up with a new image of him, as J. A. T. Robinson twenty years ago wanted us to do, but as a summons to apprehend the essence of traditional theism more perfectly, and expound it more clearly, than sometimes we have done in the past.

Finally, the phrase "God the Image-Maker" has the further advantage of pinpointing what is distinctive in the Christian concept of God as over against that of the ethnic religions. I am no prophet, nor a prophet's son, and no doubt I am as inept with the crystal ball as anyone else; but it seems fairly clear to me that whereas the battle for the meaningfulness of Christian language against the positivist critique of it has been fought and won, and while process theology has run out of steam and will not trouble theists much more, pressure on conservative theology is still building up from exponents of religious relativism and pluralism, both within the church (where some think that the more theologies there are, the livelier, healthier, and merrier we shall be) and outside it. I expect over the next few decades to see the quest for a transcendent synthesis of world religions gain impetus, with consequent attempts to assimilate Christianity to other faiths all along the line. As it took nearly a century after he started for Kierkegaard to have his day, so I suspect that Troeltsch's day is just beginning to come, and that we can expect a generation of debate on his program of moving through and beyond syncretism to a nobler religion than any that has yet been seen. Here, too, by calling attention to the key element in Judeo-Christian belief about God—that he is our Creator, and that he made each human individual in his own image so that he might communicate cognitively with us, mind to mind in order that it might be heart to heart, for everlasting communion in joy and love—our phrase does us good service, reminding us what centrally this debate is, and must be, about. I offer it to my readers, therefore, believing it to be a slogan, or masthead, that we Christians need at this time, to crystallize for us essentials that we must stand for in what, if I am right, will be the next round of the church's unending task of defending and propagating the gospel. If I am wrong in my prognosis, no great harm will be done; but if I am right, we shall I fear be badly at a disadvantage if we have not taken pains to develop our theism more profoundly along the lines for which this slogan calls, and for which I have been arguing in this chapter.

2B

Images of God

Cornelius Plantinga, Jr.

At first glance, the image of God strikes a person as one of those theological oddities, like revelation,[1] that seems somewhat more important to theologians than to writers of the Bible. Augustine uses the concept of image to pivot his Trinity theory away from a social view.[2] John Calvin employs it to summarize human salvation as well as creation and fall.[3] Christian ethics routinely present human dignity, rights, and obligations under the same rubric.[4] The image of God has enjoyed a prestigious place in Christian theology and ethics.

This may seem initially surprising given the often cryptic, sometimes casual, and altogether infrequent use of the phrase "image of God" in Scripture.[5] The most important and perhaps notorious case, at least of the cryptic sort, is the primary nest of references to image and likeness in Genesis 1:26-27. Here dominion (v. 26) and maleness/femaleness (v. 27) might be apposite explanations of the image. On the other hand, perhaps the mention of these things simply adds further information about the task and sex of humanity, leaving the image of God itself magisterially unexplained. Or perhaps only one of the two addenda explicates the image. The Genesis writer is in any case "terse and enigmatic."[6] As to the content of the image of God, he does not answer the question unambiguously.

Theologians have been far more obliging. One can often gain access to main lines of a theologian's system via his concept of the image. Indeed, as Hendrikus Berkhof notes, one could sketch a good piece of European cultural history since Christ from a connected account of the meanings theologians have poured into Genesis 1:26-27.[7] At least traditional theologians have shown a relish for inscripturating their best ideas.

But beyond such zeal, why has the image of God achieved so prominent a place in Christian theology? One reason is that the image, like the kindred concepts of son of God and children of God, links humanity to its Creator and Savior not only by likeness but also by derivation, by an "of" or "from" relation. One can thus see that if theology's object consists of the Triune God, creation, and their relation, then image of God serves as an apt connective for the three.

Further, the general concept of God-likeness not only in humanity but also in Christ, salvation, and church figures centrally in Scripture—whatever may be meant here or there by the specific phrase "image of God."[8] It is therefore theologically attractive, especially given the cryptic biblical uses of the key phrase, to gather the various scripturally indicated God-resemblances under one concept and call it the image of God. The image of God is then the conjunction of all God-likenesses.

Indeed, despite occasional protests to the effect that such a move lacks methodological chastity and restraint,[9] it is entirely proper to make it. For this is the sort of thing systematic theology naturally does. It inherits themes or motifs from biblical theology, elaborates them, discerns conceptual relations among them, and then proposes fruitful and apposite theories of God, creation, and their relation that are generated by these procedures.

Suppose, in the present case, that the Bible presents God-likeness as a motif. It does this with a variety of language and in a range of contexts. What follows for theology is that the image of God may plausibly be said to consist not merely in dominion, or capacity for fellowship, or "concretely visible sanctification," or "respondability to love," or rationality, or self-consciousness, or self-transcendence— each of which has been isolated and championed by one or another theologian as the image of God—but rather in the whole set of these (and many more) likenesses. God is not simple and the ways of resembling God are not few.

Of course one must not insist, or even assume, that such a rich array of God-likenesses was ever had in mind by any particular Bible author. Neither was the doctrine of the Trinity. The theologian is nonetheless perfectly justified in developing a *systematic* concept of the image of God, one including the whole range of respects in which human beings (perhaps even angels and other nonhuman creatures)[10] resemble, reflect, manifest, reproduce, represent, or otherwise show likeness to God.[11] And she may confidently refer to this set of likeness respects as the (systematic) image of God.

The image will thus emerge as a rich, multifaceted reality, comprising acts, relations, capacities, virtues, dispositions, and even emotions. It will also include such homely and obvious properties as *being an object, being alive, being a personal object, being at least one member of the Creator/creature pair,* and (in the case of images of the Trinity) *being a complex object of persons and relations.* I should add that one can speak of each God-like act, relation, property, and so forth, as an image of God. But one can also speak thus of any person or group that exhibits such an image, or a sufficient range of such images. Humans can either bear or be an image of God. *The* image of God, is, correspondingly, either the whole set of God-resemblances, as above, or else the person (Jesus Christ) or group (the church) that displays these resemblances *par excellence.*

We must concede at once that only some God-likenesses are scripturally highlighted and existentially crucial to the Christian life. Among these the top rank would include those benefits of Christ and fruits of the Holy Spirit that exemplify the new life. Other likenesses, such as those traditionally comprised in the "broad" image,[12] stand somewhat in the scriptural background as assumptions rather than explicit teaching.[13] Theologically one ought therefore neither to deny nor to linger over them. Possession of the broad image really functions as a necessary but not sufficient condition for expressing the narrow image. And it is the latter that more clearly interests the biblical writers. Thus, even if the image of God includes a welter of God-resemblances, one properly picks out for discussion those that show scriptural accent marks, or have suffered theological neglect or distortion, or that need special attention in contemporary society and culture.

Accordingly, I will make a run across the biblical field, quickly harvesting some of the central scriptural yield on the image. Then I will develop more fully one often misunderstood and underestimated dimension of it, namely, the communal image of God the Trinity. Finally, I will offer some reflections on the importance of the image of God theme for life in the church and world today.

DOMINION

The phrase "image of God" appears famously as climax to the creation account in Genesis 1. Vegetation, birds, fish, and livestock are splayed from the hand of God "according to their kinds" in a creative salvo whose rounds the biblical writer connects with the formulas "and God said" and "Let there be" or "let [the water, the land, etc.] produce. . . ." Then at the end of creation, at the peak of its account, the verbs shift from intransitive to transitive forms and from third-person singular to a stately first-person plural.[14] Now something weighty and sublime is to be issued, something produced not according to its kind but according to God's:

> 26. Then God said, "Let us make man in our image,
>   in our likeness, and let them rule. . . ."
> 27. So God created man in his image,
>   in the image of God he created him;
>   male and female he created them.
> 28. God blessed them and said to them, "Be fruitful. . . ."

The statements are grammatically, lexically, and narratively highlighted. At the apex of creation stands a creature that is impressively like God.[15]

In what way? As suggested above, it is not immediately obvious that ruling, to take the first candidate, is intended by the Genesis author as an explication of image and likeness. One cannot tell from syntax alone. Perhaps the author has God saying something like this: "Let us make man in our image. . . . In addition, let them rule. . . ." In that case, divine image-making and human dominion would be discrete items of interest.[16]

This reading is, however, unlikely. Biblical scholars who have studied the function of the text in its setting mostly judge that the context is royal.[17] In deliberation with his heavenly council God the King issues a cohortative: "Let us create." What follows is a complex statement of image and ruling in which the ruling part of the sentence probably functions as a purpose clause. Creation in the image of God is at least *for the purpose of* ruling.[18] Extrabiblical literature and recent archaeological discoveries heighten this likelihood: in remote parts of their domain ancient Near Eastern kings would sometimes place a statue, a *ṣelem,* an image of themselves, to represent their dominion.[19] In Genesis 1:26 the divine king similarly adorns his human vice-regents. They are equipped to keep, control, and care for the earth. As the firmament is for dividing, the luminaries for enlightening, so humans are created for ruling.[20]

No doubt such dominion, to go a step further, itself images God. Likely the Genesis author had this in mind; he would probably not have distinguished sharply between the nature and task of humanity.[21] (Indeed, in the ancient Near Eastern situation, a statue of a ruler could probably fulfill its function only if it actually looked something like the ruler.) In any case, in the larger context of the Scriptures the likeness part of representation comes clear. An agent or ambassador is sent as an almost literal representative, or representation, of his superintendent. The sent one, the *šāliaḥ* or *apostolos,* must represent the will, word, and deed of his sender as accurately, as transparently, as possible. For as rabbinic Judaism had it, "the one sent by a man is as the man himself."[22]

So, very likely, in Genesis 1:26 the God-likeness and purpose of human beings turn out to be hard to distinguish. Humans rule. Though servants to God they are landlords to the rest of creation.[23] They are at once God's agents and patented images.[24] And their dominical agency is a part of the image of God.

FELLOWSHIP AND FRUITFULNESS

But what about the maleness/femaleness statement of Genesis 1:27? Could one make a similar case for it as an imaging of God? Could anyone else do this, that is, besides Karl Barth?[25]

Rabbis, church fathers, and medieval to modern theologians have puzzled over this matter, offering views ranging from bizarre to sublime.[26] Another look at Genesis 1:27 in its setting prompts the following four observations.

First, it is somewhat less clear than in the case of dominion that the writer sees maleness/femaleness as a distinct goal of human creation. Clearer and larger are the provisions for fellowship (Gen. 2:20-34) and procreativity (Gen. 1:28) that sexuality permits. "Male and female he created them" fits, then, not so much with what precedes as with what follows it, namely, "Be fruitful and increase in number."[27] Sexuality permits fruitfulness, multiplication, earth-filling. This connection is reinforced at Genesis 5:1-3, where the male and female *adam* bring forth a son in Adam's (and, no doubt, Eve's) likeness.

Second, as the just-cited passage indicates, procreation duplicates the image of God. For after God makes humans in his image they, in turn, produce another image-bearer. Seth possesses at least a human likeness. But given Genesis 9:26 (in which the murder prohibition is based on a continuing presence of the image of God) Seth must be thought to bear God's image as well.

So, beyond dominion, what is this image? In the context of Genesis 1–5—and this is the third observation—procreation itself is presented as a God-likeness. The very process of duplicating God's image images God. In Genesis almost everything brings forth fruit after its kind: animals, plants, birds, fish—all procreate. In his own way God procreates in Genesis 1:26. He brings forth creatures after *his* kind. God issues a kind of person, a kind of ruler. And, as Genesis

4 and 5 make plain, humans follow suit. Humans reproduce in kind. All creation depends on God; all is ordered by God. All animate creation resembles God in fruitfulness, reproductiveness, procreativity. It is a *speculum*.[28] But in all creation only humans are both creators and lords.

Let us return now to this section's original question of maleness/femaleness as a possible God-likeness. There is no evidence in the text, as Barth knew, that sexuality itself images God. For God apparently has no sex. We have seen, however, that one reason for sexuality, procreation, does imitate God. What about the other reason? What about personal fellowship, harmony, mutuality?

A fourth observation, then, is that fellowship is not clearly a Genesis image of God—at least not in the Barthian intra-Trinitarian sense. There may be hints of fellowship in the God-and-his-council plurals, but the connection between these and the companionship of Genesis 2 is oblique at best. There is nothing explicit about the Trinity in Genesis. Even divine-human fellowship, thought legitimately assumed as a created excellence given the alienation of Genesis 3 that disrupts it, is out of the center of the picture. In any case there is no Genesis warrant for connecting it to an image in humans.[29] (Still, we have less doctrinal loss here than meets the eye. For what Genesis lacks John provides. The Barthian analogy of relations appears, as we shall see, very richly in the fourth Gospel.)

Genesis yields, all told, dominion and fruitfulness. If one finds the themes of glory and honor in Psalm 8 implicit in dominion, then they belong to the harvest as well.

JESUS CHRIST AND THE RESTORATION OF THE IMAGE

In the New Testament Jesus Christ appears as the preeminent image of God the Father (Col. 1:15; 2 Cor. 4:4). He is the "exegesis of God" (John 1:18) who bears the very stamp of the divine nature (Heb. 1:3) and who prekenotically exists "in the form of God" (Phil. 2:6). Believers are in turn to be conformed to the image of this Son and Lord (Rom. 8:29; 2 Cor. 3:18).

Some of these conformities appear in the context of those "renewal of the image" passages that connect vast tracts of Pauline redemption teaching to the image theme. In these passages (Eph. 4:24; Col. 3:10) knowledge, righteousness, and holiness stand for the whole new life in Christ that Paul wants believers to "put on." These three virtues are either summaries or samples of the spiritual hygiene, the moral *shalom,* that results from renewal of human communal life. Paul is talking in these passages especially about self-giving love, the ligament of the new community (Eph. 4:15-16; Col. 3:14). He is talking, most generally, about the luminous and weighty Christ-likeness that allows believers to present *his* image to the world and to each other. For, as Paul can say alternately (Rom. 13:14), it is somehow Christ himself that we put on like a garment.

One properly concludes from these passages, as does G. C. Berkouwer, that the New Testament image of God in believers includes not only loving, forgiving, and being perfect—all specifically linked to God or Christ by "just as" clauses (Eph. 4:32; Col. 3:13; Matt. 5:48). It also includes the whole array of ways we obey God by imitating Christ. It includes all the virtues, all the fruit of the Spirit, every generous lifting of a cup to someone's thirst, every resourceful attempt to shore up a sagging spirit, all compassionate attempts to struggle and suffer with a person whose life seems flat, sad, lost, and over. After all, Paul's lists of virtues are only exemplary. The image of God is every conceivable holiness: it is "concretely visible sanctification."[30]

New Testament conformity to Jesus Christ also includes certain likenesses, however, that believers may not wholly appreciate at first. Central in Paul's teaching is that Christ-likeness includes suffering as well as glory, frustration as well as liberation, death as well as life.[31] In fact, in each of these cases the former seems to be a condition, or at least an antecedent, of the latter. What Abraham Heschel says eloquently about the pathos of the God of the prophets[32] comes home to us in Jesus Christ. God suffers; so will those who are God-like and Christ-like. God the Son dies; so must those who hope, like him, to be raised to new life.[33]

This biblical theme of pathos and death in God has, of course, attracted considerable discussion in contemporary theology. With genuine excitement and an air of discovery, a number of theologians have reminded us that God feels, God cares, God commiserates; God shows compassion. God is a moved mover, a God of sorrows who is acquainted with grief. God is the eminent displayer not of apathy but of passion and compassion.[34]

One can view this welcome recovery of a major scriptural theme as the product of nineteenth-century de-Hellenization movements translated into biblical theology. One can see it as a salutary contribution of process theology—or as a place where process and liberation motifs converge.[35] One can see it as the triumph of the *via eminentiae* over the *via negativa*,[36] or even as the recovery in contemporary context of the Lutheran theology of the cross.

For Luther, as Paul Althaus observes in a purposely ambiguous claim, God is known only in suffering.[37] That is, God is known in his suffering (in Christ) only by those who suffer with him. A disciple is not greater than his master. For both, strength is displayed in weakness: he who loses his life will find it; she who is humbled will be exalted; the one who dies shall live.

The point for the image of God is that sin changes its face. Creation images of glory and sonship, for example, now appear as recovery or even as self-surpassing redemption images against the dark backdrop of sin and misery.[38] One can understand the New Testament images of glory, sonship, freedom, exaltation, and life only when one has felt the intervening force of sin's slavery, suffering, and death. In a unique convergence of such themes John's Gospel portrays the Son of God as *exalted* on a cross (12:32-33).

One cannot help pausing at this point to observe how such biblical ideas render poignant our general perception of God and evil. God's power in pitched battle with evil revises our notion of dominion and lordship: it seems to include less by way of sheer God-almightiness than by way of patient, agonizing, sometimes even hesitant, hard work.[39] It looks less like the power of Eisenhower than of Gandhi, less like the power of a pantocrator than a suffering servant.

Admittedly, we have to factor in the gracious self-limiting of God. God the Son empties himself. God the Father entrusts the fiercest work in the world to his handicapped Son. The result is an apparent disproportion in Godly effort between creation and redemption. Evil turns out to be harder to overcome than nothingness. In creation God simply speaks and it happens. But redemption takes terrible pains.[40] Redemption shows the Son of God going flat out, working at his limit. If evil, as the church fathers always said, is privative, parasitical, and secondary, it is at any rate stubborn, cunning, formidable, and frightening—even to the Son of God. Sin and misery change his image from creation mediator to suffering servant to vindicated Lord. The whole drama of creation, fall, and redemption in human beings is thus an image of the parabola-shaped career of God the Son.

THE FOURTH GOSPEL
AND THE SOCIAL IMAGE OF GOD

In main strands of the New Testament (Paul, Hebrews, John) the general picture of deity presented is that of three distinct, yet closely associated, divine persons—the picture being both richer and sharper with respect to Father and Son than with respect to the Spirit. Indeed, the very terms *Father* and *Son* suggest combined distinction and close relation. The Holy Spirit meanwhile appears not as a "family member," but rather as an agent of Father and Son. "Spirit of God" and "Spirit of Christ" are capsular for the distinction-within-unity relation of the Spirit to the two other divine persons.[41]

Yet if there is an overall relational picture emerging from a number of New Testament witnesses, some of those witnesses contribute far more to it than do others. Arthur Wainwright sketches a Trinitarian blueprint according to which there are at least three levels of New Testament development of the relation of Father, Son, and Spirit (or Paraclete) and of some problems associated with their relation.[42] John raises this development to its highest level. For in John lies the fullest recognition of the need to *account* somehow for the distinct personhood and divinity of Father, Son, and Spirit, and to do so without compromising the unity of God. There can be little doubt that this Gospel offers the richest vein in the New Testament for the church doctrine of the Trinity; it offers the "supreme biblical pattern of trinitarian thought."[43]

Let me briefly spell this out. John's Gospel presents an apparently simple text, full of innocent-looking identity statements, repetitions, and sentences in regular paratactic syntax—a simplicity that hides knotty problems of provenance, authorship, audience, and meaning.[44] It also hides a subtle and rich account of divine distinction-within-unity. In John, Father, Son, and Spirit are distinct divine persons who play different, and differently ordered, roles in the enterprise of life giving and life disclosing. Yet their primordial, unexplained divine unity or "inness" (10:30; 14:31) is revealed and exemplified by common work, word, and knowledge, and by reciprocal loving (except for the Spirit) and glorifying. The same super-to subordination that yields main differences among the three also serves simultaneously to bind them together. This is the emphatic *para-doxa* expressed by Jesus himself in the juxtapositions of 10:29 with 10:30 and of 14:10-11 with 14:28.[45] There is one divine work but several roles to play in it; one general level of divinity, but degrees of priority in it; one divine society embracing a Father, Son, and their agent.

What John presents, in short, is all the materials for a truly social doctrine of the Trinity. And because of the links John makes between heavenly and earthly communities, his Gospel presents as well a pattern of social relation between God and the community of believers. For in believers abide not only Paul's faith, hope, and love, but also John's Father, Son, and Paraclete (14:23, 17).

For John, however, Father, Son, and Spirit are not only in believers; they are also *as* believers. That is, they are social beings whom believers image. In an impressive heaping up of relational statements, many of them employing *kathōs* clauses, John directly and uniquely compares the *Wechselbeziehungen* of Father and Son (and, occasionally, the Spirit) with those of the disciples or members of the Christian community.[46] Already at 8:17-18 there is an explicit two-man analogy. But, beginning in chapter fourteen and climaxing in seventeen, we find what Mark Appold calls a "unique" and "massive concentration of reciprocity statements," including believers with Father and Son.[47] Though the fourth Gospel would qualify as a Trinitarian social gospel just by virtue of presenting three fully personal and distinguishable divine beings, these reciprocity statements take us a step further. For now we are not left to make the analogical link ourselves (Trinity to humanity); John makes it for us. In perhaps the best known of these analogy statements, the Son, who assumes his own unity with the Father, prays for the future and analogous oneness of believers: "that they may be one as we are one" (17:22).[48] What we have here is a social image of God within the church.

What are the terms and categories of John's social image? Precisely those same internally divine categories of distinction-within-unity mentioned above: works, word, knowledge, love, glory, and "inness." Using these categories, John not only presents two sets of analogically related horizontal relationships—that is, heavenly and earthly—but with the Son as pivot and mediator, he links these two sets of horizontal relations vertically—primarily, heaven to earth—to round out the threefold *analogia relationis* of which Karl Barth has rightly made so much.[49]

Let us note the use of social image in the six key Johannine concepts just listed. First, in the area of works or mission, we find not only that Father, Son, and Spirit perform different roles within the one large life-giving enterprise; we also find that the disciples will do what the Son has been doing—and more (14:12). As the Son and

Spirit obey, so the disciples must do what the Son commands (14:15). The sent one himself sends his followers in the "small Pentecost" or insufflation of the age of the Spirit (20:21-22). Just as the Father consecrates the Son for mission (10:36), so the Son (13:20; 17:19; 20:21) and the Father (17:17) do this for the disciples. And as the Son serves the Father, and the Spirit the Son, so the disciples are deliberately and incarnately taught to serve one another (13:12-15).[50] The Johannine mutuality of work even goes a remarkable step further. For as the disciples are taken up into the divine mission, they are entrusted with the power to make requests of Father and Son. True, they do not command. They ask. But, in return, the Son (14:13) and God (1 John 5:14-15) do what they are asked.

Second, in the closely related category of word, the disciples' proclamation arises from and mirrors the word the Paraclete delivers to them from the Son who is the Word of the Father. The Son's word "abides in" the disciples (15:17) when the Paraclete teaches them, but they in turn must "testify" (15:27). In fact, the "newer believers" of chapter seventeen are precisely those who come to light "through their word" (17:20). Surely the things written in the Gospel as a whole (20:31) represent and elaborate this very word passed to and through and from the community—whether or not the Gospel is primarily a missionary document.[51]

Third, knowledge is reciprocal not only among Father, Son, and Spirit but also between Son and sheep or disciples (10:15).[52] The disciples are known; they also know both their shepherd and the Father because the Son has mediated knowledge to them.[53]

Love is a fourth category. Here the threefold *analogia relationis* becomes vividly clear. In a chain of loving obedience, the Son is bound to the Father, disciples to Son and Father, and disciples to each other (13:34-35; 14:21; 15:9, 12, 17; 17:23).[54] Given this explicit linking of human love to Father/Son love, Barrett makes the social analogical conclusion: the disciples' love for each other is the community style. Disciples resemble "members of the divine family." They represent "an extension of the social personality of the Godhead."[55] Communal love is an explicit image of God.

Fifth, if the Father and Son glorify each other, and if the Spirit glorifies the Son, Jesus is also glorified in or through his disciples (17:10) and, reciprocally, glorifies them. This glory is, in fact, a condition for the disciples' oneness with each other (17:22).

Finally, the primordial divine "inness" or oneness is itself mediated to the community of believers by the Son who already enjoys it in relation with Father and Paraclete. Through the Paraclete, the Father/Son "inness" is (or is to be) transmitted to those who else would be orphans (14:18). They and the Son who is in the Father are mutually in each other (14:20). In the vine *mashal* of chapter fifteen this mutual "remaining in" is repeated ten times in seven verses (4-10).[56] Jesus in the disciples gives life; they in him produce such fruit as mutual love (vv. 12, 17), joy (v. 11), and the glorifying of the Father (v. 8). In chapter seventeen this "inness" concept expands to include the disciples in the Father/Son relation! The remarkable eschatological goal is that the disciples may be "in us" (v. 22; cf. 1 John 1:3, 7).

The equivalent term and concept "one" *(hen)* confirms this Johannine presentation of communal unity. Because the disciples have the divine word and do the work assigned to them, because they have been allowed to know and have been given to love Father and Son, because they share the life of the Son from the Father through the life-giving Spirit, they in turn will remain protected in the world "so that they may be one as we are one" (17:11). In the expansion of the church, others will become believers through the word of life. Jesus' last will is that *"all of them* may be one" (17:21).

Oneness/"inness" emerges as the overarching communal image of God, expressed or exemplified by work, word, knowledge, love, and glory. John clearly presents the early community's oneness as a participation in and reflective reproduction of a primordial and heavenly divine unity. In fact, it must be emphasized that John's conceptual order is crucial. He never models heavenly unity on earthly relations: just the opposite. Divine unity is given and assumed; it is the model. Earthly unity must be *achieved* and is hence to be prayed for. The model is always primordially divine. The community becomes, by grace, more and more like its model, and therefore continuously a better image of it.

Two final remarks about social image need to be made. First, John's "oneness" relation is dynamic. Father, Son, and Spirit *do* things with and for each other. Each acts; each is acted upon. Moreover, they overflow in zestful mission to humankind—who, in turn, reproduce the divine mission among themselves. The energy, purpose, outreach—the sheer activity in John—is impressive and unmistakable. This activity both reflects and further constitutes divine, divine/human, and human oneness. Second, the Johannine unity presents itself not only as social but especially as organic. John's central soteriological concept is life. And the unity of Father, Son, and Spirit, of divine and human interaction, and of human community is that of shared life. The presentation of the vine, of the bread and water, of rebirth, of revivification and resurrection from death, of the light which is life, of earthly flesh and blood and heavenly food, of children of God—all these things speak of life. And the concepts of "inness," withness, abiding, dwelling, making one's home—all speak of life *together.* John has no sheer existence; he has rather coexistence, inexistence, with-existence. He has a social life of Father, Son, and Spirit; of these with a hungry and lost humanity; and of the revivified humanity together. He has both a social view and social image of God.

SUMMARY AND IMPLICATIONS

Created and, particularly, redeemed human beings display a host of God-likenesses and Christ-likenesses. This essay has presented some main samples, some particular images of God. Hence its title. I have claimed as biblically central such images as dominion, fruitfulness, and suffering, and such especially communal images as concretely visible sanctification in Paul and oneness or "inness" in John. In the latter case the proper biblical analogy of the Trinity is the church. Just as each member of the Trinity, let us say, images God the Father, so each member of the church images each member of the Trinity. But the whole church images the whole Trinity. The church, like the Trinity, is a complex of persons and relations. And in its cluster of God-given works and virtues the church progressively achieves the kind of integrity,[57] wholeness, hygiene, *shalom,* oneness that eternally characterizes the divine society. The image of God thus emerges as both individual and social.

But what is especially pertinent about noting all this? To what conclusions or relevant observations does the biblical and theological doctrine of the image of God lead us in the contemporary context? Let me suggest four.

First, though the Scriptures do not accent personhood as an image of God it is everywhere assumed and in every case crucial for things the Scriptures *do* accent. For instance, the fact that humans are persons—living centers of rationality, will, emotion, responsibility, and freedom—secures human rights. It secures the right to life and life support, to a certain quality of life. It secures the right to work and to enjoy relative freedom, including the freedom to delight in creation.[58]

Personhood as an image of God secures as well the right to respect from others, for all humans carry by design a weight of glory. Human beings have poise, a divinely given center of gravity: they have weightiness, value, *dignitas*. They deserve due respect. You cannot spit on a person who wears a crown.[59] He or she has divine rights. Such affronts as racism, sexism, and classism must accordingly be seen as insulting not only to humans but also to the God they represent. The same must be said for making and glorying in war, for sexual, psychological, and physical exploitations, and, indeed, for all human abuses: they are all condemnable iconoclasm.

Further, this weight of glory calls to account the various greasy human degradations that smear the image. All sad indignities, indelicacies, indecencies, and pornographies of the human spirit are called to account. Every frightening video image of humans as slaves, snakes, slobs, or sleezebags, all attempts to objectify humans as mere bedfellows, manufacturing devices, career stepladders, or disposable inconveniences—all these things are called to account.

Humans are, after all, God-like. Because of the acids of sin they are nobility in ruins, but they are nobility who will, one way or another, live forever. They must therefore be handled with care, for "it is a serious thing to live in a society of possible gods and goddesses."[60]

As a matter of fact, the created image of God positions humanity between extravagant and demeaning estimates, between humanisms and naturalisms, between the view that we are gods in need of occasional therapy and the view that we are "naked apes" or "digestive tubes." For (to use the Barthian pattern of alternating emphases) against all Promethean or pathetic presumptions of ultimacy we are not God but only secondary *images* of God. Yet against all materialist images of animals and machines we are images of *God*. And if one adds the eschatological promise of eternal glory of a kind that we cannot now imagine, since "what we will be has not yet been made known" (1 John 3:2), then the concept of the consummated image of God places humanity beyond, not just between, humanisms and naturalisms.

Because of this last possibility owed to the work of Jesus Christ, all human beings are to be viewed not only seriously but also hopefully. This is the second observation. All human beings are by creation children of God. Sin betrays and disrupts this relation, but it does not destroy it. Further, because Jesus Christ's redeeming work ranges universally across the human race (Rom. 5:18), all humans are to be *seen* in Christ unless they give final and decisive evidence to the contrary.[61] They are to be regarded as brothers and sisters, as fellow children of God. They are to be called to the appropriate responses of faith and obedience. And in any case we must try to find in them the signs, even the quirky and distorted ones, of *eros* for their Maker, even when such signs are larded over with sin and self-deception.

The fact is that because they have been made by and for God, all human beings are incurably religious. They want God even when they are not aware of it.[62] They hunger and thirst for righteousness so much that they can seldom cease rationalizing or scapegoating unrighteous behavior. People find Christ-likeness appealing even while rejecting it; they strive for at least the *form* of godliness even in the midst of pathological wrongdoing.[63] Human beings are incorrigibly concerned about their image.

Third, we should see suffering with Christ not merely as agonizing but also as affording a painfully unique perspective on the life of God. For when we suffer, or when we show compassion to those who do, we are *like God*. God is the *dios probre,* the God of the poor. And God is the one who tends and succors the fruit of her womb like a mother (Isa. 49:15) or spares his miserably disobedient children like an exasperated, but finally compassionate, father (Hos. 11:8, 9). Suffering has the power to move believers to what black theologians call "a place of epistemological privilege." We begin in that place to understand the agony and loss in God that sin inflicts. We begin to understand the grim determination of a godly Son who "sets his face" to go to Jerusalem (Luke 9:51).

The suffering of God serves a further purpose—one that explains why pastors and counselors often refer Christian sufferers to the cross of Christ for support. Why do they do so? How does the sheer fact of Jesus' passion and death explain suffering or our particular case of it?[64] In fact it explains very little. What the suffering of God does is to reassure human sufferers *that God can be trusted.*[65] God is not aloof. God is not oblivious to the groans of a world in uproar. God's suffering is the sign of God painfully at work to call our madhouse to order.

Fourth, the church image of God the Trinity presents a number of striking reminders and obligations. The overcoming of estrangement from God and humanity is in Pauline perspective both the graceful accomplishment and goal of the Christian community. In our fellowship and *koinonia,* in our *ens sociale,* in such modest endeavors as telling each other the truth and doing such "honest work" as will help "those in need"—above all in that love which "binds everything together in perfect harmony"—we not only demonstrate that we are "members one of another," but also that we as community, we-in-the-plural, constitute the restored image of God.

Here we find a close theological link between what might be called the Johannine intra-Trinitarian "deference," on the one hand, and the Pauline recipe for organic harmony in the church on the other. John presents a general picture of the priority of the Father. The Son imitates the Father, and the Paraclete acts as agent of Father and Son. The Spirit defers to the Son who defers to the Father.

But it is not all a one-way street. It is not just that the Spirit points to the Son and the Son to the Father. Rather, as several strands of the New Testament assert, the Father also points to the Son—especially in baptism and transfiguration (Mark 1:11; 9:7). And the Son points to the Spirit, who in the new age will be teacher and life-giver (John 3:5; 6:63; 14:26). If Jesus is God's servant in the apostolic preaching in Acts, it is also the case that God has exalted his servant (2:33; 3:26). In John's Gospel, Father and Son *mutually* glorify each other (13:31-32).

In Philippians 2, Paul presents and reflects on the profound need in the Christian community to defer to and exalt the other members of the community; he does so on the pattern of the Christ whose selfless and powerful servanthood links the other-regarding Trinitarian life with the *koinonia* of the church. We in the church are to have "the same mind," and "the same love":

> Do nothing from selfishness or conceit, but in humility count others better than yourselves. Let each of you look not only to his own interests, but also to the interests of others. Have this mind among yourselves, which you have in Christ Jesus, who, though he was in the form of God, did not count equality with God a thing to be grasped, but emptied himself, taking the form of a servant, being born in the likeness of men. (Vv. 3-7)

Thus the summit of church membership is being membered with others not only by common love or loyalty for the same Lord, but also by having the divine *mind*—the servant mind, the deferring-to-others mind. Membership in the church implies the high goal of imitating the divine life by glorifying and exalting others and so doing by "taking on the form of a servant."[66] What Augustine says of the physical body of Christ may then be properly extended to the church: even the communal body of Christ is a sort of sacrament, for it is a visible sign of an invisible reality.[67]

Perhaps the most general value of the social image of God the Trinity in the church is that it testifies to the social nature of ultimate reality—the social nature of that God by whom and toward whom we exist. Reality is at its core not only personal, but tri-personal. What is for some atheistic individuals a kind of hell[68] is for God and God's community an ultimate reality and joy—the presence of *others*.

Healing Old Wounds and Recovering Old Insights: Toward a Christian View of the Person for Today

C. Stephen Evans

BETWEEN REDUCTIONISM AND SELF-DEIFICATION

The post-Christian world cannot make up its mind about the human person. Like the Socrates of the *Phaedrus* (229e) it cannot decide whether the human person is a monster to tamed or a divinelike creature who must simply be freed to express or "realize" its own innate potentialities. It cannot decide whether human beings must be reengineered (Skinnerian social conditioning) or freed from all forms of social control except their own unique "experience" (Rogerian natural development). The post-Christian view of the person is still up for grabs.

The "war" generally can be characterized as a struggle between *reductionism* and *self-deification*. The reductionism of Pavlov and Skinner thankfully is somewhat *passé* in psychology, but nevertheless the lingering effects of stimulus-response and operant conditioning as basic tools in understanding human behavior continue to linger. Freud, while never accepted in the psychological establishment, continues to have a wide cultural impact. Newer forms of reductionism abound. Sociologists such as Richard Dawkins assure us that "we are survival machines—robot vehicles, blindly programmed to preserve the selfish molecules known as genes."[1]

The most sophisticated and alluring forms of reductionism today play on our growing obsession with the digital computer. From this perspective human beings are simply extremely complex automata. Soon, it is claimed, scientists will produce fifth-generation computers that will exhibit such "human" properties as consciousness and general intelligence. Already the computer has had a tremendous impact on the human self-image as we project human characteristics on machines, which then supply us with metaphors for reinterpreting our human characteristics.

The upshot of reductionism is still that human beings are seen as products, as mere objects of nature, not as subjects, responsible beings with an interior life and the power to make choices. The uniqueness and dignity of human beings is undermined. If this were all there were to the story, the Christian response to the post-Christian view of the human person would, I think, be clear.

Unfortunately or fortunately, the post-Christian mind is as taken with self-deification as with reductionism. The same human person who is seen as a meaningless accident in the vastness of the cosmos, a machine that is ultimately the product of blind, impersonal forces, is also seen as a god! This human person is the creator of values and meanings, the source of right and wrong. What is striking is not so much the conclusion that if God does not exist, then we humans must try to assume his functions and give to our own lives value and meaning; the really astounding thing is the confidence of the secular mind that humans can pull off the trick and "become as gods." It is hardly surprising that beings who thus see themselves as the authors of their own moral universes should practically express this in the numbing narcissism and egoism that have so dramatically increased in Western society, particularly among younger people.

Obviously it is not the task of Christians to take sides in this internal quarrel within secular culture. Perhaps a first task of Christians is to help secular culture see this quarrel as a quarrel, since only too often the secular thinker cheerfully combines the two mind-sets with no awareness of tension.

However, the more fundamental, long-range theoretical task (and I hasten to add that the problems in our human self-understanding are not merely theoretical and cannot be solved merely through theoretical analysis) is to analyze the source of these one-sided, erroneous interpretations of human personhood and present a diagnosis for healing.

To accomplish this task it is helpful to recognize that the problem is not entirely new. The major alternatives to an authentic Christian view of the person have always been idealism and naturalism. From Plato onward the idealist has always seen the human person as divine or quasi-divine, a manifestation of a supreme spiritual principle, an essentially immaterial being whose true home is an ideal realm of Truth and Beauty. From Democritus onward the naturalist has always seen the human person as essentially a product of an impersonal universe.

From the Christian perspective, both views have survived and prospered because each is a one-sided appropriation of truth. The truth is, as many Christian thinkers have noted, but especially Pascal and Kierkegaard, the human person is a paradoxical fusion of godlike and animal-like characteristics. Humans occupy the "mid-point of creation," but they do so by embodying characteristics of those above and below them in the great chain of being.

The biblical teaching that human beings are creatures made in God's image is, when properly understood, the surest safeguard against both reductionism and self-deification. The Christian knows that he or she is made in God's image. Regardless of how the *imago dei* is understood, this means that humans are special creatures. Furthermore, since this special status is given to humans by God, it is not something with which we endow ourselves, though in our sinful pride we would rather bestow an illusory dignity on ourselves than accept the proper dignity of being special creatures.

And creatures we are. We can be comfortable with our creaturely status, with our physicality, our undeniable links to the animal, since that physical universe is not a product of blind chance or blind necessity, but the work of a personal being, with plans and purposes.

The secular mind, however, is not really comfortable with either pole of the human situation. Insofar as the uniqueness of the human person bespeaks the origin of human nature from transcendent personal reality, the secular mind flies toward reductionism, refusing to see anything truly unique about human beings, a refusal that sometimes approaches the comical as the most sophisticated and elegant expressions of the human spirit are employed to deny that there is anything spiritual in humans. But when facing the bleakness of an impersonal universe, bereft of meaning and value, the same secular mind hurries to affirm that meaning and morality can be securely established on the basis of the decisions and actions of a fragile race of creatures.

Never in history has there been a greater need for a clear reaffirmation of a Christian view of the person. Yet by and large Christians are not effectively communicating their vision of human personhood. We are not clearly expressing the powerful and relevant notions of human beings as created in the image of God, fallen, and redeemed in Christ. The reasons for this are clearly complex and doubtless exceed our full understanding. To some degree they probably lie in factors over which Christians have little or no control.

Nevertheless I believe we are partly to blame for the situation. We have done what we ought not to have done and left undone what we ought to have done. More specifically, we have hastily and carelessly abandoned central elements in the Christian view of the person, in order to make our views "relevant" and "contemporary." At the same time we have failed to show the genuine relevance of classical truths to the contemporary situation, contenting ourselves with reiterating those truths in a mechanical fashion. We have generated new, unnecessary squabbles within the Christian family, blurring and confusing our message. At the same time we have failed to resolve long-standing disagreements that rested from the beginning on misunderstandings and misperceptions on the part of both sides. In what follows I shall try to give some specific examples of the above, together with some recommendations for changes.

SUBSTANCE ANTHROPOLOGY
VERSUS RELATIONAL ANTHROPOLOGY

Classical Christian anthropologies were built around Greek philosophical categories, particularly the category of *substance*. The discussions focused on human beings as spiritual creatures who are a unified compound of soul and body. Human beings have a definite human nature, as a consequence of which they possess definite powers, and they exist as individual persons who are essentially related to God and other persons in various ways, particularly through such institutions as the family. All of these categories show the Greek imprint. They are either terms for substances or they are thought of in a substantial fashion. They are either enduring entities or enduring structures or aspects of entities, which enter into various relations. The *imago dei* is thought of as a property or complex of properties that humans possess.

Though there are notable exceptions, by and large contemporary Christian anthropology seems oriented away from substantial categories toward what might be termed "relational categories." This is the case whether we look at popular or technical presentations, whether we look at theology proper or turn our attention to views of human beings that have been developed by Christian social scientists.

On this sort of view the uniqueness of the human person is not to be found in the possession of a soul of a certain type, or in a particular set of qualities that constitute the *imago*. Rather, humans are special because of the relationships of which they are a part, or of which they can be a part. Our dignity stems from the social roles and functions we play, including especially our roles in relation to God.

This view of selfhood is most clearly associated with existentialism, which affirms that the self is more an achievement than an entity, something we become rather than something we are. What is striking, however, is how much this kind of view has permeated thinkers who are in other ways worlds apart from the existentialists. There are multiple examples of this. For instance, Donald M. MacKay, the distinguished British scientist of brain physiology and communication theory, answers the question "What is so special about man?" as follows:

> The biblical answer is that what makes us special is the amazing fact that our Creator was prepared to do for us all that Christ did and suffered in his incarnation, crucifixion, and resurrection. Our dignity has nothing to do with our occupying a geographic hub of the universe, or being the product of a special process, or being constructed of special materials, or being inexplicable at one or another scientific level.[2]

A little later MacKay says simply that "what is special about each man is the role to which he is called. We will be quick to distinguish dignity in this sense from *superiority,* whether measured psychologically, physically, or in any other way."[3]

MacKay here echoes Karl Barth's famous expression that the fact that "man is man and not a cat" is "quite unimportant."[4] The same sort of view expressed in a more positive vein comes from Stephen Neill: "What is it that makes man really human? The answer is, the knowledge of God."[5]

We can also see this contemporary swing toward relational and away from substantial categories in the swing from dualism to monism. The traditional view that human beings are a compound of body and soul (or body, soul, and spirit) is widely derided as a Greek intrusion on the "Hebraic" biblical view, which more holistically affirms the unity of human beings and views "soul" and "spirit" as capacities of bodily human beings rather than as substances.

The merits of this contemporary approach are considerable. One important factor is that a Christian anthropology becomes almost immune to scientific refutation. If human dignity lies in the fact that God cares about us, or in the possibility of our knowing about him, rather than in some unique human quality, then the theologian is saved from making any potentially embarrassing claims about the differences between human and other animals. As MacKay affirms, our dignity does not lie in our superiority. Nor must the theologian affirm any nonmaterial soul or spirit as a factor in understanding human behavior. In light of the directions of contemporary science this looks increasingly attractive.

But the move from a substance anthropology to a relational anthropology is attractive for internal theological reasons as well. It is frequently argued that relational, functional categories are more biblical, closer to Hebraic modes of thought. The substance categories represent the pervasive, corrupting influence of Greek thought on Christian theology. In fact, a strong case can be made that relational anthropology is really the fulfillment of a trend begun by the Protestant Reformers, who rejected the scholastic equation of the *imago* with rationality and instead viewed the *imago* as the original righteousness people possessed by virtue of their relation to God. The whole Reformation attack on the medieval categories of nature/supernature was rooted in a suspicion of any qualities or virtues humans might be said to possess independently, on their own. The thrust of Reformation anthropology was clearly in the direction of understanding everything about human beings in terms of their fundamental dependence upon God, a thrust that was motivated by soteriology but that permeated theology as a whole. Even Emil Brunner, who is ultimately sharply critical of Barth's anthopology, sees the Barthian-type view as a consistent, logical development of the Reformation view.[6]

The advantages of immunity from scientific refutation and of being a theological barrier to human pride and autonomy that relational anthropology possesses are real. But they are purchased at a price. The price of immunity from scientific refutation is the danger of lack of relevance to contemporary thought-forms. What cannot be refuted by science also cannot be supported by science, and may be difficult to relate to science. The theological advantages also carry a price—namely, an inability to answer certain questions that were answered by traditional Christian anthropology, questions that are not merely speculative but have significance for the practical piety of the church. Specifically, questions about the nature and significance of human *origins* and human *destiny* are not being answered, and an understanding of the empirically evident capacities of "natural man" for knowledge and "virtuous action" is blocked. It is, I think, for these reasons that Reformation theology did not go all the way toward a relational anthropology but preserved, whether consistently or inconsistently, the substantial category of the soul, and even the view that sinners possess a "relic" of the image of God.

My thesis is not that we should reject relational categories and return to substance categories. It is that both kinds of categories are needed to do justice to the Christian view of the person. The correct balance is nicely illustrated, I believe, in Kierkegaard's Christian anthropology. In *The Sickness unto Death* Kierkegaard apparently adopted a purely relational view of the self: "The human self is such a derived established relation, a relation that relates itself to itself and in relating itself to itself relates itself to another."[7] Here Kierkegaard sees the self as a relation of self-consciousness, which is mediated through a relation to an other, the ultimate "other" being God. This "relational" view of self is quite consistent with the strong Kierkegaardian insistence that a self is something that I must *become,* not just something that I automatically acquire, like teeth or a beard.

This relational view is not the whole story for Kierkegaard, however. He also recognizes that in one sense we are all "something of a self" and that to choose to become a self I must *be* a self. This latter kind of self seems a substantial category, and Kierkegaard makes it clear that this natural self (which contains the *possibility* of selfhood in the richer relational sense) is rooted in God's creative activity. So the self here is both an entity and a relational achievement. A closer look at specific issues will make this kind of view more plausible.

THE *IMAGO DEI:*
REFORMATION VERSUS MEDIEVAL THOUGHT

Medieval theological perspectives on the human person were rooted in the distinction Irenaeus drew between the image of God and the likeness of God. Irenaeus identified the likeness of God with the original righteousness Adam and Eve possessed before the fall. (To be sure, he believed they possessed that quality in an immature way, partly as a set of potentialities to be actualized.) The image of God was seen as a set of "natural" capacities that man possessed as a rational creature. These capacities were not lost in the fall, though they were harmed. This perspective clearly implies a distinction between what is natural, achievable by humans even in their fallen state, and what is supernatural, open to humans only through God's grace in the work of Jesus.

The Reformers repudiated this dualism of nature and supernature for a variety of reasons. Fundamentally, they wanted to deny human independence of the Creator, together with any ability to achieve virtue by natural means. An additional reason was a concern for the unity of human nature. Man's need for God must be seen as fundamental to his whole being, not an "added bonus."

Luther therefore denied the distinction between the image and likeness of God in Genesis 1:26, on exegetical grounds but for theological reasons as well. Instead, he equated the *imago* with the "original righteousness" and affirmed that this was lost in the fall. Calvin essentially followed Luther here, in the heat of polemical controversy, and both Reformers were capable of statements that implied that the image of God had been completely destroyed.

Catholic theologians responded to this Protestant attack with indignant accusations of their own. The Protestant view denuded God's creation of its value and made it impossible to understand how God's redemptive activity can be a restoration of his creation, insofar as nothing of that creation remains to be transformed. God's redemptive work implied no real change in human nature at all, but only an "imputed righteousness" that is completely external to the life of the believer.

I believe, however, that this dispute has outlived its usefulness. The differences were never as great as they appeared to be, and are today largely illusory. To continue it merely hampers both sides in their struggle to communicate a Christian view of the human person today. For various reasons the bad effects are especially noticeable on the Protestant side. For the most part, each side was right in what it affirmed. Similarly each side was for the most part unjust in its criticisms of the other.

Catholic theology was quite right to maintain that human beings, even in their fallen state, retain dignity and value. They were quite right to maintain that even unredeemed humans are capable of rational knowing and acting, and that their abilities rested on powers given to humans by God in creation. In the end, Luther and Calvin do not really deny these things, although in the heat of controversy the acknowledgments were sometimes unwilling. Nevertheless, they too recognized the value and distinctiveness of humans, even in a fallen state. They, too, affirmed that humans in their fallen state were capable of amazing achievements that ultimately pointed to powers given to humans by God the Creator. This is why ultimately both Luther and Calvin admitted that the *imago* was not completely destroyed; a "relic" remained.[8]

The Reformers, on the other hand, were quite right to maintain the unity of human nature, and the dependence of that nature on God. As originally created, human beings were what they were because of their relation to God; as fallen the break in that relation deforms every aspect of their nature. However, the Reformers did not perceive that at bottom Catholic theology agrees with this. From the Catholic perspective what belongs to man in "nature" belongs to man because of God. Indeed what is called "human nature" is not an entity that exists independently of God but is rather the outcome of God's continuous creative activity. Its stability is due to the stability of God's creative purposes; its flexibility to the freedom and openness that has been given to humans and for which God has called them to account.

Catholic theologians do *not* wish to claim that some aspect of human nature is unaffected by the fall. Aquinas, for example, clearly recognizes the effects of sin on man's rational powers. Nor do Protestant theologians really want to claim that unredeemed humans can accomplish nothing that has meaning or significance. Catholic theologians do *not* wish to claim that humans can by their own unaided natural powers attain salvation or fulfill their ultimate destiny as humans. (And their natural powers are not really "unaided" either.) Protestant theologians do not really want to deny that there is a "point of contact" in the natural man for God's redeeming grace. If humans had no natural ability to make judgments about right from wrong, no ability to hear a message and understand, no power to reflect on their own lives, the gospel could not be preached to them.

None of this implies, of course, there are no genuine differences, nor that those differences are unimportant. But a clear understanding of areas of agreement would surely go a long way toward putting those disagreements in proper context. Such shared areas could lead to a genuine theological ecumenicism, an ecumenicism that would enable us to present the essentials of historic Christianity in a clearer and more convincing manner.

The heart of the matter seems to me to be this. Whatever else the *imago* is, it must be a resemblance between God and human persons. I do not see how a relationship could be this resemblance. Whatever resemblance there is between God and humans may be—indeed must be—*derived* from a relationship to God. But the relationship cannot itself be the resemblance.

Protestants have been squeamish about giving humans credit for any good qualities, fearing that this might justify or serve as a pretext for human pride. But there are two ways for rebellious humans to dishonor God. One is, with arrogance and pride, to pretend that the gifts they have received from God are simply the result of their own achievements. The other is to deny or depreciate the gifts themselves. Avoiding the former error is no excuse for the latter. Protestants must recognize that God is not exalted by the depreciation of his human creation. To think otherwise is the flip side of the Marxist error that an exaltation of God automatically abases man.

It is quite true that man possesses all he possesses because of God, and that humans are fully human only when they consciously recognize and acknowledge their dependence on God. The opposite of sin is not virtue but faith, as the great Reformation thinkers from Luther to Kierkegaard rightly stressed. This implies that even the virtues of the pagan are "glittering vices." To the extent that these virtues are seen as autonomous human achievements, they turn humans away from faithful dependence upon God toward prideful self-sufficiency.

Relational anthropology is thus right in its aims and concerns, but it is wrong if it sets itself up as a replacement for a substance anthropology. Human beings have no genuine identity independently of God, and their humanness is tied to their recognition of this truth. The image of God is derived from God through the relation of the Creator to the creature, and can be healed only in the relation of redemption.

But to say that humans possess no good qualities independently of God does not imply that they do not possess any good qualities. To say that they cannot rightly develop and exercise those qualities except in a relation of conscious dependence on God does not imply that they cannot exercise those qualities. Relational anthropology has clearly taught us to see human "natures" as the stable outcome of God's creative purposes, rather than as a closed "form" existing independently of God. It is time to incorporate that insight into an anthropology of human *being*. We need to think again about where the *imago dei* can be seen in human nature.

Notice that I have not here attempted to defend the traditional view that the *imago dei* can be identified with rationality (though the distastefulness of that view to our generation says more about the narrowness of our conception of rationality than it does about the plausibility of the view). The more fundamental issue is a willingness to think of the *imago* as expressing itself in distinctly human qualities at all.

BODY AND SOUL: MONISM VERSUS DUALISM

The contemporary retreat from classical Christian anthropology is even more pronounced with respect to the issue of soul and body than was the case with the *imago dei*. But the main thrust of contemporary thought here is similar. Just as there has been a swing away from viewing the *imago* as an enduring quality (or qualities) of human nature toward viewing it solely as a relation, so there has been a definite swing away from seeing the human soul as a substantial entity toward seeing "soul" (and "spirit") as terms for the whole person that emphasize certain functions or relations. This is one area where evangelicals have been as "modernist" as liberal theologians, in that a perspective that was unhesitatingly accepted by almost the whole church for centuries has been abandoned in a breathtakingly brief period.

The reason this has been possible, of course, is that the swing from dualism to monism is not viewed as an alteration of Christian dogma to accommodate modern thought but as a return to a more biblical, "Hebraic" view of the person. The traditional teaching of the church is viewed as a corruption, due to the influence of Greek philosophical ideas on theologians. Now a case can be made for this, and we will consider it in a moment, but two things should give us pause. One is that the "Hebraic" view that is being urged happens to be strongly in line with contemporary secular thought, which is overwhelmingly and relentlessly monistic. While it is very possible that traditional theology was distorted by Greek philosophy and science, it is equally possible that contemporary theology is being distorted by contemporary philosophical fashions.

The second thing that should give us pause is that a dualistic view of the person *was* the overwhelming view of the church. It was, for example, an issue that played no part in the Reformation controversies, precisely because all parties to the disputes, Protestants as well as Catholics, unhesitatingly agreed that human beings were composed of a mortal body and an immortal soul.

A few citations from classic creeds and catechisms perhaps could serve as reminders of this. Question 57 of the Heidelberg Catechism from 1563 asks, "What comfort does the resurrection of the body afford thee?" The answer is forthright: "That not only my soul after this life shall be immediately taken up to Christ its Head, but also that this my body, raised by the power of Christ, shall again be united with my soul, and made like unto the glorious body of Christ."[9] The Belgic Confession (1561) is even clearer: "For all the dead shall be raised out of the earth, and their souls joined and united with their proper bodies in which they formerly lived."[10] The Westminster Confession (1647) is more philosophical: "After God had made all other creatures, he created man, male and female, with reasonable and immortal souls."[11] Later, in Chapter XXII, the Westminster Confession spells out the eschatological implications of this in a manner similar to the other confessions. The Lutheran Formula of Concord (1577) is equally prone to dualistic language.[12]

Now what is the biblical case against dualism in favor of monism? There are three main strands to the bill of indictment, I believe. First, it is alleged that dualism dichotomizes the person, whereas the Bible sees human beings as unified organic wholes. Second, it is claimed that anthropological dualism is linked to a variety of other dualisms that are also unbiblical. Last, it is said that dualism undermines the biblical view that life after death is not a natural possession, but a gracious gift of God. Each of these charges is linked to the "Hebrew versus Greek" motif. Let us consider each of them in turn.

The first is the claim that the Bible stresses the unity of the person, particularly in the Old Testament, while Greek thought (which in these discussions usually means Platonic thought) views soul and body as contingently joined substances. There is no question that the Bible does teach that human beings are unified. But why should this be thought to settle the matter? Dualists claim that human beings are unified also, and that their view allows for this. To make a biblical case against dualism one must show more than that the Bible teaches the unity of the person; one must show that this unity is incompatible with dualism.

Now it is easy to show that some forms of dualism, such as Plato's, are difficult to reconcile with this biblical teaching. However, there are many other forms of dualism. Thomas Aquinas, for example, developed a form, drawing on Greek thought, in which the union of soul and body was so intimate that he had some difficulty in explaining how the soul could survive the death of the body. Perhaps contemporary Christian thinkers, instead of simply repudiating dualism, should give more thought as to how to develop a biblical dualism.[13] Even granted a difference between Hebraic and Greek thought on this issue there is no reason why the difference must be monism as opposed to dualism. It could be Greek dualism as opposed to biblical dualism.

The second major point in the attack on dualism is the claim that anthropological dualism goes hand in hand with other objectionable dualisms. For instance, it is said that a soul-body dualism inevitably leads to a value dualism in which the soul is valued and the body, along with all that is physical, is depreciated. Or it is argued that a soul-body dualism goes hand in hand with a secular-sacred dichotomy, in which religious truth only affects the "spiritual" dimension of life and has no impact on our day-to-day existence.

There is no question that these latter unbiblical "dualisms" sometimes have been linked with anthropological dualism. Indeed, they may even be logically linked to certain versions of dualism, such as Plato's. However, when we think clearly about the issues we will see that these issues are logically distinct.[14] A person may believe that human beings are unified compounds of body and soul, and yet that both body and soul are equally valuable. (In rejecting an unbiblical depreciation of the body, we should recognize that those who make this error may base it on a genuine insight, which is that the Christian values certain goals—e.g., furthering God's kingdom—more highly than the satisfaction of his or her own natural bodily needs.)

Certainly there is no basis for equating the "soul" with the religious, "spiritual" dimension of life, and the body with "secular" life. Human beings act as a unified whole in all dimensions of life. They worship as bodily beings; they chop wood, pump gas, and vote as beings who are more than purely physical.

The final charge against dualism is that it leads to an unbiblical view of the afterlife. Dualism leads to a belief in immortality as a natural human possession. The Bible, on the other hand, does not teach a doctrine of immortality, but one of resurrection, which is not a "natural" possession but a gracious gift of God. This issue is the most complicated of all, and yet the most crucial, since the case *for* dualism is closely tied to life after death.

Once more it is crucial to distinguish between various kinds of dualism. A Platonic dualism that sees embodiment as a "prison" and life after death as the soul's release from the body is obviously in tension with the Christian doctrine of resurrection. Christian dualism, of the sort expressed in the Westminster Confession, is obviously very different, since it is clearly affirmed there that the souls of the righteous dead, though they enjoy communion with God and are "made perfect in holiness," still eagerly await "the full redemption of their bodies."[15]

Murray Harris, in his very fine study *Raised Immortal*,[16] has convincingly shown that immortality *is* a biblical concept, but that the biblical concept of immortality is very different from the Greek concept. So, for Harris, it is not a question of resurrection versus immortality but rather resurrection *and* immortality in the biblical sense versus immortality in the Greek sense.

The primary differences, as I see them, between the Greek and biblical concepts of immortality are three: (1) Biblical immortality is not mere survival, though it is that too, but a qualitative transformation. (2) Biblical immortality is not a natural possession, since only God is essentially immortal, but a gracious gift made possible by participation in the life of God. It is therefore conditional and not universal. (3) Biblical immortality is an immortality of the whole person, body and soul. The *body* is to put on immortality (1 Cor. 15:53).

Given these significant differences, how is it that Calvin and so many other Christian theologians continued to accept the "Greek" notion of an immortal soul?

Confusion here is often caused by the fact that when classical theology speaks of an immortal soul, it clearly is using these *terms* in a Greek sense, rather than in their biblical sense. But the crucial issue is not one of terminology (though clearer terms would certainly help here). The question that must be asked is whether classical theology is being true to biblical *teaching* here. And I believe the answer is essentially "Yes."

In affirming that human beings have immortal souls "naturally," the tradition was not affirming that humans have natural immortality in the biblical sense. Biblical immortality is, as we have seen, a possession of the whole person and a gift of God. Biblical immortality is a state of deathlessness that the whole person, body and soul, enjoys. Natural human beings with immortal souls are *not* immortal in the biblical sense; obviously they will die.

What then was the classical tradition affirming? Its claim was that human beings are not merely physical creatures. Human beings are not identical with their bodies; they will in fact survive the death of their bodies and they are capable of receiving new bodies. This is not *called* "immortality" in the New Testament, because the mere fact of survival is not very interesting, since it is not necessarily a state to be desired. (It is in fact possessed by the wicked as well as the righteous.) This does not mean, however, that the Bible *denies* survival in this sense. It is closer to the truth to say that it simply is taken for granted in the New Testament.

So there is no contradiction on the part of the Reformation and Catholic theologians when they affirm that humans have a soul that is naturally immortal (in the sense that the essential core of the person will survive death) and yet that human beings as a whole are *not* naturally immortal, but are granted immortality when they are given resurrection bodies. The Scriptures do not emphasize the former conception since it has little value in comparison to the second and it was more or less taken for granted. In a materialistic age such as ours, however, where the very possibility of life after death is hotly disputed, even the former conception has some significance.

But is it not unbiblical to regard even the soul as "naturally" immortal? Does this not suggest that human beings are not dependent on God for their continued existence? Here the concept of "nature" is misleading. A thinker such as Calvin would have unhesitatingly rejected the idea that any created thing, including the human soul, could exist independently of God. To say that the soul is naturally immortal (in the survival sense) means simply that it is natural or normal for it to survive the death of the body. God created it (and sustains it) as that sort of thing, and it has whatever "natural" characteristics it has because of God's will. Once more, as in the case of the *imago dei,* we must learn to understand a "nature" as a relatively stable outcome of God's purposive constancy in creation.

One area, though not the only one, where all this makes a crucial difference is the problem of the intermediate state between death and the resurrection. The Scriptures clearly seem to teach both that the resurrection is a future, historical event, *and* that the believer is consciously "with the Lord" immediately upon death. Whether that intermediate period be conceived as a disembodied state or as an embodied one, it seems evident that the person will not have the old, earthly body, which lies in the grave. It follows from this that the person cannot be identical with that body, though in this life personhood is intimately fused with the body.

We should not think, incidentally, that the issue of the intermediate state is an abstract, speculative one, with no practical consequences. To deny the intermediate state is to deny the possibility of that "mystic sweet communion with those whose rest is won" about which the hymnwriter wrote so movingly. One cannot commune with someone who does not exist. And it does not seem correct to me to say, as advocates of "soul-sleep" or gap theories do, that it makes no difference from an individual perspective either, since "subjectively" their view implies that the next moment of consciousness after death will be with Christ. For the individual cannot help but consider the matter from an objective point of view as well, and from that point of view "the next moment" will bring temporary extinction.

But even if one denies the intermediate state, one cannot really avoid dualism. Those who believe that at the resurrection human persons will be "reconstituted" must answer the question as to what makes these reconstituted persons, with their new, vastly transformed "spiritual bodies," identical with the old persons who died. Among the various answers given are continuity of memories, personality, and so on. Whatever answer is given, it appears that the essence of the person is being identified with something that is not simply identical with his former body.

It may well be that the terms *soul* and *dualism* are a lost cause, because they have so many misleading and pejorative connotations. If so, let us give them up and talk instead of the "self" or "the personal core of the individual." But whatever terminology is adopted, let us not rashly abandon the traditional teaching of the church. The essence of that teaching is that a person is not strictly identical with the earthly body. If God wills a person to continue to exist after death, that person will continue to exist. Such a one is not merely a physical entity.

THE PERSON AS A SUBSTANCE
AND AN ACHIEVEMENT

I have already urged that if the Christian view of the person is to be clearly presented to the post-Christian world, then we must see the human person as both an achievement and a substance. But can both be true? Is it possible to have it both ways?

I believe the answer is yes. The key to seeing how this is possible is to understand God as creating persons with real possibilities actually present. When God creates a person, the person is a person, a continuing substance. Yet God does not make persons fully completed, but as an essential part of their personhood endows them with possibilities, so that they may, in dialogue and dependence on their Creator, have a role in their own historical development. To actualize those possibilities responsibly is what personhood is all about. The task set for human persons is to *become* what they *are*. However, human beings have failed tragically in this arena, irresponsibly rebelling against their Creator and thereby rupturing the relationship that makes true or genuine personhood possible. Although they remain persons, they are no longer able really to function as persons.

This distinction between being a person and functioning as a person is full of important implications. It is not that being a person can be divorced from functioning as a person. If we ask what a person *is,* the answer must be that a person is a being that is endowed with certain distinctive possibilities. A person is a being intended to function as a person, at least during most of its history.

But a person who is not yet functioning as a person or who is no longer functioning as a person remains a person. All of us in some ways fail to function fully as persons but we remain persons. If we preserve personhood as a substantial category we will not be seduced into arguing about what an unborn child or infant must be able to do to be a person, nor into discussions about whether a senile individual's personhood is undermined by this lack of "social contribution." We *are* persons; our task is to *become* persons in the fullest sense.

CHRISTIAN ANTHROPOLOGY AND THE SCIENCES

Throughout most of this chapter, I have argued that Christians, in doing justice to the undeniable insights to be gained from a biblical, relational anthropology, must not throw out essential elements in their traditional view of the person to accommodate modern fashions in the world of thought. We must affirm that being made in God's image implies something about human nature, even in its fallen state, and that human persons are not identical to their bodies.

I do not mean to suggest, however, that it is not important to rethink and restate what Christians believe about human persons in the light of contemporary scientific knowledge. On the contrary, this is essential, and failure to do this leads ultimately to the abandonment of traditional teachings.

The problem lies in how the business is done. I would like to suggest that too much of what Christians have done in this area fits one of two categories: conformism or hostile rejection. Too little work has been done that can be seen as critical and creative interpenetration.

The relation between Christian theology and philosophy on the one hand and the sciences on the other has been too external. Each is "done" in a more or less autonomous fashion. When the sciences develop a perspective that seems antithetical to a Christian view, some Christians respond by rejecting or strongly criticizing that perspective. Others attempt to work out a compromise by reinterpreting the scientific finding or, as is more usual, their Christian beliefs. Given the cultural situation each of these strategies is appropriate at times. Each could be richly illustrated by looking at the relationship between Christian thought and such movements as psychoanalysis and behaviorism in psychology.

Unfortunately, however, sometimes this pattern of rejection or conformism produces new, unnecessary divisions within the church. Those who reject the new scientific findings regard the other side as traitors, while those who choose accommodation view the rejecters as anti-intellectual. The rift brought about by creation science is an excellent example of this pattern.

Christians have been largely limited to these responses of attack/accommodate because of the assumption that the sciences are neutral, independent of metaphysical and religious assumptions, focused solely on "empirical" facts. Given such a view of science, it is inevitable that theology and science will relate only in an external way.

Recently, however, philosophers of science and epistemologists, in conjunction with some practicing scientists, have questioned this view. They have argued that in all sciences, though in some more than others, metaphysical and religious commitments play a positive role. So, they have urged, we ought to allow our Christian assumptions to interpenetrate our actual work as scientists. The clearest argument for this point of view is probably Nicholas Wolterstorff's *Reason within the Bounds of Religion,* which argues that Christians ought to derive some of their basic "control beliefs" from their authentic Christian commitment. I believe that Wolterstorff's work is most relevant to the human sciences. The challenge is to go beyond rejection and conformism to doing scientific work as scientists who work within a consciously Christian frame of reference.

Obviously, this view raises difficult problems. Can science done in this vein retain a concern for truth and objectivity? Can we distinguish between genuine science and mere ideology on this view? I believe these problems can be met. Christians such as Mary Stewart Van Leeuwen in psychology and David Lyon in sociology seem to me to be leaders in developing this view.

I am not here saying that theology must dictate to Christians working in the human sciences. Too much of what passes for "integration" of the human sciences with theology has been simple-minded biblical proof-texting. What is really needed is a demonstration that basic biblical beliefs make a difference to the way Christians think of their disciplines, propose and evaluate explanations, and design and carry out research. Obviously having a Christian worldview as a basis does not necessarily make the job easier. Data must still be gathered and interpreted, new ideas must still be generated. But I believe both the sciences and theology would be enriched if it were shown that Christian teachings on the soul, the nature of the person, the basic need for God among humans, and so on, could operate fruitfully at the level of what Wolterstorff terms scientific control beliefs. In general Christians in the human sciences, and this goes for philosophers and theologians as well, must be less conformist with respect to their established disciplines, more willing to allow their research priorities and strategies to reflect their Christian vision.

What is needed is something old and something new. We need to recover old insights and heal old divisions. We need to join the contemporary conversation and participate in scholarly and scientific work, but with a healthy irreverence and suspicion of the contemporary scholarly establishments. We need clearly to tell an increasingly secular world what Christians think about human beings, and show them the power of such a perspective.

Part II
THE SELF-DISCLOSURE OF GOD

The belief that God has created human beings and implanted in them his own image is the formal starting point of evangelical faith. Even closer to the heart of that faith, however, is the conviction that God has not just made humanity but actually become human in the person of Jesus Christ. This becoming human, moreover, is but the fullest manifestation of God's disclosure of himself, his revelation, to the world he has made. Our discussion of this theme begins with Jesus' own words from Matthew 11 that point to himself as the full manifestation of the Father and that, disconcertingly, call for a childlike attitude as the precondition for perceiving that revelation. It continues with a narrative account of the divine self-disclosure that arranges the varieties of revelation in terms of God's deeds.

The three more specific chapters in this section are "position papers" in a strict sense of the term. The first argues a case against the widely held modern view that belief in revelation, as illustrated especially by the incarnation of Christ, is irrational. The second calls upon evangelicals and their critics to heed the ambiguities, as well as the possibilities, involved in interpreting the Scriptures. The third proposes a Christian way of reconciling evangelical claims about the unlimited love of God with the all too obvious fact that much of humanity has never even heard the Christian message. The positions these papers present do not necessarily speak for evangelicals as a whole, but they do indicate a common willingness to treat seriously objections to evangelical faith that are common in our day.

3

Biblical Meditation: God in Christ

John R. W. Stott

We turn now from God the Creator, the Image-maker, to worship whom is true wisdom, to God the Discloser and so to his self-revelation. The words of Jesus, as recorded in Matthew 11:25-30, take us to the heart of this matter:

> At that time Jesus said, "I praise you, Father, Lord of heaven and earth, because you have hidden these things from the wise and learned, and revealed them to little children. Yes, Father, for this was your good pleasure. All things have been committed to me by my Father. No one knows the Son except the Father, and no one knows the Father except the Son and those to whom the Son chooses to reveal him. Come to me, all you who are weary and burdened, and I will give you rest. Take my yoke upon you and learn from me, for I am gentle and humble in heart, and you will find rest for your souls. For my yoke is easy and my burden is light." (NIV)

In those very familiar final verses of the chapter, Jesus pictures human beings as a team of oxen laboring under a misfit yoke, and heavily laden, staggering under their burdens. It is not a complimentary picture, but it is an accurate one for humankind. To such people he issues two invitations. The first is that we come to him to have our burdens lifted and our yoke eased. The second is to take his yoke upon us instead and learn from him, for his yoke is easy and his burden is light. He offers us, in fact, a beautiful exchange that is greatly to our advantage. For not only do we have our misfit yoke eased and our burdens lifted; not only do we receive in exchange his light burden and easy yoke, but he who lays these upon us describes himself as "gentle and humble in heart." So we have nothing to fear in Christian discipleship.

We do not, however, always pay equal attention to the two affirmations that precede these two invitations. It is to these that our attention is required, for both of them are concerned with the knowledge of God. The word that is common to both is the word *revealed* or, if you prefer, *disclosed.*

The first affirmation, then, is that God is revealed only in and by Jesus Christ. We read, "All things have been committed to me by my Father. Nobody knows the Son but the Father. Nobody knows the Father but the Son and those to whom the Son chooses to reveal him." The Son is the unique revealer of the Father.

Consider now the extent and comprehensiveness of the claims of Jesus in these marvelous words. He began by addressing God as "Lord of heaven and earth." But he continues to call him "Father": "I thank you, Father, Lord of the universe." For the Creator and Sustainer of the universe is in a special way the Father of our Lord Jesus Christ.

Moreover, the same universe, the heaven and earth, later called "all things," has been committed to the Son by the Father. Although God remains himself, the Lord of the universe, he has appointed his Son to be its Lord and heir. More than that, not only does the Son occupy a unique position as the steward of his Father's world but there exists between him and the Father a uniquely intimate reciprocal relationship. In consequence, Jesus can say, "Nobody knows the Son except the Father, and nobody knows the Father except the Son." In the midst of Synoptic material we hear that remarkable Johannine assertion.

So each is known only to the other, and each is an enigma, or mystery, to everybody else. It is because only the Son knows the Father that only the Son is able to make him known. Unique in his knowledge of the Father, he is unique in his revelation of the Father. His claim is absolute and exclusive.

To be sure, Jesus' claim must not be taken as a denial of other and partial revelations. God is partly revealed in the ordered loveliness of the created universe. He is partly revealed in history and in experience, in the human conscience and the human consciousness, and above all in Scripture, which is the Father's testimony to the Son. Nevertheless, God's full and final self-revelation, his revelation as the Father who saves and adopts us into his family, has been given in and through Jesus alone. Therefore, "he who has seen me," said Jesus, "has seen the Father." That is the reason why every inquiry into the truth of Christianity must begin with the historic Jesus, who without any fanfare of trumpets quietly and unobtrusively claimed that only he knew the Father and only he could make him known.

If the first assertion of the passage is that God is revealed only in and by Jesus Christ, the second is equally striking, that God is revealed only to "little children" (babies, infants), for these are the people to whom the Son chooses to reveal him. Indeed, God not only reveals himself but also hides himself. "I thank you, Father, that you have hidden these things from the wise and the learned." Not, of course, that God hides himself from any who seek him, for "he is light; and in him is no darkness at all" (1 John 1:5). It is as much the nature of God to communicate and to reveal himself as it is the nature of light to shine. But God hides himself from the "wise and learned," that is, from the intellectually proud, those who dare to proclaim the autonomy of their own reason. Since they deny the possibility of revelation, revelation becomes impossible for them. They refuse it, so they do not receive it. God hides himself from those who hide themselves from him. But he reveals himself to babies, which, in keeping with the rest of the teaching of Jesus, undoubtedly means not those who are young in years but those who are simple and humble in their attitude toward him.

Some Bible readers are perplexed by this because they think Paul makes a contradictory statement in 1 Corinthians 14:20, where he says that we are not to be babies in our thinking. But there is no conflict, for Paul was opposing anti-intellectualism, whereas Jesus was opposing intellectual arrogance. In our knowledge and understanding we are to be adults; but in the humble way in which we learn, we are to remain little children.

The name of Dr. John Duncan, a professor of Hebrew in Edinburgh University during a former generation, is perhaps still known to some today. So great were his attainments in the Semitic languages that his students all referred to him as "Rabbi" Duncan. They were also convinced that he said his prayers in Hebrew. So on one occasion, a couple of them decided to find out. When they believed the professor to be at prayer, they crept along the corridor outside his bedroom to listen. What they heard was no flights of Hebrew rhetoric and mysticism, but this:

> Gentle Jesus, meek and mild
> Look upon a little child.
> Pity my simplicity;
> Suffer me to come to thee.

Still in this modern world we need to come to Jesus like little children, for he reveals himself only to such. In England at the moment we are deeply distressed by apparent denials on the part of certain church leaders of the virgin birth and the bodily resurrection of Jesus. It is not only, however, what they are saying, but how they are saying it that makes their denials the more distressing. Their manner of speech is sometimes most unpleasantly patronizing and paternalistic. "Sophisticated people," they are on record as having said that those "who know a little theology will agree with us. It is only the simple who do not understand."

Jesus turned that distinction on its head. It is the sophisticated, at least if they are proud of their sophistication, from whom God hides himself. It is the simple to whom he makes himself known.

This arrangement, Jesus reminds us in our passage, is "God's good pleasure." God has been pleased to place two limitations on his own self-revelation: he reveals himself only in Christ and he reveals himself only to babies. Once we have accepted these two affirmations of Jesus, we are ready to respond to the two invitations that follow: to come to him, and to take his yoke upon us.

We will find, moreover, that although the invitations are two, the promised blessing attached to them is one, namely, "rest." True rest, peace, freedom, or fulfillment is to be found both in coming to Jesus to lose our burdens and in taking his yoke upon us, and submitting to his teaching authority.

God the Discloser

Gabriel Fackre

The gospel speaks forthrightly of One who reveals what is hidden. The words of disclosure are about deeds of deliverance. The Good News is not that mysteries formerly veiled from the ignorant are now uncovered, but that the ultimate bondage and alienation are overcome. Whatever else evangelical faith has to say to its contemporaries within and beyond the church it is this: The fundamental question, given sin, is how can an estranged world be reconciled to God? Whatever we know about who and what God has disclosed finally comes down to that.

Modernity does not ask this question, as Karl Menninger argues persuasively in *Whatever Became of Sin?*[1] Of the perennial human quandaries, ignorance, death, suffering, and sin, it is suffering—as misery and hopelessness—that comes center stage in our time.[2] The starvation of multitudes, the oppression of the poor and powerless, tyranny that denies human freedom, injustice to class, race, sex, age, and condition, the peril of war and nuclear extermination, the ills of the flesh and the cares of the world—these in political macrocosm and personal microcosm are on the minds and hearts of our generation. And faith communities respond accordingly, whether it be in the theodicy of a Harold Kushner *(When Bad Things Happen to Good People)* that strikes a responsive cord in a Boston suburb, or a liberation theology that energizes a base community in a Latin American barrio. Both the depth and degree of human peril and the seeming possibilities of historical promise, each tied up with advances in the artifacts of modernity that occasion our fears and hopes or disseminate them globally, argue for bringing suffering and hope to the foreground of concern.

Those who name the name of Jesus in our time will understand this question and engage it. They have a Deliverer who preaches Good News to the poor, brings release to the captives, heals the sick, comforts the sorrowful, and blesses the peacemakers (Luke 4:17-21;

Matt. 5:1-9). Out of thanksgiving they want to serve in the way he served those in need. And out of sobriety as well, they know that if they pass by on the other side (Luke 10:29-37) or do not minister to the last and the least (Matt. 25:45), they must answer to a righteous God on the Day of Judgment. Further, if the technology of the time has raised sky-high the stakes of the human prospect, then Christians must read these signs of the times (Matt. 16:1-3) and speak as well as act accordingly. The Good News is a good word to those in pain and poverty, as well as a good deed. So to our interlocutors, we strive to speak the language of hope to the hopeless, indeed a sober hope, cognizant of both God's promise and the powers that militate against it.

Yet what is first in our consciousness is not the whole of the matter. In another scale of value, suffering and hope take their meaning from a larger frame of reference. What of the sin of the world before the holy love of God? What of the lethal factor that undermines our efforts to overcome suffering, and persists in the brightest of our hopes for a livable world? Here evangelical faith must risk the angry retorts ("copping out"), the knowing smiles (of course, "the opiate of the people"), and furrowed brows ("You're pushing on the brake when you should be stepping on the gas"), and ask the embarrassing unasked question. The discussion of divine disclosure that follows assumes the importance of this unasked question of *sin and guilt,* even as it regards God's deeds to deliver us from these evils as the context for all others.

Evangelical witness is important here not only because it points to the obscured aspect of the gospel but also because this very pointing serves the cause of deliverance from oppression and hope in the midst of suffering. Those liberation movements and theologies of hope that do not know of the sin that persists in every achievement of justice and peace, a sin that continues to infect the very agents of liberation and reconciliation, render their own cause a profound disservice. The evidence of history as well as the deeper perception of the eye of faith disclose the stubbornness of sin and its results. Among those consequences are the illusion of the righteous who know nothing against themselves and thus fall prey to a self-righteous fury that tramples all opposition. The same moral short-sightedness is liable to a despair that, seeing the ambiguity in both the achievement and achiever, loses all hope for historical advance and flees the struggle for justice and peace. These twin perversions are all too evident today among those eager to correct flaws in their foes but not in themselves, as in the Manichean politics of both the religious right and religious left, and in the "burnout" or ahistorical spiritualism of former visionaries and revolutionaries.[3] The unwelcome word about sin and guilt before God must be on the lips of believers because this word is true, and because this truth really does make people free.

Our discussion of God the Discloser seeks to be faithful to the fundamental issue of God's controversy with the world. At the same time that controversy can be described in motifs and metaphors that relate to this time of suffering and hope. Here a narrative idiom seems particularly appropriate. A story is a plot with characters moving over time and place through conflict to resolution.[4] A dramatic mood captures both the faith and the facts of our era. Vision and light are themes that carry the accent of hope. They also can speak to the visual environment so characteristic of modern technology (as in *tele*vision). To take seriously the suffering and hope of our age also means hearing the voice of the voiceless and honoring the presence of long-submerged constituencies in both culture and church—Third World peoples, racial and ethnic communities, women, the aged, the disabled, the poor. We confess that when representatives of these peoples and perspectives are ignored by evangelicals, our message to the post-Christian world is itself weakened. The same situation circumscribes my own efforts to be catholic. This does not mean capitulating before simplistic versions of the sociology of knowledge or the hermeneutics of suspicion. These receive a sharp challenge below. But both a genuine sensitivity to the marginalized as well as the call for a full-orbed understanding of faith, as in Paul's word to the Corinthian church (1 Cor. 12–14), constitute a forceful word to evangelicals complacent about their possession of the truth.

The modern quest for justice and peace, as well as the modern encounter with suffering, is radicalized when put in an evangelical framework with its place for the depth of sin. Thus the struggle for justice in the world confronts us also with a question of the justice of God. And before the cross of Christ the problem of human suffering becomes the anguish of God. So too other human quandaries are deepened when placed before God. Ignorance becomes error. And death, more profound than mortality, becomes separation from God. Christian faith calls into question the conventional wisdom of the world about these perennial questions. These realities take on this deepest meaning only at the point where God discloses ultimately who we are and who he is, the place where we are all known and all forgiven. A proper evangelical witness is given from the foot of the cross.

The form of this testimony is that of narrative. Such a presentation of God's self-disclosure relates to contemporary sensibility, as suggested earlier, but also has an honored history as a way of Christian communication. The first baptismal confessions of faith follow this structure, one preserved for us in the present Apostles' Creed and developed further in the Nicene Creed. Here the great drama means the acts of creation, reconciliation, and redemption, the missions of the Triune God, and thus the unfolding of the economic Trinity grounded in the inner-Trinitarian life of God. The trajectory of the narrative in one way or another is familiar in the *loci* of classical dogmatics and more recent systematic theologies.[5] And it is found in the order of Scripture itself as it runs from creation to consummation with its center point in Jesus Christ.[6]

THE NARRATIVE OF RECONCILIATION AND REVELATION

The source of the narrative of faith is in the Godhead, lying in Deity's "hidden wisdom, his secret purpose framed from the beginning to bring us to glory" (1 Cor. 2:7). This Purpose we have come to know in Jesus Christ, the divine intention, Vision, Word from the "beginning" now made flesh (John 1:1, 14). Taking a clue from Augustine's psychological analogy for the Trinity, this narrative is the account of how the Purposer exercises Power to fulfill Purpose.

The social analogy of the Trinity, a necessary companion to the psychological one that honors the inner-Trinitarian life together, is an important part of God's self-disclosure. Revelation in the economy of God is the expression of the radical openness of the Persons to one another in their common life. The coinherence of Father, Son, and Spirit is a disclosive transparency that sets the stage for the open secret to be revealed in God's history with us.

CREATION

God brings the world to be. Creation is a gift of the Creator! The stars and stones are rich in possibility, nature is blest (Gen. 1:3-24). "Being, as such, is good," as Augustine put it. Human nature, finite creature as all others yet the crown of creation, is made in the divine image: in relationship, the apple of God's eye; in capacity, given a will, reason, and spirit able to answer the divine invitation (Gen. 1:26; 1 Cor. 12:7). Trans-nature, the realm of powers and principalities, is called to special ministration in giving glory to God (Mark 1:13; Eph. 6:12). Cosmologies explaining these miracles come and go, but the fundamental meaning of God's creative deed does not change. This launches the biblical narrative.[7]

Assertions about God's disclosure are integral to God's deed. Creation in its intended state reflects God, the divine society— humanity knows its Maker, nature lives in harmony, and the powers of this world stand poised to serve their Source. Thus the light of God shines upon everything and enlightens everyone coming into the world (John 1:9). This Light and Word that form and inform the world is Jesus Christ, as "all things were made through him, and without him was not anything made that was made" (John 1:3). Creation as deed and disclosure is, finally, the work of the Triune God, the Purpose of God leaving its imprint by the Power of God.[8] The implications of this work as "general revelation" and "common grace" in the world after the fall we shall presently explore.

FALL

"The world was made through him, yet the world knew him not" (John 1:10b).[9] The world rebuffs the beckoning of God. So the second chapter in the Christian story, the turn away from the Light, the stumble and fall into the night. All across creation resistance arises to the Purpose for which the world was made. Powers turn treacherous and become the occasion for assault and temptation; human nature accedes to beguilement, seeks to usurp the place of its Maker, sullies its image of special relationship and capacity, and expresses its rebellion in an apathy and arrogance commensurate with its creatureliness and image. Nature turns red in tooth and claw, the wolf devouring the lamb, the asp striking the child, the body in pain and toil, the earth groaning. So megalomania—self-idolatry—arises to thwart God's purpose. The world shakes its fist in the face of God. And the wages of sin is death. The night of judgment falls on our day of rebellion. On these sobering facts the Christian story turns.

To "know him not" is not only "to receive him not" (John 1:16), but also to *perceive* him not. To turn from the Light is to be in the night, no longer able to see the direction in which we must go, nor empowered to pursue the journey. Here are the consequences for revelation in the fall of humanity. The Purpose in "the starry heavens above and the moral law within" no longer sends clear messages to the human spirit. The disorder of creation, prey to the demonic powers, distorted further by the darkened lens of humanity, undercuts the created ability to perceive the will and way of God and the original capacity for positive response. Sin remains separation from God, the death of the vision and the demise of creation.

COVENANT

Yet "the light shines in the darkness, and the darkness has not overcome it" (John 1:5). This narrative concerns a stubborn God, long-suffering with a rebel world. So comes the chapter that occupies two-thirds of Scripture, the enlightening work of God among the people of Israel. Here Light takes form as the pillar of fire by night, leading the people of God to a new land and toward the Day of the Lord (Exod. 13:22). In Exodus, law, patriarch, and prophet, priest, royalty, and sage, a people is selected to see and know the will of God, the Purpose of *shalom*. The love of God and neighbor for which the world was made is now etched on the two tables of "the law . . . given through Moses" (John 1:17). This covenant deed of God is a sign of the promise that the Purposer will not give up on the divine intention; it seals a people through whom that promise will be fulfilled.

While a special shaft of light pierces the darkness to rest upon an elect people, there remains even in a darkened world hints of its source and goal, and indeed enough of a residual radiance for the narrative to make its way. Where there is life there must be light (John 1:4), enough of the subdued spark in each human to discern those conditions which make life livable. Here is the elemental perception and power God gives to the divine image in us that is shattered but not destroyed. Not *the* Life and *the* Light, but life and light in a general revelation and a common grace. Keeping the promise of a Noachic covenant, a gracious Providence works to keep life human in its rudiments, though not in its fundaments (Rom. 1:19-20; 2:14-15; Acts 14:19).

Seers of a *particular* covenantal Light transmit and interpret the special deeds of God among the people of Israel. The disclosure that comes through this witness is gathered up in the prophetic testimony of the Hebrew Scriptures. What this work of the Spirit means in providing Scripture we shall explore in tandem with the New Testament witness to God's definitive deed. At this point in the narrative the "prophetic-apostolic testimony" to God's reconciling work means the inspiration of the Scriptures.

The covenant people of God prove to be as we all are, for no one loves the Light. But the purpose and promise will not be turned aside. Continuing the trajectory of the pillar of fire, there comes one from within this people who "is not the light, but came to bear witness to the light" (John 1:8). The vision will not die—the prophetic hope for the wolf and the lamb together, the child with its hand over the asp's nest, swords beaten into plowshares and spears into pruning hooks, each under his own vine and fig tree—all this comes to the burning point in a Messianic longing for the One who will not only see the light, but *be* the Light, not only reflect the glory but enflesh it.

JESUS CHRIST

And so "The Word became flesh and dwelt among us, full of grace and truth; we have beheld his glory, glory as the only Son of the Father!" (John 1:14). With this text we come to the center of the Christian story, the decisive deed and disclosure on which the narrative turns.

The deed accomplished by the Triune God in the person and work of the Son is incarnation and atonement. God reconciles the alienated parties to the divine purpose through the work done by the Word made flesh. Only the Purpose to redeem with commensurate Power to effect that redemption can bond what is estranged. The place fitting for such a reunion is the very world where rebellion has had its way. Therefore, the chief actor in this drama is One, truly God and truly human, who can wage the war and bring about the peace that removes the dividing walls of hostility (Eph. 2:14). So the eternal Son of the Father comes to us, born in a crib, growing up as a carpenter, to liberate and reconcile. From what? For what?

These questions pose the issue of atonement, the at-one-ment of the estranged parties to God's purpose, the world of human nature, nature, and transnature. What is done and what is disclosed, reconciliation and revelation, act toward and speak to this bondage in which God's partners are held. This is the fundamental meaning of liberation to which all other derivative meanings point: Jesus Christ is the deliverer from the slavery to that "No!" which creation says to its Creator. That "No!" is made up of the sin to which humans are in bondage (and the law with which it is bound up), the evil to which the powers and principalities are captive, and the death that ends in separation from God and a loss of the wholeness that God intends for humanity. In a word, that "No!" spells suffering, ignorance, mortality, and guilt before God.

God opens the way toward atonement through the birth, life, death, and resurrection of Jesus Christ. At Bethlehem God enters the realm of rebellion. In Galilee Jesus lives out the *agape* of radical love to God and neighbor, mercy for the sinner, and justice for the oppressed, manifesting the perfection of obedience to the Father. He preaches the Good News of the coming of *shalom*, the arrival of the kingdom where righteousness rules and God is all in all. He declares that it exists among them when he is near. On Calvary the world does its worst to the incarnate God, demonstrating the depth of its hate toward that Vision in the crucifixion of the Son. Yet the very cross of the world's rebellion and shame is refashioned into the instrument of reconciliation. Jesus Christ, fully God and fully human, takes into himself the punishment that the holy God exacts of sin, the final Night of death and damnation. At Golgotha, as Luther put it, the divine Love receives the divine Wrath through the vicarious work of Christ. The cross of divine vulnerability overcomes sin and its consequences. Easter morning secures and announces that victory. The resurrection of Jesus Christ from the dead demonstrates that this life and its climactic act have ended the bondage of sin, defeated evil, and overcome death. The death that Jesus conquers is the guilt and power of sin, the futility of suffering, the finality of mortality, and the blindness of fallen bondage. By the liberating work in Christ's birth, life, death, and resurrection, God has reconciled the world to the divine intention, offering life together with himself in faith, life with neighbor and nature in love, and hope for a future beyond suffering and mortality.

THE WRITTEN WORD

Since our intent in this chapter is to describe the divine self-disclosure, it is appropriate at this point to discuss the revelatory aspect of God's reconciling act. Disclosure is integral to the deed. The value of nineteenth-century theologies of *Heilsgeschichte* as well as of twentieth-century efforts to construct "biblical theology" is the positioning of reconciliation at the heart of the revelation from God.[10] In the twentieth century, however, this emphasis has often entailed the reduction of the scriptural testimony about what those events mean to the status of a "human witness" devoid in itself of any revelatory weight. This happened either through a denial of the doctrine of the inspiration of Scripture or by such a reinterpretation of it as to remove the prophetic-apostolic *testimony* from the revelatory arc.[11] The end point of this development appears in hermeneutical ventures that (a) either blur the distinction between canon and noncanonical material,[12] or (b) treat canonical interpretations of God's deeds as merely the first community reflection on the event, different only in degree from subsequent ecclesial interpretation.[13] By contrast, in the view of divine disclosure I have taken the interpretation is inextricable from the deed. Thus "inspiration" as well as "incarnation" (and atonement) constitutes the revelatory moment.[14] This commitment to the cognitive weight of Scripture is a crucial evangelical witness in theology today. A doctrine of inspiration means that the Bible is not only the occasion for "meeting" (Barth's address of the Word, Brunner's personal encounter, Bultmann's existential decision, and the current variations on these themes—Scripture as word event, performative communication, symbolic disclosure, the language game of the community, the rendering of an agent, the telling of stories, etc.) but also makes universal truth claims.[15] While the prophetic-apostolic testimony is rich in expressive and evocative language, it constantly makes statements to which the response must be Yes or No. Since these propositions concern life-and-death matters, they are more properly called "affirmations." In any case, revelation can be reduced neither to the event as such, nor the reception by it of the engaged reader or hearer, but entails as well trustworthy language with its ontological referents. For this reason a sound understanding of inspiration is fundamental to a doctrine of revelation.

That inspiration is integral to revelation is crucial to evangelical witness. Evangelicals also agree on *why* such inspiration is necessary, for they contend for its role in making propositional/affirmational truth claims of a universal nature. They evidently agree even on *what* form this disclosure takes: "verbal inspiration" means the "inbreathing" of the Spirit into the recipients of inspiration, stirring the author and bestirring thoughts appropriate to the divine intent, but also includes an "outbreathing" of the words employed to express the insights given. (Form cannot be separated from matter in the revelatory process any more than it can in aesthetic creation, as Austin Farrer has argued.)[16] Just *how* the association of words with the Word takes place is the much-disputed question among evangelicals today.

In passing we may note the diversity of these different evangelical views. They include at least the following: (1) Only a few defenders now hold to the hoary "dictation theory" and insist upon the passage of the particular words of the original text from the mind of God to the mind and pen of obedient amanuenses. (2) A cluster of opinions consider the scriptural autographs to be protected from error in all respects—science and history as well as faith and morality—but assert some role for the human agent, given the facts of varying vocabulary range, idiom, and cultural categories, on one hand, and the assumption of divine-human concurrence, on the other. Yet the degree to which human agency is acknowledged makes for variations within this position: (a) An ultra-inerrancy position declares for a grace of preservation that watches over the transmission process itself, thus assuring the reliability of received texts in virtually all respects, requiring apologetic exercises in harmonization. We might call this view "transmissive inerrancy." (b) A middle view, "trajectory inerrancy," assumes that the inspiration of the autographs continues to manifest its power after the fact, guaranteeing the infallibility of teaching for faith and morals in the received texts whatever minimal errors in other matters may be discerned in the fallible process of transmission. This view also allows a larger role for human factors in the writer, touching literary and cultural idiom. (c) An "intentional inerrancy" position asserts the trustworthiness of the written word in terms of authorial intent, when properly understood through the moderate use of critical scholarship, with special attention to the genre employed, and historical context. Here the human factor in the writing process is given greater accent along with the insistence that the standards of modern historiography not be imposed upon ancient writing. (3) A family of "infallibility" views distinguish themselves from the foregoing positions by construing Scripture as the oracle of "soteric knowledge," or as inspired by God in matters of faith and life, doctrine and morals. This view is open to the use of critical scholarship while wary of the ideological framework in which that scholarship arose. Here the human medium of inspiration receives higher profile along with an acknowledgment of biblical finitude regarding matters not of salvific importance. Yet those holding this view do not doubt the Bible's trustworthiness as an organ of God's word touching issues of "life, death and destiny." At least three subgroups are discernible within this family: (a) a conservative infallibility that assumes a unity of doctrine and morals in Scripture; (b) a moderate view that notes diversity in the theological and moral patterns found in the Bible but identifies a traditional set of evangelical essentials as the core of God's word; (c) a "Christocentric" view that acknowledges the corrigibility of any doctrinal and moral themes found in Scripture that do not cohere with the norm of Jesus Christ.

Alongside these evangelical views of biblical inspiration stand the other modern positions on the authority of Scripture. (1) Some may take an ecclesial view of the text where a teaching office or tradition mediates the authority of the Bible. (2) Some insist that the deeds of God rather than assertions about them constitute revelation, as in the various traditions of *heilsgeschichtliche* or "biblical" theology. (3) For others a Christological actualism in its various forms or a historical Jesus define the meaning of the Bible. (4) Still others hold that an experiential framework—rational, moral, aesthetic, or religious—either poses the critical questions to the text or determines the significance of it. While some of these models of revelation exist in combination with evangelical positions, they stand outside the evangelical doctrine of inspiration as I have defined it here.

Evangelicals searching for a proper word to their post-Christian world might well ask this question: Is there some common understanding of the "how" of inspiration that binds the variety of evangelical perspectives together? I believe there is. The unifying point has to do with the working assumptions of most, if not all, evangelical expositors of Scripture. Now and then it surfaces as an "of course," which happens, for example, in Carl Henry's encyclopedic defense of a trajectory view of inerrancy. While making this defense Henry alludes to the heart of the matter in a brief summary that moves from the eternal purposes of God through creation, fall, the call of Israel, the incarnation and atonement, the birth of the church, and the coming of salvation, to the resolution of all things at the end time.[17] The nonnegotiables of evangelical thinking on revelation are found right here, in the fundamentals. Whatever else the *locus classicus* of inspiration teaching may mean, it surely *must* mean at least this: "All Scripture is inspired by God and profitable for teaching, for reproof, for correction, and for training in righteousness . . ." (1 Tim. 3:16). The Scripture is of the Spirit because it teaches us these truths, it tells this story of the reconciling will and work of God. What we have taken to be the narrative of faith, its ideas and its images, its affirmations and its idiom, is God-breathed.

Inspiration in this narrative sense means that a community of those who witness this action in one of its phases captures the overarching plot conceived in eternity and played out in the rough and tumble of God's engagement with a rebel creation. These "seers" understand it, record it, and order it canonically. The Holy Spirit so worked in this journey that the textual result is a trustworthy account of the divine intention and action. Indeed the defining metaphors and motifs, stories and symbols, in which these "prophets and apostles" cast their visions and affirmations, as inspired, are the Christian's code language, a guidebook of terms, a reference point for all communication and any translation of faith. So we recognize by our weekly recourse in worship to the words of this Book. So, too, does a wider community tacitly acknowledge that same fact in its return ever again to the biblical pages as resources for the arts. This understanding of the inspiration of Scripture seems to be the functional presupposition of an evangelical perspective, whatever the differences in its outworking. The premise explicitly underlies my interpretation of God's disclosure.

CHURCH

While the fundamental deed of reconciliation is accomplished at the center of God's history with us, there remains the "application" of the benefits of Christ's work, the narrative movement from the Already to the Not Yet, from firstfruits of the new season to harvesttime. This brings us to the concluding chapters of the story: the birth of the church, the flow of the streams of salvation, and the consummation of all things. By following the biblical narrative we move from the resurrection to the record of ensuing events and thus to the ascension of Christ (Acts 1) and the birth of the church (Acts 2).

The biblical imagery of light persists and provides a potent interpretive tool for visual and visionary times. The New Testament portrays the rising of the horizon Light of Easter to its meridian in the ascent of the Son to the right hand of the Father's glory, there to rule in his own glorified humanity. But this is no tale of abstract regency, for "He's got the whole world in his hand." The manifestation of that rule is the release of the Power of the victorious Purpose of God in our midst. So comes the descent of the Spirit of the Son of God as the tongues of Pentecostal fire.

The flames that kindled a new community also cast light that show the new way. The deed of new birth is accompanied by a disclosure of new sight. The church is the people of God who are hearers and tellers of the deeds that have been done. They also point to the visions of what will be seen (Acts 2:17-18).

The revelatory characteristic of the church, with its new sight, is its gift of "illumination." Illumination is not the same as inspiration.

Inspiration is the power the Spirit gave to eyewitnesses of God's defining deeds in order to identify these actions and disclose their inner meaning (an identification and perception that binds the church forever). Illumination, on the other hand, is the power of the Spirit given over time in this community born at Pentecost to understand the inspired biblical story. The Spirit enjoys the mandate to interpret Scripture aright within the particularity of a time and place. Illumination is the church's light on the biblical map for its journey in the world. An exploration of the meaning of illumination, in turn, leads to some of the intense debates in hermeneutics today.

Illumination possesses two dimensions in its capacity to empower the church to steward both *faithfully* and *fruitfully* the Good News. In the former case, faithful stewardship means that God gives the church the responsibility of interpreting the Scriptures, and also provides means for that task. Somewhere within the church the gospel will always receive trustworthy proclamation. In the latter case fruitful stewardship means that the church is everywhere commissioned to translate the faith into terms connecting it with the issues and idiom where it lives. This aspect also carries the promise that the Spirit will somewhere be present in the church to make good this fruitfulness. The promise of faithfulness and fruitfulness constitutes the "indefect-ability" of the church. The gift and demand of transparency to the Light are the joy and burden of good stewardship.

The weakness of the church is its difficulty in keeping these twin characteristics of illumination together. Some construe the Spirit's commission to be that of preserving the purity of the gospel in its original code language. Others understand the charge to mean the task of contemporizing the faith in the language and thought-forms of our modern settings. Standing alone, each of these perspectives is an inadequate understanding of ecclesial illumination. Good News must be heard to be rejoiced in, so telling the story in a tongue unknown to the hearers does not edify (1 Cor. 14:2-25). On the other hand, an eagerness to be heard, understood, and accepted sometimes prompts the church to transform the message rather than translate it, editing out claims offensive to the ear of hearers. Depending on the temptation and challenge, it may sometimes be more important to attend to the text (in periods of acculturation and accommodation), or at other times to the context (periods of retreat and repristination).[18] But finally the Spirit's promise of illumination is bound up to both text and context and their right interrelationship.

The full light of disclosure to a community occurs when the

Evangel "hits home" in the time and place to which it is addressed, when the text meets, illumines, and transforms the context. Why is the context a partner in this engagement? Why is it not enough for the text with its inherent power to confront and overcome the hearer regardless of the nature of the setting or our understanding of it? This hermeneutical question is the counterpart in a discussion of authority and revelation to questions about the relationship of the human to the divine in Christology, ecclesiology, sacramentology, soteriology. Docetic inclinations, which accord only a "seeming" reality to the context, or Monophysite tendencies, which undercut the significance of the context in order to exalt the divinity of the text, are a constant temptation to those who perceive themselves as guardians of the divine initiative. In this case loyalty to the text may prompt defenders to obscure the role of the human context, a particular temptation of evangelicals concerned to honor the biblical word. On the other hand, an Ebionite cum Nestorian inclination, a tendency to overstress the humanity of Scripture, attends much contemporary theology that has either newly discovered the impact of context or that carries forward a long tradition that has argued for the "relevance" of faith to culture. Advocates of these views use one or another category from culture to make the faith indigenous, whether political framework, economic theory, cultural premise, psychological construct, religious sensibility, philosophical conceptuality. The result leaves the text overwhelmed by the context. When this happens faith is nothing more than the ideology of the moment dressed out in the language of piety. The most dangerous form of this hermeneutical illusion occurs when its adherents pay exaggerated homage to the text and make much of their suspicion of contextualization, but for all that, impart *covertly* a secular premise into the meaning of the text so that the modern assumption controls its interpretation.[19]

The process of translating the Scriptures provides some clues concerning the proper relationship between text and context. Thus, the translator has several options. He or she may employ either a literal equivalent or a paraphrase, or conclude that neither will do and seek an alternative. The former preserves the words of the old text in a new language but may fail to convey its intention. The latter, seeking contemporaneity, may do so by reading the framework and values of the new land and language into the text, thereby violating its intended meaning. Rejecting both approaches, many translators venture a "dynamic equivalence" in which contextual factors are taken into account by the use of other idiom, but this contextual idiom is engaged as a junior partner in the dialogue. The intention of the original text, established through rigorous analysis of its meaning and pursued by close conformity to its linguistic contours, is the clear reference point for translation.[20] Revelatory illumination happens in the communication of the gospel when translators seek this kind of faithful and fruitful communication.

These reflections carry us into the debates on the "hermeneutical circle." As an evangelical I am asserting the legitimacy of the "circulation" between text and context for the purpose of seeking a dynamic equivalence that ends in meaningful and true interpretation. However, in terms of final accountability (in contrast to the assertion of dynamism that the hermeneutical circle successfully underscores), the image of hermeneutical "arrow" is more apt. The contextual translation of the Good News must always be accountable to the text. That text is the checkpoint for all contextualization and indigenization. One of the crucial roles that the evangelical community plays within the church is its witness to this final accountability.

Another controversial question in this area is posed by the sociology of knowledge. That is, how can "the text" be normative in this dialogue with its context when that text is always "my text" or "your text," its reading controlled by one particular social location, value system, or framework of meaning? In this perspective, for example, the arguments of this entire book may be described as an ideological smokescreen for the power interests of a group of aging middle-class, white, Anglo-Saxon, North Atlantic/North American males. Such a perspectivalist critique assumes that only those who share a given social location or commitment (a) can talk to one another or (b) have access to ultimate truth.[21] Here is a post-Christian challenge of major proportions. There is just enough truth in these assertions to make this position attractive within and beyond the church, for it challenges two simple assumptions about the accessibility of the text, and it does seek to honor the practical commitment that must accompany any faithful reading of the Bible. Yet there are dire consequences if this view prevails.

The truth in the perspectival analysis is related to our overall understanding of revelation as a narrative. Our formulations of faith are truly en route, and therefore vulnerable to finitude and sin. As such they are indeed *our* affirmations about the gospel; they fall short of ultimacy; they offer "insight" not sight; they are subject to enrichment and correction. And so we must be properly self-critical of our tendencies to intrude our own agenda into our exposition of the Scriptures. The error in the perspectival view is that a radical perspectivalism disqualifies its own position as a serious partner in theological conversation. If its judgment is true, then the assertion of its own view itself becomes perspectival, a weapon in the defense of its own social location and therefore no claim to universal truth.[22] Or if its view is an honest assertion of what is believed to be so, which we are to take with due seriousness, then it exempts itself from its own perspectival premise. As such, it must acknowledge that to do so in one case makes it legitimate for others to do so in their cases; what's sauce for the goose is sauce for the gander. There are no logical grounds, therefore, to deny others the right to struggle out of the mire of distortive perspectives, or the hope that others can approach that goal.

A further objection to the conventional "orthodoxy" provided by the sociology of knowledge is just that to make perspectivalism the criterion for adjudicating issues of revelation and authority is to allow the context to control the text. A view shaped by culture with its own intellectual and social history (from Karl Marx to Peter Berger, and from proletarian cadres to university departments of sociology) becomes the magisterium for interpreting Scripture and gospel. The sociology of knowledge determines the theology of knowledge. Evangelical Christians must firmly resist this reversal.

To resist, however, is not to reject its valuable lessons. Evangelicals must be prepared to honor the sovereignty and mystery of God. They must not presume to have penetrated the ultimate reaches of divine wisdom. Further, evangelicals, who should have a sharp eye for the work of sin, especially when it is cloaked in the garment of piety, should be glad to receive criticism about their own formulations. Thus evangelicals should offer a provisional welcome to the hermeneutics of suspicion. In the same way they may embrace the role of sociology as a human science enlightening the articulation of the Good News. To do this recognizes context as the human underside of God's revelatory work. Yet a dialogue with context is not surrender to it: it is an engagement so that the gospel may stand forth in all its clarity and power.

Still another factor in assessing the significance of perspectivalism is its effect on the life of the Christian community. To assert the significance of social location does give voice to marginalized constituencies, and has enabled voiceless peoples to make their contribution to the catholicity of the church and the faith. Further, such constituencies have brought critical issues to the community's attention.

On the other hand, the doctrinal use of perspective in matters of authority and revelation, pressed to its logical end, means the Balkanization of the church, or, in more contemporary idiom, its "Beirutization." If all perceptions of the text and the gospel are legitimate only because they are construed from our social contexts, then no rationale or hope exists for sharing views across the barricades of social warfare. The only way one can understand what another is saying is to take up a stance within the other's camp, that is, capitulate to the commitments of a given locale. Or if the boundaries are drawn by sex, race, ethnicity, class, and age, there is no way to make even this transition, and we are thrown back behind our barricades. This is a very different picture of the Body of Christ than that painted by Paul in his letter to the Corinthians. There, to be sure, Paul acknowledged socially rooted particularities and checked claims by any one party in the church to speak for the whole of the Body. But Paul also acknowledged the different gifts of different parts of the church, and he expressed confidence that mutual enrichment among these different parts is possible by the Spirit's work. Thus Paul urged the *agape*, or love, of 1 Corinthians 13 upon the parts of the body in order to move beyond the boundaries of ecclesial locations and the varieties of different gifts to a mutual interpenetration and enrichment.

The Pauline counsel contains a lesson for those who claim too much for their parochial, partial perspectives, as well as for those with a hermeneutics of suspicion who have disavowed particularism but advocate their own privileged perspective as ruling out all others. While the text of Scripture is subject to our skewed perception, and while it does not deliver the ultimate vision of the kingdom, it is not inaccessible to the community. Therefore it can and must function as a reference and judge of our efforts at contextualization. The lasting gift of the sociology of knowledge is to reinforce the traditional Christian assertion that the discernment of the meaning of the text is related to the *wholeness* of perception within the community. We discern its meaning when we seek it *together,* enriched by the varieties of perspective that constitute the Body of Christ.[23]

One more thing needs to be said concerning questions of text and context, this time from the fuller perspective of the narrative of faith. By acknowledging the role of context in the revelatory process, we have assumed the continuous presence of creation, both its possibilities and limitations, in the work of the Spirit. To speak of the illumination of the gospel in each new age and place is to say that God lets the narrative go forward into these ranges of being, and therefore

Christians must take seriously the creation environment. Particular times and places provide the occasions for the articulation of the gospel just as the Word was made flesh in a crib and a carpenter shop. The task of Bible translation is important simply because the human linguistic context is an ever-present reality for a historic and incarnate faith.

Yet this underpinning of creation is no neutral terrain. It too bears the imprint of the story of salvation, its night and its light. These factors determine the priorities and functions of text and context. Because creation is fallen, context cannot control text. The bondage of the world means that the Light of God does not suffuse its exterior manifestations or automatically give spiritual sight to those who live in the world. By our natural light the Purpose of God is not self-evident. This is the reason Christian faith is narrative. The fallen condition of the world moves God to reclaim it for the divine intention. The narrative of how God has done this makes up the Good News and comes to us in the inspired canonical writings.

However benighted we are by nature, God "did not leave himself without witness" (Acts 14:17a) in this fallen world. The divine purpose has moved the world as a covenant partner in its own journey, even apart from the special story of covenant history. To preserve the world from destroying itself by sin, the Power of God gives enough clues to the Purpose of God in creation to make and keep life human. These clues are the general disclosures of truth, beauty, and goodness that accomplish this purpose, universal revelation. In the incarnation and atonement Jesus Christ takes possession of what is his own, as the Logos of creation is now joined to the accomplished Purpose. Thus the signs imparted to the world in creation now repossessed by their source at the center of history come to the church from culture as a vehicle for communicating the gospel to that culture.

This process of appropriation is manifest in various ways in the witness and theological work of the church. Thus the church uses a principle of coherent communication, the universal logic of the universal Logos, to interpret the Logos incarnate. So, too, elementary moral perceptions that make life livable are, in the proper setting, the avenue through which the hidden Christ comes to feed the hungry, clothe the naked, do justice, and make peace (Matt. 25:35-40). The graces of the Spirit of the Son at work in creation, fallen though the world is, offer reference points for the interpretation of the Bible. This is the normative reason for attention to context. In a given context the text honors the working of the incognito Christ, but always determines and defines the perception of that working by the norm of special revelation, Christ revealed in Scripture.

SALVATION

In the story of the events surrounding the birth of the church in the Book of Acts, the invitation to faith comes after the preaching of the gospel. "And Peter said to them, 'Repent and be baptized, every one of you, in the name of Jesus Christ for the forgiveness of your sins; and you shall receive the gift of the Holy Spirit. . . . Save yourselves from this crooked generation'" (2:38, 40). And again after Peter's second homily, "Repent therefore, and turn again, that your sins may be blotted out, that times of refreshing may come from the presence of the Lord . . ." (3:19). The response came. "And the Lord added to their number day by day those who were being saved" (2:47b).

Here is the deed of God in which grace works faith in those answering the divine beckoning. The Spirit takes the benefits of Christ's reconciling work and brings pardon *for* the believer and then power *in* the believer. This is salvation from sin and guilt by grace through faith. To God be the glory!

The Spirit, following the course of a grace that works faith, busy in love and energized by hope, brings light as well as life, indeed life through light. Faith arises because the Spirit opens the eye of faith to see the Light. Revelation is intertwined with redemption.

In the *personal* appropriation of the gospel, illumination becomes the concentrated ray that falls upon this life. The one who receives the Good News with an authentic "Yes!" is given an understanding of the gospel, sound knowledge *(notitia),* the power to decide for it *(assensus),* and to trust in it *(fiducia).* This enlightenment and empowerment by the noetic and fiducial work of the Holy Spirit opens the eye of faith. And so revelation reaches its personal destination, turning those made for the vision and service of God toward that end. The redeeming work of Christ, a work that particularizes the benefits of reconciliation, convicts and converts, and so gives personal insight, sight into the Purpose of God in a darkened world, illumination of the inner eye of faith.

The configuration of means and ends, ecclesial and personal illumination in this phase of revelation, receives a dramatic exposition in the Book of Acts. Thus Peter receives the gift of faithful illumination in his early sermons, for here is a trustworthy accounting of the Christian narrative, with its origins in the eternal counsel of God, its enactment in creation and covenant, with the covenant community on tiptoe toward the fulfillment of Israel's hope, one come in the life, death, and resurrection of Jesus Christ, so signaled by the pouring out of the Spirit in the new age in which Christ rules over all things, gathering a people to himself by the cleansing of sin through water and word, and pointing to a final day of the Lord (2:16-36; 3:11-26).

This is not an abstract tale, for the whole account is couched in the idiom and related to the issues of Peter's hearers who are of "Israel." Thus Peter calls on Joel as a witness (2:17-21), David steps forward to give his testimony (2:25-28, 34-35), so too Moses (3:22-23), Abraham (3:25), Samuel, and all the prophets (3:24). Here Peter marks the particulars of Israel's encounter with Christ, and he draws the hopes of Israel into view. All this is the indigenizing, or contextualizing, of the Good News, especially so in this case because this people is itself a very chapter of the story. Yet in the larger sense this is the way illumination always happens, when text is brought into living relation to context. Here is a model of how illumination happens when the church offers its faithful account of the Good News and its fruitful contextualization.

The personal consequences of Spirit-empowered communication are seen in the revelatory consequences of salvation. Fires are lit from this Light. "So those who received his word were baptized, and there were added that day about three thousand souls" (Acts 2:41). And more: "They devoted themselves to the apostles' teaching and fellowship, to the breaking of bread and the prayers" (2:42). And yet more: "Fear came upon every soul; and many wonders and signs were done through the apostles. And all who believed were together and had all things in common; and they sold their possessions and goods and distributed them to all, as any had need" (2:43-45). The early church enjoyed knowledge and courage that confused the powers and principalities of the day with truth and boldness. "And when they had prayed, the place in which they were gathered together was shaken; and they were all filled with the Holy Spirit and spoke the word of God with boldness" (4:31). Here was power and light, illumination in its fullest meaning, the application of the benefits of Christ, in community and persons, in church and in believer.

CONSUMMATION

The final chapter of our narrative points toward the consummation of the divine intention, the fulfillment of God's promise, the maturation of the Not Yet developing in the womb of the Already, incarnation and atonement. As this event is yet to be, we trust the biblical seers in their assertions about its approach and in their characterizations of its nature. The prophetic-apostolic testimony of the end gives a large place to the figural mode appropriate to the mystery of the Not Yet. Here are stained glass images that give enough light, shape, and color to serve the purposes of discernment, yet that also encourage modesty about our understanding of what lies beyond. What God grants in the visions of the end couched in the symbols of this world is the knowledge of the resurrection of the dead, the return of Christ, the final judgment, and the coming of everlasting life in its personal, social, and cosmic plenitude (1 Cor. 15; John 5:28-29; 1 Thess. 4:16; 1 Cor. 4:5; Rev. 20:12; Matt. 25:31-46; 10:28; Luke 16:19-31; John 5:25-29; 2 Thess. 1:9; Heb. 6:8; 9:27; Deut. 14:10-11; Matt. 5:8; Rev. 21:24; 5:13). And what God grants to the prophets and to us, in this time between the Times, is an assurance of this ultimate fruition, done so through signs of the Realm given in history, as well as by bonding the justified and the sanctified, when they die, with the age to come (Luke 8:52; 1 Cor. 15:20; 2 Pet. 3:4; John 3:36; 5:24; 6:40; Luke 16:19-31; 23:43; Rev. 6:9; Rom. 8:35-39).

The doctrine of revelation accompanies Christian teaching about the final act of reconciliation, reaching thereby its own point of culmination. In the end when God is all in all and the kingdom comes, the eye of faith becomes the eye of sight. While we now "see in a mirror dimly," then we shall see "face to face." "Now I know in part; then I shall understand fully" (1 Cor. 13:12). Illumination as insight is turned into illumination as "sight," the full disclosure of who God is and what God does.

Revelation in this ultimate sense is knowing God as we are known. "How blest are those whose hearts are pure, for they shall see God," said Jesus (Matt. 5:8). The vision of God is the revelatory promise. John portrays this beatific vision in the richest of images: "There in heaven stood a throne, and on the throne sat one whose appearance was like the gleam of jasper and cornelian; and round the throne a rainbow, bright as an emerald" (Rev. 4:2-3). Now the long-blind eyes are opened and we behold this ineffable Light. We face the One from whom we had turned, so that we may live and love in communion with God.

To see the Envisioner is to see also the Vision, to know its suffering and its victory. "I saw standing in the very middle of the throne . . . a Lamb with the marks of slaughter upon him" (Rev. 5:6). And to see by the Spirit the Father and the Son is to exult, "Thou art worthy, O Lord our God, to receive glory and honor and power. . . . Worthy is the Lamb, the Lamb that was slain, to receive all power and wealth, wisdom and might, honor and glory and praise!" (4:11; 5:12). To see the Light is to celebrate. The joy of thanksgiving, portended in our eucharistic worship, is the service of worship and praise that issues from seeing.

Seeing the Light is seeing *by* the Light as well. The biblical portraiture of fulfillment has a horizontal as well as vertical dimension. We see in the Light of the glory of God the brothers and sister in Christ. The estranged shall dwell in unity: "By its light shall the nations walk, and the kings of the earth shall bring into it all their splendor" (Rev. 21:24). The Vision given to us is described in Revelation not only in interpersonal metaphors of life together in joy and love, but in social and political images. The powers as well as persons of this world will come together, give obedience and praise to their Maker and Redeemer, and become agents of reconciliation instead of alienation. "He showed me the holy city of Jerusalem coming down out of heaven from God. It shone with the glory of God; it had the radiance of some priceless jewel, like a jasper, clear as crystal" (21:10-11).

The Apocalypse in its vision of things to come places "living creatures" around the throne of God. And John declares, "I saw a new heaven and a new earth" (Rev. 21:1), a revivified nature that includes crystal waters, abundant crops, and flourishing forests whose "leaves . . . serve for the healing of the nations" (22:2). Thus the New Testament continues and completes the prophetic vision of *shalom* in nature in which the wolf and the lamb lie down together, the child is a friend of the snake, and the desert blooms. The creation no longer groans but rejoices, for "I heard every created thing in heaven and on earth and under the earth and in the sea, all that is in them, crying, 'Praise and honor, glory and might, to him who sits on the throne and the Lamb for ever and ever!'" (5:13).

The disclosure fulfilled, the deeds done, these are the things for which hope yearns and to which faith points. And these are the visions love serves. Our eschatology is inseparable from our ethics. Just so, our testimony about God's disclosure is inextricably linked with our own deeds and words of mercy and justice in this time of suffering and hope.[24]

CONCLUSION: REVELATION'S GOOD NEWS OF GOD

In a play the characters are fully developed only when the action is completed. So too in the divine drama. God's final self-disclosure comes when we meet our Maker "face to face." Yet the miracle of revelation is that the eye of faith has been given a glimpse of that encounter here and now, albeit "through a glass darkly." We have traced how this disclosure takes place in our narrative: from the *impartation* of universal revelation distorted by our stumble and fall, through the central actions of the *election* of Israel and the *incarnation* of the Word, witnessed to in the *inspiration* of biblical seers, to the *illumination* of these disclosures in the life and testimony of the Christian community. Who has emerged as the chief Figure in the point-counterpoint of this action, and what has been unveiled? These are matters of "theology" in its more restricted sense. The doctrine of God, therefore, is the final meaning of the revelatory journey, and we place it accordingly in this conclusion.

The Trinity

The course taken by God's revelatory arc influenced the development of the Christian doctrine of God. The earliest thought on the pattern of God's disclosure in the writings of Ignatius, Irenaeus, Hippolytus, and Tertullian took the form of an "economic Trinitarianism." These theologians held that an understanding of God was "built up" from the unfolding of the three acts of the divine drama, three stages in the great narrative. Steeped in the heritage of Israel, and knowing that they had to do with One who entered into covenant, the patristic writers and early creeds spoke of the "Maker of heaven and earth" who providentially drew the world toward its destination. With their decisive point of orientation being the deed of God in Christ, Christian interpreters knew their understanding of God could not be exhausted by simple descriptions of "the Father Almighty," but must entail a richness of being commensurate with this subsequent act. The Father has a Son. And the sweep of events from this turning point in the life, death, and resurrection of Jesus Christ—the coming to be of the church, the forgiveness of sins, and the consummation of all things— reveals the age of the Paraclete. Here is the Spirit that proceeds from the Father through the Son.

In the biblical accounts of these three great acts, one God is at work. Yet this same recital describes Father, Son, and Spirit as personal centers of action. Each, as such, is fully God, not fragmentary aspects or partial sequences of deity, or masks behind which some fourth unknown reality dwells. Economic description requires ontological distinctions—immanent Trinitarian interrelationships as well as narrative development "ad extra." Yet we do not have here polytheism, an association of independent deities, but a "coinherence" of the Persons constituting the One who is the "Source, Guide, and Goal of all that is—to him be the glory!" (Rom. 11:36). Such a mystery of diversity in unity is the doctrine of the divine triad.

Attributes in Action

Into this Trinitarian structure is poured the content of Christian belief about the character of God. A narrative perspective brings the "communicable attributes" to the fore. So too it shepherds the "incommunicable attributes," which often stray into the hinterlands of philosophical speculation toward the fields of divine action. The language of narrative participates in the two-sided, already–not yet character of its trajectory. There is enough proximity to the realm of God, by dint of the prolepsis in Jesus Christ, to render language trustworthy, yet enough distance from the luminous end to discourage claims to replicate the discourse of eternity. Doctrinal terminology, therefore, is neither equivocal nor univocal but analogical.

The story tells us of a relentless, long-suffering pursuit of the unswerving purpose to bring all things together, a purpose accomplished against formidable resistance. At the heart of it there are two manifest qualities, inseparably joined: holiness and love. God *is* holy love.

God is holy. The narrative from beginning to end is God's, not ours. As Source, Guide, and Goal, God deserves all the glory. The sorrow of the tale is our determined effort to usurp the divine sovereignty. The majesty of God is demonstrated by our incapacity to carry out this devious intent. The justice and judgment of God are the sharp edge of a holiness exercised against rebellion. And that same majesty in its positive expression is the power to fulfill the promise of redemption.

God is love. The way and the end of divine sovereignty confutes the world's fallen perspective on power. The goal of its use is not mindless obeisance to its raw exercise, but a Life with life in freedom and peace. This *shalom* of the prophet, and kingdom of Christ, comports with the way God wages the battle against the enemy. "Christ reigns from the cross." The implacable tread of the Hound is the

sound of suffering. As Easter follows Good Friday, so the eschatological victory finally overcomes the No of the world, because "the
weakness of God is stronger than men" (1 Cor. 1:25). Love is holy
even as holiness is loving.

A special word to our generation may be found in this partnership of holiness and love. Those in our age who experience suffering
while questing in hope can understand a word of *holy* love that speaks
of a majesty that has vanquished evil and death. Knowing nothing
against themselves ("Whatever became of sin?"), they can only know
by special grace of a mercy that has overcome sin and guilt, that is, a
holy love.

God who purposes and acts as holy love is nothing less than what
we call "personal." As we are subjects of self-awareness and choosing, so God is subject. In narrative terms, "personal" means that God
is Author and chief Actor in this analogical sense. At the beginning,
middle, and end of our story is the good and majestic will and work of
the personal God.

Attributes of Implication

In a narrative framework we may view the qualities of deity sometimes called "incommunicable" or "nonmoral" as efforts to express
dimensions of personal holy Love active or implied in the history of
God with us. The twin qualities of holiness and love must be held
tenaciously in their inseparable union in order to avoid the distortions
that often appear in the doctrine of God when one or the other is elim-
inated or subordinated.

The familiar "omni's" of God (i.e., omnipresence, omnipotence,
omniscience) can be interpreted through a narrative understanding of
holiness and love. To say that God is omnipotent in the context of the
divine working along the timeline of the Christian narrative is to say
that God has the power to fulfill his chosen purpose. Such a power includes the power of self-restraint; it allows a real drama to unfold of
invitation, rejection, and resistance; yet it also bespeaks a power of
persistence that stubbornly endures until victory is won. Thus the
vulnerability at the heart of the story refutes human conceptions
about the nature of power, because it manifests the power of powerlessness.

God is omniscient and omnipresent in like manner, knowing all
that needs to be known to achieve the divine ends, and being
wherever the Presence is required to accomplish that goal.

The God of biblical history as utterly free and sovereign is self-existent, underived, the Source. As such, God is infinite, beyond and independent of all finitude, not part of, nor coextensive with the world. So, too, God is eternal, not constrained by time, beyond time and therefore "before" and "after" it. But the God of this transtemporal and transspatial holiness is a loving One who chooses to be with us—a Transcendence that risks immanence within temporality and spatiality—in it, with it, under it, while not being of it. So the amazing story goes, shattering conventional wisdom about what infinity, eternity, and aseity are thought to be.

So too the divine immutability. While the Greek philosopher, reflecting the mind of human experience, could not but think of divine majesty as impassible—incapable of suffering, invulnerable—the Good News of God is a countervision of responsiveness, vulnerability, and readiness for *long*-suffering. Yet God is immutable in the way the story reconstrues that unchangeableness in its own terms. God's purpose "to reconcile to himself all things" (Col. 1:20) is utterly unchanging, and the persistence of God in pursuing that purpose is undeviating.

The God of holy love revealed through the journey with us to the end, and shown to us in the central Light that illumines the whole track of history, transvalues all the values we bring with us to theology proper. In God's dealings with us we are turned around in mind as well as in heart. Here, as in all our doctrinal affirmations, we find our way by the light of revelation, and beyond it, to the one "immortal, invisible, God only wise, in light inaccessible hid from our eyes."

Rationality and the Christian Revelation

Thomas V. Morris

The central conviction in the New Testament as well as the conviction that is central to its affirmation about Christ is that the Word became flesh. Undiminished divinity was personally united with unqualified humanity. New Testament faith is inexplicable without this belief. And without it, Christian faith today is religion stripped of its Christian substance.

Despite this fact, the fundamental Christian claim about the divinity of Jesus has undergone a barrage of criticism in recent years. Numerous critics, including many prominent theologians who continue to align themselves with the Christian church, have alleged that well-informed and intelligent people can accept the doctrine of the incarnation only if they act irrationally. This allegation has been made in a number of ways and stands nowadays as a foregone conclusion in many centers of higher education, including numerous seminaries and schools of divinity. I believe it is a view that richly deserves to be challenged.

In this essay, I want to examine some important facets of this question as to whether it is reasonable or rational to believe Jesus to be God incarnate. In particular, I want to take a look at some considerations that have been thought by many recent critics to constitute obstacles to a positive answer to this question, and see how one can develop a perspective on the incarnation that will allow these potential obstacles to be overcome. Thus, I shall be dealing with some epistemic matters concerning the doctrine of the incarnation. My aim here, however, is not to marshal evidence or other sorts of epistemic support in favor of the doctrine. I shall not try to prove, argue, or in any other way show that Jesus was God incarnate. Nor will I attempt the more modest task of showing that all Christians ought to adopt this traditional understanding of Jesus over any of the alternative conceptions of him developed by a number of contemporary theologians, although I believe this is the case. Both these tasks are worthy in themselves of considerable attention. Elsewhere I have contributed my own efforts to what could be styled the "positive" arguments on behalf of the incarnation.

On this occasion, however, I want to direct attention elsewhere to what may be called "defensive" arguments clearing the ground for the more positive belief in the traditional Christian view of the incarnation. I shall focus on what are, in principle, only some of the epistemic dynamics of the incarnational claim—some of its logical relations to the sorts of epistemic considerations in the light of which its rational affirmation would be possible or impossible. What I do hope to indicate is that contrary to what many critics have argued in the recent past, it is possible that it be rational to believe Jesus to be God incarnate. To put it more strongly, I hope to go some way toward showing that none of the major criticisms of a philosophical nature directed against the doctrine of the incarnation in the last few years provides any good reason at all to think that it cannot be rational to believe that the pinnacle of divine revelation has consisted in God's coming among us as one of us. The belief that Jesus was God incarnate can be an eminently rational belief to hold.

The present essay will be an exercise in philosophical theology, an intellectual enterprise I take to be a necessary component in any comprehensive theology, be it evangelical or otherwise. Of course, Christian theology is not just apologetics. It is not even primarily apologetics. Yet, especially in a post-Christian world, it must prominently involve apologetics. And this is something we need not regret. For in attempting to answer our critics, we very often come to see features of our beliefs we otherwise might have overlooked. It is my hope that in taking even a brief look at each of the challenges I want to address, we shall begin to attain a richer perspective on one of our most central and important beliefs about the self-disclosure of God.

GOD IN CHRIST:
THE POSSIBILITY OF RATIONAL BELIEF

In the past, many people, including some friends of the Christian message as well as numerous foes, have believed the doctrine of the incarnation to be ultimately beyond the scope of reason.[1] Some have believed this because they have taken the doctrine to be inexpungibly obscure to the point of being without clear sense or determinate, cognitive meaning. If it were beyond the scope of reason on this ground, or on any other ground, it would not be such that belief in it could be rational, or in accord with reason.

What are we to make of this sort of view? I think it will be interesting here to quote at length a line of reasoning presented some time ago by John Wisdom:

> It has been said that once at least a higher gift than grace did flesh and blood refine, God's essence and his very self—in the body of Jesus. Whether this statement is true or false is not now the point, but whether it's so obscure as to be senseless.
>
> Obscure undoubtedly it is but senseless it is not. For to say that in Nero God was incarnate is not to utter a senseless string of words nor merely to express a surprising sentiment; it is to make a statement which is absurd because it is against all reason. If I say of a cat, "This cat is abracadabra" I utter a senseless string of words, I don't make a statement at all and therefore don't make an absurd statement. But if I say of a cat which is plainly dead "In this cat there is life" I make a statement which is absurd because it is against all reason. The cat is not hunting, eating, sleeping, breathing; it is stiff and cold. In the same way the words, "In Nero God was incarnate" are not without any meaning; one who utters them makes a statement, he makes a statement which is absurd and *against* all reason and therefore *not* beyond the scope of reason. Now if a statement is not beyond the scope of reason then any logically parallel statement is also not beyond the scope of reason. . . . The statement "In Jesus God was incarnate" is logically parallel to "In Nero God was incarnate." The latter we noticed is not beyond the scope of reason. Therefore the statement "In Jesus God was incarnate" is not beyond the scope of reason.[2]

It is not merely the case that we have no reason to believe that Nero was God incarnate; that would be compatible with our also having no reason to believe he was not God incarnate. And in that case, the claim, and claims of its type, could be beyond the scope of reason. Wisdom's point is that we have very good reason, as decisive a grounding as we could want, for believing that the wicked man Nero was *not* God incarnate. And surely to this, everyone in possession of the Judeo-Christian conception of God would agree. Any claim that Nero was God incarnate we would label as nonsense or absurd. Now it happens to be the case that many critics of orthodox Christian doctrine within the contemporary academic theological community have called the traditional claim that Jesus was literally God incarnate nonsense or absurd. But even these critics, or at least the vast majority of them, surely would recognize something clearly wrong with the Nero claim that is not wrong with the parallel claim about Jesus. The Nero claim is nonsensical or absurd on properly epistemic grounds. In an epistemic sense it stands in flagrant contradiction to what we know about God. It is Nero himself, his particular personality and character, which would make a claim to his deity particularly absurd, and markedly inferior in an epistemic sense to the parallel claim about Jesus. It is this to which Wisdom would have us attend.

The Christian claim has been said by some critics to be nonsensical or absurd in a logical, or semantic, or conceptual sense. That this is not the case can be evinced by the comparative difference in *prima facie* epistemic status between the claim about Nero and the claim about Jesus, given what we know about the two of them on the human level. Thus, as Wisdom indicates, neither of these statements is unintelligible. And neither is beyond the scope of reason.

If Wisdom has indeed successfully indicated to us that the doctrine of the incarnation is not beyond the scope of reason, has he shown that the possibility is open that it may be rational or reasonable to endorse this doctrine? The answer to this question is clearly "No," for the claim that Jesus was God incarnate could fall within the scope of reason in much the same way as would a claim that, for example, Jesus was a married bachelor, for all that Wisdom shows. Wisdom does draw our attention helpfully to a difference between the Nero claim and the Jesus claim. But the claim of deity for Nero could be absurd in a way in which the claim of deity for Jesus is not absurd without its following from this that the claim about Jesus is not absurd in any sense at all, and such that it is even possible that it be rational to endorse it.

And as a matter of fact, various contemporary theologians have thought the incarnational claim about Jesus to be patently incoherent and thus absurd in a logical or conceptual sense.[3] From this point of view, it would be possible to believe Jesus to be God incarnate and also to be rational in so believing only if one rationally could fail to see the patent incoherence of the claim. A certain significant degree of ignorance or obtuseness would be required, if this were to be possible at all. A number of philosophers have offered persuasive arguments in recent years to the effect that it is possible rationally to believe the impossible or necessarily false.[4] However, if "incoherent" means more than merely "necessarily false," if "patently incoherent" means something more like "analytically false" or "a priori impossible," then it is less likely, to say the least, that anyone would be able rationally to believe a patently incoherent doctrine, for it is highly unlikely that belief in the truth of an analytically false proposition, one that is a priori impossible, can reasonably be ascribed to a person at all. If a patently incoherent proposition is such that one cannot understand it without seeing it to be false, and if it is impossible to believe a proposition to be true without understanding it, and, moreover, if it is impossible to believe a proposition to be true while seeing it to be false, then should the doctrine of the incarnation be patently incoherent, it would not be possible rationally to believe it, because it would not be possible to believe it at all. Furthermore, understood in this way, it is clear that nothing could count as a positive epistemic consideration in favor of the truth of a patently incoherent claim. If the incarnational claim endorsed by traditional Christians had this status, there could be no positive epistemic ground for believing it true. As, for example, Grace Jantzen has said:

> If the claim that Jesus is God incarnate is on an epistemological level with "Jesus was a married bachelor" then no matter how much evidence we could discover for his having said so, his disciples and others having believed it, and the early church having affirmed it, the claim must still be rejected: such "evidence" would be strictly irrelevant.[5]

And this is certainly correct. Nothing can count as evidence or any other form of epistemic grounding for belief in a proposition the very understanding of which suffices for seeing its falsehood.

The charge of patent incoherence has been repeated in various forms quite often in recent years by critics of the doctrine of the incarnation. Basically, the sort of argument most of them seem to have in mind is roughly something like the following: On a standard and traditional conception of deity, God is omnipotent, omniscient, incorporeal, impeccable, and necessarily existent, among other things. Moreover, by our definition of "God," such properties as these are, so to speak, constitutive of deity. It is impossible that any individual could be divine, or exemplify divinity, without having these properties. To claim that some individual is divine without being omnipotent, say, or necessarily existent, would be on this view just as incoherent as supposing some individual to be both a bachelor and a married man at one and the same time. By contrast, we human beings seem clearly to exemplify the logical complement (or "opposite") of each of these constitutive divine attributes. We are limited in power, restricted in knowledge, embodied in flesh, liable to sin, and are contingent creations. Jesus is claimed in the doctrine of the incarnation to have been both fully human and fully divine. But it is logically impossible for any being to exemplify at one and the same time both a property and its logical complement. Thus, recent critics have concluded that it is logically impossible for any one person to be both human and divine, to have all the attributes proper to deity and all those ingredients in human nature as well. The doctrine of the incarnation on this view is an incoherent theological development of the early church that we must discard in favor of some other way of conceptualizing the importance of Jesus for Christian faith. He could not possibly have been God incarnate, a literally divine person in human nature.

As I have addressed this challenge to the doctrine of the incarnation in great detail elsewhere, I shall give only a relatively brief indication here of how it can be answered.[6] A lengthy response is not required in order for us to be able to see how this currently popular sort of objection can be turned back. A couple of very simple metaphysical distinctions will provide us with the basic apparatus for defending orthodoxy against this charge, which otherwise can seem to be a very formidable challenge indeed.

As it usually is presented, the sort of argument I have just outlined treats humanity and divinity, or human nature and divine nature, as each constituted by a set of properties individually necessary and jointly sufficient for exemplifying that nature either as human or as divine. Such an argument depends implicitly on a sort of essentialist metaphysic that has been around for quite awhile and recently has experienced a resurgence of popularity among philosophers. On such a view, objects have two sorts of properties: essential and accidental. A property can be essential to an object in either of two ways. It is part of an individual's essence if the individual who has it could not have existed without having it. It is a kind-essential property if its exemplification is necessary for an individual's belonging to a particular kind, for example, human-kind. Human nature, then, consists in a set of properties severally necessary and jointly sufficient for being human. And the same is true of divine nature. The critic of the incarnation begins with the simple truth that humans have properties that God could not possibly have; it goes on to assume that these properties, or at least some of them, are essential properties of being human, without which one could not be fully human; it then concludes that God could not possibly become a human being. The conclusion would be well drawn if the assumption were correct. But it is this assumption that we must question.

Once one accepts a distinction between essential and accidental properties—a distinction employed in this sort of argument against incarnation—another simple distinction follows in its wake. Among properties characterizing human beings, some are essential elements of human nature, but many just happen to be common human properties without also being essential. Consider, for example, the property of having ten fingers. It is a common human property, one had by a great number of people, but it clearly is not a property essential to being human. People lose fingers without thereby ceasing to be human. Further, consider a common property that safely can be said to be a universal human property, one had by every human being who ever has lived—the property of standing under fifteen feet tall. Obviously this is not an essential human property either. At some time in the future, an individual might grow beyond this height, certainly not thereby forfeiting his humanity. So it is not a safe inference to reason simply from a property's being common or even universal among human beings that it is an essential human property, strictly necessary for exemplifying human nature.

The relevance of this distinction to the doctrine of the incarnation should be obvious. It is common for human beings to be less than omnipotent, less than omniscient, contingently existent, and so on. Apart from Jesus, these are even universal human properties. Further, in the case of any of us who do exemplify these less than divine attributes, it is most reasonable to hold that they are in our case essential attributes. I, for example, could not possibly become omnipotent. I am essentially limited in power. But why think this is true on account of human nature? Why think that any attributes incompatible with deity are elements of human nature, properties without which one could not be truly human?

An individual is *fully human* just in case that individual has all essential human properties, all the properties composing basic human nature. An individual is *merely human* if he has all those properties *plus* some additional limitation properties as well, such as being less than omnipotent, less than omniscient, and so on. Some examples of this *merely x / fully x* distinction may help. Consider a diamond. It has all the properties essential to being a physical object (mass, spatiotemporal location, etc.) and thus is fully physical. Consider now a turtle. It has all the properties essential to being a physical object. It is fully physical, but it is not merely physical. It has properties of animation as well. It is an organic being. In contrast, the gem is merely physical as well as being fully physical. Now take the case of a man. An embodied human being has mass, spatio-temporal location, and so forth. He is thus fully physical. But he is not merely a physical object, having organic and animate properties as well. So let us say he is fully animate. But unlike the turtle he is not merely animate; he has rational, moral, aesthetic, and spiritual qualities mere organic entities lack. Let us say that he belongs to a higher ontological level by virtue of being fully human. And if, like you and me, he belongs to no higher ontological level than that of humanity, he is merely human as well as being fully human.

According to orthodox Christology, Jesus was fully human without being merely human. He had all properties constitutive of human nature, but he had higher properties as well, those constitutive of deity, which from an Anselmian perspective form the upper bound of our scale. What is crucial to realize here is that an orthodox perspective on human nature will categorize all human properties logically incompatible with a divine incarnation as, at most, essential to being *merely human*. No orthodox theologian has ever held that Jesus was merely human, only that he was fully human. The person who was God incarnate had the full array of attributes essential to humanity, and all those essential to divinity.

I am suggesting that, armed with a few simple distinctions, the Christian can clarify his conception of human nature in such a way as to provide for the coherence and metaphysical possibility of the traditional doctrine of the incarnation. Many, however, object that the use of these distinctions in explicating what Chalcedon had in mind about Jesus can only result in absurdity. For the drafters of the Chalcedonian definition, Jesus was omniscient, omnipotent, necessarily existent, and omnipresent, as well as being an itinerant Jewish preacher. But this has appeared outlandish to most contemporary theologians. Did the bouncing baby boy of Mary and Joseph direct the workings of the cosmos from his crib? Was this admittedly remarkable man, as he sat by a well or under a fig tree, actually omnipresent in all of creation? Did this carpenter's son exist *necessarily?* These implications of orthodoxy can sound just too bizarre for even a moment's consideration.

A couple of ancient claims are sufficient to rid orthodoxy of any such appearances of absurdity. First of all, a person is not identical with his or her body. Even a modern materialist who holds that all personality necessarily is embodied need not deny this. So the necessary existence of God the Son, with its implications that he cannot have begun to exist and cannot cease to exist, does not entail that the earthly body in which he incarnated himself had these properties. Second, a person is not identical with any particular range of conscious experience he or she might have. With this in mind, we can appreciate the early view that in the case of God incarnate, we must recognize something like two distinct ranges of consciousness.[7] There is first what we can call the eternal mind of God the Son with its distinctively divine consciousness, whatever that might be like, with its full scope of omniscience. And there is a distinctly earthly consciousness that grew and developed as the boy Jesus grew and developed. It drew its visual imagery from what the eyes of Jesus saw, and its concepts from the languages he spoke. The earthly range of consciousness, and self-consciousness, was thoroughly human, Jewish, and first-century Palestinian in scope.

To be as brief as possible here, we can view the two ranges of consciousness as follows: the divine consciousness of God the Son contained, but was not contained by, the earthly range of consciousness. Further, there was what can be called an a-symmetric accessing relation between the two (such as might obtain between two computer programs or informational systems, one containing but not contained by the other). The divine mind had full access to the earthly experience being had through the incarnation, but the earthly consciousness did not have such access to the content of the overarching omniscience of the Logos. This allows for the intellectual and spiritual growth of Jesus to be a real development. It also can help account for the cry of dereliction. We have in the person of Jesus no God merely dressed up as a man. No docetic absurdities are implied by this position. Nor is it Nestorian. Nor Apollinarian. There is one person with two natures, and two ranges of consciousness. He is not the theological equivalent of a centaur, half God and half man. He is fully human, but not merely human. He is also fully divine. There is, in this doctrine, no apparent incoherence whatsoever. Thus, there seem to be no good logical or conceptual grounds for thinking that there can be no rational belief that Jesus was God incarnate.

But before concluding too hastily that it is at least possible for belief in the incarnation to be rationally grounded, we would do well to consider briefly a problem raised by Francis Young. Young has said:

It is now accepted by the majority of Christian theologians that Jesus must have been an entirely normal human being, that any qualification of this implies some element of docetic thinking, and that docetism, however slight, undermines the reality of the incarnation.

I therefore pose the following conundrum:

If Jesus was an entirely normal human being, no evidence can be produced for the incarnation.

If no evidence can be produced, there can be no basis on which to claim that an incarnation took place.[8]

Young seems to assume that the belief that Jesus was God incarnate requires evidence to be considered rational, and that the sort of evidence required is unavailable in principle, given the understanding of humanity needed for avoiding docetism. That being the case, it cannot be reasonable or rational to believe that Jesus was God incarnate.

It is true that in order to avoid the docetic tendency some critics have claimed plagues traditional theology, we must maintain the full, complete humanity of Jesus. But Young has a genuine problem here for incarnational belief only if in order to avoid docetism we also would have to hold that Jesus was *merely* human, and thus different from ordinary human beings in no metaphysical way that could possibly be empirically manifested. But as we have seen, there is an important distinction to be drawn between being fully human and being merely human. Jesus can be fully human without being merely human. At least, that is the orthodox claim as I have articulated it. His complete humanity is thus compatible with his belonging to the higher ontological level of deity as well, such that his deity as well as his humanity was manifest in his life. We need not hold that Jesus was merely human in order to avoid docetism and uphold the doctrine of the incarnation. If we did hold this, it is clear that we would be fleeing docetism only to fall into the grasp of psilanthropism (Jesus as only human), and thereby relinquish the doctrine just as certainly, only in a more currently fashionable way. On a careful understanding of the logic and metaphysics of the incarnation, we can thus see that Young's "conundrum" cannot even arise. So, once again, we find that what has been taken to be a problem for the traditional position is in actuality no problem at all. None of the considerations we have examined so far has had the slightest tendency to block in principle the possibility of rationally discerning God in Christ.

But there is one more major sort of objection many recent critics have lodged against the doctrine of the incarnation, along with the beliefs about divine-human relations it presupposes. The doctrine of the incarnation is one component in a much larger doctrinal scheme encompassing the themes of creation, fall, and redemption. Contemporary critics of the traditional renderings of these themes often have pointed out that they originally were enunciated and developed in prescientific conditions and thus within the context of a very different sort of worldview from the one modern scientifically-minded people have today. They have then usually gone on to suggest that religious claims that may have made a great deal of sense in their original context have lost much, if not all, of their plausibility in the modern age. It is interesting to note that this is a general point made repeatedly in recent years by many critics both within and without the church.

In the past century there has been a marked tendency to beat a hasty retreat in the face of almost any specious argument against the traditional affirmations of the faith. Often theologians have been inclined to relinquish or "reinterpret" important doctrines on no better grounds than that those beliefs can appear to some secular critics to be somehow out of step with the march of science. Some, such as Rudolf Bultmann, for example, claim to be unable to believe in the literally miraculous while at the same time avail themselves of the comforts of modern technology. But of course such cases may be of more interest to psychologists than to anyone seeking to determine the objective status, truth value, or rationality of orthodox Christian beliefs. Occasionally, however, an interesting and even challenging philosophical or theological problem can be extracted from the often vague misgivings of such critics of orthodoxy. Let us consider various ways in which such a challenge might be thought to arise here against the doctrine of the incarnation.

It has been suggested many times during the past two hundred years that this doctrine, which made a great deal of sense to many people living within the geocentric world-picture of Ptolemaic cosmology, is rendered in some sense absurd by modern accounts of the immensity and nature of our universe. The problem seems to be something like this: During the times when the Chalcedonian understanding of Christ was developed and reigned supreme, great numbers of people, including the best educated, believed that human beings live in a relatively circumscribed universe. Its entirety has been created for the benefit of human life and represents the special crowning act of divine creation. This world is situated at the hub of the cosmos, around which all else literally as well as figuratively revolves. Within such an overall perspective, it would have seemed in no way incongruous, but rather could have appeared supremely fitting, that the Creator of all take such interest in his human creatures as to step into his world himself and take a part in the human drama, being enacted, as it was, on the center stage of the universe. An anthropocentric worldview provided the cosmological backdrop and framework for a literally anthropomorphic theology—God become a man. The importance of the earth and the importance of humanity rendered this incarnation of deity intelligible and appropriate.

However, during the past few centuries this worldview, and the framework it provided, has been destroyed by the onslaught of scientific discovery. Actually, it is quite a variety of scientific discoveries, assumptions, hypotheses, speculations, and methodological implications that have seemed to many people to have had the net result of demoting humankind from its traditionally exalted place in the universe to what can appear to be a relatively unexceptional and terribly insignificant role in the cosmic process. I shall not attempt to delineate here the variety of negative effects modern science has been perceived to have on religious doctrine. Numerous books thoroughly document the so-called history of the warfare between science and theology. But it will be of some interest to at least indicate a couple of points at which scientific developments have been thought to have this devaluing impact on our view of humanity, and thus on the system of Christian doctrines, including centrally that of the incarnation.

Some critics appear to think that the sheer size of the universe renders humanity unimportant and Christian doctrine thus implausible. Of course, it is no modern novelty to juxtapose the immensity of the universe to the religious emphasis on man. The psalmist, after all, said the same thing a long time ago:

> When I consider Thy heavens, the work of Thy fingers, the moon and the stars, which Thou hast ordained: What is man that Thou dost take thought of him? And the son of man that Thou dost care for him? (Ps. 8:3-4)

Throughout the Psalter there are frequent expressions of wonder, and perhaps astonishment, that amid the grandeur of the heavens, human beings should be especially valued and cared for by God. The attitude of modern critics, however, is that of simple disbelief. Of course, the psalmist was not aware as we are today of *how* immense the heavens might be. But it is difficult to see exactly what it is about distinctively modern knowledge of the scale of the universe that is thought to show the absurdity of any religious beliefs based on the assumption that the earth and human beings are important to the Creator of all.

Now, it is clear that in many contexts size and value are in direct correlation, the latter depending on the former. For example, all other things being equal, a large army is of greater value than a small one, if one seeks protection of one's country from an enemy. But this dependence of value on size is only relative to some contexts having to do with instrumental value, and clearly does not hold true in all or even most contexts. And when it comes to considerations of intrinsic value, the sort of value ascribed to human beings by Christian theology, questions of size or physical magnitude are simply irrelevant. It is absurd to argue that small is unimportant. Critics often accuse Christian theologians of being anthropomorphic in their thought. But here it seems to be the critics who are anthropomorphizing, or rather, anthropopathizing, with the assumption that if there were a God, he would not deign to notice or value anything as small and insignificant on the cosmic scale as the earth and its inhabitants. On the Christian picture, God is sufficiently unlike a man that his attention and care can extend fully to every part of a universe.

We are safe in concluding, then, that if any discovery of modern science undercuts the Christian belief that God so valued us that he became a man, it will not be any discovery concerning the sheer size of the universe. But as with the link between relative size and value, other signs, or even requisites, of human importance traditionally have been undercut by the advance of the sciences. For example, many primal religions equate spatial centrality with importance. Anthropologists have found many tribes who hold as a sacred belief the claim that their village, or a fire in the center of the village, is located at the center of the world, or at the center of the entire cosmos. Their importance to the gods is held to be tied to their central location. Such a view also can be seen in the Ptolemaic cosmology and in the many theological and philosophical speculations arising out of that cosmology. In light of this apparently natural equation of importance and spatial centrality, reflected also in nonspatial uses of the notion of centrality, it is easy to understand the resistance many Christian theologians and clerics once felt toward any transition away from a geocentric cosmology. But again, outside a very few contexts of instrumental value considerations, it is simply wrong to think that there is a necessary link between spatial centrality and value. Modern critics who cite the transition in cosmology from Ptolemaic to Copernican to contemporary as counting against or as undercutting traditional Christian claims that the earth and humanity are sufficiently important as to make a divine incarnation on earth comprehensible are making the same mistake with respect to value theory as the ancients whose views they deride.

EXPERIENCE AND AFFIRMATION

Given, then, that it is possible that belief in a divine incarnation is rational, we need to inquire more fully what the grounds are for such a belief. Relatively conservative theologians have usually constructed arguments with similar form, setting forth a case in two premises, from which the conclusion of Jesus' divinity is drawn. Examples include the following:

1. The Soteriological Argument
    a. Jesus can forgive us our sins and offer us salvation.
    b. Only God can forgive us our sins and offer us salvation; thus
    c. Jesus is God.
2. The Liturgical Argument
    a. Jesus is properly worshiped.
    b. Only God is properly worshiped; thus
    c. Jesus is God.
3. The Revelatory Argument
    a. Jesus reveals God perfectly.
    b. Only God can reveal God perfectly; thus
    c. Jesus is God.

Such arguments, of course, hardly ever appear in such pared down form. Usually, the (a)-premise is defended as part of the distinctively Christian proclamation throughout the centuries and as either given in Christian experience or assumed in Christian practice. The (b)-premise is seen as a product of conceptual truths concerning the concepts involved: in each case the concept of God and, respectively, the concepts of sin, forgiveness, and salvation in the first argument, that of worship in the second, and revelation in the third.

These are clearly instances of deductively valid argument forms. And if the (b)-premise in each case is a conceptual truth, it follows that it will be reasonable to accept the conclusion of each argument if it is reasonable to accept its (a)-premise. But of course, it is also true that it is reasonable to accept the (a)-premise in each case only if it is reasonable to accept the claim of deity for Jesus. And that is precisely the question at issue. Such arguments as these clearly can serve a function within the context of an incarnational Christian faith—the function of explicitly displaying important logical relations between and among various central commitments of such a faith. A function they cannot perform is that of endowing incarnational belief with a rationality or reasonableness it otherwise would lack apart from their construction.

Can there be a deductively valid argument for the truth of the doctrine of the incarnation that can function in such a way as to provide a person with a rational belief in it that, without the argument, he would not have, all other things being equal?

In one of his contributions to the incarnation debate, Brian Hebblethwaite developed several arguments in favor of the Chalcedonian characterization of Jesus as compared with the reduced claims for his status propounded in more recent times.[9] In a response to Hebblethwaite, Keith Ward wrote:

> Hebblethwaite introduces the remarkable argument that "if God might have become a man, but did not, then the reduced claims for what God has done in Christ fail to satisfy." It is difficult to formalize the argument; but it seems to go like this: "if x is logically possible; and if we think it better that x, then x." It is the sort of argument sometimes produced for the doctrine of the Assumption of Mary: "God could have done it; he should have; so he did."[10]

Consider for a moment Ward's attempt to formalize the argument he finds in Hebblethwaite. He first offers us the schema

(A) 1. x is logically possible
     2. We think it better that x; thus,
     3. x

and then apparently means to paraphrase it, or at least apply it in such a way that a parallel schema, each of whose premise-forms he apparently takes to be entailed by the corresponding premise-forms of (A), relates directly to theological argument:

(B) 1. God could have done x
     2. God should have done x; thus,
     3. God did x.

It is Ward's contention that using arguments of the form of (A) in theological matters will yield arguments of the form of (B), and will have, to say the least, untrustworthy results. Ward seems to view the sort of theological argument represented in (B) as having all the benefit of theft over honest toil, of providing an easy route to results to which we have no right. But is this so?

Ward crucially fails to see that (A) is neither equivalent to (B) and thus properly paraphrased by it, nor does it even entail (B). Since

(A) does not entail (B), (A) can be a fallacious form of argument without its following that (B) is as well. And this, as a matter of fact, is the case. Arguments of the form of (A) are obviously fallacious. The world does not necessarily conform itself to our preferences. But, interestingly, arguments of the form of (B) are not fallacious. The (B) schema is a deductively valid one, given the concept of God as a necessarily good being. If we could know, concerning some possible action, both that God could have done it and that he should have done it, then we also could know that he did it. Applying this to the doctrine of the incarnation, if we knew or had reason to believe the two premises in the following argument, our knowledge or reasonable belief would be transmitted to its conclusion:

(I) 1. God could have become incarnate in human nature as Jesus of Nazareth.
    2. God should have become incarnate in human nature as Jesus of Nazareth; thus,
    3. God did become incarnate in human nature as Jesus of Nazareth.

As I have indicated already, a couple of simple metaphysical distinctions will suffice to defend the truth of (I)-1. But, in light of the epistemic realities for religious belief with which we live, it is difficult to see how anyone might be in better epistemic position with respect to (I)-2 than with respect to (I)-3. It is thus hard to see how the reasonableness of a belief that (I)-3 could be thought to be based on or grounded in an argument such as (I) operating on an independently reasonable belief that (I)-2 and (I)-1, given the epistemic conditions we are all in with respect to God's actions, and the principles of his actions.

It seems to me that vast numbers of Christians are reasonable in believing Jesus to be God incarnate, and it is my guess that many of them have never reflected on or in any other way entertained proposition (I)-2, the claim that God should have become incarnate, and have no reasonable belief that it is true. Moreover, many who have considered it would, I suspect, maintain a properly pious agnosticism about it, while wholeheartedly and reasonably endorsing the doctrine of the incarnation. And further, I would expect that any Christians who would affirm (I)-2 would do so on the basis of, among other things, their prior belief that Jesus was God incarnate. So even in their case, the reasonableness of the latter belief would in no way depend on the reasonableness of the former. The opposite is, in fact, the case.

I have introduced this excursus into Ward's remarks in order to make a very simple point. If it is reasonable to believe Jesus to be God incarnate, that reasonableness is not likely produced by means of, or grounded in, any such deductive argument. It seems to be the case that deductive arguments for the incarnation will always have at least one premise whose positive epistemic status is no greater or more obvious than that of the doctrine itself. In the Soteriological, Liturgical, and Revelatory arguments, it will be reasonable to believe the premise in question, at best, *if and only if* it is reasonable to believe Jesus to be God incarnate. In the argument (I), gleaned from Ward's remarks on Hebblethwaite, it will be reasonable to believe the more controversial premise at best *only if* it is reasonable to believe in the incarnation. In none of these cases do we find a prior, independent reasonableness transmitted to and conferred upon the incarnational belief from more evident beliefs. So if it can be, or is, reasonable to believe Jesus to be God incarnate, then most likely that reasonableness will neither consist in nor be provided by the having of such a simple deductive argument.

It is natural to ask next whether some form of inductive, or non-deductive, argument could render belief in Jesus' deity reasonable. Consider, for example, that form of reasoning in which Nicodemus engaged concerning Jesus (John 3:1-21). We can represent the structure of his argument as

(N) 1. Jesus performed a certain class of acts M (acts such as traditionally have been classed as miracles)

2. No one can perform acts of class M unless he is a teacher come from God; thus,

3. Jesus was a teacher come from God.

Again, this is a deductively valid argument concerning the status of Jesus. As Nicodemus appears to have reasoned to the conclusion that Jesus was a teacher come from God, many conservative Christians talk as if they themselves have reasoned, or as if they are convinced that a rational nonbeliever could reason, from empirically ascertainable facts about the circumstances, character, and deeds of Jesus to the much stronger conclusion that he was and is God incarnate. They could have in mind an argument such as (N), where M now presumably would include, say, postresurrection activities of the risen Christ, and which would employ a substituted second premise such as the following:

(N) 2′. No one can perform acts of class M unless he is God. From this it would follow validly that Jesus was God. Or they could have in mind a probabilistic transform of the revised (N), in which case the simple, categorical claim of deity for Jesus would not validly follow, but the weaker claim would, that it is probable that Jesus was divine. Or it could be the case that many Christians who reason about Jesus in the tradition of Nicodemus have something in mind that cannot be captured by any such simple, two-step deductive argument. Perhaps there is a complex nondeductive form of argument to the best explanation they have in mind, which cannot be so simply represented. Thus, they would argue that the best explanation for a certain range of facts about Jesus is that he was God incarnate.

On the one hand, it is clear that most mature Christians who affirm the divinity of Jesus see their belief as anchored in the empirical realm. They see their incarnational belief as in accord with their own personal experience, with the experience of other Christians throughout the centuries, and with the apparent though sometimes elusive manifestations of deity in the empirical realm that the New Testament documents appear to record surrounding the person of Jesus. But on the other hand, it seems not to be the case that there is any single form of nondeductive argument typically relied upon to move from distinct facts about the portrayal of Jesus in the New Testament to contemporary rational affirmation. Likewise, the passage from facts about the experience of Jesus on the part of fellow believers through the ages, or from features of contemporary experience to a conclusion that Jesus is God the Son, the Second Person of the Divine Trinity, does not always conform to a single type of argument. Nor is it obvious that any account of their reasonableness in so believing must involve the production of such an argument.

It does not seem that the reasonableness of incarnational belief is provided by deductive arguments from premises it is independently reasonable to believe, nor does it seem to be provided by any single sort of nondeductive argument consciously entertained or used by believers. Could it then be a simple function of direct experience? Could it be the case that traditional Christians have just *seen* Jesus to be God incarnate, and that their belief in his deity, thus generated, is reasonable precisely in light of that experience?

Grace Jantzen once wrote:

Clearly, any doctrine which wishes to affirm that Jesus of Nazareth is God the Son, the Second Person of the Holy Trinity, is going well beyond the boundary of empirical observability. Indeed, what would it be *like* to make that sort of observation? Even the question seems misphrased. No list of empirical data, whether these are taken strictly as sense data or more broadly as observation of speech and behaviour patterns could ever entail the conclusion reached by the centurion in the Gospel: "Truly this man was the Son of God."[11]

Sense data reports underdetermine statements about physical objects. Reports about the disposition and behavior of physical objects (such as arms, legs, mouths, and even brains) arguably underdetermine claims about the distinctively mental properties of persons. And claims about the divine can seem to be even more remote from any reports about what is experienced in the empirical realm. For example, a few years ago an article appeared in which it was argued that not even God could know from observation, or even from observation enhanced by inductive reasoning, that he is God, that he exemplifies the distinctively divine attributes.[12] Consider omnipotence alone. No matter how many extraordinary tasks a being has attempted to perform and has carried out successfully with no difficulty or strain whatsoever, it will not follow from his record of accomplishments, however astounding, that he is literally omnipotent. Thus, no matter what we observe a being do in the empirical arena, a full report of our observations will not entail the proposition that the being in question is omnipotent. If seeing that an individual is God requires seeing that he is omnipotent, necessarily good, omnipresent, omniscient, ontologically independent, and the like, then the prospects for seeing that Jesus is God look pretty dim, to say the least.

But does experiencing Jesus as divine require this sort of "seeing-that" relation? Clearly, in undergoing the processes that sense data theorists have characterized as the having of percepts or sense data, we most often reasonably take ourselves to be experiencing physical objects. Likewise, in experiencing the dispositions and behavior of certain sorts of physical objects in certain sorts of circumstances, we reasonably take ourselves to be experiencing or observing the mental qualities of other persons, such as their anger, happiness, irritation, tranquility. It is true that if the observational experience of a table were to be reported in purely sense data language (supposing that to be possible), the report would not entail any appropriately related proposition about a physical object. But this does not prevent our sense experience being experience of physical objects. Likewise, the lack of entailments between reports about Jesus cast in this-worldly terms and the appropriate propositions concerning his deity need not preclude the possibility of an experience of Jesus as the infinite God incarnate through the sort of finite range of experience of him available to an ordinary human believer.

Many theologians have suggested through the centuries that there is an innate human capacity that, when properly functioning, allows us to see God, or to recognize God when we see him in the starry heavens above or in the moral law within. Would it not then be natural to suppose that he would also be recognizable in his incarnate form? It is also clear, however, that if this is right, there are widespread and deeply rooted impediments to the functioning of this capacity. Some of these impediments I have sought to address. Much, of course, remains to be said, especially on topics relating to the justification of beliefs generally and to the role of the Holy Spirit in revealing the truth about God. Nonetheless, the arguments of this chapter show the relative instability of the supposed rational impediment against traditional Christian belief. Put positively, they indicate that there is no obstacle in principle to accepting the widespread Christian assumption that it is possible to be rational when believing that Jesus is God incarnate.

Speaking and Hearing

Anthony C. Thiselton

My task here is to explore some quite specific issues in response to the question, "What is the interrelationship between evangelical theology and current issues in contemporary theories of interpretation?" We are not simply asking how evangelicals should *respond* to current hermeneutical issues, as if to imply that as evangelicals we can never lead the way but only make defensive assessments of other people's moves. Rather, we are asking how progress can be made in formulating fresh hermeneutical insights when we allow the Bible and evangelical theology to inform our own enterprise. In a chapter of this limited size, the treatment cannot be more than selective and programmatic. I therefore propose to focus attention on four particular issues: (1) problems about authority and the use of the Bible for social or religious control; (2) issues raised by diversity within the Bible and related questions about levels of meaning, the canon, and recontextualization; (3) models of understanding and communication with special reference to literary hermeneutics; and (4) the role of interpretive tradition within the community of faith as corporate interpreter.

AUTHORITY AND THE USE OF THE BIBLE

Evangelical theology regularly reflects a concern about the nature and exercise of authority that outsiders might be pardoned for regarding as verging on the obsessional. There are good and important reasons for this, but the history of ways in which the Bible has actually been used suggests that such concern about authority can lead us in equally constructive and destructive directions.

On one side, it is not only constructive but also central, basic, and nonnegotiable for the evangelical tradition that the church and its ministers preach not their own personal opinions but a message of which it can be said "Thus says the Lord." It is the aim of every evangelical pastor to be able to say, with Paul: "I did not shrink from declaring to you the whole counsel of God" (Acts 20:27). God's covenant relationship with his people spells out concrete and specific terms as a basis for a secure and defined relationship in which it is clear on what ground a human person may stand. On such a basis, the argument runs in the Epistle to the Hebrews, the believer may draw near "with confidence" (*meta parresias*, 4:16; cf. 8:10-13; 10:16-23). What makes possible this confidence or "boldness" can be articulated in the form of a confession (*homologia*, 10:23).

All the same, this claim to speak in God's name and with God's authority carries with it an awesome responsibility. The one sin even greater than that of failing to communicate an authoritative message given by God is the sin of "the prophet who presumes to speak a word in my name which I have *not* commanded" (Deut. 18:20, my italics). That such a possibility is a genuine one can be seen from the history of the use of the Bible. Some salutary examples have been collected in a recent useful study by Willard Swartley. He reminds us how Bishop John Henry Hopkins, to cite only his first example, saw the Bible as a bulwark against the supposedly "modernist" trend that sought freedom for slaves. Hopkins wrote: "The Bible's defense of slavery is very plain. St. Paul was inspired. . . . Who are we, that in our modern wisdom presume to set aside the word of God."[1] Nowadays we use sociological categories to describe this kind of phenomenon. Appeals to divine authority of this kind amount to using the Bible, however unwittingly and sincerely, as an instrument of power and domination for social or religious control. Those who would have bowed to no human hierarchy of blood, intellect, or commercial power allowed their corporate and individual lives to be shaped and directed in accordance with prescribed patterns of action sanctioned solely on the basis of certain *interpretations* of the biblical material that were equated, in turn, with God's own command. For some it is a very short step to move from calling the Bible the word of God to calling a preacher's personal gloss on the text also the word of God.

The initial response to such a problem by those who stand within evangelical theology will not be to retreat from calling the Bible the word of God. But I suggest that three principles will enable evangelical theology to stand its ground with greater integrity and responsibility both to God and to the world. First, we need to practice what Paul Ricoeur and others have called *a hermeneutics of suspicion*.[2] Ricoeur's comments on the importance of Freud for hermeneutics are noteworthy here, together with his examination of the psychological category of overdetermination.[3] We can be unaware of what lies behind phenomena that may have emerged through multiple causes. We may therefore mistake purely human concerns about the ordering of human lives for "religious" ones, or for divine commands. Long before Freud, the biblical writers called attention to this same capacity for very deep self-deception through their language about the deceitfulness and wickedness of the human heart. Hence, although ultimately the aim of hermeneutics remains constructive, there is always also the need for suspicion about the possibility of fallibility in one's own interpretation of Scripture. Our own interpretations should remain the object of suspicion and critical evaluation. How to give substance to this goal is one aspect of the study of hermeneutics.

Second, the work of Ricoeur and others on a hermeneutic of suspicion receives particular focus in the light of the category of *interest* in the hermeneutics of the social sciences, and especially in Jürgen Habermas.[4] Taking up issues raised by Otto Weber, Habermas reveals the extent to which patterns of language may function to legitimate relations of organized power within a community. Biblical texts may function, in ways parallel to written laws or constitutions, to institutionalize patterns and roles within a tradition and a community. Legitimacy formalizes authority, and thereby undergirds the exercise of *power*. But at this point interests, including those that are vested, may often shape the interpretation of the texts as they are understood within a given tradition. Interests may have a part in determining what counts as acceptable interpretation. Questions about interests, therefore, raise issues about the relations between perception, truth, and practical attitude. In other words, they relate truth to praxis in a way that is reminiscent of the wisdom tradition in the biblical writings, and especially the Fourth Gospel. Johannine language speaks of "doing" the truth (John 3:21; 1 John 1:6). This is one reason why there can never be a totally watertight division between understanding and application.

A third principle identifies a potential contribution distinctive to evangelical theology in contrast to other Christian traditions. Theology in more liberal and radical traditions has always reflected a potential tendency to *reduce* the level of the divine to the human, at least in terms of claims about authority or revelation. On the other hand, some streams of Catholic theology and even some Pentecostal or neo-Pentecostal movements reflect a parallel tendency to *elevate* human claims of authority and of revelation to the status of the divine. Reformation theology, at least in its classical forms, resisted both tendencies. This analysis perhaps represents an overly facile generalization. But there is sufficient truth in it to call attention to an important issue. On one side, for example, stands the claim of Gerd Theissen, which from an evangelical perspective can be seen only as reductionist. He writes, "There can be no recourse to privileged knowledge or authorities. . . . I shall ignore the view that it is possible to have privileged access to the truth. Instead of this I shall look for technical competence."[5] It is tempting to ask why we should not regard the disciples of Jesus as having envisaged "privileged access to the truth," while presumably the scribes and Pharisees were those who had "technical competence." However, evangelical theology today may be in greater danger of losing its balance by sliding into the opposite trend, namely, that of elevating merely human claims of authority to the status of the divine. For those of us who are evangelicals, this authority will not come clothed in priests' vestments or in power to give or to withhold the sacraments. But it may appear in subtler guises, such as claims to speak the "obvious," "commonsense," or "natural" meaning of Scripture; or, to move from this particular nuance into an adjacent evangelical subtradition, all in the interests of offering a meaning of Scripture imparted by the Holy Spirit. In yet a third subtradition the temptation will be to absolutize the ecclesial authority of the preacher, pastor, or expositor.

In all cases, evangelical Christians will continue to listen for an authoritative message. They will continue to look to Scripture as a guide through which Christ exercises his lordship. But they will combine openness, receptivity, and obedience with corporate evaluation. They will not surrender their duty to test the prophets, whether the prophet claims to mediate Scripture or to offer some different kind of oracle. One symptom of our relative slowness to hold both aspects together is often seen in the sense of disorientation experienced by many evangelical theological students who seem to feel that thinking critically about interpretations of biblical material is somehow incompatible with a more properly "devotional" attitude toward the Bible. Needless to say, different attitudes are appropriate for different occasions; and different gifts are given within the church to those to whom God appoints different tasks. But at the corporate level, at least, evangelical theology needs to retain sensitivity to both sides of the problem; otherwise the principle of *sola scriptura* becomes evacuated of substance and assumes the status of an empty slogan.

DIVERSITY WITHIN THE BIBLE

One of the most pressing hermeneutical issues facing evangelicals today is the diversity of the biblical writings and current debates on levels of canonical authority. Two principles must be accepted as a starting-point for understanding the present situation.

First, gone are the days of the 1920s and 1930s when it seemed that only evangelicals wished to lay claim to speak with biblical authority. Other traditions within the church seemed to be preoccupied with other questions at that time. Liberalism had reached a peak in the twenties and was largely preoccupied with questions about how to utilize current secular thought. Catholic movements were less concerned about the role of the Bible than they are today and placed more emphasis on *magisterium*. Almost by default, evangelicals found little competition for their claim to represent "biblical" Christianity. But after the rise of dialectical theology in Europe and more especially in the wake of the salvation history and biblical theology movements of the forties and fifties, the question was no longer *whether* a Christian should seek to be "biblical," but *how* he or she could make such a claim, and what such a claim might be said to amount to.

Following the rise and spread of redaction criticism in the 1960s, the church at large moved into a deeper appreciation of the range and variety of theological emphases and perspectives that Scripture as a whole embodied. But negative implications also emerged and many felt that a hermeneutical *impasse* had been reached. On one side, many Christians outside the evangelical tradition saw biblical diversity as a barrier to its use as a consistent or clear norm for theology and conduct. The 1967 Report of the World Council of Churches stated that the contents of biblical writings

> often stand in tension with one another. The diversity constitutes one of the main problems for the theological understanding of the Bible. . . . Attention is increasingly drawn to the diversity amongst or even contradiction between biblical writers. . . . As a consequence the hope that the churches would find themselves to have . . . the basis of a common understanding of the one biblical message has been fading.[6]

This same report criticizes the use of "proof-texts" from the Bible less on the ground that we should not seek to "prove" anything from the Bible than because "small literary units cannot be rightly used without testing and checking their functions as parts of larger complexes."[7] Countersamples might be found in broader traditions within the Bible.

It is a pity that some, although certainly not all, evangelicals met this problem defensively rather than constructively. Instead of spending labor on demonstrating the pastoral, situational, and functional roles of apparently diverse biblical traditions, they simply dismissed the problem as unreal, or as the product of unbelieving scholarship. The rich pastoral resources of the biblical writings were actually *reduced* into a flat landscape on the model of a book of timeless propositions more akin to treatises of Greek philosophy than to the Bible. We still see the effect of this reductionist and defensive maneuver in attempts to dehistoricize and decontextualize the historical and literary variety of the Bible, sometimes in the name of appeals to "logic" as the only principle of interpretation. (If God *had* wished to make the Bible like a philosophical or doctrinal textbook one might be pardoned for thinking that a better job could have been made of it.)

The present situation, however, in biblical studies is potentially a more positive and constructive one for those evangelicals who stress *both* the theological unity *and* situational pluriformity of the biblical writings. Some of the hermeneutical issues involved in viewing the Bible as canon have been opened up by Brevard Childs in studies that are widely known and discussed.[8] Yet even here what Childs provides is certainly not a "reply" to the problem of diversity; still less does he provide anyone with an excuse for failing to bother with historical inquiry, or an investigation of traditions that lie behind the text. What is far more important is the opening up of questions about *levels* of meaning within the Bible. How is meaning within a specific historical context related to the meaning of a text that has been recontextualized within a broader tradition?[9]

These problems are certainly not new. Since earliest times Christians have considered how the meaning of the Servant Songs in Isaiah might be extended or modified when they are recontextualized within the frame of the New Testament witness to Christ. But modern biblical scholarship has pressed numerous further examples upon us. When the early chapters of Acts are placed within the overall purpose of Lukan theology, do they function as accounts of models to be copied, or as Luke's conscious portrayal of a past in the church's history that cannot and should not be repeated? How does Paul's account of the law in Galatians relate to his discussion in Romans, let alone to the Paul of Acts? If Romans 1–8 is regarded as "more important" than 9–11 or 9–15, this will seriously affect not only our understanding of

Romans but also our understanding of Paul. Other more concrete issues also emerge. For example, if we look to Paul for models of pastoral or spiritual authority, we may find ourselves asking, with Brevard Childs, "Is the result of canonization that the different levels of Paul's historical exercise of power have been flattened into one form of spiritual legitimation?"[10]

It is perhaps worth reminding ourselves of the sharp contrast that exists between aspects of our work that lead us *behind* the text, those that place us *in front of* the text, and those that locate everything in a final *canonical form*. In textual criticism we seek to peel back layers of tradition to uncover the earliest readings, often ignoring the theological insights of later scribes or editors as loci of a secondary theology. Our concerns about hermeneutics often direct our attention to what Ricoeur has termed "the front of" the text. We ask what the text does; what it sets in motion. Certain forms of canonical criticism give privileged status to the final form of the text. But all these perspectives and approaches have value in relation to specific questions about a given level of meaning. We need to be able to ask questions about historical situations that lie behind the text, and indeed there is no a priori reason why these questions should be restricted to one level only. Evangelical theology will rightly accord ultimate normative authority only to Scripture as a whole and in its wholeness. But "the whole counsel of God" includes not only canonical breadth, but also historical depth. For truth, as Kierkegaard saw, involves not only where we arrive but also how we arrive. Evangelical thought has become increasingly sensitive in recent years to ways in which we are seduced into setting up "canons within the canon," and these issues must be relentlessly explored.[11]

MODELS OF UNDERSTANDING AND COMMUNICATION

The title of this chapter, "Speaking and Hearing," reminds us that speaking alone does not constitute communication. What I communicate is not what I say, but what I am heard to say. Teachers recognize this principle as a basic one in philosophy of education, and it is not accidental that the most seminal of thinkers on the subject of understanding and hermeneutics have asked questions about how a child comes to perceive and to understand.[12] But the supreme example is found in the ways in which Jesus presented his message. How Jesus preached and taught always depended partly on the nature of his audience.

I need not rehearse once again some of the philosophical and theological arguments I have put forward elsewhere in order to substantiate this point.[13] What I should like to do in brief compass here is to point out that very strong philosophical and theological arguments can be supplemented by literary and linguistic ones. It is possible to overlook the importance of the hearer-horizon in hermeneutics only if two fundamental principles in linguistics and semiotics are ignored. The first is the role of linguistic convention and reader *expectation*. The second is the double-sidedness of the *sender-receiver* model of communication.

First, all signs operate on the basis of certain shared knowledge, agreements, or conventions. In the case of traffic signals, for example, *red* and *green* perform their effective functions only on the basis of society's acceptance and understanding of the conventions that govern their use. This example depends clearly on a convention that is merely arbitrary from the standpoint of sheer logic. For there is no logically *necessary* connection between red and green, on the one hand, and directions to halt and proceed, on the other. Yet some conventions reside at such a deep and unexamined level within the corporate mind of the language-using community that they are not perceived as conventions or social customs, but rather as propositions or equivalences suggested by reason or logic. This issue was discussed many centuries ago, as long ago as in Plato's *Cratylus*. Yet even at the beginning of our own century Saussure was still having to argue for the arbitrary nature of the sign. Even so, in modern discussions about biblical hermeneutics the language-conventions that form the conceptual grid through which modern Western Christians look out at the world are very often still thought of as a *logically* grounded system that must be imposed on the Bible if its language is to be interpreted in an "objective" or "natural" way. Indeed some believe that the meaning of linguistic signs has so little to do with the mental world of the reader or hearer that we do not even need to speak of "interpreting" them.

What is "natural" in the communication and interpretation of any meaning, however, depends entirely on the nature of the conventions and expectations shared by writer and reader, or between speaker and hearer. If you ask me "How long will you be while you are in the store?" and I reply "Five feet, ten inches," what has been breached is not "natural" logic, but a convention on the basis of which you perceive certain expectations as "natural" ones. But in the case of the biblical writings, what precisely constitutes such conventions? Let me put the question sharply: Is the set of semiotic conventions that determine the "natural" meaning of statements in books of modern history or science the same as that presupposed by writers of biblical apocalyptic?

Simply to *ask* this question is to see that much of our usual talk about "plain" or "natural" meaning is not itself context-free. What was "natural" for an apocalyptist was to write and to read the genre in question in accordance with the conventions that gave form to other apocalyptic works, such as parts of Daniel, Ezekiel, 1 Enoch, and 2 Esdras. Yet clearly this may represent a different set of reader-expectations from those held by readers brought up on the modern novel, the *New York Times,* or *Christianity Today.* It is a tragic irony that some of those who are most sincerely and devoutly concerned to let the Bible speak on its own terms (and who are sometimes skeptical about hermeneutics supposedly for this very reason) often unwittingly apply standards of reader-expectation that owe more to the pseudo-objectivism of the modern world or science and technology than to the methods and conventions presupposed by biblical writers.

We need not restrict our example to biblical apocalyptic. Robert Alter has recently explored sets of narrative conventions that underlie at least some of the material in the Old Testament.[14] But if the narrative devices identified by Alter do indeed belong to a shared world presupposed by biblical writers, we need to be more cautious in our judgments about what we understand to be the "obvious," "common-sense," or "objective" meaning of the text. We must not confuse a genuine objectivity reached by historical and literary inquiry with the objectivism that measures everything by our own often modern standards of expectation. Part of what it means to be entirely open to the message of the biblical texts is the relativizing of our own expectations of what is to *count* as the "natural" meaning. To return to more philosophical issues, one of the reasons why Heidegger, in my view, has at least one thing to contribute to the hermeneutical debate is that he has demonstrated how far what interpreters *count* as truth, correctness, or validity depends on the interpretive goals and interpretive strategies they embrace for their task. To accept this principle, needless to say, is not to adopt Heidegger's philosophy. The implication is, rather, the need for openness to Scripture for the testing of everything, including those conceptual grids we sometimes impose on it without due reflection.

The second principle that emerges from linguistic and semiotic studies is the duality of double-sidedness of the *sender-receiver* model of communication. The classic formulation of this model can be found in the work of Roman Jakobson.[15] *Meaning* belongs not to one aspect of the act of communication, but to a complex of some six elements: (1) A *sender* (speaker or writer) addresses (2) a *recipient* or addressee (hearers or readers). This address involves (3) *contact* (e.g., seeing, hearing, reading). But what is conveyed is not merely vibrations in the air or marks on paper. Like the traffic signals to which we earlier alluded, signs depend on (4) a shared *code* of linguistic or semiotic conventions. Moreover, (5) a particular *context* further shapes the understanding and interpretation of (6) the *message*. All six elements, Jakobson argues, have a part to play in the single act of communication.

Jakobson's model represents no more than one possible model among others. It is more customary to indicate the importance of the reader-horizon through models that focus the problem of preunderstanding (Schleiermacher) or the role of tradition (Gadamer). But Jakobson's model helps us to see that any theory of interpretation will be inadequate that fastens exclusively only on the speaking or on the hearing alone. What is *communicated* is neither what is merely *sent*, nor what the hearer *creates*, but what the text and the hearer *share*. But this is what we should expect to be the case if the text provides an interpersonal point of meeting and relationship between God and human persons. Only if we substitute a mechanistic model for a personal one can we rest in the illusion that meaning is like a commodity merely handed over and implanted in a passive mind.

It is pertinent at this point to allude to arguments advanced in *The Responsibility of Hermeneutics* (Eerdmans and Paternoster Press, 1985), a collaborative work undertaken partly by Roger Lundin and Clarence Walhout, who contribute from the standpoint of contemporary literary studies, and partly through my own contribution from the standpoint of issues in biblical studies. This book first explores how far both literary studies and biblical interpretation have been influenced by a sharp dichotomy between Cartesian rationalism, with its inadequately objectivist notion of objectivity, and literary theories that focus on aesthetic pleasure. Confronted with this false alternative, many conservative theologians with a proper concern for truth inevitably opted for the objectivist approach, while in literary theory, aesthetic pleasure achieved the status in some circles of a comprehensive interpretive goal. We then explore the nature of textuality. On what basis, we ask, are texts often regarded as merely self-referring entities, unable to communicate truth? It might have been tempting to become simply defensive in the face of the challenges of poststructuralist theory. But we accept and value at least its emphasis on textual action and the role of the reader. Indeed, we have attempted to explore the model of action as a way forward in hermeneutics, even though we admit that this model is certainly not a comprehensive one.

The focus of the action-model for biblical hermeneutics emerged most clearly in work on the parables of Jesus, and this brings us back precisely to this section of this present chapter. Jesus did not merely lay down packaged truths to be received passively. To reduce the function of parables to that of theological assertions was the mistake of Adolf Jülicher, even though there is *also* a sense in which they may be viewed as assertions retrospectively (cf. our discussion about levels of meaning in the previous section of this paper). Susan Wittig and J. D. Crossan rightly focus attention on the active role of the reader in the process of communication. But the use they make of polyvalent meaning as a hermeneutic principle leaves little room, we argue, for *responsible* interpretation. For if knowledge needs to be correct, or if understanding needs to be adequate, acts need to be carried out responsibly. While there are different levels of textual and interpretive action, it simply is not the case that one action is as good as another, and that there can be no criteria for assessing the difference. This would bring us back, once again, to one of the two false alternatives we rejected.

The horizon of the hearer is not the decisive, let alone the only, maker of meaning. In this respect reader-response theory in its more radical forms claims too much. But neither is meaning a mere "item" to be handed over as if it were a physical object borrowed from Newton's universe. To return to our earlier arguments, messages require codes and contexts, as well as speakers and hearers. Certainly Jesus took account of the relation between language, understanding, and time. Such terms as "Son of Man" and "kingdom of God" could not be emancipated fully from inappropriate codes and contexts until they had been baptized after his own ministry in his own death and resurrection. Until that time they retained aspects of mystery and ambiguity. Every Christian pastor and evangelist understands something of what Heidegger meant when he spoke of language bearing meaning within the horizon of time. Perhaps the pastor and the evangelist can more readily appreciate the point than those who have a special liking for more scholastic kinds of theology.

ANTHONY C. THISELTON

THE ROLE OF INTERPRETIVE TRADITION

The theologian, however, cannot rest content with situational and contextual data alone. The messages of the Bible delivered to specific audiences in given situations through particular linguistic codes cumulatively enter theological tradition as the *one* gospel, the *one* message of salvation. But evangelical theology has a decidedly ambivalent attitude toward tradition. On the one side, when we encounter the minor sects, we feel that we stand in the great tradition of Irenaeus and the church fathers whereby the rule of faith determines "good" biblical interpretation. Even the authority of Scripture is often commended partly on the grounds of its central place in orthodox Christian tradition. But when we have in view not the minor sects but the issues of the Refomation, then tradition becomes more problematic and is properly judged at the bar of Scripture.

We should not be embarrassed by this dual attitude toward tradition, though we should realize its delicacy. It is wholly right that tradition should be viewed positively as embodying habituated patterns of thought and practice that express the continuity and identity of our faith. I have tried to argue elsewhere that a positive understanding of theological tradition provides an indispensable frame of reference for questions about meaning, understanding, and identity.[16] Yet tradition is never "given," once-for-all. It suffers decay, degeneration, and distortion. Hence theological tradition stands in constant need of reform, and reform must be carried out in accordance with Scripture.

At this point, however, evangelicals are often accused of occupying a self-contradictory position. All interpretations of Scripture, it is argued, occur within an interpretive tradition. How can we stand outside that which we wish to test? This question may be answered on many levels, but three issues, among others, call for attention. First, critical questioning about our own tradition must entail some kind of positive understanding of inputs from other traditions. Any theological tradition that is too defensive to listen to what others say will become inward-looking and incapable of necessary self-criticism. A balance has to be sought in evangelical seminaries between undue preoccupation with theological trends and fashions that may not in the end prove to be constructive and a narrow refusal to look for insights from outside our own tradition. Second, questions about the Bible and tradition raise matters of spirituality and spiritual vision. Although since the publication of G. H. Tavard's *Holy Writ or Holy Church* (1959) it is fashionable no longer to oppose the Bible and tradition as competing sources of truth, nevertheless traditions may easily lose sight of the goals that set them in motion. Sociologists have reminded us how traditions often pass a peak of stability and effectiveness, only to decline into a mere machinery of routine and self-perpetuation. Leadership becomes inward-looking and self-serving; those who follow run the risk of responding only to secondhand formulas and transmitted rituals rather than to the realities in which tradition's roots were grounded and nourished.

Our final comment is that every attempt to understand Scripture must remain part of a *corporate* enterprise. No single individual has a wide enough range of spiritual gifts, let alone other equipment, to do the task alone. We need both teachers and learners; both scholars and prophets; both cautious guardians and adventurous explorers. To return to our earlier discussion of Habermas, in any large and diverse community "interests" will tend to filter out unwanted voices, especially interests that have a stake in the status quo. But evangelical theology will need to monitor all inputs constructively and with sensitivity, if it is not to be trapped into reading the Bible only in ways already made comfortable and predictable through the grids and filters of our tradition. If the first article of evangelical theology is that God has spoken, the second must be that we attend to how we *hear* him to have spoken. Speaking and hearing is a two-sided event.

The Finality of Jesus Christ in a World of Religions

Clark H. Pinnock

The problem before us is an ancient issue, but one that comes to us with fresh urgency today.[1] Our Christian belief in the finality of Jesus Christ as the one mediator between God and humankind creates an explosion of questions in the modern mind. Some of them are on the theological level: How can people who have never heard of Christ be saved by him? How accessible to a large number of the people now living and multitudes who have since died is the redemption wrought by Christ? Are millions to suffer the judgment of God who never had a real opportunity to be saved? Where do the world's religions fit into God's providence over history? Other questions are on a more practical plane: What shall we make of the religious faith of persons we daily meet in the shops and at work who identify with religions other than Christianity? The world has become a global village and we feel the force of this question. Muslims are coming to our meetings, Sikhs are serving us in the health food store, and Jews are numbered among our best friends. Where do they stand before God? Do they have saving faith? It is more than idle curiosity that makes us ask these questions. We also feel threatened by religious pluralism because it seems to call into question our dearest conviction that Jesus Christ is God incarnate and the unique Savior. We find ourselves asking how these things can be.[2]

It might be good to remember in this context, too, that other religions also have difficulties with pluralism. This is obvious in the cases of Judaism and Islam, but true also even of Hinduism, which prides itself on its openness to plurality. The Hindu Vedas are taken to be divine revelation at the highest level, and are used to measure and test other claims. Hindus, too, have a problem with toleration.[3]

Now the question, like most good theological issues, is not a simple one. It is a multifaceted question that acts like a magnet among iron filings, attracting to itself a dozen important issues. It forces one to consider all manner of related subjects in the hope that help can come from them in answering our question. The effort taps the full resources of our systematic theological understanding. It is also a first-class hermeneutical challenge. For example, this issue grips me existentially at the fundamental levels of faith. On the one hand, there is the strong desire to affirm in no uncertain terms the uniqueness and finality of Jesus Christ and to regard as heretical any attempt to reduce or water down this conviction. On the other hand, there is the belief in God's universal salvific will and feelings welling up from within that God is not one to cast off millions who through no fault of their own lacked an opportunity to embrace Christ's salvation. How shall I correlate in my own mind the demands that come from my Christian tradition and my experience of life in the eighties? The hermeneutical conversation between this reader and the text is passionate and stressful.[4] Sometimes it seems as if Christianity itself is at a turning point over this issue and having to decide again about issues thought to be long settled.

The proposal I wish to develop in this chapter is in the spirit and tradition I believe emanates from the theology of St. Luke. It stems in particular from his presentation of the finality of Christ accompanied by a remarkable openness to people of other faiths as we see it in the narrative of the Book of Acts. Luke seems to be able to balance an exclusive loyalty to Christ with an inclusive appreciation of what God is doing outside Christianity. While I would not want to use Luke anachronistically to answer modern questions, I do find in him a general stance that strikes me as fruitful for us today. To be specific, I find Luke pointing me to the following triadic pattern of belief, in connection with our problem, which even resembles the faith, hope, and love triad of St. Paul's: Jesus Christ is Lord of all. This faith affirmation is basic to proper Christian grammar and cannot be watered down. But God is also at work in the world both in the mission of the church and beyond it, a belief that sustains in us an open and loving attitude toward those of other faiths. And I dare to hope, although it goes beyond the letter of Luke's own writings, for the final salvation of many unevangelized persons who longed for a Savior but never heard of Christ during their lifetimes.

Henry Cadbury once spoke of the peril of modernizing Jesus, and I would not want to be guilty of modernizing Luke. But I am not appealing to the Evangelist to support all that I wish to propose. To do that I would have to stretch Luke unfairly. His chief concern is with the entry of the Gentiles into the church and not with the salvation of the unevangelized. I use Luke only to give my remarks focus, by relating them to the inclusive finality I see in his writings, but I intend to draw upon other Scriptures to prove my case as well.[5]

In proposing such a view I am aware of venturing into controversial theology. Although from experience I would estimate that a large number of Christians are sympathetic with this line of thinking, few of them are bold enough to put it in writing because of strong opposition to it from received evangelical traditions, and from missiological leaders who have a kind of vested interest in reserving salvation for those who receive the gospel and join the church during their lives on earth. In past essays of my own along these lines, I have met with severe criticism from leaders who consider it mandatory to think that all persons not converted to Christ are without exception hell-bound. Even to open the door a crack to the possibility of salvation in the case of any unevangelized persons is thought to doom the missionary effort and to yield vital truth to the revisionist theologians.[6]

In order to head off criticisms I should admit two things at the outset. First, I prefer the thinking on this subject found in the documents of the Second Vatican Council to most evangelical treatments I have read. Second, I am aware of the danger here of what James Hunter has called "evangelical civility." Am I attracted to this position because I dislike having to appear as unfriendly as those nasty fundamentalists?[7]

Although I am sure the hardline exclusivist position is untrue, I am nevertheless modest about the quality of my own proposal. Just because the question is multifaceted, it follows that there will be many ways to construct the answer, and not only one. Therefore I put this proposal forward as a piece of disputed theology, believing it to be sound and true, but eager to learn from the opinions of others, and hoping that this essay will spark fresh evangelical thinking in an important area where I think we evangelicals may be falling behind.

THE FINALITY OF JESUS CHRIST

The rich diversity of New Testament Christology notwithstanding, when Luke quotes Peter's statement "Jesus Christ is Lord of all!" (Acts 10:36) he is enunciating basic Christian grammar. In Jesus' being Lord we have the essential particularism, and in his being Lord of all we see the universal orientation that together are basic to the Christian gospel. Jesus, whom God raised up from among the dead, has a name with saving power, a name to be preached to the whole world. Other New Testament authors speak of him as God's only begotten Son, as the one mediator between God and humankind, as the second Adam, and as the Redeemer who died for everyone once and for all. As Paul put it in a pleasing phrase: "God was in Christ reconciling the world to himself." At this point surely we are in touch with the message common to the whole New Testament. God has sent us a Savior in the person of Jesus Christ, who by virtue of his death and resurrection has made salvation available to all believers.

On this rock the spade turns. Here if anywhere we are in touch with the essence of Christianity as it was in the beginning. As surely as they believed any fact of their experience, these New Testament witnesses believed that salvation is available on account of what Jesus did and who Jesus was, and not otherwise.[8] Although it undoubtedly creates a problem for us in the area of religious pluralism, this conviction about Jesus' lordship is nonnegotiable for Christians and has to be seen as a basic rule of Christian speech. It belongs to the essential symbolism of the gospel, and cannot be given away however great the pressure to do so becomes. When we confess Christ as Lord we intend to make a first-order claim about reality as it ultimately is and cannot possibly regard it as a bargaining chip in an interreligious dialogue.[9]

In saying this, I am making only a modest point. For example, I am not requiring the reader to agree with me that this belief in the finality of Jesus Christ stems from Jesus' own impressive claims, although I believe that it does.[10] Nor am I even insisting that everyone agree with me that the Chalcedonian definition is a permanent fixture and an accurate (so far as it goes) description of Christ's true identity, although I believe that it is.[11] All I really wish to claim here is that Christians ought to confess that Jesus was and is the unique vehicle and means of God's saving love in the world, and its definitive Savior. The one who cannot confess this truth, it seems to me, jeopardizes the distinct essence of true Christianity.[12] All religions make absolute claims at some point, and Christians ought to make them in the matter of the finality of Jesus Christ. It would be slightly ridiculous for us, however good our intentions, to water down this central belief. Just as there is only one God, the Lord of heaven, the God of all the peoples, so there is only one Lord, the risen and exalted Christ. There is a kind of exclusivity here that simply cannot be given up.

Having made this point, I realize that we have to face up to the colossal pressure our culture places upon any kind of exclusivity.

What Troeltsch said about historical relativity and what Toynbee maintained about the commonality of all religions hover in the popular mind and create an enormous groundswell of resistance to the historic Christian belief in Jesus Christ. Indeed, it has led theologians to propose a major paradigm shift in the way Christians should think about the gospel. Christocentrism is an offense in the context of religious pluralism, and ought to be replaced by a concentration on theocentrism instead. Theologians like John Hick force us to decide whether to hold fast to the classical traditions about Christ or to move in a very different direction. The issue is fairly simple, but the pressure is enormous.

Historic Christianity has been simultaneously both theocentric and Christocentric. The God of the whole creation became flesh in a particularity of time-space history. What Hick has really done is to adopt Schleiermacher's doctrine of inspiration rather than incarnation. He has not moved away from Jesus as much as he has decided to think of him as a God-filled man, which does not carry with it such a weight of uniqueness. Jesus is now the ideal man, who clarifies for Christians the divine nature as love. He is a symbol of universal truth rather than the unique incarnation of a Savior.[13]

As is by now quite well known, John Hick is busy redrawing the map of the world's religions. He is trying to free Christianity of all vestiges of exclusivity. He suggests that we move from a Jesus-centered theology that shuts people out to a God-centered theology that welcomes them all in. By a move to theocentrism, Hick hopes to remove the major hindrances to dialogue and cooperation among the religions and thus contribute to a more unified and peaceful world. He is well aware that traditional Christology stands directly in the path of such a proposal. Therefore he has devoted considerable energy to reinterpreting the incarnation in mythic terms so that it can still serve as a Christian symbol but not constitute a universal truth-claim. In Jesus we see the love of God in action but we are not obliged to believe in the preexistence of the Son or the divine-human union in the creedal sense.[14] Under the terms of such a proposal one would understand the "once and for all" language of the New Testament either as a bad development in itself or else as a species of confessional language that is not meant to be pressed metaphysically. It is the manner in which the first Christians liked to express themselves, but belongs more to the medium than to the essence of the message.[15] One might think of it as the language of love, defining a meaningful personal relationship, rather than a truth-claim others have to reject.

If we assume that the New Testament doctrinal grammar is normative, then I think we would have to conclude that the strong statements made in support of Jesus' lordship and divinity make reference not merely to the feelings of believers but to underlying ontological reality. But this alerts us to an even deeper shift Hick makes. He does not regard undemythologized New Testament grammar as normative today. Rather, he sees these assertions as human symbols arising from religious experience and not divinely revealed truths. It is important to see that underneath Hick's move away from uniqueness and incarnation lies his abandoning of authoritative apostolic Scriptures. His is now a rudderless modernism drifting hopelessly on the high seas.

This radical paradigm shift is obviously the product of the desire to accommodate to cultural pressures arising from religious pluralism, and we cannot possibly accept it. It seems to me incontrovertible that when the New Testament writers and the majority of Christians today confess their faith in Jesus Christ they are not simply saying how good Christ has been to them. They are also volunteering the information they are certain is true: that Jesus is Lord of all people and wants to be recognized by them all. Christianity is both theocentric and Christocentric, and I predict the effort to reduce it to a vague theism will fail as indeed it ought to. Trying to fit Christianity into the contours of the world's way of thinking is an apologetic strategy Christians should not accept.[16]

But to avoid being misunderstood let me hasten to add that when we confess the finality of Christ we are confessing Jesus as the universal Savior. This particularism carries with it universal implications. Christ died for all, not just for the small company of present believers. God sent his Son to save the world, not a pitiful remnant of lost humankind. The finality of Jesus Christ carries with it catholic implications. We are not locking ourselves into a narrow perspective by believing this. There is a wonderful broadness in the apparent narrowness of the Christian confession. Our hearts are alive with the hope that the saved will come from all the corners of the earth and sit down at table with the Lord in his kingdom.

But this grand vision also creates for us some difficulties to which we must now turn. If the Lord is not content to sup with only 10 percent of the fallen race because 90 percent of them historically speaking have never heard the gospel, what are the arrangements for the seating of the guests? What about the other religions, and what about the fate of the very numerous heathen?

IN A WORLD OF RELIGIONS

Taking the finality of Christ as a given for Christians, how then ought we to regard the spiritual condition and eternal destiny of people of other faiths? Are other religions zones of complete darkness? Are these religions vehicles of salvation? Are they a mixture of good and bad elements emanating from humankind's religious propensity? Where according to Christian theology ought we to take a stand in this matter? Please note that I am looking at the question from within the Christian faith, and not presuming to have an expert or detailed knowledge of specific religions.

Luke is helpful to us as we seek answers to these questions because he seemed to hold together a firm belief in the finality of Christ with an openness to people of other faiths. Although it is true that he saw the dark side of religion in spirits of false prophecy and unbelief, he also presents a positive side. He had no difficulty acknowledging that God listened to the prayers of the centurion Cornelius and took account of his godly and righteous life. Indeed he quotes Peter as saying, "In every nation any one who fears him and does what is right is acceptable to him" (Acts 10:35). Surely this is a judgment remarkable for its liberality. To the people of Lystra he quotes Paul as saying that "He [God] did not leave himself without witness" (Acts 14:17). Apparently these people possessed truth from God in the context of their religion and culture, and Luke does not hesitate to acknowledge it. In Paul's speech upon the Areopagus we hear how God has providentially ordered history "that they [people in general] should seek God, in the hope that they might feel after him and find him. Yet he is not far from each one of us" (Acts 17:27). Then we can link up these tolerant sentiments with Luke's overall theology that Jesus came to save all peoples unto the ends of the earth (Luke 2:29-32; Acts 1:8). Evidently belief in the finality of Christ did not cause Luke to close himself off from an ability to relate in an open spirit with people of other religions. How is it that he could do so?

I think that the answer to this question lies in two presuppositions Luke held and the Bible generally holds. On the one hand, he held to a form of divine revelation that was accessible to all people everywhere, and gave a point of contact with them in the work of evangelism. On the other hand, he did not view history as static but dynamic so that, even though a non-Christian group might now exist in an attitude of unbelief, the situation can change and even they can be swept into the flow of the missionary ingathering. Both these beliefs encourage and support a positive attitude on our part to people of other faiths.

One of the keys to openness to people of other faiths is a firm belief in God's universal or general revelation. Contrary to Barth's theology, the knowledge of God is not limited to places where biblical revelation has penetrated. We might speak in this connection of the Melchizedek factor. When Abraham, the recipient of God's promise to save the world, met the king of Salem he recognized that here was a man who really knew God, and gave him a tithe of everything (Gen. 14:17-24). Evidently to his surprise God had more plans afoot than the great plan he had shared with Abraham a short time before. It seems to me that the reason traditional Christians often refuse to recognize genuine piety outside the church is because they persist in ignoring the scriptural truth symbolized by Melchizedek, and this creates in them a brittleness, rigidity, and narrowness in the presence of non-Christian people.[17]

Is it not curious that theologians have never questioned the propriety of conversing with non-Christian philosophers in building up their categories, but have seldom welcomed people of faith as their interlocutors? Why do we look so hopefully to Plato and expect nothing from Buddha? I think we are now entering a period in history when the world religions will begin to impinge upon theology as philosophy has always done. It is a significant moment for theology, and depending upon our response it will mean bane or blessing.

In the case of Judaism and Islam of course we are not only dealing with general revelation. These religions are in touch with the word God gave to Abraham and his seed. Therefore we would expect to find a good deal of common ground with these people. But beyond that, we cannot forget God's covenant with all flesh through Noah (Gen. 9:17). In Jewish theology we find the idea that the Noachic covenant expresses itself in the conscience, in certain basic moral commandments being written on the heart. Surely this lies behind Paul's remarks in Romans 2:14-16. There is the light of revelation beyond the message God gave to Israel and even to the church. God's kingdom encompasses far more territory than the ground presently occupied by the church. The Lord told Israel not to worship the heavenly bodies, and added that he had allotted them to the other nations (Deut. 4:19). Moses also speaks of God fixing the boundaries of the nations "according to the number of the sons of God" (Deut. 32:8). Amos underlines God's liberality in this remarkable statement: "'Are you not like the Ethiopians to me, O people of Israel?' says the

Lord. 'Did I not bring up Israel from the land of Egypt, and the Philistines from Caphtor and the Syrians from Kir?'" (9:7) For some reason evangelicals have tended to conceal God's generosity in the Bible. We feel a little uncomfortable with the fact that Daniel expected King Nebuchadnezzar to know who the God of heaven was and respect him, and the fact that the pagan sailors on Jonah's boat feared God and sacrificed to him. In order to protect, as we suppose, the uniqueness of God we have suppressed this positive witness to universal revelation. We do not find it easy to say that Jesus is the light that lightens everyone coming into the world (John 1:9). I suggest that Luke believed these things, and that if we believed them we, too, would be able to encounter unsaved people with openness and hope.[18]

In Protestant theology, however, we often meet with a very closed-minded attitude. We have to buck a strong tradition that refuses to grant any gracious element in general revelation. Blunter than most, Jack Cottrell states categorically: "We must not hesitate to condemn all non-Christian religions as part of the broad road that leads to destruction."[19] Even more moderate writers like Millard Erickson and Bruce Demarest are reluctant in the extreme to grant more than a glimmer of hope in regard to the positive character of general revelation and its potential to help anyone who responded to it.[20] Even in mainline Protestant theology this tends to be true. They, too, denigrate other religions.[21] Among the evangelicals J. N. D. Anderson stands out as a brilliant exception, but an exception is what he is—at least in print.[22] The fact is that traditional Protestants, especially the evangelicals, seem keen to acknowledge the reality of general revelation and then to deny that it does anyone any good or was even intended to. I find this appalling.

Basically I am offended by the notion that the God who loves sinners and desires to save them tantalizes them with truth about himself that can only result in their greater condemnation. Does God then delight in the death of the wicked? Surely not. Rather, God visits them with general revelation and common grace in order that they should seek him and find him. Therefore, when we encounter people of other faiths, we can acknowledge with Luke that God has given them a witness too and seek to locate the bridges that might carry the Good News about Jesus over to their side. Of course there is the presence of sin in all of us, and there are manifestations of the effects of sin in all humanity's cultural achievements. But that does not change God's will to be present in all the world as the One who desires all to be saved and come to a knowledge of the truth (1 Tim. 2:4). Let me be frank. On this subject, limitations notwithstanding, I find the tradition of Vatican II to be more evangelical on this subject, more Lukan, than the overcautious, even niggardly comments of my fellow traditional Protestants on this subject. The tradition that stems from the "extra ecclesiam nulla salus est" has a great deal to answer for in terms of turning multitudes away from listening to the Good News. In order to confess God's grace in Jesus Christ it is not necessary to deny God's grace everywhere else.[23]

Without question there is a good deal of darkness in world religions. But nevertheless there is also divine revelation to which people have to respond. As Luke says, "God never left them without witness." Therefore we enter into the encounter with other people of faith with a certain positive hopefulness that there will be lesser lights burning as the nations await the dawning of the greater Light. We might want to take Jesus' word more seriously in this connection: "He that is not against us is for us" (Mark 9:40).

The other key to Luke's openness to people of other faiths is his view of salvation history. The people he met of this type were non-Christians, but they could also be viewed as *pre*-Christians. After all, history is open and the gospel is actively at work in history. Its universal potential has not yet been realized, but one day it will be. It is only a matter of time. The decisive saving event has taken place, but its impact and implementation among all nations is part of the "not yet" that is now being realized. The banquet has been announced and the invitations are being issued. On that day all nations will come and sit down at table with the Lord.[24] If you have a victory orientation like Luke had, you are not put off by temporary rebuffs and setbacks. As Paul said, Israel may now exist in a condition of unbelief in Jesus, but that is not the last word on the subject. The day will come when Israel too will be saved (Rom. 11:25-26). And so it is by analogy with other peoples. Islam at present is militantly non-Christian, but that is not all that informs our attitude toward Muslims as individuals or even Islam as a religion. Who knows how God in his providence may decide to use Islam to bring his kingdom nearer? Is it not slightly blasphemous, as Rabbi Lapide says, for us to dogmatize over how God intends to accomplish the salvation of the world?[25] Perhaps he is planning to lure the nations into the position where they will gladly see why they need to encounter Jesus Christ. The point is, if one believes in God and his saving intentions, one is free to be open to what happens and to whoever comes across our path because God is committed to bless the nations and to bring his kingdom in. Hear what Carl Braaten says:

> The gospel is the announcement that God in Christ is drawing all people to himself. The one who is revealed in Christ is at work in all religions as the power of their eternal origin and destiny. Religions are not closed systems. They are all involved in history. They can be sprung open by the gospel on the way to a fulfillment beyond themselves, which they may have already glimpsed, albeit only in a fragmentary way. Religions are not systems of salvation in themselves, but God can use even them to point beyond themselves and toward their own crisis and future redemption in the crucified and risen Lord of history.[26]

In closing this section it should be recognized that even if we act out of the openness the gospel allows us the reception accorded us may be a cold one. After all, we have not yielded an inch on the position that Jesus is the only mediator and that all must come to him and through him, and furthermore the highest compliment we have paid to other religions is that they may prove to be preparatory in some way to the gospel and needing to be surpassed. But that is, I believe, as far as we can go.

THE ACCESSIBILITY OF SALVATION TO THE MARGINALIZED

An enormous problem remains. A large percentage of the human race has lived its life under the influence only of God's general revelation before the news of salvation penetrated into their cultural situation. If we assume, as I do, that the redemption of Christ has been provided for them, how is it possible for them to receive the benefits of that provision? If Christ died for the sins of the whole world, how do we deal with the fact that access to his atonement seems unavailable to most of the race even today when the gospel is more universally accessible than ever before? These people seem to have been marginalized by the progress of the spread of the gospel through no particular fault of their own. Better to be born nearer the consummation of the age than nearer to its inception in terms of accessibility to salvation. It is as if Cornelius had asked Peter, I am happy for my own good fortune, but what about my pious grandmother? Does the problem of evil loom any larger than in the case where multitudes perish because they lacked any opportunity to be saved? I am not much impressed by those who say God is within his sovereign rights to judge them on account of their sins. That is not the issue. The problem is that God cannot save those he would like to save if indeed it is true that there is salvation only where the gospel is preached and accepted.[27]

St. Luke gives us a little help with this problem, but not too much. He tells us how God looked with favor upon Cornelius in his pre-Christian piety and then brought him into contact with Peter the evangelist. But what we really need to know is what the destiny would be of a Cornelius who feared God but never did hear the gospel. The standard evangelical response in the spirit of the Frankfurt Declaration would be that lacking a knowledge of Jesus he would surely perish.[28]

I wish to challenge the hardline traditional view in this matter, and give evidence for a different interpretation. My proposal would be that God takes account of faith in him even if it occurs in the context of general revelation, and always sees to it that those responding to the light they have encounter Jesus Christ, whether before or after death.

The first point to establish is the fact that God does have regard for faith in him even when it is forced to rely upon defective and incomplete information. "God rewards them that diligently seek him" (Heb. 11:6). God is able to take account of faith even when it arises in a person within a pagan context. He called Abraham from within this condition, and others such as Melchizedek, Jethro, Job, Abimelech, Naaman, and Balaam all had faith in God even though they lived outside the range of Israel's revelation. In the same way today, people who are spiritually "Before Christ" even though they are chronologically "Anno Domini" can trust in God on the basis of the light they have. As Peter said, "God has no favorites" (Acts 10:34). Anderson was right to ask: "Might it not be true of the follower of some other religion that the God of all mercy had worked in his heart by his Spirit, bringing him in some measure to realise his sin and need for forgiveness, and enabling him, in the twilight as it were, to throw himself on God's mercy?"[29] Just as the Jews before Christ were saved in the context of shadows of the true and on the basis of a redemption yet to be revealed, so these others with so much less information to rely on can have called out to God to save them.

It seems to me that Paul is saying this in Romans. All people possess a sufficient knowledge of God on the basis of which they are justly condemned if they reject it. But the converse is also true—it is possible for them to renounce their sin and seek God, even if ignorant of Christ's provision, so that on the day of judgment the evidence of their conscience may "accuse *or perhaps excuse* them" (Rom. 2:15). I agree with Stuart Hackett when he suggests that there are those "who are, in spite of conceptual shortcomings, nevertheless trusting in the true God as genuinely as ourselves."[30] In this way we can believe that God's forgiveness is universally accessible to every person in every culture and epoch.

J. I. Packer puts forth this point hesitantly. On the basis of general revelation, he writes, "We may safely say (i) if any good pagan reached the point of throwing himself on his Maker's mercy for pardon, it was grace that brought him there; (ii) God will surely save anyone he brings thus far; (iii) anyone thus saved would learn in the next world that he was saved through Christ." The logic is impeccable, but Packer remains uncertain that God actually saves anyone in this way.[31] For my part I am bold to declare that on the basis of the evidence of the Melchizedek factor I referred to earlier God most certainly does save people in this way. I do not know how many, but I hope for multitudes.

My objection to the traditional Protestant treatment of general revelation is that it overlooks the Melchizedek factor and places all or most of its emphasis on the negative side of the ledger. It is time to remember that Melchizedek worshiped the true God before Abraham met him, and that Jethro, a Midianite priest, knew God and even instructed Moses before learning of Israel's commission. God is known throughout the whole world on account of his mighty acts in creation (Ps. 104). The supreme revelation in Christ is not the sole revelation of God. Dale Moody deserves credit as one of the few prominent evangelical theologians to celebrate this truth.[32]

It is possible, however, to let this insight get out of hand. Although it would be reasonable to call Jethro a pre-Christian believer, it would not be accurate or helpful to call him an anonymous Christian. The evidence does not allow us to say that Jethro enjoyed the benefits that are ours from knowing Christ and had no need of ever meeting Christ in a fulfilled relationship. Karl Rahner has gone much too far in the direction of sanctifying non-Christian religions as vehicles of salvation in the lives of those who call out to God from within paganism. In a way he has discredited my point by extending it speculatively to an unreasonable extent. I appreciate Rahner's basic insight that God takes account of faith in any and all situations from anyone, but not his many extensions of it that make it sound as if being a Buddhist is perfectly all right. It was not Rahner's intention to suggest this, but he has been read in this way and used by others in this direction. We cannot say anything that would create the impression that there are some who do not need to repent and believe the gospel.[33]

The second point to establish is the basis for supposing that the unevangelized are given an opportunity to encounter Jesus Christ as Savior after death if not before it. If pre-Christian faith is inherently prospective, how does it experience fulfillment if the gospel does not arrive in time? In one sense I suppose we could just posit it. This is what love would hope for. This is what logic would suggest. If God desires to save sinners, and if sinners have responded positively to the light they have, then it follows that at some point in the future the opportunity to encounter Christ will present itself. As Russell Aldwinckle puts it, "Why should it be deemed impossible that Socrates and the Christ will one day meet face to face and that Socrates may find in the Son of man and the Son of God the answer to his own restless search?"[34] Ladislaus Boros even suggests that death is the occasion when humans meet up with this choice and their destiny.[35] There is of course a danger of guessing what the outcome of God's judgments might be. Jesus seems to stress the element of surprise when discussing the subject, as though the unexpected is what can be expected. Naturally this works both ways. It rebukes the hardliners for insisting that they already know how God will treat all the unevangelized, and it warns us all against speculating. Nevertheless, the way Jesus treated those who came off badly in this life and showed them unanticipated mercy suggests to me that the element of surprise is likely to work in favor of the marginalized, in this case the unevangelized—the neediest of all—rather than work against them. God will surely condemn his enemies, but will he condemn those who did not know the truth and reject it but rather never knew it at all? Is it not possible that the Beatitude "blessed are you poor" applies to those who are bereft of the saving knowledge of God even though they sought after it with tears?[36]

Nevertheless, I am sufficiently suspicious of merely logical postulates to ask whether or not there is actual exegetical evidence to back up this theologically pleasing surmise. Of course there is some evidence. The most direct is what Peter says in his first epistle about the gospel being preached to the dead (3:19-20; 4:6). It seems plausible to suppose that Peter means that the gospel comes to the dead so that they "might live in the spirit with God" if they respond to the proclamation they hear. In this way the universality of Christ's redemption is vindicated and made effective.[37] I agree with Wolfhart

Pannenberg, who writes: "Salvation from future judgement is still made available to those who during their lifetime encountered neither Jesus nor the Christian message."[38] In this way Jesus truly triumphs over Satan by taking away from him even those the Enemy had thought were securely his. This is the meaning of the "descent into hell." People who through no fault of their own and who never came into contact with the gospel can have a part in its benefits by the extraordinary grace of God. With G. R. Beasley-Murray I see it as making good the universal reach of the atonement and the divine willingness that all should know it.[39] Thus Peter's teaching corresponds to the logic we have been entertaining.

I would not myself rest as much upon Matthew 25:31-46. This text has become a favorite of liberation theologians to prove that salvation comes through acts of morality even if they are not explicitly Christian. If this were its meaning, then Matthew 25 would back up my point drawn from 1 Peter. But I fear it is not. The "little ones" in the passage are clearly identified by the Evangelist as the missionaries sent out by Jesus (see 10:42). These are the poor who need assistance and hospitality. Therefore the passage has more to do with the reception of the gospel than with anonymous salvation. In some sense, though, it does imply that a person may find himself acquitted in the last judgment and be surprised by that. One wonders how many other surprises we may be in for.

But is it wise to base a hope for the unevangelized upon texts that are admittedly difficult to understand? Would it not be better to maintain silence and admit that God has not revealed to us all his arrangements with other peoples? Evangelicals have tended to deny that the idea of a probation after death is scriptural.[40] In my view they are unduly cautious. The fact of God's universal salvific will coupled with several broad hints about the postmortem probation are enough for me to hope for such a thing. I do not think of it as a dogma enjoying the kind of biblical certainty the deity of Christ, for example, enjoys, but only as a broad hint from the Lord that he will do what our hearts long for him to do.[41]

At this point I would want to emphasize that we should not let theological speculation go wild. For example, there are many who not only grant what I have been saying but press for complete universalism. God not only gives one chance to be saved after death, but gives chance after chance until everyone gives in to him. John Hick's proposal in *Eternal Life* amounts to this. William Barclay suggests that everyone goes to heaven by way of purgatory.[42] But this is out of the question. Far too many judgment texts depict the destruction of the wicked to allow any such wishful thinking.[43] All that I feel justified in concluding is that everyone will have an opportunity to be saved so that the possibility of salvation is universally accessible. Scripture permits no more. I appreciate the thinking of C. S. Lewis when he said about universalism, "How if they will not give in?" And concerning multiple choices, Lewis wondered how many they would need.[44]

Now the obvious and pressing objection to all of this in the minds of evangelicals is its impact upon the rationale for sending missionaries to all the world. Why bother with missions if it is true that God is going to give an opportunity to be saved to everyone sooner or later anyhow? Where is the urgency then? Is this not missiologically dangerous speculation on the part of an armchair theologian? Is it not the perfect excuse for us not to exert ourselves very much in world evangelization? Will it not inevitably lead to a crisis of determination among the churches?

I am sensitive to this objection more than to any other. I will not dwell upon the fact that the hardline position has not in fact always led to missionary efforts. Neither the Reformers nor the post-Reformation orthodox people are known for their missionary zeal. Apparently one can believe the heathen are perishing and still not lift a finger to help them.[45] But I will not press this point. The fact is that evangelical missionary theory in modern times has been worked out in the context not of a theory of inclusive finality (like mine) but according to the belief of exclusive finality. It would seem, therefore, if my thinking is right, that evangelicals will have to rethink the motives of missions in a new setting. In such a framework the church stands under the command of the Lord to take the gospel to the whole world. My problem is no greater than that of the Calvinist who believes the church should fulfill the Great Commission even though he knows all the elect will be saved in any case. He goes because he has been commanded to go. And there is the fact that salvation is much more than deliverance from eschatological wrath. People can enjoy eternal life now in this life if the gospel is preached to them, and this is what God wants. Just because we posit that God will not permit people to be damned because through no fault of their own they never received a gospel message, we still long to see the nations converted to Christ in this present history. The unevangelized do have access to a degree of divine revelation, but the proclamation of the gospel will fill out the measure of God's mercy and reconciliation for them and stimulate them to turn to God.[46]

CONCLUSION

What I have tried to accomplish here is to combine the historic belief in the finality of Jesus Christ with a spirit of openness and hope in regard to all the people of the earth. My position of inclusive finality will offend those who wish to surrender the incarnation to achieve good relations and also those who insist on maintaining the doctrine that there is no salvation "extra ecclesiam," outside of the church. I can only hope there is a multitude in addition to these two groups that can see that finality with openness is what the Bible teaches. In faith we confess the lordship of Christ. In love we open ourselves to the person and truths other people possess from God. And in hope we anticipate that none will perish who, through no fault of their own, lacked opportunity to embrace God's love.

Part III

CREATION AND ITS RESTORATION

The first two parts of this book have presented evangelical views on God, on humans made in his image, and on the way God reveals himself to humanity. Such discussions are big with implications for everyday life, for work, family, economic relationships, national conflicts, scientific endeavors, and much more. It is the task of this third section to examine some of these questions in "practical theology." It does so, moreover, by interweaving the insights of theologians who are interested in the world beyond the church's walls with those of laymen who are concerned about the theological implications of their disciplines.

We begin with a meditation on the dominion of God, as revealed in a biblical vision of the end, and proceed to a programmatic assessment of the ways in which evangelicals and other Christians have approached the question of daily life as a theological issue. Three chapters follow on work, poverty, and science. These are intended to suggest evangelical positions on these issues, but also to indicate the nature of such inquiry currently underway among evangelicals on many such fronts. The last two chapters describe strategies for living as Christians in the secular West and implications for believing as Christians in a divinely ordained future.

4

Biblical Meditation:
The Restoration of Creation

John R. W. Stott

As we meditate on God the Restorer of creation, it is appropriate to look beyond the present moment to the end. Consider these words from the Book of Revelation, chapter four:

> After this I looked, and there before me was a door standing open in heaven. And the voice I had first heard speaking to me like a trumpet said, "Come up here, and I will show you what must take place after this." At once I was in the Spirit, and there before me was a throne in heaven with someone sitting on it. And the one who sat there had the appearance of jasper and carnelian. A rainbow, resembling an emerald, encircled the throne. Surrounding the throne were twenty-four other thrones, and seated on them were twenty-four elders. They were dressed in white and had crowns of gold on their heads. From the throne came flashes of lightning, rumblings and peals of thunder. Before the throne, seven lamps were blazing. These are the seven spirits of God. Also before the throne there was what looked like a sea of glass, clear as crystal. In the center, around the throne, were four living creatures, and they were covered with eyes, in front and in back. The first living creature was like a lion, the second was like an ox, the third had the face of a man, the fourth was like a flying eagle. Each of the four living creatures had six wings and was covered with eyes all around, even under his wings. Day and night they never stopped saying:
>
> > Holy, holy, holy is the Lord God Almighty, who was, and is, and is to come.
>
> Whenever the living creatures give glory, honor and thanks to him who sits on the throne and who lives for ever and ever, the twenty-four elders fall down before him who sits on the throne, and worship him who lives for ever and ever. They lay their crowns before the throne and say:

> You are worthy, our Lord and God, to receive glory and honor
> and power, for you created all things, and by your will they were
> created and have their being. (NIV)

At the beginning of the Book of Revelation John is preoccupied
with the condition of the churches on earth. He sees Jesus among the
lampstands, patrolling them. In chapters two and three he records the
letters to the seven churches that Jesus gave to him. Some of the
churches he praises for their faith, their hard work, their zeal for the
truth, their willingness to suffer, and their perseverance. Other
churches he censures: the church of Ephesus because it has lost its
first love; the church of Thyatira for tolerating false teaching; the
church of Laodicea for its lukewarmness; and the church of Sardis for
its deadness.

Now in chapter four he turns from the church on earth to the
community in heaven. He sees before him an open door. He is invited
to "come up" and is promised a revelation of the future. "In the
Spirit" he peeps through that open door, and immediately his eye
lights on a throne, symbol of the sovereignty or kingdom of God. This
throne of God dominates the rest of his vision. For four chapters (4–
7) everything John sees is related in some measure to that central
throne of God.

At least ten details are relevant to our theme in John's vision of
the throne of God in this and subsequent chapters.

First, somebody is sitting on the throne (4:2-3). That somebody
is not described, for the Living God is indescribable. All we are told
is that his appearance is like jasper and carnelian, radiantly beautiful.
Later he is designated the thrice-holy one, the Lord God, the
Almighty, who was, and is, and is to come, the eternal (v. 8).

Second, encircling the throne is the emerald rainbow, symbol of
the covenant of God, reminding us that the throne of God, great and
glorious as it is, is nevertheless a throne of grace (v. 3).

Third, surrounding the throne are twenty-four other thrones occupied by the twenty-four elders, all with crowns on their heads, sharing to some degree the reign of their God (v. 4). Since the number
twelve throughout the Book of Revelation is a symbol of the church,
these twenty-four elders evidently represent the church of the Old
Testament with its twelve tribes, together with the church of the New
Testament founded upon the twelve apostles. Now they are glorified
and reigning with Christ.

Fourth, from the throne issue flashes of lightning and peals of thunder, lightning enough to blind the eyes, thunder enough to deafen the ears (v. 5). Both are tokens of the presence and power of God the Lawgiver, as on Mount Sinai.

Fifth, before the throne John sees seven blazing lamps, and interprets them as "the seven spirits of God," presumably meaning the Holy Spirit himself in sevenfold manifestation and operation (v. 5).

Sixth, also before the throne of God John sees an expanse of sea, clear as crystal, symbol of the distance of God, his transcendence as he reigns above and beyond the universe that he has made (v. 6).

Seventh, around the throne as a kind of inner circle are four living creatures resembling a lion, an ox, a man, and an eagle, symbolizing it seems now not God's new creation, the church, which has been symbolized in the twenty-four elders, but the old creation, the natural world (vv. 6-7). These living creatures are covered with eyes because they are ceaselessly vigilant and endlessly praising the holy God, ascribing to him who lives and reigns forever the glory that is due to his name as the Creator.

Eighth, John sees the Lamb in the very center of the throne, sharing the rule with the Living God, and encircled by the four creatures and the twenty-four elders, "looking as if it had been slain," the "Lion of the tribe of Judah" (5:5-6). The Lamb takes the scroll and is worshiped because he alone is worthy to take and to open it, and because he was slain and has purchased human beings by his blood for God.

Ninth, encircling the throne again, this time as an outer circle, are ten thousand times ten thousand angels, leading the heavenly singing, proclaiming the worthiness of the Lamb, and provoking all creatures throughout the universe to join in the chorus of worship.

Finally, John sees standing before the throne the great company of the redeemed that no one can number, in fulfillment of God's promise to Abraham that his posterity would be as numberless as the sand on the seashore and the stars in the night sky, "from every nation, tribe, people and language" (7:9ff.).

As we try to picture the scene that John describes, notice again that everything is related to the throne. On it, the Lord God Almighty; at its center, the slain Lamb; before it, the sevenfold Spirit of God; encircling it, the rainbow of the covenant; issuing from it, the thunders and lightnings of judgment; stretching before it, the crystal sea; surrounding it in concentric circles, God's threefold creation: the four living creatures, the twenty-four elders, and the thousands of angels; and standing before the throne, the whole international company of the redeemed.

The vision given to John is not a vision of fantasy but a vision of reality. It is, in fact, the ultimate reality. To be sure, it is described in highly figurative and symbolic imagery. Yet it is reality, both present and future, the rule of God with everything related to his throne.

This vision of the throne should lead us to a threefold repentance in relation to our way of looking at the end. First, our vision of the end and of eternity is often too negative. We tend to concentrate on the promises that there will be no more hunger, no more thirst, no more scorching heat, no more pain, no more sin, no more death. And these are certainly true. But there is something more important than these absences, namely, the central, dominating presence of the throne of God to which the absences are due. Because God is reigning these things will be no more. So it is not appropriate to think negatively of the end.

Second, many have a vision of the end that is too heavenly. They forget that there is to be a regenerated universe, a new earth as well as a new heaven. Mark Twain, in *The Adventures of Huckleberry Finn,* wrote of the Widow Douglas, who had little success in interesting Huck in heaven. "The Good Place," she called it. "She said," said Huck, "all a body would have to do there was to go around all day long with a harp and sing for ever and ever. So I didn't think much of it." But the Widow had a false view of the end. When we come to Revelation 21, he who sits on the throne rises from it and says, "Behold, I am making the universe new." There will be a new heaven and a new earth. And then John sees the Holy City, the New Jerusalem, descending from heaven to earth. Nothing impure will enter this city. But nevertheless, the kings of the earth and the nations of the world are permitted to bring their glory into it. The location of the throne of God and of the Lamb will be in the city that has come to earth (Rev. 22:3). The groaning creation, as we see it all around us, and as we share in its groans, is going to be redeemed and restored, and God will rule over it.

So our vision of the end must be neither too negative nor too heavenly, nor, third, too selfish. Many Christians seem to have a vision of the future that is as self-indulgent, and even as voluptuous, as the vision of paradise of which we read in *The Koran.* Sidney Smith, an Anglican wit in the middle of the last century, founder of the *Edinburgh Review* and a canon of Saint Paul's Cathedral, is said to have described heaven as eating paté de foie gras to the sound of trumpets! By the way of contrast, the biblical vision of the end is not, "Oh that will be glory for me" (though to be sure Christians will be glorified), but rather that God will himself be glorified.

On that day, the throne of God will be central. Throughout eternity, we shall never speak a word, or do a deed, or think a thought that is not related to the throne of God. For when God takes his power and reigns, all creatures will be subdued before his reign and will find fulfillment in their submission.

Meanwhile, we are called to anticipate now, in this life, the God-centered life of the end. The divine restoration of creation is underway. We are called to a life of godliness, of God-centeredness, because through Christ the kingdom of God has come, the end has begun, and his rule is spreading out over the world. So we are to demonstrate now the reality of God's rule in our lives and in the life of the church, until that great day when God will take his power and reign without rivals, and will be "everything to everyone."

God the Civilizer

Donald Bloesch

If humanity was created in the image of God and if God has revealed himself to humanity for its salvation in Christ, there are immense consequences for the creation itself. In spite of the impression that some evangelicals occasionally leave, Christianity is not about pie in the sky. The Christian faith is based in transcendent realities but its implications appear immanently in creation. "God was in Christ," the apostle said, "reconciling the *world* to himself" (2 Cor. 5:19). Put another way, God wants to save souls, but souls in factories, offices, farms, and the unemployment office, souls with their different amounts of money, souls engaged in the scientific enterprise—all matters treated in separate chapters below—as well as souls in political activity, souls in bedroom and boardroom, souls on the playing field, souls in the domestic order, and on and on.

Theologians have long pondered what it means for God, as another revelation of his being, to be a Civilizer, a restorer of the world he has made. The discussion in this chapter draws upon that history of theological interpretation to outline several important issues attendant to the divine restoration of the world. It explores the relationship between religion and culture, sacred history and human history, creation and redemption, human culture and the kingdom of God. It also makes the argument that God works to restore civilization primarily through the church, an argument that I set out abstractly before applying it directly to the conditions in which we now live.

This chapter and its self-conscious dialogue with theological voices offers a religious counterpoint to the next three chapters where the debating partners are modern theoreticians of work, poverty, and science. It also prepares the way for the last two chapters where Klaus Bockmuehl and David Wells expand upon the themes presented here, especially the connection between "this world" in its secular manifestations and "the age to come."

DEFINITIONS: CHRIST AND CULTURE

To assess the complex and intricate relationship between Christ and culture, we must begin with definitions. By "Christ" I mean neither the idealistic Jesus of liberalism nor the eternal Christ of mysticism but the Jesus Christ of biblical faith. It is God's self-revelation in Christ that comprises the divine side of this relationship. By "culture" I mean the sum total of the creative accomplishments of a given people, the intellectual and pragmatic ramifications of a particular philosophy, or the social expression of a life and world view.[1]

"Civilization" I understand as a higher stage of human achievement associated with great art, literature, and philosophy. This agrees very much with standard definitions, as in *The American Heritage Dictionary:* "an advanced stage of development in the arts and sciences accompanied by corresponding social, political and cultural complexity."[2] As I use the terms, *culture* and *civilization* are virtually synonymous.

H. Richard Niebuhr maintained in his pivotal study, *Christ and Culture,*[3] that since culture represents the pinnacle of human achievement, it also represents the realization and conservation of human values. Culture embodies a world of values because human achievements are always measured against ideal ends. Niebuhr also reminded us that culture is invariably pluralistic because any one civilization contains a wealth of often conflicting values.

All human culture is secular to some degree because it belongs to its own age *(saeculum)* and necessarily reflects the spirit of that age *(Zeitgeist).* At the same time a culture can be religious if it is preoccupied not only with penultimate but also ultimate concerns. In this sense a religious culture is more of a threat to the church than a merely secular one since the religious culture tends to absolutize cultural goals and values. Karl Barth once said that Christian faith frees culture from all absolutism: it leads to an appreciation but not a deification of the human.

To this sociological understanding of culture we may also add a theological definition. So defined, culture becomes the arena that God has appointed for humans to realize their destiny in service to his glory. Or as Barth phrased it, culture is the sphere that yields parables of God and his kingdom. Barth further regarded culture as something worthwhile on its own level because it is the divinely appointed means for men and women to realize their humanity: "What else is civilization than the endeavour of man to be man, and therefore to bring honour and to set to work the good gift of his humanity?"[4] Indeed, "the term *culture* connotes exactly that promise to man: fulfillment, unity, wholeness within his sphere as creature, as man."[5] On the other hand, Anabaptists such as the Mennonites often betray a profound mistrust of cultural pursuits; culture is here "the institutionalization of structured unbelief and sin."[6]

Culture is both a human achievement and a divine gift, the result of both human dexterity and divine grace. God gives motivation and inspiration; human cultural achievements are responses to this divine call. The grace that undergirds and adorns cultural achievement is the grace of preservation, however, not the grace of redemption. God acts to preserve humanity even in its sin and folly. And God rewards humanity for its creative contributions to human welfare and justice, even though such efforts fall far short of the perfect righteousness that he demands.

The motivation to realize our creative potential comes from God, but our striving for fulfillment is invariably corrupted by sin. Culture is not only a tribute to human sagacity and ingenuity but also a monument to human pride. It represents not only a flowering of human creativity but also its distortion. So much is this the case that the triumphs of human culture can aggravate as well as ameliorate the human predicament.

PATTERNS OF INTERACTION

The particular strategy for Christians in meeting the challenges and threats of the secular culture should no doubt vary depending upon the historical situation *(Sitz im Leben)* in which the church exists. In some situations where the culture has become irretrievably idolatrous, the church must sound the call to separation. Flight rather than fight is then the strategy with divine sanction, even though this kind of withdrawal must always be carried out for the sake of a return at a later time and on a deeper level. In other situations where the forces of good are not so completely overwhelmed by the forces of evil, the Christian might well work for reform so that the present civilization could be humanized.

For considerations of the Christian stance over against culture, the typology offered by H. Richard Niebuhr in *Christ and Culture* is quite helpful.[7] Niebuhr suggests that Christians have approached the larger world (i.e., "culture") from one of five ideal types: "Christ Against Culture," a position whereby people of faith try to divorce themselves from the world in all of its vanity; "The Christ of Culture," which accommodates the gospel to what the world values most dearly; "Christ Above Culture," which attempts to forge a synthesis between eternal values and the wisdom of the world; "Christ and Culture in Paradox," a dualistic stance in which believers are active in the world but not confident about success in bringing it captive to Christ; and "Christ the Transformer of Culture," where believers attempt to shape the world in every particular according to the norms of Scripture and Christian tradition.

Niebuhr's "Christ-of-culture" position identifies the highest values of the present culture with the substance of faith and thereby represents an ignominious accommodation to the spirit of the age. Niebuhr finds cultural Christianity in the Gnostics of the church's earliest centuries, in Abelard the medieval philosopher, and in the nineteenth-century theologians Schleiermacher and Ritschl. On the contemporary scene I believe it can be detected in liberationist, process, and feminist theologies as well as in the new religious right.[8] For each of these groups some value from the culture molds, informs, and even determines the shape of the faith.

Those who espouse a "Christ-against-culture" stance, by way of contrast, sound the call to separation from the evils, allurements, and compromises of the world. They argue that the Christian should be impelled to live in conscious opposition to the values, claims, and practices of culture, with the assumption that all cultures by their very nature are under the sway of the powers of darkness. Niebuhr discerns this tendency in the monastic tradition, in the church father Tertullian (who asked what Jerusalem had to do with Athens), and in Leo Tolstoy. I would add that this tendency shows up also in Menno Simons, founder of the Mennonites; in Jacob Amman, who spearheaded the Amish separation from the Mennonites; in the nineteenth-century communitarian Eberhard Arnold and dispensationalist John Nelson Darby; and in our day in the French Reformed iconoclast Jacques Ellul and the founder of the Catholic Worker Movement, Dorothy Day (though several of these manifest a strong conversionist motif as well).[9]

Those who view Christ as being "above culture" try to do justice to the cultural quest for wisdom and truth, but contend that it can be fulfilled only in Christ. Their aim is to correlate the fundamental questions of the culture with answers from Christian revelation. They therefore strive for a theology of synthesis where cultural expectations may be subordinated to Christian concerns. We see this strategy in Clement of Alexander, who over against the Gnostics of his day proclaimed Christ as the true "gnosis" or wisdom; in Thomas Aquinas with his "baptism" of Aristotle's philosophy for Christian purposes; and in our day with Paul Tillich, whose theology had not been significantly developed at the time Niebuhr wrote.[10]

The "Christ-and-culture-in-paradox" position is dualistic in that the Christian is said to belong to two realms, the spiritual and temporal, and must live in the tension of fulfilling responsibilities to both. Niebuhr lists here the apostle Paul and Martin Luther, who explicitly advocated an ethic of Two Kingdoms. An important representative of this tradition in our own time is Reinhold Niebuhr, who was especially alert to the ironies involved with life lived simultaneously in the divine and human spheres.

Finally we have those who demonstrate what Richard Niebuhr calls "Christ-transforming-culture." These are the people who try to convert the values and goals of secular culture into the service of the kingdom of God. In their thinking, Calvary must be fulfilled in Pentecost. The author includes in this category the Gospel of John and several of the more influential figures in the history of Western Christianity—Augustine, John Calvin, John Wesley, Jonathan Edwards, and F. D. Maurice, the Christian socialist in nineteenth-century Britain whose views nonetheless transcended a narrow ideological vision.

Karl Barth's position is close to this last one, the conversionist position. He presses for a transformation of the cultural vision in the light of the divine promise and commandment. At the same time, Barth sharply stresses what previous advocates of this approach had also maintained, that no cultural achievement may identify with the coming kingdom of God. The righteousness that we as Christians are called to effect is not the divine righteousness of the kingdom, which God alone can enact, but a purely human righteousness that nonetheless corresponds with and is determined by this higher righteousness. Barth on occasion appears to advocate a cultural Christianity when he endorses the values of democratic socialism as most nearly approximating the values of the kingdom of God.[11] At the same time, however, he could be regarded as a separationist because of his deepseated conviction that the demands of the gospel always run counter to the hopes and expectations of the culture. Christians will always be standing against the stream of what is popular and acceptable for the time.[12]

For Barth, Jesus Christ is the humanizer of culture. It is through his grace, which is always redemptive and never simply preservative, that men and women can move toward a more just and humane society.[13] God alone is Renewer, Reconciler, and Sanctifier, but God is Civilizer only in conjunction with human efforts toward a better world. God makes us his covenant partners in fashioning a society that will redound to his glory. He enables us to realize our vocations to be signs and witnesses to Jesus Christ.

In weighing the various stances in Niebuhr's typology, I find Barth's position persuasive. It approaches the conversionist ideal. Yet it always unites "Christ-against-culture" with "Christ-transforming-culture" in order to maintain the transcendent character of the claims of the gospel over cultural goals and expectations. Niebuhr's types are valuable heuristic tools. Neither his categorizations nor mine are to be taken as dominical classifications. What they do set up is a grid useful for making more searching judgments among the stances that Christians over the centuries have assumed toward culture.

RELIGION AND CULTURE

A consideration of Niebuhr's types raises the more general question of the precise relation between religion and culture. It is generally agreed in both theology and the social sciences that this relationship is inseparable and indissoluble. Tillich put it well when he declared that culture is the form of religion, and religion is the substance of culture.[14] Every culture has its genesis in a spiritual and moral vision, and every religion seeks a cultural incarnation. Religion is the wellspring of culture; culture is the social embodiment of religion. Culture is the bearer of religion; religion is the ground and goal of culture.

A culture can deny or cover up its metaphysical undergirding and thereby become secularized. Yet even in this situation, it cannot remain insulated against religious and moral claims. On the contrary, it will then most likely invest its secular forms and ideals with religious and moral significance. A culture closed to the transcendent will create its own equivalents of the sacred.

Tillich sees clearly that the church and culture exist within, not alongside each other.[15] The kingdom of God includes both even while it transcends both. The erosion of religion betokens the secularization of the culture, but no culture, he claims correctly, can exist in a metaphysical vacuum. When God is dead, the gods are reborn, and Christianity is once again confronted by idolatry.

Christianity is both a religon and a cultural phenomenon, but in addition it is anchored in a divine revelation. The Christian faith bears witness to a God who infinitely transcends human culture and religion even while entering into cultural and religious activity. This is the God who judges as well as blesses human accomplishments, even those done in the name of Jesus Christ. As Barth put it, God's self-revelation in Christ might well be regarded as the crisis or judgment of both religion and culture.

At their best, both culture and religion can be a sign and witness of the redemptive action of God that occurs *in* them but does not arise *from* them. Cultural and religious activity can be parables of the coming kingdom of God, though such activity must never be confounded with this kingdom.

CONFLICTING VIEWS ON HISTORY

To examine the problem of Christianity and culture means of necessity to consider as well the meaning of history. Here, too, there are many discordant voices. But as with the more general typologies, these different assessments of history aid in the construction of a perspective that, while finding meaning in the flow of human events, reserves ultimate meaning for the sovereign, providential action of God. For Reinhold Niebuhr history is a perennial tragedy—the story of human hybris and divine nemesis.[16] Such seminal thinkers as Hegel, Tillich, and Moltmann view human history as the unfolding of divinity and therefore are inclined to be optimistic about its final outcome. For process theologians such as Wieman, Meland, Whitehead, and Hartshorne, the trajectory of human history and culture marks the path of the creative process toward a more complex and humane social order, however checkered its course may be. In the thought of Augustine, Calvin, and Luther, history is best understood as a perpetual battleground between two kingdoms—light and darkness. Karl Barth presents a variation on that theme: history is the drama of the ongoing encounter between an aspiring humanity and the living God of the Bible, who both casts down and raises up kings and empires.

Drawing mostly from the latter thinkers, I suggest that history is the story of human vanity and creativity in conflict with the omnipotence of God to which every culture bears witness in some way or other (Acts 14:17). This conflict must be seen in the light of a wider and deeper struggle—that between the devil, the adversary of God and humanity, and the God of Jesus Christ. The devil is superior to humankind but drastically inferior to God. He is permitted to work his destruction in the world for a time, but only for the purpose of furthering the purposes of God to bring healing and deliverance to all peoples. God makes even "the wrath of men" to praise him (Ps. 76:10; cf. Exod. 9:16; Rom. 9:17), and in this way his work of civilizing and humanizing goes on even in the midst of chaos and disorder.

While Barth overstated the case to say that all human history is sacred history, he was correct to see God working in all history—though (I would add) preservatively, not redemptively. Only where the living God, the God who revealed himself in Jesus Christ, is acknowledged as Savior and Lord do we find the sphere of redemption in history. Yet all of history moves toward the goal of the kingdom of God, since eventually the whole of humankind will be brought under the redemptive rule of Jesus Christ.

The meaning of the world, too, is brought more sharply into focus through these conflicting approaches to human culture. For Reinhold Niebuhr, the world is most accurately portrayed as a tower of Babel in which our infinite possibilities are time and again subverted by our sin. Tillich, on the other hand, sees the world as the sanctuary of divinity, the latent church in which the Spiritual Presence is hidden rather than manifest. The Unconditioned, he says, "can be recognized in the cultural and natural universe,"[17] but this natural knowledge yields at most the fundamental question of human existence, for which the Christian revelation is the answer. In Calvin's view, the world is the theater of the glory of God, the sphere in which God's glory is advanced even in the midst of human destruction as well as human liberation. For Barth the world is the field of the redemptive action of God, but it is not the source of his redemptive activity. According to Thomas Aquinas, the kingdom of nature is fulfilled and perfected in the kingdom of grace.

In accord with some of these voices, I propose a vision of the world as the locus for the pilgrimage of faith, the crucible of probation where the people of God are tested and prepared for eternity. It is not a prison from which we need to escape (as in Gnosticism). Nor is it a ladder by which we can ascend to heaven with the assistance of grace (as in classical Christian mysticism). Instead, it is the arena in which people, all people, are summoned to work out their vocation to be servants and heralds of the one Lord and Savior, Jesus Christ. We prove our fidelity to this high and holy calling by bearing fruit that proceeds from repentance (Matt. 3:8-10).

CREATION AND REDEMPTION

The role of the Christian in human culture is best understood against the background of creation and redemption. In this, evangelical theology differs from other theological traditions. There are those like Thomas Aquinas, Paul Tillich, Emil Brunner, or Karl Rahner who see creation as essentially a preparation for redemption, and redemption as the elevation and fulfillment of creation. Nature is the precondition for grace, and grace is the perfection of nature.[18] Others have been inclined to view redemption as basically the completion of creation— even as a further or higher stage of creation.[19] In Schleiermacher's thought, the appearance of Christ "is to be regarded as a preservation . . . of the receptivity, implanted in human nature from the beginning and perpetually developing further, which enables it to take into itself such an absolute potency of . . . God-consciousness."[20] In our day Jürgen Moltmann has argued that the divine *kenosis* (or "self-emptying") begins at creation and reaches its fullness in the incarnation.[21] For those standing in the Gnostic tradition, on the other hand, redemption is an escape from creation.[22] Evangelical sectarians thus reflect a Gnostic vision when they say that this is Satan's world rather than God's. Mystics whose affinities are with Neoplatonism (pseudo-Dionysius, Meister Eckhart, Simone Weil) view redemption as the transcendence of creation.

In refreshing contrast, Karl Barth, who here represents evangelical theology at its best, argues that creation exists for the sake of redemption.[23] Redemption, to be sure, brings about the renewal of a creation that has been marred by human sin. It entails the regeneration of human nature, which is in effect a new creation (1 Cor. 5:17).

> Redemption is more than creation, more also even than (as Schleiermacher thought) the completion and crown of creation. God's creation needs no completion. It was and is complete. But we can lose that completeness of creation, and we *have* lost it. It must be restored to us inalienably, by forgiveness and renewal.[24]

Building upon Barth, one can say that redemption signifies the dawning of a wholly new reality that satisfies the yearnings of creation, but that also negates the hubris of a creation that has abandoned its ontological moorings. The possibility of this new reality lies not in creation but in a divine intervention into human history.

Barth is further correct in maintaining that one can rightly understand creation only from the perspective of redemption. The buried and forgotten truth of God in creation is only brought to light through the awakening to faith in God the Redeemer. We can truly appreciate the work of God as Civilizer only when our eyes are opened to his glorious work of redemption in Jesus Christ.

Reformed or Calvinistic theology has been accustomed to making the distinction between common and saving grace, a distinction valuable in some respects but less so for relating creation and redemption. "Common grace" signifies the general providence by which God prevents humankind from destroying itself by its own sin and that inspires people to transcend themselves in works of creative achievement. "Saving grace" is the work by which God transforms the human lust for power into the generosity of love. Calvin himself did not use the term *common grace,* but he alluded to a general grace *(gratia universalis)* that upholds human culture and mitigates the effects of human sin. The concept of common grace is not in the Bible as such, but it has a biblical basis (cf. Matt. 5:45; 7:11; Luke 11:13; John 1:9; Acts 14:17; 17:26-28; Jas. 1:17).

The danger in this distinction lies in separating the two activities of God, thus creating the deceptive impression that God calls only a select few to salvation. The distinction is helpful so long as we hold that God's preservative work is for the sake of his redeeming work. God's civilizing activity leads to and is confirmed by his redemptive activity.

From his own perspective, Emil Brunner reaffirms this truth:

> The first thing is always what God wills as Creator; but even apart from our sin—it is not the last. For He wills to lead the creation out beyond itself, into the perfecting of all things. God does not preserve the world simply in order to preserve it, but in order that he may perfect it.[25]

A further distinction, from both Catholic and Protestant theology, between the kingdoms of nature on the one side, and grace and glory on the other, is also helpful at this point. Thomas Aquinas perceived well that there is always a leap between the stages; they do not unobtrusively blend into one another. Yet, in biblical understanding, God's grace and glory are the source and goal of nature. God the Reconciler precedes God the Civilizer. God has chosen us to inherit the crown of eternal life before the foundation of the world (Matt. 13:35; John 17:24; Eph. 1:4; 1 Pet. 1:20). Before there was a cross in human history, there was a cross in the heart of God (1 Tim. 1:9-10; 1 Pet. 1:20; Rev. 13:8). Jesus Christ, the new Man, precedes Adam, the primal man. From the perspective of eternity, redemption is prior to creation, though, to be sure, on the plane of human history redemption occurs after creation.

HUMAN CULTURE AND THE KINGDOM OF GOD

Such considerations raise the larger question about the fascinating and enigmatic relationship between human culture and the kingdom of God. We may regard culture as a sign of the kingdom but not its seedbed. The kingdom of God breaks into culture, but culture does not lead to the kingdom. The kingdom is not an extension or flowering of the culture, but culture can be a parable of the kingdom. Barth puts it very well: "The Church will not see the coming of the kingdom of God in any human cultural achievement, but it will be alert for the signs which, perhaps in many cultural achievements, announce that the kingdom approaches."[26]

The discontinuity between culture and the kingdom becomes more evident when we consider the gulf between the righteousness of the kingdom and social justice. According to Tillich, human culture at its best is characterized by proportional justice, but the kingdom of God is marked by transforming justice, where justice is united with love.[27] Luther contrasted civil and spiritual righteousness, insisting that the latter, which transcends civil obligation, characterizes the new social order inaugurated by Jesus Christ, where love and forgiveness prevail. The difference, in Berdyaev's phrase, is between the common morality and the "morality beyond morality." Whereas human decency and fairness are the marks of a genuinely humane culture, holy love pervades the kingdom of God. Bonhoeffer acutely perceived the radical newness of the kingdom when he declared, "God has founded his church beyond religion and beyond ethics."

Divine grace operates in both realms: it is the elevating force in human culture and the creative source of the kingdom of God. This is why Barth could contend that the foundation of a genuinely free culture is not human potentiality but the freedom of God.[28] We are made free to realize human potential on the basis of divine grace. In the power of this grace we can strive for human righteousness, though this must always be distinguished from the divine righteousness that belongs to the kingdom of God. Yet the social righteousness that we can achieve under the impact of his grace can be a provisional reflection and foreshadowing of the perfect righteousness of the kingdom. This is why Barth could say: "The action of those who pray for the coming of God's kingdom and therefore for the taking place of his righteousness will be *kingdom-like,* and therefore on a lower level and within its impassable limits it will be *righteous* action."[29]

Barth recognized clearly that both church and state are under the rulership of Jesus Christ. Jesus Christ is Lord because he is not only Creator along with the Father but also Redeemer through his decisive and world-shattering victory over the principalities and powers of darkness.[30] This is why both church and state can be signs of the kingdom of God. The state may be envisioned as an analogue to the kingdom of God, since this kingdom is a new social order, "the city of the living God" (Heb. 12:22), not simply an assembly for worship. The essence of the state is not violence or power but justice, or power in the service of justice. To be sure, the state is given as a restraint on sin, but it is also the sphere in which justice can be realized. The human righteousness realized in the state corresponds to the higher righteousness of the kingdom, but there is still a discontinuity. It is the difference between the force of law and the freedom of love. Unfortunately, some states spurn their divinely given mandate and arrogate power to themselves, ruthlessly suppressing the hopes and wants of their citizens. A Christian does not owe obedience to a state that has become demonic in such a way (cf. Acts 5:29; Rev. 13).

This vision of the state helps determine its proper purposes. Social legislation is not only to preserve order in society but to make secure the rights of all, especially the rights of the oppressed. Yet social legislation has its limits: it can alter human behavior, but it cannot change human nature. The state can legislate against immorality and thereby curb the rapacity of its citizens, but it cannot make people more loving. It can make people law-abiding but not God-fearing. The key to social reformation is supernatural regeneration, a change in inner attitudes and dispositions that is wrought by the Spirit of God in the awakening to faith in Jesus Christ. A society can advance toward greater justice only when it contains a church that reminds it of a higher claim and a higher morality, a church that functions as an agent in bringing to people a new life orientation and the spiritual gifts that enable them to realize this orientation in their thoughts, words, and actions.

THE TWO KINGDOMS

The relationship between human culture and the kingdom of God must be assessed in the light of the cosmic conflict between the kingdom of God and the demonic kingdom of darkness. The kingdom of darkness is anticultural because it fosters disorder and anarchy. It is also the fulcrum of inhumanity because it denigrates and defaces the human. Theologians have agreed on the discontinuity between these two spheres, but they have pictured the points of conflict as well as the potential for interaction differently. In what follows, I survey some of the most compelling of these interpretations, both past and present, in order to suggest the complexity and the richness of the relationship. This survey also puts us in a position to see how the church may act as an agent of God's kingdom while it lives in the kingdom of this world.

In Augustine's famous picture, two cities are arrayed against one another—that of the world, ruled by the devil, and that of God.[31] The City of God advances in the world through its earthen vessel, the holy catholic church. Indeed, Augustine speaks of a building up of the kingdom through the word and the sacraments. At times he virtually equates the kingdom and the church, though for the most part he keeps the two distinct. Augustine gives us a "realized eschatology": the kingdom of God is realized now in history and is therefore engaged in mortal combat with the principalities and powers that presumptuously strive to control human destiny.

This contradiction between the two kingdoms was underscored by Martin Luther, who interpreted world history in light of an apocalyptic conflict between two cosmic powers, culminating in a momentous final struggle.[32] The kingdom of Christ is an island of light in a world still under the domain of the demonic powers of darkness. The world will not be flooded by light until a new divine intervention at the end of history when Christ will come again—this time as triumphant king rather than suffering servant. Christ is Lord of both church and world by virtue of his role in the creation, but he is Savior only where his rule is acknowledged in the hearts of men and women. Luther also referred to the two governments of church and state; both of these are vulnerable to penetration by the powers of darkness just as both can be vehicles of the kingdom of God.

John Calvin's eschatology is more optimistic, looking forward to the triumph of the kingdom of God over the kingdoms of this world within earthly history. This is not, however, a total or unqualified triumph (which waits upon the eschaton), but a gradual seizure of power; hence there is a postmillennial motif in Calvin. His ideal was a holy community in which both church and state cooperate to fashion a social order where the glory of God is served in every area of life.[33]

Both church and state are under the revealed law of God; the church interprets this law to the state, and the state in turn applies this law to life in society. The holy community is not itself the kingdom of God, which is fundamentally a spiritual kingdom, but it can be a means by which the kingdom of God is extended in the world. Indeed, Calvin was adamant that we, as humans transformed by grace, can extend and advance the kingdom of God through the preaching of the word, prayer, church discipline, the sacraments, and works of social service.

Reflecting a quite different orientation is Reinhold Niebuhr, who upholds a transcendental eschatology.[34] He depicts the kingdom of God as a transcendental ideal beyond history calling into question every human expectation and achievement. Niebuhr views world history as the story of human hubris and divine nemesis. While the kingdom gives meaning and purpose to human endeavor, it can never be realized by means of human endeavor. The kingdom is always coming, but it is never here. It is a religio-moral ideal by which we can measure our progress toward a higher degree of justice and mutual love. The kingdom impinges on history, but it never becomes incarnate in history. Its reality can be momentarily experienced when individuals are grasped by the power of sacrificial love, but it can never be identified with any cultural movement or achievement.[35]

While Niebuhr does not envision any cosmic conflict between two opposing spiritual kingdoms, he does affirm the polarity of the kingdom of the world and the kingdom of God. Although the first stands in contradiction to the second, it also points beyond itself to this higher kingdom where it finds both its fulfillment and its negation.

Yet another perspective comes from Paul Tillich, whose eschatology is both transcendental and inner-worldly, with the accent especially in his earlier years on the latter.[36] In his view the kingdom of God has two sides: it is both inner-historical and eternal. The kingdom is not only above history but also within history. In addition, there is a "demonic kingdom," signifying not simply a deficiency of the good but a corruption of the creative dynamic at work in all things. Tillich called for a theology of synthesis in which the fundamental questions and highest values of the culture are brought into a working relationship with the demands and ideals of the kingdom of God. In contrast to the dialectical theology, Tillich saw hope and promise in cultural endeavor and achievement. From his perspective the kingdom of God is being realized wherever people are awakened to the reality of the New Being, which appears in all genuinely prophetic figures and movements. One can also encounter the Spiritual Presence in great art, literature, and philosophy insofar as they throw light upon the human condition.

Even in the so-called dark periods of history when demonic forces seemed ascendant, Tillich was insistent that the creative power of being is at work making all things new. Whereas Barth viewed the experience of defeat and despair, the economic collapse and rising social conflict following the first World War as a crisis in the history of European civilization, a divine judgment on the nations, Tillich regarded this unsettling time as a *kairos,* a promise of new beginnings.

Notwithstanding his dour appraisal of current events, Barth's writings exude a holy optimism. He breaks with theological tradition by insisting that the triumph of Jesus Christ over the powers of darkness was so definitive and final that Christ is even now Lord and Redeemer of all creation. This is what Moltmann aptly calls the doctrine of the royal or kingly lordship of Christ.[37] Christ is even now the center of both state and church. The church is under the knowledge of Christ, the state under the power of Christ. The church's responsibility is to remind the state of its true nature and mission—to establish justice for the poor and oppressed.

Yet we are not being fair to Barth if we fail to take seriously his belief that the demonic kingdom of darkness, which spawns anarchy and disorder, is still very much alive. Though it has been divested of its power ontologically, it still wields power through deception. This is why he can refer to the lordless powers that continue to rule as rebels and usurpers. Christ has indeed demolished the demonic powers that have held the world in subjection, but until this fact is generally recognized they will continue to wreak havoc. Thus Barth can speak at the same time of a world fully reconciled to God in Jesus Christ and of a "still unredeemed world."

Though very much influenced by Barth, Jürgen Moltmann has swerved in still another direction.[38] Moltmann basically takes a positive view of culture, though he is also acutely aware of the lingering shadow over cultural achievements—that of exploitation and oppression. The division he sees in history is between the oppressors and the oppressed, and this is why Moltmann belongs in the larger circle of liberation theology. Following Hegel, he contends that all human history is taken up into the history of God. There is hope in history because God is acting in human conflict, bringing good out of evil, transmuting suffering into joyous expectation. Culture has revelatory promise because it is the medium through which the Absolute Spirit unfolds itself in history. He even says that the coming of the redeeming kingdom rests partly "in the potentialities and powers of the world religions."[39]

Whereas Barth's emphasis is on the finished work of Christ, Moltmann gives us a "theology of hope" for a world still groaning in travail, still waiting for the promised redemption. What Jesus Christ gained for us is the promise of a new world; we still wait for its fulfillment. But we can do more than wait: we can join the human struggle for liberation and thereby pave the way for the kingdom. For Moltmann, the lordship of Christ is realized wherever the hungry are fed, the naked are clothed, and unjust rulers are dethroned. Indeed, the lordship of Christ takes effect only where it is acknowledged and realized in acts of compassion, service, and social action.

Moltmann envisages the kingdom of God as a kingdom of freedom—a world free of exploitation and oppression. His eschatological hope is "the humanizing of man," "the socializing of humanity," and "peace for all creation." Although we can prepare the way for the kingdom through politics, God himself will bring in his kingdom in his own time. Yet we can cooperate with the Spirit of God in building a just society and bringing peace to all creation.[40] We can thus anticipate and facilitate the coming of the kingdom. The real presence of God is experienced wherever there is release from economic or political captivity, bread for the hungry, and security for the disinherited. The goal of liberation is "the ultimate dignity of man."[41]

I see in Moltmann a mixture of "Christ-transforming-culture" and "Christ-of-culture." He calls for the transformation of the social order even through revolution, but he betrays an unwarranted dependence on Hegelian and Marxist philosophy in the attempt to render the Christian hope intelligible and credible to an age in the throes of turmoil and upheaval. He loses sight of the transcendent and otherworldly dimensions of the kingdom of God, so that in his effort to do justice to the millennial promises of Scripture he transmutes the kingdom into a this-worldly practopia.[42] The Christian hope "is not directed towards 'another' world, but towards the world as it is changed in the kingdom of God."[43]

The centuries between Augustine and Moltmann have witnessed dramatic shifts in the position of the church over against civilization. In our own day the hard theoretical labor of the theologians has great practical importance as Christians attempt to exemplify the values of God's kingdom while living in the kingdom of this world.

GOD AS CIVILIZER AND RECONCILER:
THE CHURCH AND SOCIETY

The cultivation of the arts and sciences would not be possible apart from the work of God as Civilizer. It is God who educates and enlightens so that humans can realize their potentialities for culture and wisdom. It is God who leads humans beyond provincialism and tribalism into a social existence that makes room for human sublimity.

Yet the benefits of civilization mean little unless we maintain a deepening communion with God. We must not forget that God is Reconciler and Sanctifier as well as Civilizer. Unless his reconciling and regenerative work takes place in our lives, we will be prone to resist and deny the light of God in nature and conscience that makes civilization possible.

Cicero contended that justice is necessary for order in society, but Augustine maintained that piety, the fear of God, takes precedence over both justice and order. Unless people learn to know and fear their Creator and Lord, their efforts to build a just society ultimately will be self-defeating. Sanctity is necessary before education, for otherwise we will misuse the skills and knowledge we acquire. Repentance is a necessary precondition for genuine peace among peoples.

No enduring civilization or culture, in the highest meaning of the terms, is possible apart from the light of the gospel and the leaven of the church. The church provides the spiritual and metaphysical foundation for culture, and the Spirit working through the gospel endows people with the motivation and power to pursue peace and justice.

Our goal as Christians is not the Christification of the universe, as Teilhard de Chardin contends, nor is it simply humanization, as Barth and Bultmann sometimes seem to say. Instead, it is Christianization in the sense of bringing people into a saving relationship with Jesus Christ. We cannot realize our humanity in the way God intended until we come to a right knowledge of the living God and what he has done for us in Jesus Christ.

What I am calling for is not an imperial church, which imposes its peculiar beliefs upon an unwilling people, but an obedient church, which tries to live in the light of God's promise and in fidelity to his commandment. The weapons of the church are spiritual: the word of God, prayer, and works of mercy. It is not by law or coercion that people are brought into the kingdom but by the preaching and hearing of the word of God and by deeds of love.

Today, as in the past, what the world needs is a prophetic, not a triumphalist church. Such a church will see itself as the moral monitor of the state, not as a state within the state. It will serve as the conscience of the state, not a power structure wielding a club over the state.

Our protest, as Christians, is not against the secular culture, for culture deserves a certain autonomy, but against secularism, the enthronement of cultural values and ideas. The church combats idolatry when it brings the law of God to bear upon human pretension through its preaching and teaching.

A prophetic church should also be contrasted with a servant church, whose preeminent concern is to meet human need, to alleviate social ills. We must never forget that the mandate of the church is to bring the Good News of salvation through the cross and resurrection of Christ to a dying and lost humanity; in so doing the church will satisfy the deepest of all human needs—peace and reconciliation with God. The servant church carries out its witness by Christian presence rather than by the kerygmatic proclamation. The prophetic church will insist that deeds accompany words, but it will labor in the conviction that the key to the new creation is the gospel united with the Spirit.

In opposition to certain strands within Protestant liberalism, we must insist that the church of God is neither a humanitarian agency nor an ethical culture society. Instead, it is the social embodiment of the new reality of the kingdom of God. Its gospel is neither the social gospel nor the privatistic gospel of interior peace, but the biblical gospel of reconciliation and redemption through the atoning work of Christ on the cross and his glorious resurrection from the grave. It must never be forgotten, however, that such a gospel has far-reaching social and political implications.

Karl Barth has said that the Christian is called to be a *witness* rather than either a *crusader,* one who tries to set the world right, or a *monk,* one who withdraws from the fray in order to follow personal spiritual pursuits.[44] Yet this same theologian acknowledges that Christians are free to join, even to initiate, crusades as well as to embrace monastic-type vocations so long as their primary aim is to hold up Jesus Christ before a sinful and ailing world and so long as their trust remains in divine grace and not their own efforts.

The church has a spiritual mission and a cultural mandate. Its primary goal is to bring the glad tidings of reconciliation and redemption to all races and nations, but it is also responsible for teaching people to be disciples of Christ in the very midst of the world's plight and dereliction.

Church and state should be separate regarding specific roles and obligations, but both should be seen as under the rulership of Jesus Christ. The church must generally refrain from dictating to the state, but it can be a goad that spurs the state to fulfill its obligations to the poor and disinherited.

At its best, the church should be a leaven that turns the world in a new direction by changing attitudes and ideas, by altering hopes and goals. It is not primarily a battering ram that breaks down the walls that keep culture intact, though on occasion it may have to assume this role as well.

The church of God is not anticultural but transcultural. It is not iconoclastic but transformative. Its aim is not to tear down but to refocus. In the Christian perspective, human culture should not be overthrown or uprooted but relativized and demythologized.

Worldliness, not civilization, should be seen as the main foe of the gospel. Civilization is something to be appreciated, even celebrated, but worldliness is something to be spurned and combatted. Christianity, says H. Richard Niebuhr, rejects "the ascetic and romantic efforts to solve life's problems by flight from civilization."[45] Our Lord does not call us out of the world but sends us into it—though to conquer, not to succumb (cf. John 17:15-19). Worldliness takes the form of both ideological deformation and pusillanimous conformation to the values and goals of secular culture.

In our world, as in all previous ages, the overriding issue is idolatry. People are tempted to absolutize cultural forms and ideals instead of treating these things as means to a higher end. The higher the level of civilization, the greater the peril of culture-idolatry. As Richard Niebuhr put it, "The temptation to idolatry and lust is the greater the more man is surrounded by the works of his own hands."[46]

By far the most insidious type of idolatry is the elevation to divine status of the religious ideals, values, and practices that find general acceptance within a culture. Barth with his usual perspicuity observed, "Godlessness appears in a worse form in religion than it does in theoretical atheism, for here it does not make open confession as it tries to do in atheism, but thinks it has sought and found a positive substitute for what is lacking."[47]

The older Protestant liberalism did not fully consider how easily cultural achievements can become towers of Babel that foster confusion or new Molechs that hold people in servile subjection. In some quarters, civilization was even regarded as the condition for apprehending the truth of faith. "Christianity," declared Lynn Harold Hough, "has a great stake in the recovery of the civilized mind. The modern preacher confronts a major task in the remaking of the mind of his congregation. When minds become civilized, they can understand the Christian message."[48] But this is to reduce the gospel to the wisdom of the world. The church today is confronted by various temptations. On the left are those who are all too ready to identify the cause of human liberation with salvation and movements of liberation with the kingdom of God. Such ones should not forget the lessons of the twentieth century. A great many social idealists were attracted to the program of the German Christians, that segment within the German church in the 1930s that sought to accommodate the gospel to National Socialism.[49] They, too, protested against our profit-loving, capitalistic civilization, but their substitute was not a proletarian but a National Socialist utopia.

On the right, we have those who hold that America is the New Israel with a special destiny to be a light to the nations. More than one TV evangelist has proudly declared: "It is religion that has made America strong." But when religion is appreciated primarily for its social utility instead of for its truth, we have succumbed to a secularist mentality.

There is no purpose in attempting to establish a self-consciously Christian nation in which Christian symbols are invoked to justify social policy or sanctify imperial ambition. Instead, we should press for a just nation—but one informed by a Christian life and world view. Our goal for our nations should be to see them steadily becoming more Christianized and therefore at the same time more humanized, but we must never presume that any nation in this aeon can be wholly or even genuinely Christian. There is a difference between a nation suffused with Judeo-Christian values and a nation that actively promotes the dogmatic beliefs and practices of a particular church. Our membership as Christians is not in the New Israel as a Christian America but in the New Israel as a spiritual church.

The demands of the gospel impel us to strive for a nation characterized by justice and caring; yet such a nation cannot come into being unless it is grounded in and nurtured by piety—reverence for the living God. Piety is never the outcome of social planning, though it provides the fabric for social order. True religion is something interior, not something for exhibition. True religion cannot be enforced by civil law, but it ought to be respected by civil authority.

Richard Neuhaus has complained of a growing metaphysical vacuum in the public arena of life, which he describes as the "naked public square."[50] There is considerable merit in his charge, but the remedy is not a civil religion, much less a popular or folk religion. Instead, nations need to rediscover the culture-transcending vision of Jonathan Edwards, Abraham Lincoln, and Herman Melville, or in Britain of Wilberforce or Gladstone, a vision that keeps alive the infinite distance between the holy God and man the sinner.[51]

Our choice today is between a prophetic religion and a culture religion. The first is anchored in a holy God who infinitely transcends every cultural and religious form that testifies to him. The second absolutizes the cultural or mythical garb in which God supposedly meets us. A prophetic religion will keep a nation humble but at the same time hopeful, knowing that its destiny is in the hands of a living and sovereign God. A culture religion makes a nation vain and ultimately foolish, tempting it to yield to the deception that the gods are in its power and service.

We must steer clear of both a theocracy, where the church actively wields political power, and a rationalistic, egalitarian democracy, where the voice of the people is equated with the voice of God. Democracy in the Christian context is based on the axiom that all people are equal before God—all are created in his image and all have sinned and fallen short of his glory. Liberal democracy, on the other hand, which has its roots in the Enlightenment, is based on the infinite value of humanity. We need today a democracy anchored in theonomy, in which ultimate authority is assigned to the living God rather than to the nation or religious institution. A truly theonomous culture acknowledges that only the God revealed in the sacred history of the Bible is sovereign and that, above the civil law, there is a higher law to which all people are subject.

Yet we should keep in mind that a democratic society under the moral law is not yet the kingdom of Christ, nor is its justice to be confounded with the righteousness of the kingdom. At the same time, a just society is not possible apart from the providential and superintending work of God, which preserves people from their own worst natures and prepares them for faith in Jesus Christ. A righteous state is not possible apart from the redemptive work of God in Jesus Christ, which gives such a state a viable spiritual center and a righteous nucleus that will make it more sensitive and knowledgeable concerning the needs of the poor and oppressed in its midst.

Christians as citizens of the state are obliged to work for justice, meaning equity or fairness, as a penultimate ideal. As members of the Body of Christ, we are called to herald the coming of his kingdom, which is not of this world (John 18:36). Justice is made possible by God's universal grace; the righteousness of the kingdom is made possible by the grace revealed in Jesus Christ.

The Christian lives between the times, between the collapse of the kingdoms of this world and the dawning of the messianic kingdom of Christ. We can earnestly seek this kingdom, but we cannot create it. We can herald it, but not procure it. We can prepare the way for it by the preaching of the word in the hope that God may deign to work in conjunction with our broken and feeble witness.

Our divinely appointed task is to be witnesses and servants of the word. But it is also incumbent on us to be doers of justice, since our witness must be in deed as well as word (Rom. 15:18). Through our prayers and godly lives we can hasten the day of the Lord, though we cannot force the hand of God (cf. Acts 3:19-21; 2 Pet. 3:11-12). God may use our efforts to call attention to his kingdom, to deepen our yearning for his kingdom. But they are not the necessary means by which God brings in his kingdom.

The criterion for social justice is divine justification, the act of unmerited forgiveness made available to us in Jesus Christ. The evidence for our justification is a commitment to social justice.

The coming of the kingdom of God involves the elevation and transformation of human culture. But it also brings about the negation and purification of cultural achievements. Human culture is elevated through the conversion of the attitudes and expectations of its people. It is negated through a divine judgment on its idolatrous trust in its own accomplishments and panaceas.

Because our values and attitudes need to be constantly refashioned and overturned by divine grace, the kingdom of God might well be described as a "permanent revolution."[52] What is important to understand is that even the regenerate or the elect need to be converted and renewed by grace. Even their values and expectations are suspect, for they too are sinners, though the power of sin is, for the most part, checked in their lives.

The hope of the world rests on God as Civilizer, Reconciler, and Redeemer. God's work of civilizing presupposes and is carried forward on a new level by his work of reconciliation and redemption.

His civilizing work is done for the sake of his reconciling and redeeming work.

The perfect social order, the kingdom of God, should be welcomed as a new social order that displaces the old. By no means is it to be seen as the crystallization or maturation of the old. Nor does it build upon the old. At the same time, it fulfills the quest for meaning and purpose and the hope of justice and peace that pervade the old. What has genuine value is taken up into the kingdom of God and made to serve his glory.

The perfect social order is a goal, not a present possession. But it can be anticipated now in fellowships of outgoing love and missionary concern that exist within and apart from the institutional church. The *koinonia* is a visible and poignant sign of the *parousia,* when Christ shall come again to claim his own and to set up the kingdom, the civilization, that shall have no end.

Calling, Work, and Rest*

Paul Marshall

If we wish to address the problems and questions of the world, we must, among other things, see those problems and hear those questions. Consequently before trying to outline an evangelical view of work and rest I will sketch the history, nature, and problems of the dominant modern views of work. Then, while also trying to deal with the topic somewhat systematically, I will tailor my own constructive affirmations as a response to these problems.

There are many ways we could and should address the matter of work. We must pay attention to the problems of unemployment, including growing structural unemployment in the industrialized world, and the vast unemployment, or exploitation, in much of the two-thirds world; the often deadening monotony of labor; and the modern demeaning of voluntary and household work. Yet, despite these real and urgent needs, I wish here to address the apparently more abstract matter of a theology of work, of work in relation to God and to belief in God. I stress a theology of work for three reasons. One is the particular focus of this book. The second is that the basic issues in any area of life are always in some sense religious. The third is that, as my survey of modern views of work will reveal, work has a highly religious, indeed soteriological, significance in our secular society.

I will outline the modern view of work and trace its roots to the Bible and to Greek culture. I will then outline a theology of work, paying particular attention to the high value that the Scriptures put on work and to the relation of work and the "cultural mandate." I will then explore what this biblical view implies for the healing and restoration of work in our own day. After praising work, I go on to argue that work should not be overvalued. Our lives should include more

* I would like to thank Bill Dyrness, Douglas Kelly, Stephen Evans, and Lee Hardy for suggestions and comments on this paper.

than, and other than, work. In particular we must recover a genuine pattern of rest.

One final introductory word. I am not attempting to define work. I find available definitions unsatisfactory, and I believe that tight definition is not always important in essays of this kind. What I mean throughout is similar to the popular understanding of work; it includes such things as one's job, or repairing the faucets, or helping the kids with their homework, or making the bed. It would not include play, or sleeping, or eating, or relaxing, or contemplating, or certain types of prayer. What I mean by rest will become clearer as we go along.

MODERN VIEWS OF WORK

Introduction

Modern views of work can best be understood as a peculiar combination of two components. These components are, first, the ancient and, to a lesser degree, medieval disdain of work as the creature of necessity, a disdain that is coupled with a praise of leisure as the expression of a free, human existence; and, second, the Jewish, Christian, and Protestant acceptance of work as a calling from and a blessing by God that is itself a source of human fulfillment.

Work and Necessity

In Greek and Roman culture those who had leisure took a low view of work. Xenophon said that "the illiberal arts *(banausikai),* as they are called, are spoken against, and are, naturally enough, held in utter disdain in our states."[1] Aristotle thought that "leisure is a necessity, both for growth in goodness and for the pursuit of political activities." Later Cicero described the occupations of artisans as *sordidi.*[2]

Doing something with one's hands was not itself necessarily degrading. Homer's Odysseus could build his own boat and Penelope could spin and weave; Paris of Troy helped build his own house while Nausicäa did her brothers' laundry.[3] But what was important about this type of activity was that it was freely chosen; it was independent; it was free. What was objected to was work based on dependency and necessity—the absence of autonomy *(autarkeia).* Freedom was "status, personal inviolability, freedom of economic activity and right of unrestricted movement."[4] Slaves lacked all of these, and artisans lacked the last two for at least a limited time. Consequently, Aristotle thought that artisans were really part slaves, and therefore less than fully human.[5] These views permeated the language itself. The Greek word for leisure was *skole*, but there was no word for work. Work was "un-leisure," *ascolia*. Latin was similar in its use of *otium* and *negotium*.[6] Work, although necessary, was peripheral to real human concerns. Work formed only a base, a substratum, upon which genuine human activities could flourish.[7]

The views of work that developed in Christian culture after its first centuries tended to draw more heavily on these classical motifs than they did on specifically biblical teaching. Following Aristotle, Augustine distinguished between an "active life" *(vita activa)* and a "contemplative life" *(vita contemplativa)*. The *vita activa* took in almost every kind of work, including that of studying, preaching, and teaching, while the *vita contemplativa* was meditation upon God and his truth. Both kinds of life were good, but the contemplative life was better: "the one life is loved, the other endured." "The obligations of charity make us undertake righteous business *[negotium]*" but "If no one lays this burden upon us, we should give ourselves up to leisure *[otium]*, to the perception and contemplation of truth."[8] Similarly for Thomas, the *vita contemplativa* was "oriented to the eternal" whereas the *vita activa* existed only because of the "necessities of the present life." The active life was connected to needs of the human body shared with animals. While both lives had their place, the active life was bound by necessity; only the contemplative life was truly free. In short, "the life of contemplation" was "simply better than the life of action."[9]

This sort of distinction, focused around a polarity of freedom and necessity, formed the basic pattern of medieval Christianity. It resulted in a view according to which the only true Christian calling, or, at least, the highest calling, was a priestly or monastic one. In fact the terms *calling* and *vocation* came to be used to refer only to such pursuits. A calling was something different from everyday work.[10]

Work and Calling

The other principal component of modern views of work is the emphasis of the Protestant Reformers on calling. Their views, I believe, were largely accurate portrayals of biblical teaching. Nevertheless at this juncture I will not try to outline a biblical view but only treat Protestantism as a historically significant influence on the present.

Almost without exception the Reformers rejected the view that the *vita contemplativa* was the more truly Christian life. They taught that work as well as leisure and contemplation was a good gift of God. Almost without exception they maintained that all forms of work were of equal worth in the sight of God. One of the articles of heresy for which William Tyndale was arraigned was his conviction that "there is no work better than another to please God; to pour water, to wash dishes, to be a souter [cobbler], or an apostle, all is one; to wash dishes and to preach is all one, as touching the deed, to please God."[11] Luther taught that God in his providence had put each person in their place in society to do the work of that place:

> If you are a manual laborer, you find that the Bible has been put into your workshop, into your hand, into your heart. It teaches and preaches how you should treat your neighbour. . . . Just look at your tools . . . at your needle and thimble, your beer barrel, your goods, your scales or yardstick or measure. . . . You have as many preachers as you have transactions, goods, tools and other equipment in your house and home.

Even Adam had "work to do, that is . . . plant the garden, cultivate and look after it." "There is therefore nothing which is so bodily, carnal and external that it does not become spiritual when it is done in the Word of God and faith."[12]

Calvin was perhaps the strongest in his exhortations on work. Above all, he stressed *useful* work; his God was "not such as is imagined by the Sophists, vain, idle and almost asleep, but vigilant, efficacious, operative, and engaged in continual action." In his commentary on the parable of the talents (Luke 19:11-27) Calvin related the talents to everyday work and calling, the particular example he considered being trading *(negotiara)*. He stressed the concrete nature of these gifts and, in so doing, shaped the modern meaning of the words *talent* and *talented*. André Biéler described his position thus:

> Companionship is completed in work and in the interplay of economic exchanges. Human fellowship is realized in relationships which flow from the division of labour wherein each person has been called of God to a particular and partial work which complements the work of others. The mutual exchange of goods and services is the concrete sign of the profound solidarity which unites humanity.[13]

Work and Capitalism

Max Weber emphasized that "only in the Protestant ethic of vocation does the world, despite all its creaturely imperfections, possess unique and religious significance as the object through which one fulfills his duties by rational behavior according to the will of an absolutely transcendental God."[14] Weber also emphasized that Protestantism, especially Calvinism, "caused very specific psychological premia to be placed on the ascetic regulation of life."[15] The result was an "innerworldly asceticism" that created a *psychological* disposition toward continual, rational, restless labor. This disposition continued and provided an impetus for the "spirit of capitalism" even after the religious spirit and teaching that had given birth to it had passed away.[16] Neither Weber's nor any other writings clearly show how Protestantism actually brought about such a disposition. Nonetheless, the relation that he tried to describe is a real one: in some manner Protestantism did indeed create "the religious motivations for seeking salvation primarily through immersion in one's worldly vocation."[17]

In the development of capitalism and a market economy this stress on work and calling continued. But in the process it became focused on production and money. Benjamin Franklin's declaration that "time is money" captured the heart of this attitude. Work came to mean a job and unpaid work was downgraded. "Real" work was work that was paid. Activities that may have pleased the Puritans, such as Bible study or visiting the sick, were no longer thought of as work, but as "free time" activities. What women did in the home was no longer work: work became the province of men. The economists accepted and promoted this categorization, and proceeded to define work as a disutility that was done only for external reward. Other activities, those concerned with creating what Marx calls "use-values," disappeared from their purview.

With the development of capitalism work devoted to the production of commodities has become the central activity of human life. The formation of a labor theory of value shows this most clearly. This theory appeared in Locke, was refined by Adam Smith and David Ricardo, and reached its apogee in Marx. According to the theory, what is of value in human life is ascribed to work. More work is required to create a more valuable life. The transformation of nature through work becomes the key to a more human future.[18] The result of this process is a society focused on, even obsessed with, work.

A focus on the virtues and promise of work was not restricted to Victorian capitalists. The same theme was propounded by the radical opposition to capitalism of the philanthropist Robert Owen as well as Saint-Simon, Comte, Proudhon, and Marx.[19] Marx was most emphatic on this point. For him labor constituted history: *"The whole of what is called world history* is nothing but the creation of man by human labour, and the emergence of nature for man."[20] But Marx was also highly critical of labor, and not just labor under capitalism: "Labour itself, not only in present conditions but universally in so far as its purpose is merely the increase of wealth, is harmful and deleterious."[21]

The reason Marx was so critical of necessary labor and yet also sang its praises was, of course, because he believed that necessary labor would lead to its own transcendence. The labor that builds up capital is self-alienation, but this self-alienation also provides the basis for the freedom of communism. Marx condemns the capitalist, but he also praises him highly as the one who "forces the development of the productive powers of society and creates those material conditions which alone can form the real basis of a higher form of society, a society in which the full and free development of every individual forms the ruling principle."[22]

Marx here expressed in radical form the new work ethic shaped by capitalism. Through continual, rational, productive labor the world can be transformed. Labor is the key to history, the key to a new society, a new nature, and a new man. Through the products of work we will achieve freedom—our core and our salvation. It is no longer a Protestant or Christian salvation, but it is a salvation nonetheless.

Work and Salvation

Our view of work now, a view common to the right and the left, is composed of elements from both our Greek-Roman-medieval and our Judeo-Christian-Protestant backgrounds as these elements have been combined in the specifically modern project of transforming nature. As with Greek thought we view work in terms of a polarity between necessity and freedom, but now we try to ascend from necessity to freedom by means of our work. This ascent is no longer envisioned as merely a personal matter, a dialectic of our own work and rest. It is now a major social project—to take humankind from the realm of necessity and bring it into the realm of freedom. We will achieve our salvation within history by producing a realm of universal freedom.

Marx is clear on this point. In his writing on "Alienated Labour" he argues that this kind of work is unfree, based on necessity, and on a par with the activity of animals. In opposition he proposes that man's essential activity is consciously directed and truly produced because the producer is free from physical need. This much could have been a gloss on Aristotle, who said about the same thing. But Marx departs from Aristotle by basing these two lives no longer on a vision of nature but rather on a vision of history. Instead of a vertical hierarchy of human lives, he posits a historical flow of lives. He moves from "above" to "ahead." Humankind now lives in the realm of necessity under capitalism and, more broadly, the technical division of labor. In the *future*, growing beyond this necessity, the true life of freedom can begin. In *Capital,* sounding somewhat like Augustine, Marx writes:

> The realm of freedom actually begins only where labour which is determined by necessity and mundane considerations ceases; thus in the very nature of things it lies beyond the sphere of actual material production. . . . This realm . . . still remains a realm of necessity. Beyond it begins . . . the true realm of freedom, which . . . can blossom forth only with this realm of necessity as its basis.[23]

Nor is such a dream confined to the more eschatological moments of Marxism, for it is the capitalist dream as well. In his "Economic Prospects for our Grandchildren" John Maynard Keynes flatly contradicts the Sermon on the Mount in articulating the same future hope for capitalism:

> We shall once more value ends above means and prefer the good to the useful. We shall honour . . . the lilies of the field who toil not, neither do they spin.
>
> But beware! The time for all this is not yet. For at least another hundred years we must pretend to ourselves and to every one that fair is foul and foul is fair; for foul is useful and fair is not. Avarice and usury and precaution must be our gods for a little longer still. For only they can lead us out of the tunnel of economic necessity into daylight.[24]

Our society lives with a relentlessly future orientation. Work, with science and technology as its handmaidens, will usher us into a new world of consumption, leisure, and freedom. Meanwhile, we alternately praise work for the future it will bring or condemn it for the pain it causes us in the meantime. But, either way, work is essential to our understanding of the meaning of life. The project we are engaged in, the society we live in, is focused on and centered around work. Our hope is a hope in work. Work defines our ultimate concern. And that is why we must address work in a fundamentally religious way.

A THEOLOGY OF WORK AND REST

The Cultural Mandate

On making the first man and woman God blesses them and, as part of this blessing, tells them to "be fruitful and multiply, and fill the earth and subdue it" (Gen. 1:28). This "cultural mandate" includes far more than is usually described as work, but the terms of that mandate must define our calling to work.

This command of God to the first man and woman, and through them to all humanity, comes as the culmination of the story of the creation of the heavens and the earth.[25] God's acts on the sixth day are not just the last items on the list, they are the *climax* of the story. The mandate shows God's *purpose* in creating the man and woman in and on the earth. Not only the timing but also the way that God creates the man and the woman is significant. On the sixth day we are told, for the first time, of God planning (v. 26), and then carrying out the plan (v. 28). The plan is to make humankind "to be our image and to have dominion." Thus "having dominion" is itself part of God's creative act. The "cultural mandate" is part of God's plan of world creation. Human molding of the earth is the continuation of God's creative acts.[26]

Even the word *mandate* is something of a misnomer, for the emphasis at this point of Genesis is on the *creation* of humankind as the stewards of the earth. It is not as though humankind were made and then given instructions. Rather God *made humankind* in order to fill and care for the earth: it is how and why we were made, it is built into who we are. If we do not take up the care of the earth as service to the Lord, then we defy the very purpose for which we have been created.

This mandate also shows something of what it means that we are made "in the image" of God. To be in the image of God is to be like God in some way. There are several expressions of this image—the New Testament mentions righteousness, holiness, and knowledge. In Genesis the image seems specifically to refer to lordship and creation, to having dominion over the world and being creative in it. We are those who are called to image God by our activities in shaping, forming, and caring for God's creation.

Genesis goes on to describe how humankind responds to the mandate and thereby manifests the image of God. We are told of the fall (3:6), casting out from Eden (3:23), murder (4:8), the beginning of cities (4:17), the development of herding and nomadic life (4:20), music (4:21), metalworking (4:22), and so forth. The structure of the earliest chapters of Genesis is centered around an account of human beings as the *shapers of history:* they tell us what those who have been called to fill and subdue the earth actually have done in response to their mandate, whether sinfully, as with Cain, or obediently, as with Noah.

Despite the catastrophic effects of sin, the fall did not suspend the cultural mandate. Adam still works the ground, Eve still brings forth the generations. Even after God drowns the earth and saves a remnant with Noah, he renews the mandate (Gen. 9:7). In fact humankind could not cease trying to fulfill this task, even in a perverted way, for that is how God made us. We cannot even survive if we do not fulfill it. Consequently with Noah the cycle of human culture begins once more and immediately we read that "Noah was the first tiller of the soil" (9:20) and that from his children "the whole earth was peopled" (9:19).

In Jesus Christ this mandate is renewed, is being redeemed, and will be perfected. After proclaiming that we are heirs of God (Rom. 8:15-17), Paul rushed on to show the full significance of this restoration—that it is a promise to the creation itself: "the creation waits with eager longing . . . the creation was subjected to futility . . . the creation itself will be set free" (Rom. 8:19-20). God remembers the covenant with the creation (Gen. 9:8-11). The creation will be set free just as, and because, the children of God are set free.

The same theme is present in Revelation. John writes "And I saw the holy city, new Jerusalem, coming down out of heaven from God, prepared as a bride adorned for her husband" (Rev. 21:2). Here John portrays the reconciliation of God with God's people as taking place no longer in a garden, as in Paradise at the beginning, but in a city, the creation of human culture. What had been begun in sin by Cain and at Babel is here portrayed in its perfection. John also sees the bride, not naked, but "richly adorned for her husband." Whereas Adam and Eve clothed themselves with fig leaves because of shame resulting from their sin, the appearance of the bride shows clothing perfected in and presented to Jesus Christ. Human stewardship of the earth is made perfect at the coming of Christ. The flow of human history, the outworking of God's act of creation, is redeemed and is taken up in the creation of the new heavens and earth. "The kingdom of the world has become the kingdom of our Lord and of his Christ" (Rev. 11:15).[27]

Work

The importance of the cultural mandate shows the importance of the work to which humans are called as stewards of the earth. The Scriptures are full of praise for the work of human hands, hearts, and minds. Even God is described by analogy to human work, as the one who makes, forms, builds, and plants (Gen. 2:4, 7, 8, 19, 23). Work skills are described as gifts of God: "the Lord has called Bezalel . . . and he has filled him with the Spirit of God, with ability, with intelligence, with all knowledge and with all craftsmanship" (Exod. 35:30-32; see also Pss. 65:9-13; 104:22-24; Gen. 10:8-9).

Nor is this a theme that diminishes in the New Testament. Here we find Jesus immersed in the life and problems of working people. The apostles were mainly of humble background and sometimes returned to their work after being called by him. Jesus was a carpenter for all but the last few years of his life. His parables refer to sowers (Matt. 13:3), vineyard laborers (Matt. 13:30), harvesters (John 4:35), house building (Matt. 7:24), swine tending (Luke 15:11), and women sweeping house (Luke 15:8).[28]

Paul criticized idleness and exhorted Christians to work (2 Thess. 3:6).[29] He made no distinction between physical and spiritual work and he used the same terms to refer to both the manual labor by which he earned a living and also his apostolic service (1 Cor. 4:12; 15:10; 16:16; Eph. 4:28; Rom. 10:12; Gal. 4:11; Phil. 2:16; Col. 1:29; 1 Thess. 5:12). Often it is quite difficult to know to which he was referring, or whether he himself was making such a distinction. For Paul, all types of work originate in faith and are service to God. When he outlines the "new nature . . . created after the likeness of God," he urges "doing honest work with his hands." The new creature, restored in Christ, in God's image, is to work in God's world to supply the needs of others and shape the development of human life (Eph. 4:17-32, esp. v. 28; 2 Cor. 11:9; 12:13; 1 Thess. 4:9-12; 2 Thess. 3:8; Acts 20:35).

Paul himself worked with his hands so as not to be a burden to the church; he worked to support others and he urged this practice on other Christians.[30] His advice to slaves, that they should work willingly as slaves of Christ, illustrates the same theme. It shows that he regarded even slave labor as service to the Lord on a par with his own work. He summarized his position in the remarkable assertion that "there is neither . . . slave nor free . . . you are all one in Christ Jesus" (Eph. 6:6-7; Gal. 3:28). Similarly, his declaration "if anyone does not work, let him not eat" was not an expression of callousness toward those who could not support themselves—his program for deacons, collections on behalf of the poor, and sharing of goods show that this was not the case. Rather, Paul was concerned not with those who could not find work but with those who refused to share the burdens of their fellows. He was asserting that a life of leisure, religious contemplation, or eschatological abdication was a deficient life—that all members of the church should work (2 Thess. 3:10). Clearly this view was in radical opposition to the attitudes of Hellenistic culture. Paul did not regard religion as a "spiritual" activity separate from work. He regarded all aspects of life as equally religious, as equally noble, when done in loving service to God.

Even the New Heavens and the New Earth will include work. Isaiah prophesies that

> They shall build houses and inhabit them;
> they shall plant vineyards and eat their fruit.
> They shall not build and another inhabit;
> they shall not plant and another eat;
> for like the days of a tree shall the days of my people be,
> and my chosen shall long enjoy the work of their hands.

> Isa. 65:21-22[31]

When we read that "they will beat their swords into ploughshares and their spears into pruning hooks" (Mic. 4:35), we should remember not only the destruction of implements for war but also the (new) creation of implements for work.

In short, human beings are made, *inter alia,* as workers: this is part of what it means to be created in the image of God. We are called to work, and we are to find fulfillment in our working. Work has fallen under the curse of sin and so is torn with pain and suffering. But the curse is not the core of work: it is a cancer upon it. Work can be and will be fully redeemed as in the new creation it becomes an authentically free human action.

The Restoration of Work

The biblical teaching on work has three immediate implications. First it shows that all human activities are equally God-given, are equally religious. No one type of human activity can claim religious priority over another. Therefore we must echo Tyndale's declaration that "to wash dishes and to preach is all one, as touching the deed, to please

God" and we must reject the semi-Gnosticism that has pervaded much of the Christian church, and especially its evangelical wing. Human beings are not apprentice angels better suited to and waiting for an existence on another spiritual plane. We are those whom God has made to tend the earth and serve one another through work. While sin has caused and will cause pain and frustration, work has not lost its character as service to Creator and creature.

Second, work must not be regarded as the antithesis of human fulfillment. We are not creatures destined for freedom who are now trapped in an alienated realm of necessity.[32] We are called to manifest the image of God and, hence, to be free precisely *in and through* our work, in and through the necessities of life. This emphasis opposes the drift of our society where, while certain professions are thought to be fulfilling, work is generally treated as what economists call a "disutility," something to be minimized. It can fairly be said that the modern world underestimates economic life. As Sander Griffioen notes, the modern world treats material production as "a condition for the development of the individual, rather than being part of this development."[33] Consequently, for Marx, as for others, "the shortening of the workday" and never good work itself is portrayed as the entrance to the "realm of freedom."[34] Pope John Paul II well expresses a Christian response when he emphasizes that work is essential for any genuine subjective human development.

> For when a man works he not only alters things and society, he develops himself as well. He learns much, he cultivates his resources, he goes outside of himself and beyond himself. Rightly understood, this kind of growth is of greater value than any external riches which can be garnered.[35]

Third, work is the act of a creature made in the image of God. Consequently work should be an action of responsibility carried out by a free image-bearer. This too can be contrasted with dominant social patterns, for an understanding of work as an activity reflecting the *imago dei* necessarily brings to the fore the theme of human responsibility as well as the theme of human freedom. We must concentrate not on wages as a "compensation" for work (though all people have a right to be sustained in and through their work) but on making work genuinely responsible. As R. H. Tawney emphasizes, this is necessary for any just economic order:

> Both the existing economic order, and too many of the projects advanced for reconstructing it, break down through their neglect of the

truism that, since even quite common men have souls, no increase in material wealth will compensate them for arrangements which insult their self-respect and impair their freedom.[36]

The development of such responsibility has a subjective side that requires a renewed sense of vocation and willingness to rejoice in servanthood. But we must beware of portraying the relationship of work and responsibility only as a question of personal renewal. Our work does not depend merely on our own motivations: it depends also on the attitudes, motivation, and actions of others, especially those who came before us and those who have power over us. Such attitudes have *already* been built into our property relations, into the factories and workplaces we have designed, the types of products we manufacture, the types of machines we work with, and the rhythm and pace of our work itself.

Individuals in an auto factory in Detroit conceivably can have a strong sense of their vocation to make good, relatively cheap cars that people will be happy to drive. But it is almost impossible to maintain such a sense if all you do is endlessly repeat the same mechanical action on an assembly line amid howling noise. In fact, in this type of situation a sense of vocation may be out of place because it is out of touch with reality. You are not being treated as a responsible person, an image-bearer of God. You are not being allowed to serve your neighbor. Work has ceased to be a calling and has become a pain, and money is the compensation for it.

We must restructure work so that it can honestly be a service and calling. We need to design workplaces and corporate structures so that we both exercise genuine responsibility and are treated as God's image-bearers. This means a concentration on good work and a rejection of the notion that "labor" and the worker are commodities to be bought and sold in a "labor" market. Those who work in an enterprise are to be responsible for it and need authority commensurate with that responsibility.[37]

The Limits of Work

I have stressed the biblical teaching on the goodness and the redemption of work. But, given the modern secular stress on the salvific nature of work, we must also stress that work is not the means of salvation. Work is not the mediation between God and humankind, it cannot eradicate sin, it cannot produce a new creation. We cannot achieve happiness and security through the control of our human and nonhuman environments.

Nor can we identify work as the totality of our calling. When Paul tells the Corinthians to "abide in the calling in which [they] were called" (1 Cor. 7:20), he tells them that regardless of their state in life, slave or free, they are to remain in their calling as Christians. He treats even slavery as comparatively unimportant. Compared to this high calling, our actual situation in life is secondary.[38] We are called to be and to live as Christians: work is only one part of this.

The Scriptures teach that salvation is by grace; it is the gift of God, not the result of labor. The most radical words we can say to our technological society are, contra Keynes:

> "Do not be anxious about your life, what you shall eat or what you shall drink. . . . Consider the lilies of the field, how they grow; they neither toil nor spin. . . . But if God so clothes the grass of the field, which today is alive and tomorrow is thrown into the oven, will he not much more clothe you, O men of little faith?" (Matt. 6:25-30; cf. Josh. 24:2-13; Deut. 8:11-20; Luke 12:13-32)

The healing of our lives is a gift of God to those who trust God and keep the commandments.

The Scriptures couple their rejection of salvation by works with a denunciation of overweening pride in work. The sin of Adam and Eve, that they wished to be gods and no longer human beings, was replayed in the construction of the tower of Babel "with its top in the heavens." Babel symbolizes a lust for power and greatness that rejects God's limits and so drives people apart from one another. Isaiah repeats this theme:

> For the Lord of hosts has a day
> > against all that is proud and lofty,
> > against all that is lifted up and high;
> . . . against every high tower,
> > and against every fortified wall. . . .
> And the haughtiness of man shall be humbled,
> > and the pride of men shall be brought low;
> > and the Lord alone will be exalted in that day.

> > > > > > Isa. 2:12-17

Such pride becomes idolatry, the worship of something within creation, particularly the worship of the work of our hands—"the workman trusts in his own creation when he makes dumb idols."

(Hab. 2:18-19).[39] As Paul warned the men of Athens, God is not "like gold, or silver, or stone, a representation by the art and imagination of man" (Acts 17:29; see also Rom. 1:24). We, in turn, start to become like our idols. As the Psalmist says:

> The idols of the nations are silver and gold,
> the work of men's hands.
> They have mouths, but they speak not,
> they have eyes, but they see not,
> they have ears, but they hear not,
> nor is there any breath in their mouths.
> *Those that trust in them are like them!*
> *Yea, every one who trusts in them.*
>
> Ps. 135:15-18

If we trust the work of our hands, then we will be controlled and shaped by that work: we will be remade in its image. Indeed, this process takes place in our world. As J. K. Galbraith has pointed out:

> If we continue to believe that the goals of the industrial system—the expansion of output, the companion increase in consumption, techno-logical advance, the public images that sustain it—are coordinate with life, then all of our lives will be in the service of these goals. What is consistent with these ends we shall have or be allowed; all else will be off limits. Our wants will be managed in accordance with the needs of the industrial system; the policies of the state will be subject to simi-lar influence; education will be adapted to industrial need; the disci-plines required by the industrial system will be the conventional morality of the community. All other goals will be made to seem pre-cious, unimportant or antisocial.[40]

This is very much the situation of our societies. It is a situation where "the economy" is hallowed. It is a situation where unemployment has the overtones of excommunication. It is a situation of captivity to idols.

Because we must worship God rather than idols, we must find our true end in what God has given, not in what we can achieve.[41] Consequently we must continually be aware of the limits of human achievement. We remain creatures, and we cannot become gods either through our work or through anything else.

The limits on our work and on our achievement arise from two sources—the nature of created reality, and the consequences of sin. We must be aware of both of these. And we must also distinguish them carefully lest we identify creation and sin and, in consequence, either accept the triumph of sin by identifying our present broken situation with the will of God, or deny our status as creatures by attempting a Promethean struggle to escape our creaturehood.

Because of who we are in the creation, we will always need to work, our work will always present challenges, and it will always call us to responsibility. This necessity will remain a necessity; neither diligent labor, advanced technology, radical insight, fervent repentance, nor political revolution will overcome it.[42] An attempt to do away with such limits is hubris, a replay of Babel.

But we must also emphasize that, because of sin, the good things that God has given in the creation have become distorted. Work has become toil, it is enmeshed in pain and suffering, it is long, and it can reduce us to automatons, or to scarecrows, or kill us. We are called to fight against these evil consequences, just as we, because of Christ's victory, are called to fight against all the effects of sin. Though pain in work will not finally disappear until the Lord's return we can never accept it passively: we are called continually to the struggle to transform the work of all human creatures into secure, free, and joyful service.

Rest

As creatures made in the image of God we are called to do many things other than work. We are called to be Christianly responsible in all our relationships: we are called to be good husbands, wives, parents, children, neighbors, friends, and citizens. Our mandate and calling is to image God in every dimension of our existence—including worship, intimacy, play, and rest. While the *vita contemplativa* is not a higher kind of life, it too is an essential part of our life. Our work has, per se, no prior claim to our time. As Thomas Aquinas says, "the essence of virtue consists in the good rather than in the difficult."[43]

One part of our calling is the calling to rest. Even God rested after creating the world. The commandment not to labor on the Sabbath carries as much weight as the commandments not to kill or steal. During the time in the wilderness and also in the exile Israel was promised rest in the land (Deut. 3:20; Jer. 46:27), a rest that was also a respite from their enemies (Deut. 3:10; 2 Sam. 7:11). Israel's life was ordained as a rhythm of work and rest. Each seventh day, each seventh year, and each seventh of seven years was a Sabbath for people, for animals, and for the land itself.

This cycle of work and rest was intimately tied to Israel's trust in God. If Israel rested in the seventh year, it needed to trust God's promise that the land would produce a surplus to see them through (Lev. 25:18-24). In the fiftieth year, the year of Jubilee, Israel's faith was tested even more. As they celebrated the Day of Atonement they needed to put aside the work of their hands for two years: they would live off the gifts of God (Lev. 25:8-12). In a similar vein the New Testament often pictures salvation as entering into rest (Hebrews 3–4). And Jesus promised rest to those who came to him.

This rest is more than recuperation from and preparation for work. It is a God-given human response in its own right. "It is not simply the result of external factors, it is not the inevitable result of spare time, a holiday, a week-end or a vacation. It is . . . a condition of the soul."[44] Indeed, rest and work may involve similar activities, but activities done in a different spirit. For me reading is a part of work and a part of rest. Resting is tied to faith—which is one reason why most of us avoid rest. It is also why medieval Christendom pictured it as a higher way. The Scriptures frequently relate lack of rest to unbelief (Ps. 95:8-11; Heb. 3:7–4:10).

When we rest we acknowledge that all our striving will, of itself, do nothing. It means letting the world pass us by for a time. Genuine rest requires acknowledgment that God, and our brothers and sisters, can survive without us. It requires a recognition of our own insufficiency and a handing over of responsibility. It is a real surrender to the ways of God. It is a moment of celebration when we acknowledge that blessing comes only from the hand of God. This is why rest requires faith. It is also why salvation can be pictured as rest. When we rest we accept God's grace: we do not seek to earn, we receive; we do not justify, we are justified.

This biblical picture can be contrasted with the industrialized world's drive to escape from work. We manufacture distractions and entertainments, we live for Friday and Saturday nights, we count days to vacations. These activities try to negate work and, hence, are controlled by it. Our most characteristic "leisure activity" is consumption, an activity that, through the manufacture of "life-styles," has itself become more hectic and more akin to work. The shortening of the working day has not produced what Marx hoped for, a nation of fishers and critics, a flowering of culture; it has produced a nation of consumers.[45]

The spare time of the *animal laborans* is never spent in anything but consumption, and the more time left to him, the greedier and more craving his appetites. That these appetites become more sophisticated, so that consumption is no longer restricted to the necessities but, on the contrary, mainly concentrates on the superfluities of life, does not change the character of this society. The outcome is what is euphemistically called mass culture.[46]

Our society finds itself ever more distant from rest. Its manufactured "holidays" (including "Labor Day") are becoming mere excuses for novel forms of consumption. The notion of a Sabbath rest, or even of Sunday, is shouldered aside not only as an affront to the secular belief that God is irrelevant to social life, but also, in what amounts to perhaps the same thing, as an impertinent obstruction to the voracious mores of the market.

It is possible to suggest several practical steps for the restoration of rest, but here we will merely point out that genuine rest can never rest on a skill or technique, it must flow from living faith in a Savior, the One who takes up our burdens.

CLOSING

I have tried to outline some theological reflections relevant to work and rest, and to relate these reflections to the suffering and problems of the modern world, especially the industrialized world. I have emphasized that our calling embraces a rhythm of both work and rest. In doing this I have not really addressed the question of how we should divide time between them, or how we decide (if we are in a position to decide) between different types and amounts of work.

It is certainly true that our particular situation will determine a large part of the proper response we give to these questions. Yet even beyond this situatedness, I would like to stress that biblical teaching is not really designed to answer these types of questions.

It does not tell us how many hours of work or rest, or how hard, or at what. Certainly it is possible with responsibility to work sixteen hours a day on a project that must be done or for only a few hours in order to free up time for reflection; to work for a high salary in order to give away to those who need money, or to work at subsistence because the work itself needs doing; to devote most of our time to a paying job, or else to voluntary work, or the church, or the family; to excel in a profession, or to break out of a profession's self-interest and arrogance (Bernard Shaw, remember, once described a profession as "a conspiracy against the laity"): to search for work that is genuinely fulfilling and responsible, or to take up work that is personally degrading but helps others, or to take anything that will bring the money in; to work in an existing organization, or to start a new one.

This does not mean that our choices, if we have choices, are only relative or situational. Rather, it means that our direction is not toward principles or a rule, but toward an honest response of faith shaped by a wise discerning of the spirits of the age. The Bible does not, in the first place, give us a theory of work, or an ethics of work, or a systematic theology of work. What the Bible says about work it says in relation to Jesus Christ; what we do is in relation to him, what he has done and what he will do. The Scriptures point us to Jesus Christ with the promise that through him we can be reconciled to God. And so we can work and rest. The integration point of work and rest is Jesus Christ, who says "Come to me, all who labor, and I will give you rest. Take my yoke upon you. . . ."

Toward an Evangelical Theology of Poverty

Richard J. Mouw

In the preface to his book *God So Loved the Third World,* evangelical theologian Thomas D. Hanks reports that when he set out in 1969 to prepare a lecture about the biblical teaching on poverty, he searched in vain through the existing technical literature for serious treatments of the topic. A person setting out on a similar assignment today is likely to have a very different problem: we have been blessed in recent years with—as it were—an embarrassment of riches on this topic. Hanks's own book contains, for example, an extensive and highly nuanced study of biblical terminology relating to the nations of poverty and oppression.

In addition to the technical exegetical materials produced in recent years, a large body of related writings has appeared on the scene. Some of this can also properly be considered technical—such as important works in biblical theology and ethics and Christian economic and political analysis. In addition are more popular books and articles that have, in some cases, reached a very large Christian audience.

It is possible to discern, in this flurry of scholarly and practical Christian interest in biblical economic-political thought, a shift in where the "action" is happening on the ecumenical spectrum. Until rather recently, most North American thinking in the area of Christian "social ethics" occurred—or at least has been widely perceived as occurring—primarily among mainline "liberal" Protestants. But significant changes have now taken place. While mainline Protestant scholars have not been completely absent from recent social-ethical discussions, they have had to yield their privileged position to Roman Catholic and evangelical scholars and activists. Thus, *Sojourners* magazine has come to be taken at least as seriously as its liberal Protestant counterparts, and the political and economic deliverances of Roman Catholic bishops are considered much more significant than those of the National Council of Churches. An important sign of change can be seen in the fact that one of the most widely discussed books about biblical teachings concerning poverty, Ronald J. Sider's *Rich Christians in an Age of Hunger,* was originally published jointly by an evangelical and a Roman Catholic publisher. In short, in both the practical realm (as is evidenced in the sorts of religion-and-politics disputes that have emerged during recent political campaigns in the United States) and in scholarly discussions, Roman Catholic and evangelical perspectives have moved to center stage—even to the point, as some would have it, of nudging the mainline Protestants off to the wings.

Thus, there can be no doubt that the influence of Roman Catholicism is being strongly felt these days in dealing with social-ethical matters—more specifically, in formulating an understanding of the biblical address regarding the poor and the oppressed. The strong impact of Latin American liberation theology on recent North American theological discussion has made Roman Catholic concerns and themes very visible—a visibility that has been reinforced by the increasingly activist role of the North American Roman Catholic hierarchy with regard to questions of public policy.

Nor can there be any real doubt about the growing influence of evangelical thought in this area of concern. If, then, it is the case that Roman Catholics and evangelical Protestants have assumed a prominent place—or as some would have it, *the* prominent place—in present-day social-ethical discussion in North America, this state of affairs presents us with some important opportunities. Not the least of these has to do with the continuing need for serious Roman Catholic–evangelical dialogue. There are many very important items on the agenda for this dialogue. Not all of these matters, of course, relate directly to questions about how the Christian community is to carry out its extensive obligations with regard to a mission of peace and justice. But a focus on these matters—in which Roman Catholics and evangelicals talk together about how they may better join in a common witness to the full power of the gospel of Jesus Christ—is certainly an important item for joint exploration.

The significance of such a North American dialogue is heightened when we turn to a consideration of the community of poor in the larger world—those people who are most likely to be affected by the North American discussions. To put it bluntly: there are very few Protestant liberals among the poor and the oppressed of the earth. If the Christian poor of the Third World were to engage in theological discussion of the doctrinal differences that exist among them, that exchange would be, in effect, a Roman Catholic–evangelical dialogue. Roman Catholic and evangelical Christians in North America have an obligation to help to clarify the issues as they arise (or where they lurk just beneath the surface) at the front lines of social-ethical concern.

But it is not merely a recognition of the need for this kind of ecumenical dialogue that should compel us as evangelicals to engage in extensive discussion of our obligations to the poor and the oppressed. Quite apart from how we come off in discussion with others, evangelical Christians have to engage in self-correcting thought and action of these matters. Evangelical shortcomings in this area during the twentieth century have been significant.

To be sure, the failings have not been as significant as is often claimed. It has become common practice in the popular press, and even in seemingly more sophisticated quarters, to tell a story about a North American evangelical community with forty to fifty million members that has only recently begun to awaken to the need for "social action"; having been thus aroused, the narrative continues, this sleeping giant has developed both right-wing and left-wing tendencies, thus running the risk of being torn apart by strong internal tensions.

Such a story distorts the facts. If the awakened giant is as large as the commentators claim—and the forty- to fifty-million figure seems necessary to make the tale worth telling—then the evangelical community has not completely ignored the poor and the oppressed of North America in past decades, simply because of the fact that many evangelicals themselves have been numbered among the poor and the oppressed. The expansive assessment of the size of North American evangelicalism includes, for example, millions of members of black churches, many of whom are desperately poor, as well as persons from other low-income groups.

Furthermore, this way of counting also includes evangelical churches and organizations—such as the Salvation Army and various Mennonite and Brethren groups—that have consistently placed a strong emphasis on serving the needy. Indeed, even the record of those white middle-class Christians who seem to come most quickly to many minds when the word "evangelical" is mentioned—even their record is not as consistently bad as many of the present-day narrations imply. This history of "rescue missions" in twentieth-century North America, for example, displays examples of outstanding evangelical commitments to the poor and downtrodden. And even given many of the mistaken attitudes and strategies that shaped the evangelical pursuit of missionary activity, there can be no questioning of the fact that many families involved in the work of "faith missions" manifested a firm commitment to identify with the poor and the oppressed—a commitment that required of them the kind of voluntary poverty that would stir the heart of the most dedicated follower of St. Francis.

But for all of that, evangelicals have much to do by way of self-correction with respect to their understanding of, and commitment to, the biblical message of Good News to the poor. Part of this self-correction must be theological in nature, since the evangelical community does not presently have a widely accepted, coherent, biblically faithful, theological understanding of this important dimension of the gospel. For a people who speak much about the importance of "sound theology" this is an important defect.

A theology of poverty can serve at least two important functions. For those evangelical Christians who ignore the concerns of the poor and the oppressed, theological reflection on this topic can provide the means for demonstrating the link between a concern for the needs of the destitute and those matters of theological emphasis already taken for granted in the evangelical community. But perhaps more important, a theological understanding of this topic can provide those who are already attending to the issues with a coherent account of the variety of biblical data on the subject.

And there is indeed a variety—enough so, at least, for Christians with very different attitudes toward the poor to be able to sustain their perspectives by the selective citation of favorite biblical passages. Thus, for some people, the words of the Psalmist have a very special status in formulating the Bible's perspective on poverty: "I have not seen the righteous forsaken or his children begging bread" (Ps. 37:25); on this reading those who are poor would do well to heed the warning of Israel's sages:

> How long will you lie there, O sluggard?
> When will you arise from your sleep?
> A little sleep, a little slumber,
> a little folding of the hands to rest,
> and poverty will come upon you like a vagabond,
> and want like an armed man.
>
> Prov. 6:9-11

For others, the supreme assignment of the Christian life is to prepare for the day when the divine King will say to his servants: "As you did it to one of the least of these my brethren, you did it to me" (Matt. 25:40).

Evangelicals ought not to be content with this kind of proof-texting stalemate. The standoff can be avoided only by a systematic study of the biblical data regarding poverty and oppression. A coherent theological account of poverty should be especially attractive to evangelicals, who are otherwise quick to insist that the Bible does not contain a plurality of incommensurable "theologies." The formulation of a theological account of poverty, then, in which the tensions between apparently conflicting accounts of the causes of poverty are shown to be elements in a larger and consistent scheme, would seem to be highly desirable from an evangelical point of view.

In spite of our widely advertised love of orthodoxy, evangelicals have not always been diligent in promoting sound and careful theological reflection. We have been especially lax in this regard on matters of social and political concern; on such questions we have often settled for the kind of prooftexting just illustrated.

To be sure, there are important exceptions to this pattern of theological neglect. Nor are evangelicals the only Christians to experience stalemates in dealing with the topic of poverty. Indeed, the general ecumenical situation seems now to be characterized by a stalemate of sorts. Polarization has set in on this subject—the most visible recent expression of which is the trading of accusations between defenders of liberation theology and Christian neoconservatives.

Perhaps this is a time for evangelicals to take on the topic of a theology of poverty, thereby aiding others in making a fresh start at dealing with difficult issues. Needless to say, it may turn out that polarization is inevitable in this area of concern. Perhaps differences of class orientation and economic ideology are such that it is unthinkable that a broad consensus could emerge as an expression of the Christian community's understanding of biblical teaching regarding poverty and oppression. But if so, then this too is a very interesting conclusion to reach. To acknowledge an impasse here would itself compel evangelicals to rethink some of their cherished assumptions—such as a belief in the perspicuity of the Scriptures.

But it is also possible that some kind of broad consensus can be achieved—at least on the basic issues. One helpful way of conceiving of the attempt to find such a consensus is to observe the example of the Roman Catholic bishops of the United States, who have structured the discussion of economic issues, in their recent pastoral letter,[1] along these lines: first they discuss "Biblical and Theological Foundations" for a Christian perspective on economic life; they then outline a set of "Ethical Norms" for evaluating institutions and practices; finally they turn to a discussion of "Policy Applications" in the light of these norms.

This is by no means a noncontroversial approach. A number of Third World liberation theologians have, for example, condemned any way of setting up the discussion in which there is a distinction made between "timeless principles" and the ethical "application" of those principles to concrete historical problems.[2] The alternative they seem to suggest is one in which the choice of norms or principles—even the formulation of a theological perspective—cannot, or ought not to, occur until one has already immersed oneself in a concrete "praxis."

Unfortunately, it is not clear to many of us exactly what this proposal comes to. If we really are to think of the immersion in a "historical praxis" as the result of a normless choice, then we can legitimately wonder why these same theologians can be so certain that the kind of praxis associated with identification with the poor of the Third World is preferable to, for example, a praxis-immersion in the life of North American Yuppies.

Perhaps, however, what is being suggested is not the radical—and highly questionable—epistemological thesis that theological and ethical reflection is necessarily shaped by a normless choice of a specific praxis, but rather the more plausible claim that we tend to bring the biases of the praxis-situation in which we are involved to our theological and ethical reflection, and that we are often, consciously or unconsciously, influenced by those biases. Again, this is a plausible claim, and we would do well to take it as a legitimate warning that we try not to be unduly influenced, as theologians and ethicists, by cultural and class prejudices.

But if this is the nature of the warning, it is difficult to see what could be wrong with the approach taken by the Roman Catholic bishops. They have outlined their biblical-theological framework, and have then gone on to lay out their ethical norms and their specific policy proposals. If their theological principles or ethical norms are in fact shaped by the praxis represented by their policy proposals, the way to demonstrate this is to show how alternative proposals would be related to more adequate theological foundations or ethical norms. And for that task, it would seem that the bishops have provided just the right kind of format against which to formulate a critical response.

In this discussion I am assuming that the issues can be treated in the context of a similar format. I am taking it for granted that the first step is to get clear about theological foundations, before articulating the ethical norms that in turn enable Christians to address questions of specific policy. A concern with this first step is my primary focus in this discussion. If it should turn out that our very formulation of theological matters is shaped by prior policy-commitments—by a "historical praxis"—then we must still be convinced that such biases have led us to adopt an inadequate theology. And *this* question— about theological adequacy—must ultimately be decided by a critical assessment of our theological claims in the light of divine revelation.

I have already observed that evangelicals have not been consistently diligent in their efforts to construct a theology of poverty, often set-tling instead for a prooftexting kind of approach to the issues. But it is a well-known fact that on those matters where evangelicals *have* chosen to engage in theological reflection they have regularly dis-played certain stubborn habits of mind—even a kind of theological crankiness. We must be careful not to celebrate this evangelical crank-iness too enthusiastically, as if it were an unadorned virtue. But to be an evangelical is to nurture some degree of fondness for these stub-born habits of mind. With reference to our present topic this means that one will not want the evangelical community simply to adopt, without modification, someone else's theology of poverty—whether it is an old-fashioned "social gospel" liberalism or Roman Catholic liberation theology or the neoconservatism of those former liberals and radicals who have recently become disenchanted with the leftist orientation of the mainline churches.

What will a properly cranky evangelical approach to the the-ology of poverty look like? Or, more modestly, what stubborn ques-tions will have to be raised at the outset of an evangelical quest for a biblically faithful perspective on the needs of the poor and the oppressed of the earth?

The most basic formal condition that evangelicals will stipulate has already been mentioned: a proper understanding of these matters must treat the Scriptures as presenting a consistent and coherent mes-sage on this subject. The biblical account of these issues may very well be complex and nuanced, but it will also be a supremely trustworthy word from the Lord, offered to human beings as a sure guide for belief and action in the political-economic realm.

On a more substantive level, many of the specifically theological qualms that evangelicals experience when they approach a topic such as poverty have to do with a legitimate fear of a thoroughgoing "horizontalism." Horizontalist thought can be expressed in a variety of ways. I will mention here a few manifestations of horizontalism as it affects discussions of the Christian mission on behalf of the poor and the oppressed. These manifestations overlap; indeed some of them are mere variations on a single theme.

One manifestation of horizontalism is political-economic reductionism. This pattern of thought is present when the attempt is made to squeeze the rich diversity of human life into constrictive political-economic categories of explanation. Thus the impression is sometimes given by Christian thinkers that all sins, or most sins, or the most interesting and offensive sins, are political and economic in nature.

This will not do. What seems more plausible and helpful is to stress the fact that political-economic life is one very important arena for the playing out of human rebellion. This thesis cuts two ways. It points to the fact that the political-economic dimension of life is only one of the areas in which sin manifests itself. For example, evangelicals have surely often spent too much time thinking about the sexual sins of their neighbors, thereby ignoring or downplaying other forms of unrighteousness; but they have not been wrong in thinking that the Bible is very specific in its condemnations of sexual sin—which sin cannot, in turn, be reduced to a form of political or economic disobedience.

But the thesis also points to the fact that the political-economic realm is one very important area where people, including Christian people, have sinned seriously against their neighbors. Political injustice and economic oppression may not be the only patterns of sin in the world. But they are very real patterns of human rebellion against the living God.

A second manifestion of horizontalism can be seen in the exclusive emphasis on "praxis" that sometimes occurs in various contemporary "radical theologies." We are indebted to the Latin American liberation theologians for their insistence that we attend to the kind of plea found in a passage such as Jeremiah 22:15-16:

> Do you think you are a king
> because you compete in cedar?

> Did not your father eat and drink
>   and do justice and righteousness?
> Then it was well with him.
> He judged the cause of the poor and needy;
>   then it was well.
> Is this not to know me?
>   says the Lord.

This call to do justice is an important biblical theme. And there can be no denying the fact that the prophet is pointing to a close link between doing justice and being familiar with God. But it is wrong to take the biblical writers as somehow *equating*, in some basic sort of way, "knowing God" and "doing justice"—in the sense that anyone who performs acts of economic justice *ipso facto* knows God. As Ronald Sider has rightly observed, "To say that God is on the side of the poor is not to say that knowing God is nothing more than seeking justice for the poor and the oppressed."[3] There is more to knowing God than engaging in certain patterns of political-economic praxis.

For one thing, elsewhere in the Bible the writers point to different "praxical" elements of the knowledge of God. When the apostle warns that the one "who does not love, does not know God" (1 John 4:8), he is not making a claim that competes with Jeremiah's—even though the "love" he refers to here may not be exclusively political or economic in nature. What the biblical writers give us is a variety of components of the knowledge of God; the doing of justice and the exercise of faithful love toward others may be necessary conditions for having a proper knowledge of God—as also may be adherence to certain cognitive claims. To treat one or another of these components, whether an item of praxis or doctrine, as if it alone *constituted* the knowledge of God—as is suggested in the "orthopraxy, not orthodoxy" motto of some Christian radicals—is to distort the biblical message.

A third manifestation of horizontalism shows up specifically in the way in which the person and work of Jesus Christ is often portrayed by Christians who want to view Jesus as the liberator of the poor. A strong emphasis is placed on the incarnational elements in Jesus' ministry: his identification with the despised and the destitute, his willingness to take the sufferings of the poor upon himself, and so on. This emphasis is often spelled out in such a way that other important elements of Christ's redemptive ministry are ignored.

Thomas Hanks has argued the evangelical case in this area very effectively. Using the fourth Servant Song of Isaiah 52:13–53:12 as his reference point, Hanks shows how Pentecostal theology portrays Jesus as enduring the suffering of physical affliction in order to expedite a ministry of divine healing, and how liberation theologians emphasize the political-economic suffering of the Servant who comes to liberate the oppressed. Hanks insists that each of these is a legitimate emphasis, with significant biblical support. But he also argues convincingly that one must not highlight these themes to the exclusion of the very important, biblically grounded emphasis—found both in traditional Roman Catholic and evangelical theology—on the penal substitutionary work of Christ, whereby the righteous Son of God bore human sins in his own body in order to satisfy the demands of divine justice on behalf of sinners.[4] This crucial "vertical" element of the work of Christ constitutes, from an evangelical point of view, an absolutely necessary transaction between the First and Second Persons of the Trinity, without the occurrence of which all human beings would still be lost in their sins, hopelessly condemned to eternal punishment.

A fourth manifestation of horizontalism can be discerned in the tendency on the part of some to blend together the classifications "poor and rich," "oppressed and oppressor," and "saved and unsaved." It may be that the first two sets of distinctions are not simply to be run together. But it is certainly the case that the last of these three ways of classifying human beings must be kept distinct from the first two pairs. The biblical distinction between saved and unsaved is a fundamental one; it points to the eschatological sorting-out of human beings into their final groupings. These two classes of persons, the saved and the unsaved, are not coextensive with the classes pointed to by the terms *poor* and *rich,* or *oppressed* and *oppressor.*

This is not to say that there are not intimate links among these modes of classification. The Scriptures give us every reason to believe (Matt. 25:31-46 is an obvious case in point here) that those who are numbered among the saved are fully expected to act in certain ways toward the poor and the oppressed. But there is also every reason to think that there are poor and oppressed persons who are not saved; it also may be the case that there are wealthy persons and persons who qualify in important respects as "oppressors" who are granted salvation by the mercy of God. The categories "poor," "oppressed," and "saved" are simply not coextensive; nor are "rich," "oppressor," and "lost."

Evangelicals should insist that these cranky concerns be taken seriously in formulating a theological understanding of poverty. But for all of that, any Christian who takes the Scriptures with utmost seriousness must acknowledge that the God of the Bible cares very much about the poor.

To acknowledge this is not, for those who claim to be loyal to the traditions that have shaped present-day evangelicalism, to endorse a novel theme. It is difficult to find a historical theological stream that has fed evangelical thought in which there is not a strong emphasis on serving the needs of the poor. For example, John Calvin in his *Institutes* points with admiration to the examples set by the bishops Acacius and Ambrose, each of whom sold the sacred vessels from their churches to feed the hungry and to ransom prisoners. Calvin goes on to endorse some rather strong claims made by Ambrose, such as: "The church has gold not to keep but to pay out, and to relieve distress"; "Whatever, then, the church had was for the support of the needy"; "The bishop had nothing that did not belong to the poor."[5]

Similar emphases are found in other evangelical traditions. Those recent historians of continental pietism—such as Ernst Stoeffler and Dale Brown[6]—who have done so much to rescue the reputation of the seventeenth-century pietists from the schemes of those for whom "pietism" is synonymous with "world flight religion," have provided us with convincing accounts of the deep concern that the early pietists had for the poor and the destitute. And we find much the same concern when we look to other traditions in which evangelical heroes and heroines of the past are to be found: British and North American Holiness groups, the Dutch "Kuyperians," the black churches, the Anabaptists, the Restorationists, the Franciscan spirituality that some evangelicals are claiming these days as an expression of "evangelical Catholicism," and so on.

The strong expressions of concern for the poor that come from the evangelical past are echoing today on the leadership level of the evangelical community. These contemporary expressions of commitment to the poor and the oppressed are not just coming from the *Sojourners* people and Evangelicals for Social Action. Expressions of concern are also being voiced by persons who oppose what they view as a "leftist" bias among many evangelical activists.

For example, in a recently published criticism of some of Ronald Sider's views on Christian obligations to the poor, Ronald Nash remarks that every Christian has to recognize "that he or she had better be on the side of the poor and oppressed." This is so obvious, Nash suggests, that it needs no elaborate proof; the important question is "how this support and concern for the poor should be translated into practice." An adequate answer to this question, says Nash, requires the formulation of "a new liberation theology that will recognize the fundamental role of free markets in any economic system."[7]

Similarly, in a recent report issued by Grove City College's Public Policy Education Fund, L. John Van Til denounces Latin American liberation theology as "a fraud if it is passed off as a Christian doctrine." But he immediately adds: "Still, there is a lesson to be learned from its creators. It is this: the world hurts, it aches, it is hungry, and it cries for help. Implicit are important questions: Who will help? Who will heal? Who will feed? Who will educate? Who will reach out with a hand to help?"[8]

Clark Pinnock, who has recently repented of his earlier espousal of "radical Christian" schemes, nonetheless assures us that he still believes that Christians must defend the concerns of the poor—although Pinnock now thinks this can best be done by promoting a democratic capitalism understood in "neo-Puritan" theological terms.[9]

Some of the harshest evangelical criticisms, then, of liberation theology are being accompanied by the insistence that evangelicals demonstrate the kind of strong commitment to the poor that is characterized by what the critics view as saner and more Christian economic sensitivities than those exhibited by liberation theologians. These calls to identify with the poor and the oppressed suggest that for a growing number of Christians today the question is not *whether* concern for the poor is a central biblical mandate, but *how* we are best to fulfill that mandate. That is, the debate seems to be not about goals but about strategies.

In an earlier attempt to shed light on this subject, I myself proposed that participants in Christian debates over how to identify with the poor should accept in good faith each other's professions of concern for the poor, treating their debates as legitimate arguments over the proper strategies for achieving the agreed-upon goals of bettering the lot of the poor.[10] I still endorse this proposal. But I am also convinced that the discussions of strategy cannot avoid dealing with what are in fact different understandings of the formally agreed-upon goal.

The disagreements that arise when Christians spell out their conceptions of the biblical mandate to identify with the needs of the poor are complex ones. I cannot hope to address all of the issues involved here. The remainder of this essay will focus on two important questions that arise in this area: Who are the poor for whom the God of the Scriptures expresses his deep concern? And what does it mean for us to respond in faithfulness to God's expression of concern for the poor?

The biblical writers not only speak in general terms about God's concern for the poor and the oppressed; they also regularly mention certain types of persons who fall within that category of people who are the special objects of divine concern. Thus, the writers refer to God's care for the widow, the orphan, the prisoner, the sojourner, and the beggar.

Why is it that these types are often mentioned when the Bible refers to those people "whose help is the God of Jacob" (Ps. 146:5)? These are types of individuals who, in the social setting addressed by the biblical writers, lack a legal "voice." They have no social power to make claims that others must take seriously, nor do they have automatic access to advocates who will take up their causes. God's people are constantly admonished to hear the cries of those whose claims have no official status; they are to do so because God graciously heard the cries of the people of Israel when they had no rightful claim on his mercy:

> The stranger who sojourns with you shall be to you as the native among you, and you shall love him as yourself; for you were strangers in the land of Egypt: I am the Lord your God. (Lev. 19:34)

> If your brother, a Hebrew man, or a Hebrew woman, is sold to you, he shall serve you six years, and in the seventh year you shall let him go free from you. And when you let him go free from you, you shall not let him go empty-handed; you shall furnish him liberally out of your flock, out of your threshing floor, and out of your wine press; as the Lord your God has blessed you, you shall give to him. You shall remember that you were a slave in the land of Egypt, and the Lord your God redeemed you; therefore I command you this today. (Deut. 15:12-15)

A recognition of the close link between the helplessness—the "voicelessness"—of the poor and God's concern for them can help to solve at least some of the issues that arise in Christian discussions of poverty. For one thing, it enables us to see the continuity between those passages in which the biblical writers "spiritualize" the notion of poverty and those where poverty is treated as a straightforwardly political-economic condition. This is the way, for example, in which we can see the complementarity of the Matthean and Lucan versions of the poverty Beatitude. As Julio de Santa Ana[11] and others have argued, poverty in the New Testament has both a spiritual and a material aspect, and it is important to take both into account. People who have been deprived of the basic means of material support, and who know their helplessness, have few "crutches" to discard in order to throw themselves completely upon the mercy of God; it is in this fundamental openness to the promises of the kingdom that their "blessedness" resides—thus the Lucan formulation. The "poor in spirit" of Matthew 5:3 are not necessarily the economically deprived. But they can find blessedness only if they, like the "poor" of Luke 6:20, know their total dependence on God's sovereign grace. This is why it is merely difficult, and not impossible, for the rich to enter the kingdom.

We must keep in mind this helplessness motif in our attempts to understand God's actions on behalf of the oppressed in the biblical narrative. For example, Ronald Nash has taken Ronald Sider to task for claiming that the exodus event exemplifies God's commitment to liberating the poor and the oppressed.[12] Nash counters Sider's claim with the insistence that God's reasons for delivering the Israelites from Egypt "transcend the fact that the Israelites were poor and oppressed." Thus, he argues, their "poverty and oppression" was "an essentially accidental feature of the exodus," since God's real purposes in the exodus have to do "with some other end (such as the deliverance of human beings from sin)."[13]

As we have already seen, however, the biblical writers themselves regularly remind the people of Israel that in delivering them from Egypt the Lord had mercy on them in their helplessness. And these same writers use this reminder to urge the Israelites to show mercy toward—to take up the cause of—the sojourner, the slave, and the orphan, since the Israelites themselves were sojourners and slaves and orphans in the land of Egypt, when God heard their cries.

The specific form of political-economic destitution that characterized the Egyptian condition of the Israelites may be, then, as Nash suggests, "an essentially accidental feature of the exodus." But that God's people were met by him in their helplessness and that they ought to view their own past helplessness as akin to that part of the widows and sojourners of their own society seems to be an important part of their experiences as a people of the exodus. Thus, Sider and others have some biblical support for their portrayal of the exodus, at least insofar as they are making the modest claim that God's deliverance of the people of Israel is of a piece with his concern for slaves and sojourners and orphans.

A recognition of the connection between helplessness and poverty also gives support for the making of some kind of distinction between the "deserving poor" and the "undeserving poor." It seems clear that the Scriptures condemn idleness—as in Proverbs 6:10-11, quoted above. Those impoverished people whose poverty is due to their own refusal to work are judged by the Lord. But the idle poor are not to be confused with those persons—like the widow and the sojourner—whose difficulties are not due to a refusal to accept responsibility for their lives but to the oppression of unjust economic and political structures. Here the divine judgment is directed toward the wielders of power. Some sort of distinction between "worthy" and "unworthy" poor seems necessitated, then, by the Scriptures. Such a distinction has also been constantly present in Christian thought.[14] And although some Christians may find it an offensive practice to make such distinctions, it is difficult to know how to avoid them—as, for example, in a situation in which one must decide whether to use one's limited resources to help the impoverished and disabled widow next door or to come once more to the rescue of a brother-in-law who constantly wastes his earnings on booze and gambling.

Another distinction many, especially in the evangelical community, insist has crucial relevance in assessing the biblical message regarding poverty is that between the "believing" and "unbelieving" poor. They argue that the Bible does not portray God as having a concern for the poor as such, but only for the believing poor: the poor of Israel and the poor of the Christian community.

In spite of the fact that many discussions of "the Bible and the poor" never even hint at the relevance of such a distinction, it is not a silly point to raise. Christian people who are economically well-off have very special ties to Christians who are poor, ties that result from having been incorporated together into the community of blood-bought sinners. There can be no doubt that many of the New Testament reminders about the needs of the poor are appealing to these very intimate ties and the obligations that arise from them.

But the Scriptures offer at least two grounds for thinking that God also requires his people to manifest a concern for the non-Christian poor. One has to do with Christian witness. Believers are called to show a concern for the poor outside of the church as a means of demonstrating the power of the gospel to them. The command to feed our enemy, in Romans 12, may be linked to an expression of divine judgment: "By so doing you will heap burning coals upon his head." But this in no way cancels or moderates the mandate: "If your enemy is hungry, feed him."

A second ground has to do with God's concern that justice be manifested, even where the doing of justice does not necessarily result in the salvation of those who benefit from the establishment of just policies. Thus, Amos denounces not only the economic unrighteousness of Israel but also the unjust practices of the surrounding pagan nations. And Daniel commands the king of a pagan nation to "break off your . . . iniquities by showing mercy to the oppressed"— not so that the nation might be saved, which is the kind of promise offered to Israel, but so "that there may perhaps be a lengthening of your tranquillity" (Dan. 4:27).

This "general" concern for the poor is not as clear a matter as it is sometimes assumed to be. Evangelicals, who rightly place an important emphasis on the saving mercies of God, have some reason to be nervous about a concern for the poor that is separated from a desire that the poor acknowledge the One who, though he was rich, became poor for our sake, so that we might receive the riches of his kingdom. We have a right, I say, to be nervous about such an understanding of our "general" obligations to the poor. But the Bible does seem to suggest that the Lord delights in works of justice on behalf of the poor, even when those poor folks do not receive the Savior. Here, perhaps, we must simply allow the Scriptures to keep us nervous!

While mentioning distinctions that are sometimes introduced into the discussion of this topic, we must also acknowledge the legitimacy of Jacques Ellul's complaint, in *The Betrayal of the West,* that concerns for the poor often get expressed along faddish lines—lines that, in turn, are drawn sometimes for ideological purposes.[15] Ellul is right to point out that there are "truly poor" peoples, such as the Kurds and the Tibetans, who are systematically ignored by those who claim to be champions of the oppressed. In light of this fact, it seems clear that a Christian concern for the poor and oppressed must be expressed in terms of a constant calling into question of popular ways in which the "truly poor" are identified, so that attention might be drawn to those destitute individuals and groups who would otherwise be ignored.

Needless to say, if we are to acknowledge the complexities of the biblical address to the human predicament, we will have to operate with a highly nuanced understanding of who "the poor and the oppressed" are. Indeed, it seems fair to suggest that from a biblical perspective we cannot permit the distinctions between "rich" and "poor" and "oppressor" and "oppressed" to function as strict and rigid categories. Even Karl Marx recognized some degree of fluidity in the proper use of such terminology. In commenting on the oppressed role of women in capitalist societies Marx observed that a kind of class-conflict occurs in miniature within the bourgeois family, where the husband "is the bourgeois; the wife represents the proletariat."[16]

Christians must be at least as flexible as Marx in this regard. Very few people are *simply* "oppressor" or "oppressed." The male slave who is oppressed by his owner may in turn oppress his wife; the wife may oppress her children in significant ways; the children may grow up to become oppressors of their parents; and so on. "Oppressor" and "oppressed" are relational terms; the roles they denote may shift from relationship to relationship. With regard to these matters too it is important to talk about "contextualization."

If we keep these nuances in mind, we can acknowledge some legitimacy to the kind of plea issued by Richard Neuhaus, in a book addressed primarily to clergy:

> Those who are called "liberation theologians" today tell us that we should read the Bible through the eyes of the poor and the oppressed, and they are right. We should also read the Bible through the eyes of the more elegantly and complicatedly poor who make up the churches of North America. It is easier to cheer the liberation struggles in distant lands than to anguish over the liberation of ourselves and others with whom we cross paths and cross swords every day. The Church may be the pilgrim people of God on their way to the New Jerusalem, but they are still pedestrians, and it is to the pedestrian Church that we are called to minister.[17]

These urgings of Neuhaus are well taken, especially where church leaders may be tempted to ignore the needs and struggles of Christian people on the home front, in the manner described by Neuhaus. For example, people who live in North American suburbs also experience important forms of helplessness—a defenselessness in the face of family breakups, a desperate inability to articulate their hurts and fears, a sense of hopelessness caused by disease or addiction; here too are patterns that deserve to be called "oppression." Here too is a helplessness that the Son of God died to overcome. One does not approach such situations in an appropriate evangelistic or pastoral manner simply by telling such people that they are fortunate not to be natives of Haiti or Ethiopia.

But there are important differences between the kinds of oppression that we experience in our North American context and those that characterize the life of people in situations of desperate poverty. We well-off Christians in North America must be reminded of these differences. To be sure, these reminders ought not to be couched in terms that suggest we are, in some unqualified sense, "oppressors," while people in the Third World and in our own ghettos are *the* oppressed." Rather, our relationship to those whose destitution is more consistent than anything we have experienced must be spelled out in the terms the Lord used in speaking to his people in the Old Testament: We must listen to the cries of those who are more consistently helpless than we are, and must act with charity and justice toward them. For we were helpless in our sickness, our marital trial, our addiction, our time of temptation, and the Lord heard our cries for help.

How ought Christians, especially Christians who have some degree of social leverage, to respond to the fact of God's concern for the poor and the oppressed of the earth? What ought to be the patterns, the shape, of our attempts to identify with the destitute?

These questions cannot be answered adequately without dealing in great detail with many complicated issues. I will not do that here. This is a time of much ferment and excitement in Christian economic discussion. There was a time in the not too distant past in North America when it was virtually unthinkable that evangelicals would be anything but strong supporters of the "free enterprise" system. In recent years the popularity of liberation theology has led many to develop some sympathy for, or at least openness to the legitimacy of, socialist programs. Even more recently defenders of "democratic capitalism" have launched a detailed and impressive counterattack. This is not the place to settle those debates. Instead, I will offer a few observations about the significance of these ongoing arguments, with some suggestions regarding questions to which further attention ought to be given.

First, there are many important issues at stake in these debates that cannot be settled decisively within the context of *theological* exploration. Some of the points of contention are empirical in nature; others have to do with matters of theoretical formulation that go well beyond the bounds of theological discussion. All we can hope for is that the discussion of such matters by Christians will be shaped by appropriate theological sensitivities.

Second, it seems to me that these economic debates ought at least to be welcomed with enthusiasm by evangelical Christians, as God-given opportunities for creative self-examination. Most of us, especially those of us in the scholarly world, have had to change or modify enough of our sincerely held positions of the past to know that it is a good thing to be called to account for the political and economic hopes that we nurture. This is not a time for us to "harden" in our economic convictions in such a way that we refuse to engage in self-critical discussion.

Third, perhaps there are even good theological reasons for remaining principally skeptical about the more hard-line espousals of both socialism and democratic capitalism. In a recent article Stanley Hauerwas and William H. Willimon express their misgivings about the views of those who are involved in "the neoconservative enterprise":

> While with them we raise questions about theological integrity and share their low view of religious liberalism, we are more pessimistic about this culture than they, much more radical and much more optimistic about the church's intrinsic worth.[18]

Hauerwas and Willimon may be onto something. This is certainly not the time for evangelicals to be pursuing the obviously defective theologies and strategies of Protestant liberalism. But neither is it a time for an uncritical endorsement of the programs of those who are inclined to portray "the free market system" or "the American Way" as vehicles of hope for all humankind. Perhaps these schemes are not worthy of the same degree of skepticism with which we should greet the announcement that a "Marxist socialism with a human face" has now been discovered. But a healthy skepticism is called for nonetheless.

In a provocative essay on "Exodus and Exile," John Howard Yoder has warned against a "neo-Constantinian" perspective, according to which Christians feel compelled to promote "a theocratic takeover of the land of bondage by the brickmakers." Instead, Yoder encourages us to *be* the "non-conformed, covenanted people of God," thereby offering the world the kind of "liberation" that comes from "the presence of a new alternative."[19]

It is this new alternative—and not capitalist or socialist schemes—to which we as Christians are, in the final analysis, committed. Our primary emphasis, then, must be on living together as a people who long for the kingdom that is already present among us, but is not yet here in its fullness. To yearn for this kingdom, and for the appearance of the King whose blood has liberated us from the bondage of sin, is to do everything possible, within the life-contexts in which the Lord has placed us, to promote charity and justice—associating with the lowly and seeking the well-being of all humankind.

Christian economic thought and action, then, will not be inspired primarily by a commitment to this or that ideology or program, but by a vision of what God has called human beings to be. Thus Michael Novak has rightly prefaced his own defense of democratic capitalism with the asking of those questions which ought to stimulate the economic reflections of all who possess the Christian vision: "Which ethos, which virtues, and which institutions must be prized and nourished in order to ease the sufferings of the poor? We must help the poor, but how?"[20]

Novak is right: the basic question is one of the "ethos," the "virtues," that will breathe life into our economic institutions and programs. To propose this is not to retreat to the simplistic "changed hearts will change society" slogan of the evangelical past. "Hearts" themselves, as we should all have learned by now, often are shaped extensively by the ethos of the age. Rather, the recognition of the importance of ethos provides the framework for seeing that we can only hope to challenge the reigning "virtues" of the larger society in which we live by developing a proper communal ethos for the "nonconformed, covenanted people of God" of whom Yoder writes.

That such an ethos may not comport well with the major economic schemes being bandied about these days is hinted at by Gertrude Himmelfarb in her recent ground-breaking work, *The Idea of Poverty: England in the Early Industrial Age.* She finds it odd that R. H. Tawney, in his famed *Religion and the Rise of Capitalism,* "having made so much of Puritanism, should have done so little with its counterpart in the eighteenth century—Wesleyanism." But then she herself goes on to find some "anomalous" features in the thinking associated with the Wesleyan revival. Wesleyanism, she observes, preserves "so many features of a pre-capitalist or anti-capitalist ethic . . . while advocating a Puritan ethic often associated with capitalism."[21]

Perhaps—just perhaps—there is nothing anomalous here after all. Perhaps the anomalies make their appearance only when someone looks at the evangelical ethos from the outside. It may be that from within that kind of Christian ethos, properly understood, what the contemporary economic mind views as a curious juxtaposition of pre-capitalist, anticapitalist, and capitalist virtues is in fact the stuff of a coherent life of discipleship. If so, then we will all serve the poor most effectively if we refuse to jump onto someone else's ideological bandwagon and get on instead with the important evangelical task of bringing our economic thoughts and deeds into submission to the authority of the One who came so that the poor might finally hear Good News.

4D

Farewell to Arms: Reflections on the Encounter between Science and Faith*

David N. Livingstone

Viewers of BBC television's 1984 series "The Sea of Faith" were lately treated to an uninhibited display of scientific imperialism. Don Cupitt, whose weekly broadcasts and accompanying book might have been christened rather more appropriately "The Faith at Sea," told listeners and readers alike—and in no uncertain terms—that the whole fabric of traditional Christian theism was in need of radical restatement in the light of modern scientific insight. Supernatural beliefs, the Dean of Emmanuel College Cambridge insisted, were simply outworn as science systematically shredded and discarded belief in a moral world order, the idea of a world beyond this one, and the very possibility of truth. "Scientific knowledge," he asserted,

> is so different from religious knowledge that it might seem that the two could easily co-exist without coming into conflict. However, in practice, as everyone knows, conflict does occur at many levels. Science-based culture is activist and progressive, tending to see change as a good thing, and from its standpoint religion often appears to be obscurantist and morally backward. By contrast religion often sets its golden age in the past and tends to regard any change as being for the worse. . . . More generally, religion promotes an accepting and acquiescent temper of mind, whereas science promotes and requires analytical and critical habits of mind.[1]

I certainly do not propose to let Mr. Cupitt set the agenda for our

* I am grateful to Frank Gourley, David Hempton, George Marsden, Mark Noll, Patrick Roche, Colin Russell, and Thomas F. Torrance for their comments on an earlier version of this paper.

present discourse; but it is well to remember that his sentiments, whether ingenuous or artful, are widely shared by members of Western society at the present time. What is of moment is that this interpretation of the encounter between science and faith is thoroughly contested by a number of alternative historical reconstructions that have surfaced in recent years. Some reflections on these major approaches to the historical question will, therefore, help sketch in the context for the substantive issues facing Christian theology and practice today, and at the same time clarify the role played by evangelicals in the advancement of scientific culture.

TELLING THE STORY OF SCIENCE AND FAITH

Traditional histories of science, Whiggish in spirit and triumphalist in character, conventionally resorted to the language of warfare and struggle in their reconstruction of faith's encounter with science. This *conflict* model, with its military metaphors and campaign veterans, was enshrined in the celebrated best-seller, *History of the Conflict between Religion and Science,* published in 1875 by John W. Draper who had earned, among other things, the distinction of witnessing firsthand the legendary clash between Wilberforce and Huxley at that infamous Oxford meeting of the British Association for the Advancement of Science in 1860. Clever metaphor that it was, the book provoked a whole spate of similar crusade reveries most conspicuous in Andrew Dixon White's *A History of the Warfare of Science with Theology in Christendom* (1896) and James Y. Simpson's *Landmarks in the Struggle between Science and Religion* (1925).[2]

As the documents of the scientific past have been ransacked, however, the whole apparatus of this "conflict" arsenal has been dismantled with forensic precision by a squad of historical revisionists.[3] It has long been recognized, for example, that the vocabulary of controversy is just simply inappropriate for the periods before 1850. The new science of geology, to take one case, happily counted among its advocates such perfectly orthodox English clergymen as Sedgwick, Buckland, and Coneybeare, and somber Scottish Calvinists like Playfair, Hugh Miller, and John Fleming.[4] Again, the pervasive influence of natural theology, sustained with vigor throughout the entire nineteenth century (and *a fortiori* earlier), has had to be taken more fully into account[5] while, at the same time, many nineteenth-century evangelicals like Gray, Dana, and Wright in science, and Warfield, Orr, McCosh, and Strong in theology found the conceptual resources necessary to absorb any shock-waves emanating from the Darwinian revolution.[6] Even the Wilberforce-Huxley melodrama at the 1860 meeting of the British Association for the Advancement of Science at Oxford may not have been all that it has been made out to be. Popularists like William Irvine in *Apes, Angels, and Victorians* colorfully portray Bishop Wilberforce congratulating himself on not being descended from a monkey, and the skeptical Thomas Huxley replying that he would rather be descended from a monkey than act like Wilberforce, who turned his gifts against those who were wearing out their lives to find the truth. But the accounts of careful historians have shown this incident to be more the product of historical predisposition than a description of what really happened. J. R. Lucas and Sheridan Gilley, recently raking over the ashes of this supposed fracas, have succeeded in finally dispelling the disarming simplicity of the so-called Victorian crisis of faith.[7]

All this is not to deny the secularizing role that science has played since the late Victorian period. As a source of religious skepticism, though, science probably did rather less harm than the ethical revolt against Christian convention, the explosion of radical biblical criticism foreshadowed in *Essays and Reviews* (1860), working-class defection from institutional religion, and interdenominational feuding.[8] Nor is it to suggest that no one felt a tension between the call of faith and the practice of science. Among evangelicals, to take a random example, Alexander Winchell, a prominent nineteenth-century American geologist and Wesleyan Methodist, devoted a four-hundred-page volume to the *Reconciliation of Science and Religion* in 1877—a title evidently assuming mutual antagonism.[9] And certainly the accommodationist ethos of theological modernism only makes sense against the background of a perceived need to reconstruct the Christian ethic along lines dictated by scientific overlords. The cosmic holism of a John Fiske, the psychic science of a Frederic Myers, and the synthetic idealism of a Henry Ward Beecher represent just some of the efforts at credal reformulation, a strategy that has found its nadir in the scientific dogmatics of a Teilhard de Chardin or a Don Cupitt.[10] Besides, there is just the hint of suspicion that the images of conflict were deliberately fostered by those antitheistic polemicists who had vested interests in using science to displace the church from the center of the social and cultural stage. Again, the fact that the vocabulary of hostility and conflict is not far from the lips of latter-day creationists and their evolutionary opponents should caution against a too facile expulsion of the warfare analogy to the mists of historical imagination. Recent reruns of the 1925 Scopes "monkey trial" in California and Arkansas—spectacles presented in the media as a kind of atavistic *déjà vu*—have done little to dispel the noise of battle from popular and journalistic ears.[11]

Still, the warfare model has, by and large, done little to advance our understanding of the relationship between science and faith in history, and it is precisely because of its ambiguities and crudities that some historians of science have recast it in a much more restricted vein. Here, the conflict is transmuted into a *competition,* and is applied not so much to science and faith per se, but to the "struggle" for cultural ascendance in society contingent on the appearance of the scientific professional. Frank Miller Turner is the leading architect of this interpretative realignment, and he has made out the case for a Victorian battle for preeminence between the ecclesiastical hierarchy and the new, thrusting scientific elite. The "conflict," then, is to be seen in terms of the shift in intellectual authority—involving of course epistemological factors—from the preprofessional clerical sage to the middle-class professional intelligentsia. The amateur parson-naturalist who had hitherto played a noble role in the advance of science's discoveries and institutions was somehow, by late Victorian days, a quaint anachronism in the "laboratorial" world of the emerging disciplinary specialist.[12] So when Victorian men and women fell on hard times—whether because of the threat to harvest, cattle plague, or typhoid in the royal household—it was questionable whether they should obey the clergy's call to prayer or turn to the agricultural, veterinary, or medical experts. If the choice was initially hazy, it was rapidly resolved in a predictable direction. The manifest success of sanitary engineering, preventive medicine, and the surgeon's knife heralded an increasing privatization of religious observance, and an accompanying transfer of societal kudos into the hands of a willing scientific fraternity. As Turner concludes:

> If the movement from religion to science in western culture represented, as some would contend, the exchange of one form of faith for another, it also meant the transfer of cultural and intellectual leadership and prestige from the exponents of one faith to those of another. In this regard the long debate over the nature of prayer suggests that the Victorian conflict between religion and science was something more than a dispute over ideas. It manifested the tension arising as the intellectual nation became more highly differentiated in functions, professions, and institutions. It was a clash between established and

emerging intellectual and social elites for popular cultural preeminence in a modern industrial society.[13]

All this, moreover, has been reinforced in the writings of another student of Victorian intellectual life, T. W. Heyck, who finds at least one locus of the "conflict between science and theology" in

> the effort by scientists to improve the position of science. They wanted nothing less than to move science from the periphery to the center of English life. . . . And the scientists' general desire for a scientific culture was only half the story; the other was their powerful impulse towards the professionalization of science.[14]

This analysis certainly does throw light on several infernally stubborn problems in the history of the science-religion saga. It helps explain, for example, the rise of the Wilberforce-Huxley legend. For the later passion to purge the British Association of the stain of clerical dilettantism would evidently favor a reconstruction of that debate in the baldest religion versus science, medieval versus modern, terms. At the same time, it may help to explain the willingness of the Old School Princeton Presbyterians to negotiate a *modus vivendi* with the new evolutionary paradigm. Occupying a place of cultural prestige throughout the entire nineteenth century, a position soon to be swept away with the rise of a militant fundamentalism, the Princetonians could happily engage in the task of keeping the marriage of science and faith alive, for their professional representatives in geology, geography, biology, and so on, shared the self-same religious worldview of their theological colleagues.[15] The competitive reading, too, I think, clarifies much of the otherwise ambiguous rhetoric on the lips of scientific publicists. Huxley's craving for a molecular teleology, Galton's hankering after a "scientific priesthood," and Geddes's substitution of Darwin for Paley certainly invite such exegesis.[16]

This approach has certainly much to commend it; but it surely is worth emphasizing that by itself it cannot accommodate all aspects of the science-religion question. Its advocates, of course, have been far from expansionist in their claims to the interpretative territory. Still, it is in connection with the model's greatest strengths that most care must be taken. Religious knowledge, to be sure, cannot be cut loose from religious knowers, nor scientific theory from scientific practice; both *are* rooted in society and it is well to remember that they can be manipulated to serve particular group interests. But this in and of itself tells us really very little about the *nature* of religious and scientific understanding, nor about the adequacy of the grounds for resorting, say, to surgical operations rather than to spiritual observance, or for that matter to the sorcerer rather than to the doctor. Such theoretical questions would clearly have to be resolved by other criteria whatever the legacy of historical judgment may have been. Then too, by focusing on the *social* struggles of religionists and scientists, the "competition approach" solidly ties both enterprises to the moorings of popular culture. This clearly has its advantages in explaining the flowering of Victorian naturalism. But since the average "hip ecologist" knows as much about environmental science as the average "Jesus freak" knows about theology, we may well be justified in wondering how Victorian folk religion is to be related to biblical Christianity. The occultish and superstitious tincture of much late Renaissance churchdom,[17] for example, would arguably incur the judgment of New Testament religion as much as of scientific rationalism. So the substitution of popular confidence in hygiene for the faith of vernacular supernaturalism leaves quite untouched the relationship between Christian theism and scientific naturalism. Of course, as I have tried to make plain, theoreticians like Turner and Heyck have focused on the strategies of the intellectual hierarchy; but that struggle for cultural power is necessarily earthed in the functional value of the religious and scientific merchandise to the populace at large.

Predating this rereading of the record is an alternative historical hermeneutic characterized by its emphasis on the *cooperation* science has received from Christianity. This interpretation was spearheaded, in large measure, by the early sociologists of science, particularly Robert Merton, who sensed a direct correlation between the advent of Puritanism and the rise of science in seventeenth-century England. Institutionally, he felt he could point to a predominance of Puritans within the "invisible college" that was to become the Royal Society, while intellectually, he believed the Puritan temper to be particularly congenial to scientific pursuits.[18] This sociological rendering was complemented by the theological reflections of those who, like Hooykaas, found in the doctrinal thought-forms of the Reformation specific principles foundational to the very possibility of experimental science.[19] Themes like the love of nature, the glory of God, the welfare of humanity, and the priesthood of all believers, Hooykaas argued, were so entwined in the nexus of Puritan thinking that their thoroughly empirical science was merely one expression of an anti-authoritarianism equally displayed in their distaste for ecclesiastical hierarchies and the "divine right of kings" in civil government.[20]

Science, to them, was grounded in experience, not in the authority of the Ancients. So, for Hooykaas, the spirit of philosophical liberty that pervaded the scientific writings of the Puritan geographer Nathanael Carpenter is symbolic of the entire Puritan venture out into the territorial waters of science.[21]

Supporters of this cooperative exegesis, as it may be styled, have come from many quarters. On the philosophical side Michael Foster presented an early defense in an influential piece entitled "The Christian Doctrine of Creation and the Rise of Modern Natural Science"; from the ranks of the theologians T. F. Torrance has added his support, underlining in particular the displacement of Medievalism by the Reformation's rediscovery of a contingent creation; and then again, the Marxist historian Christopher Hill found close links between religious dissent and scientific progress in Restoration England; while A. N. Whitehead long felt that it was the unique synthesis of Greek and biblical thought-forms during science's gestation period that encouraged a growing sense of an intelligible nature and repudiated the world-denying extremes of Gnosticism and asceticism.[22] Space does not permit me to rehearse the volume of literature basically in agreement with the thrust of this diagnosis.[23] But I must point out that the general thesis recently has been subject to criticisms and is now held rather less confidently than in the past. For one thing it has long been recognized that social and economic forces also played a part: the navigating needs of a maritime nation—what Eva Taylor once called "the haven-finding art"—cannot be ignored, nor can the domestic needs of agriculture or the structural transformation of society due to the growing strength of its manufacturing class with a capitalist ethos.[24] Then Michael Hunter has most forcefully expressed his reservations in a superbly documented study pointing out, among other things, how elusive precise definitions of Puritanism in the earlier literature really were. "Puritans, like others," he writes, "may have contributed to scientific enterprise, but Puritanism can claim no preponderant share of its achievements."[25]

Be this as it may, it is certainly true—as even critics admit—that Puritans played an honorable role in the rise of English science. And the cooperation between natural science and Christian faith did not end there. James Moore's monumental study of Protestant responses to Darwin suggests, as a broad generalization, that orthodox believers who retained a firm hold on Calvin's doctrine of Providence experienced the least religious nervousness. Indeed, I have discovered a vibrant tradition of evangelical evolutionism, particularly in the United

States, which has been ignored or suppressed by certain propagandists. Moreover, we must not overlook the Wesleyan affirmation of science, and one or two students of John Wesley himself have sought to redress the balance.[26] Finally, bringing the story up-to-date, several scientist-theologians, of both Protestant and Catholic persuasion, have argued that developments in post-Einsteinian physics have done much to confirm, and indeed have been confirmed by, the witness of Judeo-Christian theism.[27]

This general scheme of interpretation is plainly attractive. It accommodates, for example, both theoretical and social dimensions of our subject, by engaging both the theological ideas and the human networks in which scientific practice was ultimately rooted. Even for controversial periods like Darwin's century, it redraws our attention to aspects of that drama that have laid hidden beneath the veneer of positivist rhetoric. But it clearly cannot be sold wholesale as a panacea for all theological ills. Its undoubted value in explaining *some* of the facts only highlights the areas where it fails to improve our understanding. The secularizing ethos of the scientific worldview, science's reductionist and materialist inclinations, and the sense of cosmic loneliness with the breakup of the natural theology canopy are some of the more prominent topics needing resolution. Besides, there is the ethical challenge forthcoming from those quarters frankly critical of scientific rationality itself, and therefore of its philosophical underpinnings. The advanced state of environmental pollution, the unprecedented threat of nuclear holocaust, the exhaustion of the soil by agricultural mismanagement, and the undreamt horrors of biological warfare are just some of science's nasty gifts that have to be weighed in the balances against the evident benefits of modern engineering, agriculture, and medicine.

Perhaps the most coherent effort to transcend the emphases on conflict and cooperation is the argument for ideological *continuity* most forcefully articulated by the Marxist historian of science, Robert M. Young. In a number of influential and impressively documented articles, Young advanced the proposal that "conflict" readings of the great Victorian debate on "Man's place in Nature" have only obscured the fact that both religion and science are socially sanctioned ideologies.[28] And in developing his critique he has made use of the old idea of theodicy, a doctrinal move originally designed to diffuse the problem of evil. What Young suggests is that the theodicy grounded in natural theology (justifying the ways of God to humanity) has been replaced by a scientific theodicy (justifying the laws of nature to society). In both cases the existing social order is ratified and therefore science, no less than religion, continues to support the principles of adjustment and conformity. Darwin, in other words, is merely a secular Paley.

Whatever the inadequacies of Young's ultimately Marxian program, he has nonetheless compiled an imaginative travelogue to guide us through the maze of the Victorian intellectual landscape. The much vaunted talk of a Church Scientific, lay sermons, a Scientific Priesthood, and what not, begin to make sense in the context of a transition to a new theodicy. Then the ultimate imprimatur of establishment acclaim—burial in Westminster Abbey—which was accorded to Darwin, thanks to the frenetic string-pulling of John Lubbock, can now be read in a new light. Moore, following the broad sweep of Young's portrait, finds much symbolic significance in the solemn bearing of Darwin's body "up the nave by Huxley, Wallace and other dignitaries . . . to its resting place a few feet from the monument to Sir Isaac Newton." It was, he suggests, "the Trojan horse of naturalism entering the fortress of the Church."[29] Besides, Young's arguments do full justice to the pre-Darwinian roots of secularization and to the way in which a rising tide of intellectuals casting about for some new consensus took advantage of the rising prestige of science. That a number of religious believers shared many of these credenda only seems to strengthen the case.

It is worth citing one particularly dramatic instance of this kind of conceptual maneuver where the pressing of science into the service of ideology is all too clearly paraded. Throughout the last century—and in some cases a good deal later than that—numerous individuals were intoxicated with the hope of isolating some scientific measure of racial differences. A whole subfield of anthropology—anthropometry or somatometry—emerged to satisfy their needs. This subdisciplinary specialism had no necessary ideological undertones, but many practitioners believed that the inferiority and superiority of particular races could thereby be unambiguously established. Scientific racism, drawing from disciplines as diverse as evolutionary biology, physical anthropology, the new human geography, and certain schools of history, rapidly contributed ammunition for a battery of social policies ranging from eugenics to immigration restriction.[30] Here, the "constitutive role of evaluative concepts" in science, to use Young's own terminology,[31] is all too clear. Nor were evangelicals immune from such machinations. Consider, for example, the judgments of two prominent evangelical scientists in nineteenth-century America. In the case of

Arnold Guyot (Princeton University professor of physical geography and guest lecturer to the Seminary's students), it was the Creator who had "placed the cradle of mankind in the midst of the continents of the North . . . and not at the center of the tropical regions, whose balmy, but enervating and treacherous, atmosphere would perhaps have lulled him to sleep the sleep of death in his very cradle."[32] For Alexander Winchell, by contrast, it was "Nature," conscious of the "irremediable estrangement" of the black races, that had condemned them to inhospitable and inaccessible regions of the globe.[33] A more dramatic shift from a theological to a scentific theodicy within a religious frame of reference can scarcely be envisioned.

Still, for all that, Young's treatment is open to objections both technical and philosophical. The relative *in*coherence of the natural theologians' strategies in the pre-Darwin period have been highlighted by some historians,[34] and Young's "common context" begins to look in disarray. Fundamental disagreements over the theological significance of everything from animal instinct to the geological column show the supposed shared framework of discourse to be rather less than unified. There is too, I think, some sense of the overdetermination in Young's theoretical framework. To say that science and society are closely related, indeed that scientific theory is often socially determined, is one thing; but to claim that values and politics are necessarily constitutive of scientific explanation is quite another. Philosophy of science, surely, cannot so easily be resolved into the sociology of knowledge, nor science transmuted into ideology.

And yet, at the same time, Young's trenchant questioning of scientism, scientific idolatry if you will, is certainly timely. Surely it is right to demand, as he does, that the philosophical, ethical, religious, and political factors invariably assumed or promoted in the practice of science are brought out into the open and discussed for what they are, rather than being concealed behind the facade of scientific jargon. For as Colin Russell has recently reminded us, it is "the sacralisation of science (or the secularization of society by putting science in the place of cultural leadership once occupied by institutional religion) [that] has meant a burgeoning of the uses of science as an argument for justifying, or delaying, changes in society."[35]

UPDATING THE STORY

These historical foragings, I believe, perform a dual service. Not only do they uncover factors endemic to the secularization of the Western mind over the past two centuries, but they also enable us to pinpoint some of the issues to be faced squarely in any serious Christian engagement with science. Only with the benefit of hindsight, which comes from looking to the past, can we begin to distill many of those taken-for-granted assumptions that continue to permeate the management of the modern scientific project. By now it is certainly clear that we cannot construct a viable Christian framework for science on the purely cerebral or theoretical plane. Of course we must resolve epistemological questions, but if history teaches us anything it surely is that that pursuit cannot be severed from the social, ideological, and ethical contexts in which science as a cultural enterprise is embedded. As to policy, it would be as wise to build upon the specific contributions already made by Christian theology and by Christian scholars to the advancement of the scientific industry, as it would be foolish to work in a temporal vacuum. We must take into account current problematics, for theology—no less than history—must be translated into the idioms of each generation. So we turn now to three areas of concern, all of which are already revealed in the historical survey to one degree or the other, where the guidance of Christian principles is urgently needed.

Epistemological Issues and Scientific Explanation

In the past half century or so, revolutions in the philosophy of science have come thick and fast.[36] Naive inductivism inherited from the seventeenth-century Baconians saw science as knowledge derived from the empirical observation of the facts of nature. By painstakingly scrutinizing the multitude of discrete data, formulating initial hypotheses, and testing them against reality, inductivists believed that the universal laws of nature could be laid bare. In the 1930s, a group of continental philosophers—who came to be known as the Vienna Circle—sought to give greater conceptual rigor to this formula and spawned a philosophical movement described as Logical Positivism. By using the criterion of verifiability, they hoped to distinguish meaningful from meaningless statements. Their endeavors soon brought on a severe batch of theological headaches, for whereas a proposition like "Those rocks contain quartz" can be empirically tested, "God is love" is hardly subject to normal scientific warrants. At a stroke, theology and metaphysics were swept out into the ocean of literal nonsense.[37]

Or so it seemed. Logical Positivism itself was soon to be scuttled with the realization that "scientific observations" were not themselves free from theory dependence. Deduction, not induction, was seen to be the only available strategy. The setting up of an experiment, to take just one case, clearly assumes distinctions between relevant and irrelevant processes—a theory-based demarcation right from the outset. Besides, as Karl Popper made clear, the universal propositions of scientific theory cannot be verified; but they can be falsified by the specification of counter instances. "All swans are white" can never pass the verification test (how could we observe every single case?), but the discovery of a single black swan can falsify it. This, Popper claimed, was the only viable scientific method, and therefore science was the art of being precisely wrong.[38] The seeming elegance of Popper's principle, however, only obscured the fact that its simplicity was more apparent than real. The difficulty of finding cases of absolute refutation in theories above the level of the trivial concerned some of his critics. For science operates far more with notions of probability than with absolute certainty. Moreover, it suddenly became apparent that to say that some theories were falser than others was not exactly the same as telling which were closer to the truth.

Any concern that Popper had to keep such relativist tendencies in check were hastily jettisoned (at least so far as ontological questions were concerned) in Thomas Kuhn's *The Structure of Scientific Revolutions*.[39] In his idea of "paradigms," historians, philosophers, and sociologists of science found a new toy to engage happily their imaginations. By "paradigm" Kuhn roughly meant—and he was confessedly ambiguous at least initially—a tradition with historical exemplars. In other words, a mature science is conducted with a conceptual framework that sets the standard for relevant research, stipulates the puzzle-solving objectives, coordinates the disparate work of its member scientists, and socializes its rising students in the ways of the tradition. Now, Kuhn went on, scientific revolutions occur when the paradigm is replaced by another that gives rise to a new systemic approach. The changeover is like a Gestalt switch, and the reasons for the shift just as mysterious. The new model may accommodate more information, be more aesthetically pleasing and more psychologically satisfying. But there are no independent rational criteria for discriminating, because they themselves are dictated by the paradigm itself, and practitioners in different traditions are caught in the trap of incommensurability. The guts of post-Einsteinian physics, Kuhn would say, cannot even be expressed in the language of the Newtonian paradigm.

The thoroughly relativist temper of the Kuhnian interpretation, moreover, has been pushed to the very limits by the anarchist philosopher Paul Feyerabend.[40] To him, science is a completely freewheeling business, for without the logical apparatus for comparison implicit in Kuhn's story, literally anything goes. This of course means that *everything* goes, and Feyerabend has unapologetically rejected any suggestion that science is superior to any other form of knowledge whether it be poetry or drama or more fringe pursuits like astrology or Voodoo.

The relativists, needless to say, have not had it all their own way. Realism in various guises has had its willing advocates. Such philosophers as Imre Lakatos, Hilary Putnam, and William Newton-Smith have sought out a number of routes by which to defend a rationalist position. One is by seeing the history of science as a tale of increasing approximation to the truth, its theories always provisional certainly, but ever more refined and sharply focused. Another is by the simple fact of science's pragmatic or instrumental success and by its amazing predictive powers.[41] These, it is argued, are signs of the increasing correspondence between scientific statements and physical reality. Yet another tactic is the insistence that successful research programs lead to the discovery of novel, quite unexpected phenomena on at least some occasions[42]—reality, as it were, speaking through the filter of our presuppositions. And even those sympathetic to Kuhn's paradigms have felt that, as in the Gestalt switch, "there are lines in the picture which do not change."[43]

It is time to stop and ponder how the Christian is to respond to all of this. Clearly the arguments involved are often highly technical and necessitate a level of detailed evaluation far beyond the scope of this discussion. Nevertheless a few signposts along the scientific road are surely discernible. At the outset we must recall that evangelical Christians have taken rather different stances on the question of value-free knowledge. Some, and I have Cornelius Van Til and his disciples in mind, have grounded their epistemology in the presupposition-ladenness of all theoretical knowledge. The filtering role of tinted spectacles is an analogy to which they have persistently reverted.[44] By contrast, the British philosopher Paul Helm has welcomed the realist emphasis as most congruent with Christian theism, while Donald MacKay has argued for the normative role of value-free knowledge, at least for the exact sciences.[45] My own instinct, therefore, is to resist the temptation to pin Christian colors to the mast of one particular brand of scientific philosophy. Clearly we will want to balance the intelligibility of the Creator's world with the defects arising from a human fall from grace. We might also be careful neither to deny the theoretical possibility of objective knowledge nor to be too mesmerized by the epistemological promises of the cocksure scientist. The contrast between divine revelation and scientific investigation will be worth maintaining.

Every claim to scientific knowledge will have to be judged on its own merits. For example, consider the "Copernican Revolution." We now know that Copernicus's heliocentric theory was not in any narrowly empirical sense a scientific discovery, at least as judged by the quality of his observational data. These in fact were every bit as compatible with the old geocentric universe and were therefore not decisive. What *was* important were the philosophical assumptions with which his theory was impregnated; it was shot through with a distaste for the complications of Ptolemy's system and a sympathetic awareness of pre-Aristotelian scientific theory.[46] In any meaningful sense, therefore, the Copernican theory was not the outcome of value-neutral reflection. But that in itself did not make it false. Clearly scientific theories can be presupposition-laden, and still make substantive claims to truth.

For this reason, then, I am inclined to resist those blanket proposals that are issued from time to time in the effort finally to clinch the deal on how to relate science and faith. To banish each to eternally separate spheres fails to take account of the divine management of the natural order. To press for mutual modification in the light of current discoveries ignores the real distinction between technology and theology. To find solace in the argument for two language systems trivializes both science and faith by decomposing them into useful fictions.

More positively, what recent developments have shown is the need for a broader understanding of what constitutes "rationality." The realization that metaphorical insight lies at the heart of scientific model-building—subatomic particles, we are told, behave as if they are miniature orbital systems; human brains function like computers; light is thought of as waves or particles—has served to reintroduce to science such "artistic" qualities as imagination, creativity, and elegance.[47] In many ways this conception of truth is closer to Hebrew wisdom than to Greek rationality, and may suggest that a coherence view of knowledge is more insightful in the long run than patching up the traditional correspondence formula. Via the paths of science, human beings have achieved a stunning mastery of complex nature, and indeed, in turn, have had their conceptual forms pried open as they have encountered a universe breath-taking in what Torrance calls its "coherent singularity."[48] But science is an ever-changing endeavor, a wholly human artifact, and for that reason a good servant but a bad master.

Ideological Issues and the Scientific Enterprise

However contested the claim that social conditions determine scientific theory, it is nonetheless apparent that science is practiced in a social context. This indivisibility is evident, for example, in the role of foundation research funding, government sponsorship, and the growth of what is often called "big science." At the everyday level, too, the output of the scientific industry has transformed our lives. "Science and technology," writes Charles Rosenberg,

> have produced both the hard tomatoes we encounter every day in our supermarkets and the hydrogen bombs that recur in our nightmares. The ideas and authority of science and technology are not mere mystification; they have created the possibility of new social choices even if they do not determine how these choices are to be exercised.[49]

In our scientifically impregnated society we can scarcely avoid the conclusion that "scientific knowledge" is a cultural product and a political resource. Indeed some, notably those historians and sociologists of science collectively known as the Edinburgh group, have pressed on to the view that social goals and political aspirations directly shape the content of scientific knowledge.[50] On all of this I find myself in substantial agreement with Martin Rudwick when he writes:

> This view need not in fact reduce scientific knowledge to "nothing but" a product of social circumstances; but it is understandable that some of its critics fear its apparent relativism. This is not least because it makes increasing use of explicit analogies from social anthropology.... But the more general point is that the anthropological perspective is seen as breaking through what is otherwise an impenetrable barrier to a realistic view of science, namely the "sacralization" of modern scientific knowledge. It provides resources for studying science realistically as a social institution and as a cultural product, without assuming *a priori* any intrinsic uniqueness that would preclude or limit the scope of such a study.[51]

Any hint at the sacralization of a human endeavor ought to put us immediately on guard. Indeed, such ideological uses of what was once unselfconsciously described as "The Faith of Reverent Science"[52] is manifest in a range of styles from the explicit to the covert, from the declared to the unconscious. The most vulgar displays of unadorned scientism are easily spotted and just as easily scotched. When Sir Peter Medawar tells the British Association for the Advancement of Science that "the deterioration of the environment produced by technology is a technological problem for which technology has found, is finding and will continue to find solutions,"[53] he is simply mistaken. Scientific discoveries by themselves can never "solve" our ecological problems. Economic, moral, political, and administrative dimensions of that quest cannot be so easily erased, nor can science *qua* science solve the evils of human greed or the lust for power.

What is perhaps more disturbing and at once more enlightening is the resort to science by religious unbelievers and believers alike to justify their own worldview. Eileen Barker has sociologically wandered through the meetings of every sort of scientific gathering from the fundamentalist Institute for Creation Research via the orthodox Victoria Institute and the American Scientific Affiliation to the Marxist British Society for Social Responsibility in Science. Concluding her delightfully caricatured vignettes of each body, she shows how all in their own way have turned for self-vindication to the "new priesthood of science."

> The Biblical literalist, the Evangelical revivalist, the political visionary and even the slightly perturbed old priesthood of the established theologies turn to the new priesthood for reassurance that their beliefs have not been left behind in the wake of the revolutionary revelations of science. The new priesthood has not been found wanting. Sometimes with formula, sometimes with rhetoric, but always with science, the reassurance is dispensed.[54]

In this case, as in the former, a tighter rein on scientific histrionics and a larger measure of self-criticism might temper the extravagances of those claiming scientific vindication for their own party line.

Ultimately more sinister, I believe, are those "theodicean" pronouncements presented in the guise of innocuous academic neutrality. One sphere where this is particularly evident is biological determinism. Here we are told that as science has excavated back through the layers of human values, it has found them to be embedded in the very laws of nature. Unpacking behavioral traits one by one, scientism has relocated their source neither in social nor transcendent realities, but in biology. This theme has run like a high voltage current throughout the human sciences. Whether in the grosser forms of a brutally manipulative scientific racism, in the excesses of behaviorist psychology, in the various schools of environmental determinism, in functionalist social science, or in psychoanalytic therapy, reductionist maneuvers have been in vogue. In all of these, as the Marxist Bob Young has argued, "metaphysical belief, in its religious sense, has been replaced by a set of scientistic concepts, analogies and reductions which, in turn, are employed to explain the religious belief itself."[55] Besides, under the guise of neutral scientific description—whether drawn from genetics, ethnology, archaeology, or anthropology—such popularizers as Lorenz, Ardrey, and Morris have continued to write ideologically prescriptive works, accounting "scientifically" for everything from aggression to altruism, from industrial management to intelligence quotients. These are dramatic cases, but there is little reason to believe that the sanitized world of the specialist is de facto any less captive to group loyalties, personal motives, and social prejudices.

My point, again, is not that science is all ideology. But the fact that it can be and often is so is surely sufficient grounds for it to feature high on any Christian agenda for science. The Christian call to self-awareness and self-judgment is particularly cutting at this point. Evangelical scientists, of course, no less than others, have been hostages, albeit unconscious, to ideological science in the past, and doubtless are today. And if the Christian critique of the naturalization of human values is to be heard, it will need to be presented with all due humility and critical reflexivity. Then we can continue the task of discerning the legitimate role that scientific explanations play in the understanding of human evolution and social development while retaining the vitality and integrity of discourse about morality, politics, freedom, and grace.

Ethical Issues and Scientific Practice

Holding a finger up to the wind of social opinion, J. R. Ravetz has sensed a "sudden shift in the public image of the morality of science."[56] Once lauded as a pursuit lofty in ideals and ennobling in actions, science has come of age with a crisis of ethical identity. The apocalyptic visions of nuclear holocaust, the chilly winds of environmental decay, and the human face of technology in assembly-line alienation, not to mention the unscrupulous fixing of results and the petty partialities of journal refereeing are just a few of the stern reminders that the ethical dilemma is inescapable. The most heinous crimes of the technological imperative ("If it can be done, it must be done") are all too familiar, and lest our memories should be too short-lived, Theodore Roszak compiled some years ago a brief but grotesque catalog of experiments carried out by advocates of "objectivity unlimited."[57] Everything from the gruesome neurological testing of the "feeble-minded" to the truly prurient psychological scrutiny of prisoners facing impending death by execution finds its way into Roszak's morbid inventory. In most of these cases, to expound is to expose.

But the ethical dimensions of science cannot be restricted to those clear-cut instances of agreed misconduct. Moral questions and judgments insinuate their way into scientific discourse at many points. Genetic engineering, biomedical ethics, the technology of war, and animal experimentation are just some of the spheres where tough issues have to be confronted. In these areas it is science itself that has raised the moral dilemmas, and if it is wrong to expect science to answer them, it is equally wrong to exclude moral discussion from the life of the scientific community. Consider, for example, the case of the ecological problem. At this point I am not concerned with the charge that our environmental crisis is the direct result of human technological mastery of nature. My claim, rather, is that to speak of an "ecological problem" is to make a moral pronouncement, a judgment that society would be better off without it. This, of course, is what makes the perception of what *is* an ecological problem a contested issue, and *a fortiori* what constitutes a satisfactory solution.[58] Words like *reduce, diminish,* or *abolish* are notoriously value-laden, as is the view that at a certain level pollution is a cost not a scourge. In an enlightening contribution to this subject, Rowland Moss has shown how a series of archetypal metaphysical systems held by environmentalists—Christian, Marxist, humanist, pragmatist, mystical, and so on—influence their descriptions of environmental problems and their prescriptions for their resolution. As he concludes, "To insist that to conduct the debate about environmental problems in particular, without examining the ideological presuppositions of the major contenders, is to ignore the most significant factor in the debate."[59]

Of course it is possible to claim as a purist that science should not be concerned with judgments of this kind: that its role is to describe and explain some aspect of nature in a morally neutral way. Certainly the answers to purely technical questions (How does DDT find its way into the fat of Antarctic birds?) are fundamental to understanding dimensions of the problem. But to dismiss as a categorical mistake the propriety of raising the ethical question is, I believe, to ignore the fact that scientists—people who perceive problems, knowers who obtain knowledge—practice science. From the Christian perspective at least, the biblical insistence on the responsibility of knowledge—doing the truth, not merely knowing it—strikes a chord that we all need to hear. Indeed, evangelicals have already made helpful contributions to this whole debate.[60] This naturally does not mean that the *modes* of exercising moral accountability are self-evident or clear-cut: should it be left to the individual scientist, to peer groups, or to society at large? What sanctions need to be invoked? Where is the line between censorship and academic freedom? There are no easy answers to these questions, but the concern to open up the scientific subculture to ethical dialogue is an aspiration consonant with the spirit of the Judeo-Christian tradition.

RUDIMENTS OF A THEOLOGY OF SCIENCE

As historians, philosophers, and sociologists have plied the tools of their trade, both the status and image of science have needed a thorough revision. Science's claims to cognitive privilege, ideological autonomy, and ethical immunity, once taken for granted, have all been seriously contested in the effort to develop a more realistic understanding of the achievements and limitations of the scientific experience. The need for a corresponding theological reevaluation is a real *desideratum*. Such an endeavor, I firmly believe, will be careful to retain the real gains already won by Christian theology, to take into account fully the critique of the scientific revisionists, and to re-mine the quarries of the Christian heritage in the search for a viable conceptual and ethical framework. This is, plainly, a formidable task, and precludes all but a few programmatic statements in the present context. Still, there are extremes evidently to be avoided. The doctrinal doubletalk of those reformists who pour new meanings into old words is no more satisfying than the cheap certainties of those rearguard reactionaries who squeeze scientific theories out of biblical texts.

In our own day, no doubt because of the environmental panic and a corresponding scientific *volte-face,* the doctrine of creation has been under reconstruction. To anaesthetize Christian guilt-feelings over the technological mess of modern society, some have called for a new biblical theology of nature. By claiming to respect the rich lore of Scripture, Conrad Bonifazi, for instance, can literalize Isaiah's metaphor of mountains breaking into song to mean that nature is imbued with vital energy.[61] And just as he finds solace in the speculative metaphysics of Teilhard de Chardin, so H. Paul Santmire has reinterpreted the biblical record in such a way that the earth and humanity are seen as "brothers" in God's creative venture.[62] The sheer modernity of this hermeneutic alone makes it suspicious. For, as Thomas Derr has put it, "if theology is to be redone to make it acceptable to each newly popular study or cultural mood, it squanders its integrity in hopeless promiscuity."[63] Besides, even if the Bible is most interested in the world of nature as it impinges on human history, that does not *per se* prevent its rendering a viable ecological ethic. Only if people are separate *from* nature can they assume real responsibility *for* it. And this, I think, cuts clean across the remystifying temper of much process theology. Building on the earlier philosophical reflections of Whitehead and Hartshorne, modern process theologians have spawned neologisms like *panpsychism* and *primordial oneness* to emphasize the need for "binding sentient and non-sentient things into an essential unity."[64] Certainly the consonance of process thought with the indeterminacy of modern physics has made it attractive to many, but its sacrificing divine transcendence to immanence and fudging the bifurcation between nature and humanity stretch biblical exegesis beyond reasonable limits.

Even for the ecologically-minded the biblical portrait is surely more satisfying. I do not say this with any naive prepossessions as to the simple coherence or unity of the biblical conception of nature. Nevertheless I feel quite sure that the doctrine of creation embodies insights that we jettison at our peril, and the recovery of which was formative, to a greater or lesser degree, during the inauguration of modern science in the west. The first of these is surely its secularizing ethos, its dedivinizing of the world of nature. Now I am quite ready to admit that the desacralizing implications of biblical creation must be interpreted with rather more care than in the past. The supposed animistic cast of nonbiblical Near Eastern religions, for example, as James Barr has insisted, "seems to depend excessively on purely theological and philosophical analysis of what it *must* have been like, and too little expert historical analysis of what it *was* like."[65] Still, as even he admits, there are aspects of historical religions that can be understood only as proposing divinity in nature. For the Hebrews, by contrast, the very fact that nature is created implied that it was not divine, and their cosmology is therefore as distant from ancient pantheism as it is from our vernacular tendency to imbue nature with personality ("Nature shows . . ."; "Nature teaches . . ."; "Nature selects . . ."). And even if we can no longer go so far as to say that it was this disenchantment of nature that provided an essential precondition for the emergence of natural science,[66] we can certainly agree with Archbishop Temple that "it may be safely asserted that it [science] can never spontaneously grow up in regions where the ruling principle of the Universe is believed to be either capricious or hostile."[67] So, if we are to discard the Reformation view of creation in favor of mysticism or cosmic holism or concretion or Zoroastrianism, we will have to do so in full knowledge that it was, as a matter of historical fact, the dedeification or secularization of nature that gave us the mechanical philosophy so central to the emergence of Western science. The epistemological implications of following the path toward the *re*mystification of nature in the face of the cultural debt already owed to its *de*mystification is surely a cost too great to bear. For if nature is divine it is to be worshiped and feared; if it is created it is to be analyzed and controlled. This does not mean, of course, that the created order has no value. On the contrary. It has value, a derivative value stemming from the character of its Creator. Besides, within the Christian tradition are other grounds for affirming nature's worth. The doctrine of the incarnation is nothing less than a divine declaration of God's solidarity with the material world. For in Christ we see the earthly, and earthy, face of the Creator God himself.

Whatever the historical significance of nature's desacralization, the conceptual significance of the biblical idea of creation's contingency must also be taken seriously. As Torrance puts it, this theme "is the direct product of the Christian understanding of the constitutive relation between God and the universe which he freely created out of nothing, yet not without reason, conferring upon what he has made and continues to sustain a created rationality of its own dependent on his uncreated transcendent rationality."[68] More than ever, modern science surely assumes both the contingence and orderliness of the universe: contingent, because it does not exist of necessity, and orderly, because experimental replicability presupposes that the universe is neither chaotic nor precarious. To this extent, Norbert Wiener, founder of cybernetics, was quite correct to speak of science's initial faith in the order of the world. "Without faith that nature is subject to law," he wrote, "there can be no science. No amount of demonstration can ever prove that nature is subject to law."[69]

In another sense, the order of nature stems from its historicization in the biblical cosmogony. By the offices of providential management, the natural world has a history and a future. It is neither eternal, nor a cyclical system of recurring states, but rather dynamic, eschatological, evolutionary. Indeed the created world participates no less than its human occupants in the soteriological drama, for in the messianic kingdom its predatory relationships are to be transformed in the final consummation of all things. So it is no surprise that some have tried to describe the providential government of the world as "continuing creation." Moreover, if the structure of the universe displays the marks of its maker, there is no reason to suppose that the history of life on earth should not equally exhibit some discernible pattern.

This growing sense of nature's contingent rationality and its linear historicity throws some light on the reinstatement of the arguments of natural theology in the writings of some philosophers and scientists. The characteristics of the quantum mechanical world have forced some physicists into religious language to find adequate expression for their empirical findings.[70] Others, notably evolutionary biologists, have tried to transmute the idea of teleology into "teleonomy" in the effort to preserve purpose without finalistic implications. This is indeed, as Bowker declares, "one of the curiosities of recent writing," for the new terminology "has been evoked by the sheer pressure of data—by the sort of universe this appears to be, and by the evolutionary process being the sort of process that it is."[71] Still others have marshaled design arguments into a much fuller defense of the traditional claims of natural theology.[72] So, even if like Thomas Chalmers—surely the most reluctant of natural theologians to write two books on natural theology—we agree that it raises questions even if it provides no answers,[73] we should surely welcome the testimony of its latter-day exponents as celebrating the rationality and purpose of God's world.

The doctrine of creation, it would seem, is still as foundational to the scientific enterprise as it was in the past. But it needs all the while to be supplemented by a theology of humanity. The Genesis picture is at once denigrating and dignifying, humbling yet elevating. Human beings, we see, are dust through and through, and herein lies our continuity with nature. But men and women are equally made in the image of God and this is what differentiates us from the rest of the organic and inorganic worlds alike. Moreover, what the Christian tradition also teaches is that this image is defaced, scarred, distorted through rebellion. The effect has been disastrous. We have a congenital bias to revolt against what is good and true and right. Scientists, no less than other mortals, certainly fall within the universal limits of what Paul calls the "reign of sin." So if the doctrine of creation teaches us the objectivity and rationality of the universe, the theology of the fall reminds us that the claim to any particular piece of scientific knowledge is not automatically immune from the taints of sin. The ideological captivity of science to particular group interests should therefore come as no surprise, nor should the scientific voyeurism that casts all moral sense to the winds. Christian scientists, it goes without saying, are no less inclined to partisanship than their secular colleagues, but the implication of biblical anthropology is surely that they should be in the vanguard of scientific self-criticism. At the same time, aware of humanity's constitutional disfigurement, Christian scientists should best understand the irrepressible idolatry of humankind that has resulted in the transfer of the sacral from the spiritual to the scientific realm.

Besides these are the moral repercussions of original sin. Indeed, Christianity speaks so clearly and realistically about humanity's ethical illiteracy that the counterculture guru, Theodore Roszak, grasping for words to express his revulsion at the evils of technocracy, is forced to resort to the language and images of Scripture to give adequate voice to his sense of moral outrage.[74] In the spheres of science and technology the Christian revelation would certainly underscore the prime importance of our "stewardship" of the Creator's world, the need to preserve human freedom and dignity vis-à-vis the hazards of research, and the individual and social responsibility of scientific knowledge. If these were to be taken more seriously the antinomian spirit of much scientific inquiry would be curbed and the world of science opened up to the cathartic inflow of transcendental values.

The Christian agenda for science certainly does not stop here. There are still items of unfinished business on our theological order paper. There is, for example, the need for a coherent hermeneutic of Scripture that will allow it to be heard fully as canon and yet remain sensitive to modern scientific discoveries. Our work on Genesis and geology, and its wider implications, is not as yet complete. The doctrine of God's relationship to his creation in providence and miracles still requires further elucidation so as to integrate what we know from science about, say, human origins and natural law, with what we derive from our chosen theological sources, especially Scripture. Besides, there are the pastoral problems of diffusing those emotional and theological obstacles to modern science that linger in some circles by enabling people to face the issues squarely without sacrificing their theological or scientific integrity.

In the last analysis, I believe, a Christian theology of science must be both confessional and critical. It will encourage us to confess our commitment both to theology and to science, to the God of creation and to the creation itself. Yet it will invite us to be as critical of the limitations of theology to fathom the unsearchable judgments of the Creator as of science to penetrate the ultimate mysteries of his Creation.

Secularization and Secularism: Some Christian Considerations

Klaus Bockmuehl

In the present situation a primary concern of the Christian church should be to understand the secular and define an attitude toward it. Bryan Wilson, the British sociologist of religion, is quite right to marvel at a theologian who can declare that the problem of ecumenism is the order of the day. An independent observer would have thought "that the problem of secularization could much more suitably have been chosen as the special problem of contemporary Christianity."[1] And indeed it is. A church that was destined by its Founder to be evermore in a process of consolidation and expansion must be disturbed when it experiences uncertainty of heart and, in many places, a dwindling of adherents.

Nonetheless, the church in the West where these developments primarily occur does not seem to have given serious thought to the problem. With a peculiar belief in providence, some authorities persuade themselves that secularization, the movement away from the church to the world, is essentially a salutary move somewhat comparable to the incarnation or *kenosis* of Christ. Others, evangelicals among them, focus their attention on the future of their respective groups, and seem to be well content if they add to their own numbers even if the overall state of Christianity deteriorates. Others again fight evangelicalism as their foremost enemy, and pay no attention to the general ascent of secularism. Against each of these, the sobering observation of the sociologist points to the fact that secularization and secularism concern the very existence of religion and its institutions, especially, as the figures show, in areas traditionally Christian. What then is secularization and secularism and how should the church respond to them? Attempting to answer these questions, we shall first examine the nature of secularization, secularism, and the secular, then consider their prospects, and finally try to determine possible responses by the church.

THE NATURE OF SECULARIZATION AND SECULARISM

Historical Observations

To understand the meaning of secularization and secularism, it is not enough merely to sketch the history of the concept, for the history and extent of the subject matter itself is the real concern.

Karl Heim, together with J. H. Oldham and the participants of the International Missionary Council's 1928 meeting in Jerusalem, was one of the first to address the problem directly. Heim especially sought an answer to the question why secularization and secularism would spring up and spread so extensively in the areas of Christendom itself. His suggestion was that Scripture allowed for creation, the world, to act as an agent by itself, in relationship with but also over against God. By contrast, other religions pictured the world as an extension of the deity incapable of acting on its own. Only where there is a duality between God and world, God and man, can a dualism develop, a corruption of the original and intended community.[2]

This may be part of the explanation, although it does not explain why secularization and secularism failed to originate also, and with the same intensity, in Judaism and Islam, which share the presupposition of the transcendence and aseity of God. In fact these faiths, by not allowing for the incarnation, hold to the divine transcendence even more vigorously.

Within Christendom itself the medieval antithesis between the holy and the secular certainly deserves consideration in the development of secularism. Monastic theology, for instance, fiercely contrasted the "angelic" contemplative life of monk and nun with the drudgery and uncleanliness of the ordinary Christian in the world. It is well known how the monastic ideology could ravage the traditional doctrine of the Christian life, until the monastery became the church, vows became rebirth and the second baptism, and the monk was the only true Christian, leaving nothing for the believer whose walk was "in the secular."[3]

Out of this juxtaposition of church and world, *sanctum* and *saeculum,* grew the process of secularization. It begins, in the Middle Ages, when the withdrawal or dismissal of an individual monk from the monastery or a priest from the ranks of the clergy is called an act of "secularization." During the Reformation monasteries and church estates came into secular hands, became secularized. In the peace negotiations ending the Thirty Years' War in 1648 the French delegate suggested the "secularization" of certain church territories. The year 1803 witnessed the dissolution of the Holy Roman Empire of the German Nation and at the same time the alienation (or "secularization") of the remaining ecclesiastical territories with which Napoleon meant to compensate the princes whose lands he had taken for himself and the members of his family. We observe thus, on the level of laws and institutions, an ever-growing circle of objects drawn into the process of "secularization."[4]

We may observe a similar development in the history of ideas. F. X. Arnold[5] has pointed out the secularizing implications of the philosophical school of Averroism in the Faculty of Arts of the University of Paris during the thirteenth century. This school postulated the liberation of philosophy from the supremacy of theology, and the disjunction of rational and revealed truth; its representatives spoke of "twofold truth"; and they already held most of the tenets in the modern catalog of unbelief.[6] The intellectual movement of the Italian Renaissance continued this effort and in the famed *Principe* of Machiavelli proclaimed, in effect, the secularization of political ethics. Thomas Hobbes and Hugo Grotius established the framework for a secular conception of political theory and the law, and Adam Smith as well as Karl Marx effectively did the same for the whole world of economics. The materialists of the eighteenth and nineteenth century from Holbach to Haeckel looked after the secularization of the philosophy of nature while historians during the same period did the same for their own field of endeavor.

It has been observed frequently, however, that the secular viewpoint is largely independent of empirical argument both in the natural sciences and in history.[7] Rather, it is very much the consequence of an existential attitude, what could be styled "voluntative secularism." Owen Chadwick pointed out that "the onslaught upon Christianity owed its force . . . not at all to the science" (i.e., of the nineteenth century). It was made "not in the name of knowledge, but in the name of justice and freedom."[8] Karl Marx reacted against the concept of creation (in favor of the self-generation of the universe) precisely for reasons of human independence and autonomy. In his early notebooks he picked up on the argument of the French materialist Holbach who, resurrecting the pre-Christian critic Lucretius, described religion as man's undignified subjection to, and worship of, the deities of nature, lightning, and thunder. Marx correspondingly heralded Prometheus, the ancient symbol of rebellion against the gods.[9] Sharing Marx's refusal to distinguish between religions, Feuerbach, Bakunin the anarchist, and Buchner the materialist all proposed similar arguments at the end of the nineteenth century.[10]

The nineteenth century is remarkable for yet another development in the thrust toward secularization. Earlier, in the second half of the eighteenth century, the Enlightenment was the undertaking of the intellectual elite. Voltaire among others refused to talk atheism "in front of the maids" because he felt that religion upheld the morality of servants; and this could only result in his own profit.[11] The same attitude prompted the notorious edict of 1788 written by F. W. von Wollner, the Prussian minister, in which enlightened pastors were constrained from preaching anything in discord with the teaching of the church, notwithstanding their own personal convictions. Secularity of viewpoint is here a private matter, of the individual, not of the public mind; neither the masses nor the institutions are as yet secularized. The situation is quite different at the end of the nineteenth century, at least in the European continent, which seems to have pioneered the development. As Chadwick has shown, this is likely due to the victory of Marxism over other schools of thought within the European workers' movement. Workers took a long time to be convinced that social renewal could be achieved only by the defeat of religion. But with the ascent of Marxism, socialism as well as the liberalism of the bourgeoisie became the vehicle of secularism. Thus Chadwick can say: "Marxist theory is the most influential of all symbols for the process of secularization in the nineteenth century."[12] Unlike the situation in the Enlightenment, a century later secularism has reached the general populace. It is one of the ideas that, as Marx put it, "become a revolutionary force as soon as they grip the masses." The final deinstitutionalization of religion was then only a matter of time.

Definitions

Although, as David Martin has well said, "the range of meaning behind the term secular" can include all sorts of things, for example "assimilation to established power, an overtly materialist doctrine, hedonistic indifference, religious propaganda based on psychic utility," even the phenomenon that the bishop is a warrior—"we have the paradox of secularization always with us"[13]—the historical survey can nevertheless aid in defining the concepts under consideration. Taking into account the different levels of development, one can say that secularization is the withdrawal or emancipation of social institutions, worldviews, and individual lives from instruction by, or responsibility to, ecclesiastical or divine authority.

Both the secularization of social institutions and public life (which sociologists primarily seem to study)[14] and the secularization of ideas, human consciousness, and "ideation"[15] (which historians seem to be more concerned with) are important. It is also important to perceive the process of secularization as a mass departure of individuals from church and religion. Just as statisticians can, as it were, give us a day-by-day breakdown of the growth of Christianity in certain countries, so we must think of the loss of faith as a concrete process made up of individual people, even though these are not marked with visible symbols that, like baptism, designate conversion to the faith.

Secularization and secularism seem to differ one from another in that secularization denotes an actual *process* of "becoming worldly"—it can affect individuals or groups—whereas secularism denotes the *program,* the intention of worldliness, or "the will to secularization" as a practical worldview.[16] As such—and similar to other "-isms"—it is unified (we don't tend to think of secularism in the plural) and limitless in its thrust.

Secularism in itself seems to be the "positive equivalent" of atheism, a de facto atheism, a forgetfulness of the things of God as compared with the belligerent denial of God in atheism proper. It is rather an attitude on the other side of atheism, of "let's get on with the job," the practical stance Marx and Engels advocated when they berated their atheist mentor Ludwig Feuerbach, who couldn't seem to leave religion alone even after he had effectively criticized it. Secularism bespeaks the intention to live "without God in the world" (Eph. 2:12).

We are now in a position to interpret the final distinction in the definition above, and so to determine the meaning of "the secular." For this purpose a distinction between ecclesiastical authority and divine authority is indispensable. Many authors fail to distinguish between the two, a failure that creates havoc in the perception of history as well as in the discussion of contemporary concerns. We are faced with a cluster of problems that need careful sorting out.

To begin with, the Latin root of the term *secular, saeculum,* occurs not infrequently in the Vulgate translation of the New Testament, taking the place of the Greek *aion*. One particular occurrence, Titus 2:12 *(abnegantes impietatem, et saecularia desideria, sobrie, juste, et pie vivamus in hoc saeculo)*, shows that the term can be used both in a negative ("worldly desires") and a morally neutral sense ("live in the world"). In this it resembles the notorious ambiguity of its synonym *kosmos/mundus:* the "world," fallen into sin as well as God's creation and object of his love.

When the Reformation toppled the monastic antithesis between the secular and the holy, it recovered the Christian relevance of lay life in the secular world, for example in one's civil vocation. Overcoming the monastic devaluing of life in the normal workday, the Reformers moved from the holy precinct into the marketplace. They did so not to live an unholy life, but to claim even this sphere for the holy God. As is well known, Luther in the course of his career changed from the Augustinian doctrine of the two kingdoms, the kingdom of heaven and the kingdom of this world, to his own teaching that distinguished between the kingdom of Christ and the kingdom of God, the realm of salvation, gospel, and church on the one hand, and the realm of creation, law, and state on the other. The secularization that took place during the Reformation (Luther's adversaries accused him of making the whole of Christianity "profane") was not therefore a denial of the divine ordinances but of ecclesiastical tutelage and the church's dominion over the life of society. Breaking away from Rome (and from some imaginable Protestant clerocracy as well) was quite different from breaking away from God and his commandments.

This distinction is often overlooked. Many authors, Protestant as well as Catholic, portray the Reformation as the beginning of the modern process of secularization. Some do so because the Reformation broke Christian unity (and thus created the movement toward modern pluralism and the consequent possibility of confessional or religious neutrality). These interpreters do not, however, regard the earlier schism of Christendom into the Eastern and Western churches in a similar manner. Others credit (or debit) the Protestant Reformation with the invention of the modern principle of moral autonomy.[17] The whole debate over secularization and secularism revolves indeed around the question of autonomy. But for the Reformation, the autonomy of the "secular" was set over against ecclesiastical authority, not over against the authority of the divine commandments. The secular was not emancipated so that it could advance according to its own discretion (that is a modern concept, originated with accommodation to subsequent secularism). The "secular" was rather subjected to a different set of rules *("Andersgesetzlichkeit,"* not *"Eigengesetzlichkeit"*).

Luther occasionally (e.g., in "The Bondage of the Will") stressed the role of human reason in earthly concerns, but only to denounce it the more for questions of God and salvation. He elaborates, as it were, on the famous dictum of Ecclesiasticus 15:14 (also perused by Thomas Aquinas): "God made man from the beginning and left him in the hand of his own counsel." But, as at least our forefathers were well aware, the text continues: "He added His commandments and precepts. If thou wilt keep the commandments . . . , they shall preserve thee." *That* is the framework of God's "Kingdom at the left hand," his order of preservation that is to determine the life of society.

Of course, one can take the view that Martin Luther, religious appearances to the contrary, was really a proponent of the Renaissance and its thrust toward secularity. But that does not fit with the historical observation, emphasized repeatedly by Troeltsch and others,[18] that in terms of social ethics the Reformation, both in Lutheran and Calvinist versions, very much represented a continuation of the medieval synthesis, not a "Copernican revolution" away from it. It is also a fact that the secularization of the mind (and later of the state), in recapitulation of the ideas of the Renaissance, originated in France and Scotland, and not in Luther's native Thuringia.

Indeed, the Lutheran doctrine of the two kingdoms should be considered as a viable third option between an ecclesiastical hierocracy and a secularism regarded as an inevitable reaction to it. This doctrine clearly differentiated between "Christianity" and "Churchianity." As it eventually developed, it allowed for a pluralism of confessions within one and the same state, "one nation under God, not under Catholicism or Anglicanism or Presbyterianism."[19] Within this perspective it is possible to distinguish between deconfessionalization, the disestablishment of a church, and the demise of the divine laws. This notion also defines a kind of desirable secularity for a state that was previously (or still is) confessionally Muslim or Hindu; indeed, it can serve as a common framework for people from different religious communities living together.[20] Increased attention to the Reformational doctrine of the two kingdoms would also go a long way to remove the painful uncertainty in the United States concerning the separation of church and state. The Fathers of the Constitution

seem to have been well aware of the difference between a decon-
fessionalized state and a secularist state.

We therefore need to distinguish throughout between two types
of secularization, between emancipation from ecclesiastical tutelage
and withdrawal from one's responsibility to the judgment of God.
The former was the intention of the Reformation, the latter the program of more recent centuries. Only the latter is an unlimited proposition; only it is "secularism."

PROSPECTS OF THE SECULAR
AND OF SECULARISM

Our own time appears to be dominated by the mindset of secularity.
One finds it difficult to say what is still left to be secularized. Before
we can come to suggest a Christian stance toward these developments, it is necessary not only to survey their past but also to probe
into their future development as that future is prefigured in earlier
events, or as it unfolds in the present. Certain evolutionary patterns
are discernible, both in mass psychology and in social structures.

Two Phases of the Secular Mindset

The development of the secular mind seems always to begin with eu-
phoria. We have the testimony of exhilaration in the heyday of
Enlightenment at the beginning of the second half of the eighteenth
century. The same mood seems to have pervaded Western culture
around the turn of the nineteenth to the twentieth century when the
educated elite consciously espoused the Enlightenment and its optimistic view of human nature. Owen Chadwick quotes an advertisement for the *Encyclopedia Britannica* of 1898 that exalts "the
wonderful story . . . of modern progress in the arts, sciences and in-
dustries" and promises to "tell how the light was spread." Spirits are
waking everywhere: how glorious to be alive! Humanity is seen to be
potentially almighty. However, these sentiments do not last. The
atrocities of the French Revolution and its tyrannical pursuit of virtue
had a sobering effect. Later, it is surprising to see, for example, how
the mood of French historiography changed from the optimism of
Michelet to the dejection of Hippolyte Taine, and how the public reception of Darwinism turned sour.[21]

World War I had similar effects. Evangelists of materialism
around the turn of the century made way for culture critics who
brooded over the relativisms and meaninglessness of the technologi-

cal age. Karl Heim has observed the sobering of mood in the leading scientists.[22] Already at the time, many people felt that the "Roaring Twenties" was a dance on a volcano that was ready to erupt. They attempted, as Thornton Wilder characterized the mood, to "eat their ice cream while it is on their plate." One theologian of the time captured the cultural climate in a startling manner: "Fear of God has died. But a new fear replaces it, fear of everything *(Weltangst)*. . . . Adoration of culture turns into disdain. The dark gate, to which all secularization leads, is pessimism."[23] Humanity, having abolished God, now bemoans its fate as a "cosmic orphan."

Peter Berger, the eminently readable sociologist who has a wakeful eye on intellectuals, observes that such individuals "are notoriously haunted by boredom." For whatever reason, Berger feels that on the other side of secularism, "there is no telling what outlandish religiosity, even one dripping with savage supernaturalism, may yet arise in these groups."[24] Ultramoderns develop a new belief in fate, turn to superstition in search for "meaning," and make enlightenment perfect in a new obscurantism.[25]

The most remarkable instance of such a change in mood is the recent collapse of secular optimism in western Europe. Whereas the 1960s with their booming economies encouraged a confidence in limitless progress and human abilities, the first oil crisis, the public awakening to seemingly untractable ecological problems, a period of economic decline, and the renewed perception of threatening nuclear war completely changed the picture. Today visitors from overseas marvel at the weariness and melancholy, the doom and gloom that rule Europe. Problems may be far greater in India or in Latin America, but it is "Euro-pessimism," "the disappearance of hope," that characterizes the old countries. People speak of themselves as the "no future generation." All creativity is gone. Humanity has lost its moorings—after people discarded faith in God, they now also doubt the confidence they were to have in themselves. Sartre's prophecies of "Huis clos" and "La nausée" are fulfilled. One wonders what happened to the "Principle of hope" and the "Theology of hope" that were hailed in the sixties—could they have become "old hat" in less than twenty years?

Disorientation and despondency again give rise to new eccentric faiths. David Martin observes: "Amsterdam . . . one of the most secularised areas in Holland . . . at the same time is besieged by minor cults."[27] People begin to meddle again in witchcraft and necromancy. Astrology is "a burgeoning industry in the most 'advanced' countries of the west."[28] Where God and man have been abandoned, humanity discovers that the cult of Satan is next: it begins to dominate whole sectors of cultural expression, as, for example, in the rock scene. Secular society quickly becomes a victim of fear and superstition after people abandon the ground that does not shift with the moods of the day. These perspectives make the question "After secularism what?" mandatory.

"Anomie"; or, The Prospects for the Social Structures

The same question is well worth asking about the consequences to social structures of a secularity that denies any allegiance to God. Secularism proves a terrifying solvent of social bonds. Secular sociologists today are the foremost witnesses to the fact that religion provides both identity and bonding, and also to the effects when religion is lost in a largely secularized milieu. "That religion has been a carrier of identity is axiomatic"; it also engenders organic solidarity and looks after the "coherent relation" of one's social and personal identity "to a whole."[29] Sociologists are aware that religious ethics constitute a running endorsement of the ancient teaching, "God said to them: 'Beware of all iniquity' and commended to everyone his neighbour" (Ecclus. 17:12).

It is even more remarkable that modern sociology, beginning with Emile Durkheim, should have chosen a term—*anomie*—for the secular dissolution of social bonds that figures prominently in the eschatology of the gospel: "Because *anomia* (lawlessness) will abound, the love of many will grow cold" (Matt. 24:12). Sociologists, philosophers, and historians have charted this disintegration of the social network in the progress of secularization. For example, in the field of economics emancipation from traditional religious ethics and the renunciation of the proprietor's responsibility before God has resulted in the theory and practice of an utter individualism, with a resulting fragmentation of society and with overt acts of unmitigated class warfare that bring misery to millions of people.[30] Others observe the ominous rise of nationalism concurrently with the maturing of secularity, another fragmentation for which the world has already paid dearly in two world wars.[31] The desacralization of religion can quickly turn into a sacralization of politics.

In more recent times we are faced with a mounting disintegration of the family, the social unit sociologists fifteen or twenty years ago still thought to be highly resistant to the acids of secularization. But here, too, social disorganization is under way.

The overall result is "anomie," an atomism of social life. Only now do we recognize the prophetic character of the arts, music, painting, and literature from the first half of the twentieth century, which are dominated by the same principle. This *anomie* expresses itself in the abolition of moral consensus, a phenomenon that gleams at first as the opening up of individual freedom. Liberals like J. Stuart Mill postulated that the individual can be trusted, indeed must be trusted, to take responsibility for morality. But what if others, like Nietzsche, proclaim that not only religion but also morality is "opiate for the people," only a design to stifle genius?[32] How shall we then live together? Where there are no absolute values, all behavior is arbitrary, and Adolf Eichmann and Mother Teresa only represent different individual predilections.

Nietzsche knew that secularism and anarchy go together in the same way as faith in God and belief in structure: "I fear we won't get rid of God since we still believe in grammar."[33] Only the dissolution of all structure, social or otherwise, seems able to give the individual that total autonomy that supposedly facilitates the ultimate self-realization and gratification claimed as entitlement.

The Enlightenment took individuality, a boon from the inheritance of Christianity, severed it from its organic links, and it became individualism, an uncontrollable cancerous growth. The same thing occurred when brotherhood was blown up into collectivism. A paradigm of the whole development occurred in the evolution of individuals known as the "Young Hegelians" after they rejected Hegel's synthesis of Christianity and culture. Each position coagulates, as it were, in the stance of an individual thinker, the whole presenting an instructive genealogical tree: D. F. Strauss combines the extremes of Bible criticism with the veneration of humanity; L. Feuerbach combines the overall criticism of religion with the worship of the I-Thou relationship; the Bauer brothers are atheists and anarchists; and the end product is Julius Stirner's philosophy of "solipsism," neatly expressed in the title of his book, *The Only One and His Property.* The road that began with the Enlightenment must end with Stirner. But already at its start, the life of Rousseau provided a glimpse about its end. The historian James Hitchcock shrewdly observes: insofar as "the ultimate demand of the secularised individual . . . is absolute personal moral autonomy," "the most fundamental disease of the modern psyche is solipsism, the need for an empty universe to be filled by an infinitely expanding self."[34] Stirner's *The Only One and His Property* is also the secret of Adam Smith's political economy. The logical conclusion, since we cannot afford to depopulate the globe for the benefit of the Only One, must be civil war, even if a cold one. In this light Marx's desperate scramble to evade these consequences through the proclamation of socialism is easily understandable.

The consequences of such a secularism, however, are not merely logical extrapolations of theory. We are beginning to feel the palpable burden of the rising spiritual and material costs of social disintegration, in the international order as well as in the family, in the social expenditure for which the taxpayer answers. There comes the moment when people are no longer willing to bleed. Attempts at setting up new goals on the basis of this-worldly human responsibility fail. The consensus of perception that prevails for mechanics and the "How to" of science cannot be repeated for morals and the "What for?"[35] The impasse to which pluralism comes, when the realization dawns that no social system can exist without a basic commonality of norms, can be met by growing institutionalism. Even more blatant is the emergence of an unsurmountable public desire for new ideological reintegration, even by force if necessary. Robespierre, master of purges in the French Revolution, may serve as a classical example for the reversal of secularization into sacralization.[36] Reintegration here involves the idea of a "salutary" dictatorship that will make on our behalf the decisions of renunciation and frugality to which we can no longer bring ourselves. This is the type of the beneficent dictator who steps in when a majority, facing the confusion of goals and values, begins to feel that "It cannot go on like this." A change of mood is sometimes recognized in the shifting place of the concept of freedom. Always a prominent slogan at the beginning of secularization, it can become obsolete, almost an embarrassment, before the advent of the benevolent dictatorship. In the same way confidence in the potential of man is replaced by fear and a feeling of powerlessness over against the pressing social problems, a feeling that also serves the purposes of impending dictatorship.

Sociologists are only too aware of these historical consequences of "anomie." At the end of his book *Religion in Secular Society,* Bryan Wilson, the Oxford sociologist, testified to a remarkable change of mood. Throughout the book Wilson appears to take lightly the demise of religion and to fend off any justification for its meddling in public affairs again, as if to say "the secular world can do very well without it." Toward the end, however, a more thoughtful tone intrudes. Wilson observes that Christianity has brought into our culture "the extension of kin-group and neighborhood affectivity into generalized and impersonal goodwill," "a strong internalized sense of impersonal individual honesty," as well as "disinterested devotion to one's calling"—all qualities that reduce the need for external social control and that may well have been decisive in making our present culture possible.

Wilson goes on to note that when the church's liturgy, its theology, or its social life deteriorates, that is of concern to the church only. However, with ethics, things are different. These moral guidelines now appear "as a type of moral capital debt which is no longer being serviced." Therefore, "whether indeed our own type of society will effectively maintain public order, without institutional coercion, once the still persisting influence of past religion wanes even further, remains to be seen." What can be seen already, and must be further expected, is the increase of crime and public disorder.[37]

Wilson's colleague David Martin comments on the disorientation in the wake of European secularism:

> The extension of pluralism can create the conditions under which either the older forms of integration will try and reestablish themselves in control, or the pluralistic tendency will be pushed dangerously close to anarchy and atomism, or the monism of the Eastern European system will come to seem attractive by virtue of the ideological vacua and disintegrations which have been created. . . . Anarchy in any context is frequently a prelude to totalitarian reintegration.[38]

The state must then take over the enforcement of morals and replace God as the guarantor of the morality of social life; that is, the state must become totalitarian. It must inspire awe and reverence and must establish a secret police that if possible could know everything and even read the thoughts of the heart, just like God did, and so become a replacement for conscience as the representation of objective moral law within the individual subject.

One can already see what ideology would be favored by such a state. It must be socialism or nationalism, as attempts to recover social cohesion and to legitimate outward enforcement of the commonality of life, or preferably a mix of the two. The German reintegration of 1933 is a telling example.

Thus, the secular sociologists of today are most aware of the threatening corollaries of secularization: less religion must logically mean more coercion. They substantiate William Penn's dictum: Nations must be governed by God, or they will be ruled by tyrants. If that is the truth to be gleaned from the pages of recent history, then secularism is the enemy not only of religion, but of humanity.

The problem that surfaces everywhere in these explorations is the old question of whether there can be legality without morality, and whether there can be morality without religion. Concerning the first question, the secularists of a hundred years ago were convinced that one could not (as J. Stuart Mill had proposed) leave the basic moral decisions in the hands of the individual. They therefore demanded that morality be taught in schools. Then, of course, the problem of motivation arose. Their materialist worldview and a natural history of accidents would not support the quality of mercy. It could not rule out Auschwitz. Nietzsche derided D. F. Strauss in his later attempt to combine a naturalist worldview of causality and contingency with the exhortation to humanism and brotherhood. Marxism still labors with this dilemma. Voltaire had quietly endorsed the necessity of faith as the foundation of morality when he refused to "talk atheism in front of the maids." Kant examined the problem under laboratory conditions, as it were, and decided that morality must always lead to religion and rely on religion.[39] One French intellectual, F. Brunetière, as Chadwick relates, went through this argument existentially in the course of his life, beginning as an atheist, but returning to the church under the conviction that "society cannot dispense with religion in its acceptance of moral axioms."[40] It cannot dispense with it because responsibility, the backbone of morality, is a theological concept, and the group or the state cannot serve as its point of reference.[41]

Cycles

In our historical survey we have seen the cyclical character of the secularization process. That is, the optimism of the Enlightenment, at the turn of the nineteenth to the twentieth century, and in the decade of the sixties, gave way to repeated periods of social disorientation and decay. Karl Heim thought that the mindset of secularism was an age-old problem, only compounded in Christian culture.[42] Indeed, already the Psalmist was faced with a milieu ignoring God: "Help, Lord; for there is no longer any that is godly; for the faithful have vanished from among the sons of men" (Ps. 12:2).

What this cycle reveals perhaps is the "natural" process of moral corrosion in a fallen world, a tendency to corruption (Eph. 4:22b) that would finally tear down humanity if it was not for measures of divine preservation, disinfection, expurgation, and renewal. These measures may be called the visible historical counterparts to the renewal of creation praised in Psalm 104:30: "You send forth your Spirit . . . and You renew the face of the earth."

These measures are of different kinds. In addition to the dispersion of humankind in Genesis 11, the calling of Abraham in Genesis 12 must be seen as God's response to man's rebellious undertaking exemplified in the Tower of Babel. In more recent history, the secularist exultations sometimes ended in wars on an ever more terrible scale. But perhaps there is another possibility, of a culture, a nation, a creative minority, returning to the mercy of the Eternal God. Christ's parables of the Mutinous Tenants and of the Prodigal Son seem to suggests two possibilities as the outcome of secularization. The latter parable describes a cycle of apostasy and conversion as already experienced on a rational scale by the people of Israel during the time of the early Judges.

With this cycle in view, the most "advanced" group of people in our day might be those Russian intellectuals who, having gone through the empty promises of rationalism, nihilism, the Marxist reintegration of society, and finally through the utter disillusionment and mortification of an aging Marxist society, are now in growing numbers turning to the orthodox Christian faith. Of them we have recently been given a first glimpse in Tatiana Goricheva's disturbing and fascinating book, *Dangerous to Speak of God*.[43] Through their witness, Western society is once more given the gracious opportunity to choose between the Road of Light and the Road of Darkness.

CHRISTIAN RESPONSES

Available Responses

How have church and theology in modern times responded to their new environment of commitment to secularism that does not allow for any further input by religion to leaders who claim to "do without God as a working hypothesis"? In fact, a number of well-tested responses are available. We are in the fortunate position of being able to examine them not only as theologians but also with the eyes of sociologists of religion, for these outside observers have already been studying the options.

Bryan Wilson distinguishes three organizational responses of

Christianity to contemporary secularization, from the mainline churches, the "denominations" (free churches), and the "sects." He sees the mainline churches withdrawing into esoteric pastimes like reform of the liturgy when public proclamation and interaction are no longer welcome, or trying to buttress their flagging strength by way of mergers (the ecumenical movement is a special object of Wilson's scorn), or through bureaucratization. Denominations may have a different history, but appear to long for the same future that the churches are already experiencing. Only the "sects," a concept Wilson understands in sociological instead of religious terms (i.e., as small groups sustaining a high level of commitment, identity, and life together), may as yet have a true future and a contribution for society in general.

Peter Berger defines three other "possibilities of religious affirmation," that is, theological attitudes: Deductionism (the "neoorthodoxy," e.g., of Karl Barth), Reductionism (the theology of Rudolf Bultmann), and Inductionism (following Schleiermacher). We will look at these options and Berger's own meanderings among them in due course.

First, however, we need to consider the position Berger, perhaps due to his orientation to the mainline churches, does not describe as a separate option. This is the position of *withdrawal*. This attitude may shape the earlier Anabaptist tradition, which teaches believers to separate from society and live the Christian life in a small circle of disciples, perhaps even in physically separate settlements. Some strata in evangelicalism hold to a similar view, only allowing for occasional forays into the world in order to save individual believers as "brands plucked from the fire." The same attitude can also develop as a reaction to overinvolvement in society where high hopes for a Christianization of the world have been frustrated. Those who pass through these stages sometimes withdraw into private life and refuse to give any further moral leadership in the public square.

All attitudes of withdrawal, however, appear to neglect the duality in the biblical concept of "world." The prophets do not shrug their shoulders saying, Atheism and destruction set the course for this world; I told you so. They rather enter the cosmic courtroom as God's representatives, in order to argue with the world. Jonah has to learn mercy with Nineveh as God himself feels it. Jesus sheds tears over Jerusalem; he does not wash his hands of its transgression. The true Christian attitude is characterized by difference with, not withdrawal from, the world. And it is also marked by radiation. Christians are to be not only a "light in the Lord" (Eph. 5:8) but also the "light of the world" (Matt. 5:14) and "lights in the world" (Phil. 2:15). In a similar vein, the view of "snatching from peril" must be complemented by the bringing of gifts, "the glory and honor of the nations" (Ps. 72:10; Rev. 21:26; cf. Matt. 2:11), into the kingdom of God. Defense against secularism needs as its correlate the employment of all created human abilities in the service of God (2 Cor. 10:5).

The second possible stance is *surrender* to secularism. Peter Berger makes many shrewd observations about this stance, for which, in the initial, self-confident phase, secularism is not so much a contention as an assumption, the unquestioned critical standard against which the Christian tradition is examined and found wanting.[44] Historian James Hitchcock has argued that great damage is done when church dignitaries and theologians, who manifest this attitude, openly espouse the cause of secularism, ridicule or destroy the tenets of the Christian faith, and nevertheless retain their respectability in church and society.[45] Berger points to the self-defeating effect of such accommodation. It is equal to surrender: if a person can have all the alleged benefits of modern worldliness, why encumber them with an additional Christian label?[46] This attitude can appeal only to those who still struggle with inherited Christian sentiments, a special group that must die out in the near future.

Next comes the response that Berger characterizes as *Reductionism;* that is, an accommodation of the message to the standard of secularity at the expense of the integrity of the message. Berger here deals very energetically with the program of demythologization set forth by Rudolf Bultmann, a program Berger calls a "strategy of orderly retreat" of theology before the forces of modernity. Berger rightly attacks the way in which those like Bultmann uncritically accept some assumed standards of modernity to which the biblical material must be subjected: "secularity here is taken as (cognitively) superior." Demythologization, therefore, is also secularization. With a perceptiveness and circumspection not always characteristic of modern theologians, Berger concludes that Ludwig Feuerbach's critique of religion as human projection "hovers over every . . . program of secularizing the religious view of reality (including the programs of thinkers who are unaware of Feuerbach)."[47] Close to Bultmann stands Friedrich Gogarten, who considered secularization as a legitimate development from Christian origins. Gogarten wanted to "christen" the secular so long as it did not idolize itself, a condition he thought had taken place in full-blown secularism as distinct from secularization.[48] Harvey Cox in his panegyric of the new freedom of

"The Secular City" took his cue from Gogarten. Both Bultmann and Gogarten in so many words conceded the "proper autonomy" of the secular, thereby showing that they abandoned the reformational understanding of the two governments of God.

Gogarten's thesis, proposing the end of hostilities between Christianity and secular culture, was widely acclaimed although some of its earlier advocates, like the Protestant H. Thielicke and the Catholic J. B. Metz, later had second thoughts about the seemingly unlimited emancipation and authorization of the secular.[49] A warning about the fate of this attitude was present when Gogarten earlier proposed roughly the same arguments in accommodating his theology to the advent of National Socialism.[50]

Peter Berger himself has become a case in point for this stance of accommodation through reductionism. In his earlier, more sociological book, *The Sacred Canopy* (1966), he had disposed of Bultmann and Tillich as quite unacceptable theological reductionists. At that time, he criticized Schleiermacher's "Speeches on Religion" for exactly the same reason, that is, their "defensiveness" over against the seemingly definitive "truths . . . of secular reason, outside the Christian sphere," which, "rather than the sources of his own tradition, now serve the Protestant theologian as arbiters of cognitive acceptability." His criticism of Bultmann was similar: "Theology adapts itself to reality presuppositions of modern secularised thought."[51] In a later book, *A Rumor of Angels* (1968), Berger attempted to recover ground apparently lost to the secularists, through the presentation of a quite remarkable kind of natural theology with which he, setting out from general human experiences like order, play, hope, moral damnation and humor, tried inductively to argue for transcendence. In the third book of his trilogy, *The Heretical Imperative* (1979), he is back to claiming the special religious experiences upon which Schleiermacher based his theology. The latter book seems to throw Berger's fortune in with this hero and prototype of all modern liberal theology.

Berger now believes in an inductionism of "controlled accommodation," although he is aware of having entered a procedure that "all too often ends in reductionism."[52] One fears that Berger has fulfilled his own prophecy. It would have been good had he also consulted Schleiermacher's "Two Letters to D. Lucke," in which the great theologian expounds with all desirable clarity that he is indeed engaged in a "strategy of orderly retreat" from the advances of a modern worldview, and willing to lighten the Christian baggage by dispensing with objects like the Old Testament as well as doctrines like creation, the divinity of Christ, the biblical miracles, and so on. As early as in his "Speeches" of 1799, Schleiermacher, prefiguring the decisions of Bultmann and Gogarten, had "renounced" all claims of religion to codetermine anything that belonged to the fields of metaphysics and morality. In his recent book, however, Berger goes far beyond Schleiermacher. Not only does he now vindicate the modern resemblance he had earlier deplored between religious truths and consumer articles in a supermarket, maintaining that we moderns must "pick and choose" (whence "The Heretical Imperative")—he now also proposes to stock the shelves with products of other religions ("My understanding of 'ecumenicity' has expanded very greatly").[53] And he makes this move even if it means that he cannot maintain statements like "once-and-for-all" and "no-other-name"; that is, the exclusive attributes of Jesus. Give up historical Christianity, retain generic religion—that is the outcome of Berger's "controlled accommodation."

These options are so clearly unsatisfactory from a Christian position that one is almost eager to reassess the virtues of Berger's further model of "Deductionism" (representing Karl Barth and "neoorthodoxy") and to explore James Hitchcock's statement that attempts by the church to mollify usually have the opposite effect. "Paradoxically," as he puts it, "a firm purpose . . . often makes the church more credible even in the eyes of the skeptic."[54]

Desirable Responses

Having surveyed the main specimens of available responses, we would like, in conclusion, to add a few remarks concerning desirable responses.

1. It is necessary to expose the mechanisms of secularization and secularism so as to beware of their inherent pitfalls. The recognition of a diffuse and hidden peril is of immense value. It needs to be said that secularism is the adversary of the gospel, that it will never engender love of God and love of neighbor but only love of self, and that there is no future for faith in its appeasement. Such an analysis of secularism and its working can act like a necessary disinfectant.

2. However, we propose at the same time that a "response" should not merely be shaped by an analysis of the opponent, inducing accommodation or rejection. The "response" should not be a reaction; it should be determined not by the milieu but by the word of God. Taking an example from Barth's "Theological Existence

Today," written during the political crisis of Germany in 1933, Christian proclamation must in the last analysis go on "as if nothing had happened." Accommodation concerns the form of speech. Christians need to focus rather on the difference of the contents of the message, the incommensurability of the gospel with any secular epistemology. The church, furthermore, must not withdraw from the world but, according to its marching orders in the New Testament, aim for holy living even in unholy places (Eph. 4:17ff.; Tit. 2:12ff.).

3. On this basis, three transactions are necessary to sustain Christian identity and vitality: prayer, sustenance of the fellowship, and proclamation.

a) The first task is to strengthen the center of Christian identity, that is, a person's relationship with God. This is done through prayer. Prayer is the expression of respect for, and love of, God, clearly the extreme antithesis to secularism. In prayer, the Christian holds up humanity and its current course.

Prayer engenders steadfastness and independence and yields the necessary orientation. The German author Ernst Jünger noted this in the days of the turbulent dissolution of the National-Socialist Empire:

> What could one recommend to help people, especially simple people, to avoid conformism with, and standardization by the system? Nothing but prayer. This is the point of leverage, even for the humblest. . . . It yields uncommon gain and tremendous sovereignty. This is also true apart from all theology. In situations where the most clever ones fail and the most courageous look in vain for ways out, you sometimes see a man quietly counsel the right and do what is good. You can trust that that is a person who prays.[55]

Prayer helps to recover perspective and teaches us what Os Guinness has called "a basic requirement of contemporary discipleship": to be "ready to 'think globally but act locally.'"[56] Perspective is a fruit of perceptive prayer. As such, it is the prerequisite of ministry to fellow believers and to the world.

Moreover, prayer must be accompanied (2 Tim. 2:19) by a life of sanctification, by the willingness to "live soberly, righteously, and godly in this world" (Tit. 2:12); that is, to live differently from the rest, to stick to God's absolute moral standards and not yield to general permissiveness, to live conscientiously, and yet not turn one's back on humanity, to withdraw from evil although not from people. There can be no Christian life without the struggle against secularism, a struggle against the will to autonomy and the forgetfulness of the things of God that characterize the *Zeitgeist*. This is part of the daily battle to awaken to God and to the hallowing of his name.

b) *Diligite dominum, agite viriliter, et confortetur cor vestrum* ("love God, act bravely, and He shall strengthen your hearts") is the Vulgate translation of Psalm 31:24-25. The whole psalm speaks confidently of the possibility of courageous action in an alien environment and reminds one of Paul's words of encouragement for Christians in 1 Corinthians 15:58: "Therefore, my beloved brethren, be steadfast, immovable, always abounding in the work of the Lord, inasmuch as you know that your labor is not in vain in the Lord." The second task, combining the interests of identity and outreach, concerns the "strengthening of the brethren" (Luke 22:32; Acts 14:22; etc.). It endeavors to "fan the flame where you find it," to support any discernible movement in the direction of faith, and to strengthen Christian commitment.

This will find expression in the conscious cultivation of cell groups, small circles that support those purposes. Bryan Wilson felt that any good that might still come from religion would come from "the religion of the sects," by which he seems to mean the unpolluted Christianity of small groups of committed people not associated with the churches. He may have underestimated the network of such groups *within* today's churches and denominations, successors of the *ecclesiola in ecclesia* of early pietism and of Wesley's "bands," which successfully countered institutional torpor and the dissolution of social bonding. David Martin seems to be fascinated with the wide-reaching effects of Haugeanism, the corresponding movement within the Norwegian church.[57] Faith here proves once more not only the guarantor but the source of salutary human relationships.

c) Finally, proclamation. This concerns Christian outreach. In the first place, it is the calm reannouncement of the reality of God, both of his righteousness and mercy, to a secularity forgetful of these facts. In a secular environment religion may perhaps still be allowed as a topic, but the question of God (like death) has almost become something to be ashamed of. It is of utmost importance that individuals, as well as society as such, be faced, in a matter-of-fact way, with the question of its relationship to God. The church's task is to announce God again to "a crooked and perverse generation" (Phil. 2:15). The church is to remind the world that God "has appointed a day on which He will judge the world in righteousness by the Man whom He has ordained" (Acts 17:31) and that this Man, Jesus Christ of Nazareth, at the same time is the one ground of our salvation. We therefore support Bishop Newbigin's plea for "a genuinely missionary approach to post-Enlightenment culture."[58]

In the pursuit of these tasks the church will be the light of the house (Matt. 5:15) she shares with the rest of humanity. The church will act like leaven in the dough, and resemble the mustard in its surprisingly abundant growth, making it the nesting-place for many. In the pursuit of these tasks, as well as in the work of their callings, Christians will not only "help to build the temple of the Lord" (Zech. 6:15) but, in the meantime, also unwittingly participate in God's work of sustaining his own creation.

4F

The Future

David F. Wells

What awaits us?

There are few Americans who are indifferent about the future, despite the fact that the national lust for personal affluence is chronically myopic, its purview extending neither forward nor backward but existing only in and for the pleasurable moment. This reverie is not, however, uninterrupted. The future intrudes upon the present with regularity and insistence, whether we like it or not.

This intrusion of the future upon our experience is not, of course, a uniquely American phenomenon. Its main impetus, as Peter Berger has argued,[1] arises out of the process of modernization, a process affecting all of the industrialized nations in the West. Modernization has, however, affected America more deeply and profoundly than the others. By its very nature it powerfully shifts our attention from the present to the future. It does this by requiring of us that we plan and by planning to anticipate the future in the present. In our secular context this anticipation of the future almost invariably becomes an attempt to control it, rendering it more manageable and less capricious. This planning usually goes far beyond the kind of preparation that prudence requires and becomes a form of secularized providence in which those in the present attempt to capture and control the future.[2]

Although the future is a permanent factor in our present experience, it registers upon our consciousness in different ways.[3] For some, what awaits us is terrifying since, in this view, the future will be the aggregate and confluence of existing trends realized in terms of exponential growth. For others, what awaits us is enormously exciting because the technology that has already overcome so many threats to human survival will continue its work and lead the world to an entirely new threshold of existence. In both form and function, these visions of the future are frequently eschatological. The first sees a multiplication of present problems bringing a terrifying judgment; the second sees the growth of technology bringing an exhilarating

285

salvation, secular as it may be in its nature. Each has been given powerful expression in recent years.

The pessimistic outlook, in which the future evokes only despair, is grounded on the belief that most nonrenewable resources will have been depleted within the next fifty years. At that point, Harrison Brown declares, our present industrial development will be seen to have "flourished for awhile, only to become extinct as its needs outstripped its supplies and as the complexities of its organization outstripped its capacity to organize."[4] The first report of the Club of Rome issued in 1972[5] likewise concluded that, given population growth, declining natural resources, and the growing difficulties with pollution, only a concerted, worldwide effort at planning could avert the catastrophe that otherwise lay on the horizon.

The Club's second report[6] intensified this pessimism and argued strongly that only a new world order with a new global economic system and diversification of industry could save humankind. The blueprint suggested in this report was enlarged in 1976 under Jan Tinbergen's direction.[7] Population growth must be stopped immediately, the report urged, as must all industrial and economic expansion. The manufacture of arms must also be halted and, in place of the current disorder, we must seek a new international order. This would require the abolition of the current economic system, tearing down the "poverty curtain" between the rich and poor nations, transcending territorial boundaries and narrow nationalistic interests, sharing power between the first and third worlds, and instituting central planning for the whole world.

Against this bleak forecast, an optimistic outlook that regards the future as containing the hope for survival has been clearly articulated by, among others, Herman Kahn. He suggests that we are to find the resources fundamental to human survival not in the earth but in human creativity. It is human genius that produced the industrial revolution, the agricultural revolution, and, as population began to outstrip the food-producing capacity of the earth, the green revolution. This same human genius has produced the medical and technological breakthroughs that remove human beings from the mercy of nature. The process will continue. Technology will move the giant Western economies into a postindustrial phase where humans will be liberated from work and many, in time, will colonize space.

These two eschatologies are not without their detractors. Much of the criticism has predictably focused on the assumptions shaping the projections. Can we realistically project population when we cannot anticipate the effects of war, famine, and disease? Do we really know what nonrenewable resources may lie at our disposal? Can we include in our figures, for example, minerals garnered from the ocean beds or gathered from outer space? Are the problems that have followed industrialization, such as pollution, the result of too much technology or too little? But leaving aside these questions, there are other issues of greater importance for both eschatologies.

Those who view the future as the source of human salvation usually think that technology will make it possible. Such persons, however, must come to terms with the kind of critique Jacques Ellul has made. First in his classic, *The Technological Society,* and then in its sequel, *The Technological System,* Ellul has argued persuasively that technology creates a worldview with its own rationale for existence, that warps and distorts the very nature of humanity. Technology does not merely create the means of productivity and innovation, but also structures a unidimensional and naturalistic life system that is all enveloping and has abundant capacity to destroy the humans it was created to serve.[8]

Those who despair about the future and turn to the creation of a new, centrally controlled world order would do well to ponder the brilliant dystopian novels of Aldous Huxley and George Orwell. Both *Brave New World* and *Nineteen Eighty-Four* explore the dilemma thrust upon the world as to which personal freedoms are to be exchanged for what kind of social stability. And they capture with intense imagination the possible results of such changes. The assumption in both novels is that social stability is impossible without central control and that central control demands the surrender of individual autonomy and individual responsibility.[9] The conclusion to which both arrive is that humans can obtain the desired tranquility, but only at the cost of destroying what it means to be human. They do not, therefore, believe in this beatific vision of a new social order. The social engineering that is undertaken to achieve it, whether in Marxist (Orwell) or Western (Huxley) forms, will only produce a nightmare version of utopia.

The inverted utopias of Huxley and Orwell are intended to remind us that modernity is a two-edged sword. We may possess the technology to create a rational and abundant world. But do we have the discipline of spirit, the values, to check our selfishness and our drive to power as we rush to lay claim to this abundance? Lewis Mumford has noted that in the transition from the medieval to the modern capitalist world only one of the seven deadly sins remained an evil, and that is sloth. The others—covetousness, anger, lust, envy, gluttony, and pride—have all become positive virtues. What is the outcome when technological brilliance is not disciplined by wisdom, when knowledge is divorced from morality, when power is exercised without conscience? Every advance in the modern world seems to be attended by a corresponding loss. The medical genius that has banished and controlled so many of our diseases also poses a major threat to human life. In the very hospitals where heroic measures are taken to save some children, others join the 1.6 million who are killed each year before birth. If we enjoy abundance, we must now also reckon with scarcity; if our technology has emancipated us from some of life's drudgery, it has also enslaved us to the processes and the worldview it creates; if we have solved many problems, our solutions have generated at least as many in their place.

This contradictory character of modernity, this fearful ambiguity, should give us pause before using secular projections of the future as a buttress for our Christian perspective, and in particular for an interpretation of the millennium. The pessimistic outlook may coincide with forms of premillennialism because both picture an awful devolution in the quality and conditions of life before the end. It should be noted, however, that if there is to be a centralized world order, premillennialists would regard it as the Antichrist rather than the last means of human survival. Likewise, the optimistic projection seems to comport well with the postmillennial outlook. Yet, if there are grounds for hope about the human race, these are not to be found simply in technology as Kahn imagines, but also in the presence of the kingdom of God and, perhaps, of common grace.

And there are better reasons not to identify interpretations of the millennium with secular visions of the future. Such interpretations are often selective in what they see. They employ a way of thinking about the future that owes at least as much to twentieth-century secular debate as to the categories of Scripture, and considers only some parts of the human story and ignores others. It is important, then, for Christians to view the future in careful conformity with the biblical categories and emphases. In this regard, I wish to explore three propositions. First, the future in the New Testament is a way of existence that is already penetrating the present. Second, this future is inseparable from Christ. Third, this future has moral implications for the world, but does not justify speculation about events to come.

THE FUTURE IN THE PRESENT

The witness that biblical revelation makes in the midst of current debate over the future has less to do with what events may or may not take place and much more to do with how the future is to be conceived. In the biblical perspective, the future is already being experienced. It is already penetrating this historical moment. The future, then, is not so much the series of earthly events that flow in a lineal and chronological relationship from the present out into an unrealized time. It is, rather, a qualitatively different mode of life that is already intersecting the horizontal line of chronological existence. This future sometimes stands as an antithesis to that normal chronology, sometimes as paradox, sometimes as reformation, and sometimes as transformation. This divine future is radically different from the human future; as different, indeed, as eternity is from time and God from the creatures who bear his image.

To say this only recognizes a distinction that has always been intrinsic to Christian thought. Augustine spoke of it in terms of two realms of allegiance, two cities.[10] For him the collapse of Rome under barbarian assault was but a symbol of the larger passing of sinful life called the City of Man. Only the City of God had any lasting future. Luther, too, spoke of two kingdoms sharply divided against one another. To a minister sore pressed by fellow clergy sympathetic to Rome, he wrote:

> Outwardly we are living in the kingdom of the devil, and so we should not expect to see and hear good things on the outside. But inwardly we are living in the Kingdom of Christ, where we may behold the riches of God's glory and grace. This is what it means to "rule in the midst of thine enemies." Because it is a kingdom, there is glory there; and because it is in the midst of enemies, there is offense there. But we shall make our way through glory and shame, through good report and evil report, through hate and love, through friends and foes, until we arrive where there are none but friends, in the Kingdom of the Father.[11]

This commonly accepted distinction between the two cities, the two kingdoms, led all of the Reformers to picture also two churches, the one visible and the other invisible. The invisible church is made up of those who belong to Christ by faith and who, Calvin said, are led into a "denial of themselves and contempt of this world and this earthly life" and "into a devotion to righteousness in order to aspire to heaven."[12] This orientation is neither identical with, nor is it always served by, the life of the organized church. The visible communion, Martin Chemnitz said flatly, cannot assume as a matter of course that it is "always and indubitably the true church."[13] As a result, in both continental Europe and in England, Reformers developed tests through which the presence of the invisible and spiritual reality could be discerned in the functioning of the visible, ecclesiastical organization. In turn, this had the effect of relativizing the church's organization and its functioning even as Augustine's conception of the City of God relativized all social, political, and cultural life.

With the passing of time, however, intense perception of God's immediate reign, especially as something qualitatively different from present earthly existence and human organization, waned. In the liberal Protestantism of the nineteenth century, with its commitment to divine immanence, the two realms of existence merged. The divine future became coincidental with the evolution of the human present. In the twentieth century neoorthodox critics battered this liberal conception until it seemed almost dead. But recently Jürgen Moltmann and Johannes Metz have breathed new life into it in Europe, and the liberation theologies adapted it to their own purposes in South America. Thus Moltmann has proposed that divine transcendence is not a realm "above" but one that is "beyond."[14] It refers to a future in lineal continuity with the present that God is going to bring about. In this future, social and political conditions will arise that are qualitatively different from the present. This conception is really quite different from traditional premillennialism, which also sees such a future, but argues that it will be ushered in suddenly and supernaturally by Christ himself. In Moltmann's conception, the future emerges out of the human potential of the present. Moltmann's internal principles seem to accord with those of Karl Marx, although Moltmann ascribes to them the name of "God."

The liberal Protestantism of an earlier age, as well as the Moltmannianism of ours, are alike indistinguishable from humanism, a humanism that is not made more palatable because it is cloaked in religiosity. The fundamentalists who protested this amalgam, this confusion of God's kingdom with human development and planning, therefore once again reasserted the older cleavage between the two cities. Yet where this fundamentalism was allied with a dispensational interpretation of the Bible it invariably shifted the distinction between these cities from the present to the end of time. When time had run its course, they declared, the divine conditions of Christ's rule upon earth would come crashing into human existence. Until that time,

Christians should assume a posture of alertness and preparation, awaiting this awesome finale.

Fundamentalism, and that part of evangelicalism which grew out of it, therefore forged a sharper distinction between Christ and culture, but in the process it sometimes became overtly anticultural in its bias. In its premillennialism it announced a miracle of such gigantic proportions that even benign and muddled-headed humanists had to take offense. Premillennialism, especially in its dispensational variant, became as important, it seems, for its sociological function as for its theological affirmation. It was a key instrument, perhaps *the* key instrument, in creating a cognitive dissonance from prevailing cultural, humanistic assumptions. So completely did dispensational fundamentalists identify the surrounding culture with the antithesis of the coming heavenly kingdom that they sometimes even rejoiced in its tragedies, wars, disasters. This is also why, in dispensational literature, amillennialists were so consistently berated as closet liberals. They had given away *the* miracle that would, once and for all, close the door on all liberalism, humanism, and naturalism!

This substantial, if not total, relocation of the "age to come" to the end of time and its complete identification with the millennium almost reverted to the Judaism the New Testament had sought to correct. It was a mistake of very large portions. For the New Testament is insistent that the "age to come" is not, as Judaism thought, an era of earthly tranquility and righteousness following the Messiah's arrival, when present earthly conditions will be renovated, but it is already coexisting with and penetrating this present "age." This "age to come" has already intruded into and is now being established in this "age" through the incarnation, atonement, and resurrection of Christ and the extension of his work by the Spirit. In this sense, all theology that is Christian is theology that is necessarily eschatological.[15]

To be sure, the word *aion* ("age") as used in the New Testament does not have a single, unvarying sense. Yet the different usages sharpen, rather than blur, the distinction between the time of mankind and the future of God.

Taken by itself, *aion*[16] refers simply to a life span, to the course of world events, to life running through successive epochs and, if the epochs are infinitely successive, to eternity. But when it is used of life as we know it in this fallen world, it becomes charged with ethical significance. This significance is often implied by the use of *toutos*: blasphemy against the Spirit will not be forgiven in *this* world (Matt. 12:32); *this* world is full of cares (Matt. 13:22); *this* world has its own god (John 14:30; 16:11; 1 John 5:19; 2 Cor. 4:4). "This age," or "this present age," or, in the Johannine equivalent, the "world" are therefore terms used with a frequently pejorative sense (1 Cor. 2:6-8; 2 Cor. 4:4; Gal. 1:4; 2 Tim. 4:10; John 1:9, 29; 3:16-17, 19; 6:33; 8:12; 12:31; 14:17; 16:8; 17:14-16; 18:36; 1 John 2:15-17; 5:4). Although Paul's use of *kosmos* ("world") is occasionally neutral he frequently equates it with *toutos aiōn* in meaning and infuses it with all of the characteristics of life lived in separation from Christ and in defiance of his word and kingdom (Rom. 3:6; 1 Cor. 1:20-21; 2:12; 3:19; 2 Cor. 7:10; Phil. 2:5).

The relationship between "this age" and the messianic "age to come" can be viewed in different ways. From an ethical point of view, scriptural writers often set them in sharp antithesis and define a relationship analogous to death and life. From a chronological point of view, however, the ages overlap and coexist with a measure of interpenetration. That these ages occupy the same period of time so that both are experienced simultaneously led Geerhardus Vos to speak of a "semi-eschatological" period. It is not a felicitous phrase because it implies that there is a mutual contamination of the ages and not simply a shared chronological life. It is important to observe, however, that though the ages are experienced together, their essential characters remain unchanged. The "age to come" is that realm of divine, redeeming existence, that sovereign rule of the Triune God, that heavenly form of existence which has come in and through Christ. "This age" is life characterized by rebellion and sin that in all of its dimensions—existential, social, political, and natural—is doomed to pass away under the judgment of God. These realms may be experienced simultaneously but they do not modify each other's character. The unbeliever who lives in "this age" does not need mere improvement in order to enter "the age to come," but to die and be resurrected through union with Christ. Hence the antithesis between the ages is always preserved (Eph. 1:21; cf. Rom. 12:2; 1 Cor. 1:20; 2:6-8; 3:18, 22; 2 Cor. 4:4; Gal. 1:4; Eph. 2:2; 1 Tim. 6:17; Tit. 2:12; Rom. 8:30).[17]

There seems to be little doubt, as Seyoon Kim has argued,[18] that what led Paul to recast the traditional Jewish apocalyptic so radically was his own encounter with Christ on the Damascus road in which he experienced a glory that he had associated only with the "age to come." And from that encounter, he could look back on Jesus' death, "an eschatological event brought forward into the period before the

[Jewish] Age to Come,"[19] as C. K. Barrett put it, and see in it the End to which that apocalyptic had pointed.[20]

The precise relationship between the two ages during the period when they coexist is not easy to define. The arrival of the "age to come" in Christ was obscured, his true character remained incognito. But equally certain is the fact that Jesus' relationship to "this age" will culminate in an overt, public, and cataclysmic expression of judgment (Rom. 2:16; 1 Cor. 6:10; 2 Cor. 5:10; Gal. 6:7; 1 Thess. 1:10; 5:9; 2 Thess. 2:12). Whether this final convulsion will include the intrusion of an anticipatory reign of Christ, whether it will be preceded by a growing assertion of the messianic "age" within the worldly process, or whether the worldly process will simply end without other spiritual accompaniments are debated questions among Christians. What is strikingly clear, however, is that the eschatological age of the future is already present, that Christian hope is grounded in its invincible and absolute character rather than upon a moral elevation of "this age," that though these ages coexist for a period of time and are experienced together by God's people they are in their essential nature completely and radically different. In the purview of the New Testament, therefore, the future is not a sequence of chronological events that is yet to reach us, but the presence, indeed, the triumphant presence of that divine kingdom whose existence is as eternal as the God whose rule it is.

THE FUTURE AND CHRIST

This "age," this divine future, is one that only God can bring into existence. Since this new "age" requires, as a condition of its existence, the destruction of sin, death, and the devil, the only ground on which this can be done is the incarnation, death, and resurrection of Christ. For that reason, the "age to come" could only arrive, and has only arrived, in and through Christ.

The gospel writers make this clear in teachings about the kingdom. As George Ladd observes,[21] we can search for the kingdom, look for it, and pray for it, but only God can bring it about (Luke 12:31; 23:51; Matt. 6:10, 33). The kingdom is God's to give away; it is ours only to enter (Matt. 21:43; Luke 12:32). We can inherit it and possess it, but we cannot build it or destroy it (Matt. 25:34; Luke 10:11). We can preach it and work for it, but only God can construct it (Matt. 10:7; Luke 10:9). This is, in fact, one of the strongest arguments for Christ's divinity. He must have been divine to do what only

God could do in establishing the kingdom, bringing into history the conditions of the messianic "age to come." Those who have disputed his divinity inevitably have had either to dissolve the reality of the kingdom or to dissolve Jesus' link to it. This link, however, cannot be destroyed. The kingdom has come in and through Jesus. In his life are seen the very acts of God and in his words are heard their interpretation. In him were revealed the character, will, and purposes of God because it was God himself who was revealing his character, will, and purposes.

The discussion of the "age to come" in the Epistles is more complex,[22] and language about the kingdom less frequent. The writers retain the "two age" terminology (Rom. 8:18-23; 12:2; 1 Cor. 1:20; 2:6, 8; 3:18; 10:11; 2 Cor. 4:4; Gal. 1:4; Eph. 1:21; 1 Tim. 4:1) and also the conception that God is bringing a reality into existence whose genesis lies solely in his grace and power and never in human potential, resources, and ingenuity. An inbreaking into the horizontal plane of human existence has begun. God is now sending out clarifying shafts of light, exposing the present in its dying and pointing forward to the future that has already arrived, even if it is not fully come. The New Testament Epistles develop this theme in new ways and with new language.

Paul, for example, explores Christology and soteriology in five major areas. First, he establishes the parallels between the first and last Adams and the humanities they represent (Rom. 5:12-21; 1 Cor. 15:21-22).[23] Second, he expands Jesus' substitutionary death in a variety of ways to show how sin, death, and the devil were defeated at the cross. Third, Paul develops an entire spirituality around the notion of being "in" Christ, because he acted in the place of sinners at the cross.[24] Fourth, he develops far beyond even what we have in John 14–16, a deep and complex theology of the Spirit.[25] The giving of the Holy Spirit was one of the signs that Jews believed would declare the arrival of the messianic age; not only has the sign been given but in some 120 references, Paul explores the significance of that gift for Christian life. Finally, he points to the dawning of this new age in Christ as the explanation for the church that exists as the human exegesis of the divine future.

One of the most striking features of modern theology, in both its Catholic and Protestant expressions, however, is its destruction of that distinction between the ages the New Testament insists upon preserving. In different ways, modern theologians have fused the ages into one another because, in different ways, they perceive the human and the divine as fused in one another. Human potential, therefore, becomes the quarry out of which God is making his new age, and this new age is the end result of human or of societal development. This also means that theologians have become disenchanted with Christian particularism and now search for a world spirituality coextensive with all of human experience.

Perhaps the most conclusive evidence that this is theology's present preoccupation lies in the fact that Harvey Cox has written a book about it! Whenever culture rubs religion a certain way, Leonard Sweet has observed, out pops Cox with a book to announce it.

> A theology for a secularized, urbanized America? *The Secular City* (1966). A theology for those fed up with a secularized, urbanized America? *A Feast of Fools* (1969). A theology for meditation, play, theatre of the absurd, nude baths, science-fiction, cryonics—in short, a theology for a wet Saturday afternoon? *The Seduction of the Spirit* (1973). A theology for hope, social revolution, and Marxism? *On Not Leaving It to the Snake* (1967). A theology for a global village and guru hunters? *Turning East* (1977).[26]

And now we have *Religion in the Secular City* (1984), a book that supposedly points forward to a "post-modern theology" but actually points back to the old liberal Protestant search for a world spirituality predicated upon confusion of the human and divine, upon evolution, and upon cultural adaptation as theological methodology. The very ideas that Emil Brunner struck down in *The Mediator* are being breathlessly announced as an exciting new discovery. Cox, however, always keeps a sharp eye on those around him. He wants to be the advance guard provided there is a wave of troops behind him. These troops, however, are surprisingly diverse, but whether existential, liberation, or process, they share a common commitment to finding, describing, and acting upon a spirituality of this world.

One of the more intriguing aspects of the theology of the Second Vatican Council, for example, was the apparent differences in methodology between the Constitution on the Church and the Pastoral Constitution on the Church in the Modern World. The former spoke of the Trinity, the church, revelation, tradition, the magisterium, the sacraments, and Mary. Within this context it spoke of salvation. The latter constitution passed by these matters in silence. Instead, it grounded its affirmations and its understanding of salvation upon the human being who in his or her religiousness is the center and summit of the universe.[27] The human being *as* human being has what the council called "a profound religious sense,"[28] arising from the "unutterable mystery that engulfs our being."[29] This sense is plainly not the equivalent of a Protestant's understanding of natural revelation, for the constitution went on to declare that "by His incarnation the Son of God has united Himself in some fashion into every man."[30] Commenting upon this, Bernard Lambert observed that if humankind is in Christ, then faith in human progress has been taken up into faith in God, for the work of culture and of civilization are not estranged from the reality of Christ.[31] What this means, M. Dournes added, is that our knowledge of Christ grows out of and is coextensive with our knowledge of ourselves.[32]

These affirmations of Vatican II were, nevertheless, left somewhat vague, as the theoretical basis for this anthropology was not declared. Karl Rahner later said, however, that the council had been seeking ways of affirming a universal spirituality. In his own work, he laid the basis for this by modifying the old scholastic distinction between nature and grace, blurring it with elements of a Heideggerian existentialism.[33] Nature is never to be confused with grace, he said, thus conforming with the biblical position; nature, however, is never dislocated from grace in actual fact, and thus he departed from the biblical position. Nature is never "pure," for it is always infused by grace and thus contains an orientation toward the divine that is intrinsic to its naturalness. This appetite for the divine, inarticulate as it may be, is what Rahner called the "supernatural existential." This concept also appears to be what underlay the council's affirmation that it is possible for a person to be an atheist at a cognitive level but to be in a condition of grace at an ontological level such that eternal salvation will be the result.[34] Thus the new age is divine in its origin and in its results, yet access to it is not through the historical Jesus but through human nature. The connection between "this world" and the "age to come" is not in the exercise of faith but in the organic union with the divine that is already forged within human nature.

A significant variation on this theme has emerged among the Catholic liberation theologians in South America. Although there are differences among them, especially in the extent to which Marxism is used as a tool for social analysis and the conditions under which violence is appropriate, these theologians usually agree that the link with the new age is neither naked faith nor human nature but social action. In action where we identify with the poor, oppressed, disenfranchised, and marginalized we are also identifying with God, for he also takes the side of the aliens and the outcast. In North America, James Cone and Carl Braaten have argued the same point.[35]

In his five-volume *Theology for Artisans of a New Humanity,* Juan Segundo proposes two modes of salvation that, in fact, correspond very closely to the methodologies proposed by the two constitutions on the church from Vatican II. The one is a traditional Catholic notion of salvation through the church; the other is a proposal that salvation comes through social action, which is what Segundo feels is taught in Matthew 25:31-46. The question that haunts Segundo as it did Rahner is whether there is a means to salvation that is correspondingly universal. If the means is limited, as is the church, salvation will not be universal since only a small percentage of the world's population is knowledgeable about Catholic faith. Rahner found the universal means and the basis for a world spirituality in human nature; Segundo finds it in social action.

What such theologians do not make so clear, however, is that the identification between human and divine liberation is only partially ethical. Most assume that the ethical is itself also ontological. The philosophical foundation is Hegelian.[36] They presuppose that the divine is permeating the human, that the divine in conjunction with the human is in motion, and that the presence of the divine is to be detected not so much by what Kierkegaard called the "cud-chewing process with three stomachs" (thesis—antithesis—synthesis) but by ethical eruptions in which social justice triumphs. The emergence of this justice, understood in an evolutionary framework, is the emergence of the divine future. And this is why the political theology of Johann Metz and Jürgen Moltmann as well as the liberation theologies of Segundo and Gutiérrez have all had such affinities with Marxist ideology.[37]

Theologians in the political and liberation schools have regularly disparaged existentialist thought and sometimes the advocates of process theology. The underlying conceptuality in process thought, however, is not greatly different since it too is a variation on Hegelianism. Whitehead proposed that all of reality, visible and invisible, conscious and unconscious, is interlaced and interlocked. Moreover, created reality is itself creative inasmuch as it elicits from God his potential. At the same time God, through "lures" placed within the world, entices from it an unfolding and development of its potential. In this sense, we know God only as he acts in and through the world, the world itself being the expression of the divine. Process thought is, therefore, monistic and evolutionary. Where it seeks to be biblical, as in the case of Norman Pittenger,[38] it glimpses the dawning of the divine future in gathering expressions of human love.

What these theologies share, then, is a search for a universal spirituality. What they have all found, they believe, is an *entrée* to it. The secret for Rahner is human nature existentially conceived; for Segundo, politically oriented human action; for Pittenger, a mystical experience of the creation. These schemes all build upon the notion that the divine is infused into the human, that nature is the means to the supernatural, and that human experience is itself divine experience. Thus Christ is important, even unique, as the microcosm to which universal human experience is the macrocosm. Jesus is what *interprets* the whole; he is not what constitutes the whole. Thus the human future runs out into the divine future.

Those who embrace such theological positions, however, do not always perceive that, in fact, one can obtain the same religious wares purveyed in these various theological forms under strictly secular auspices. That is always the price extracted from religion when it plays the game of cultural relevance. When that culture is secular, it leaves the proponents of such religion in the hapless position of offering benefits encumbered with the high price of needing to be religious when those same benefits are available at no cost in their secular form. A comparison between the strictly secular Human Potential Movement and those variants of a this-worldly new age makes the relationship obvious.

Apocalyptic ideas have usually flourished in ages marked by suffering and anxiety.[39] The resulting visions are attempted answers to the problem of evil, for all of them propose that the wearying conditions of life are neither permanent nor ideal. A different mode of existence can be had. Apocalyptic schemes differ only in the way in which they see this occurring and in what they see as the result.

Ours is an age of anxiety in which the resulting stress and suffering have produced numerous false eschatologies. In the Los Angeles area alone, for example, there are over six hundred "New Age" groups. While many of these employ Eastern ideas, they are also part of a wider and more significant movement within our society established on the conviction that within each person resides all the potential needed to overcome life's hardships and sorrows.

Although this Human Potential Movement[40] is related to a tradition that was given expression by Mary Baker Eddy, modified by Norman Vincent Peale and more recently by Robert Schuller, it also has its own theorists. Principal among these are Abraham Maslow,

Carl Rogers, and Wilheim Reich. The operating assumption of the movement is the essential innocence of humankind, each member of whom has enormous and untapped capacities for love and constructive behavior. The structures of an ossified and authoritarian society imposed on the individual are responsible for guilt and frustration. While the radicals in the 1960s sought to eliminate the offending structures, the Human Potential Movement works within the offending psyche that resonates with those structures. What is right and wrong is no longer a moral issue per se. Questions of good and evil yield to an analysis of whether an individual's potential will be realized through a given action. The self and its actualization are the keys to reality. Indeed, the discovery of the self is the equivalent of conversion: its actualization is the "age to come." One of the results has been an entirely new conception of death, which some devotees deny is real. Thus the Human Potential Movement has proposed that a change in being is possible, one with physical, ontic, and epistemological dimensions, a change that already anticipates what Christians foresee only at the return of Christ (1 Cor. 15:51-52; Heb. 1:12; 2 Cor. 3:18). It has made the future a present reality, but it has grounded the arrival of the new conditions not upon Christ but upon the hidden potential of the human being.

From a Christian perspective, the assumptions of the movement are naive. The human being is neither innocent nor a reservoir of untapped spiritual potential. The old adage "Physician heal yourself" is here stripped of its irony. Self-salvation is a reality to be realized through psychological manipulation. In such a view, what the New Testament calls "this age" contains within itself "the age to come." Indeed, the "age to come" is merely an extension of "this age" ushered in by a cadre of benign psychologists.

While Scripture recognizes a continuity in revelation between God and human beings, rooted in the universally present *imago dei*, it also teaches a soteriological discontinuity resulting from our sinfulness. New Testament theology locates the two ages in the framework of discontinuity; much contemporary theology locates them along a line of continuity. For modern theology, the divine future is incipiently present in human nature; for New Testament teaching it is not. For modern theology, the divine is hidden in the human; for New Testament theology the divine is separated from the human. For modern theology, Jesus is a striking example of how the divine manifests itself within human experience in general; for the New Testament writers, Jesus was the point and means, the *only* point and means, of the inbreaking "age to come," since this age could only come in and through the one who was divine.

THE FUTURE AND ETHICS

There is an important distinction between what is apocalyptic and what is eschatological. The apocalyptic, a vision of the "age to come," cast a dark shadow over this present age. To believe in the "age to come" was to be filled with despair about the "present age." Apocalyptic literature always pictured salvation as emancipation from this world, this "present age," and was therefore always ethically passive; it looked for deliverance, not involvement and engagement. The New Testament understanding of eschatology also employed the terms and concepts of the two ages—but with an important difference. Because the "age to come" is now present in "this age," an incentive for Christian ethics exists that was absent in the apocalyptic vision where "the age to come" did not intrude into this "present age." Eschatology, in fact, provided one of the major motivations to ethics in the New Testament.

In the New Testament, then, as Helmut Thielicke notes, ethics has its place "in the field of tension between the old and new aeons, not in the old alone, nor in the new alone."[41] Believers retain some continuity with this "present age," because they live within its social, political, and economic structures while also partaking of the "age to come" by living within its spiritual power and moral life. It is not so much a position of ambiguity as of multiplicity.

The tension between the two has frequently been resolved by emptying "this present age" of significance out of concern for the "age to come," or—as is more common—by absorbing the "age to come" into this "present age" and, in the process, domesticating it. Karl Barth once observed[42] that ethical systems, as they relate to society, must be justified in terms of a desired goal that has not yet been attained. In the post-Enlightenment world, this goal has often been restricted to this-worldly earthly progress. In this sense, socialists like George Bernard Shaw, as well as Marxists, have envisioned a millennium, but it is a secularized, this-worldly *telos* to which human life is evolving naturally.[43] For the New Testament, however, this goal is not *within* the social fabric but *above* it. It is "above" in terms of its nature and genesis, but its presence registers categorically and insistently upon the worldly process in the present.

Jesus asserted that his followers would remain in the world. He also declared that all authority had been given to him and that the god of this world was being ousted. It therefore follows that while ethics has a personal and interior dimension, it must also have a public and exterior proclamation arising from Jesus' authority and based upon his conquest.[44] This proclamation is the gospel of Christ whose rule is not postponed to the chronological end of the ages, but has even now begun.

There is, to be sure, a sequence of events that will occur immediately prior to Christ's return, but it is doubtful whether the events themselves, as distinct from Christ's actual return, can exert any spiritual or ethical significance upon Christian life prior to that time. It is true that Christians have always been perplexed as to where they are in the divine calendar of events. In certain periods, the impulse to interpret present worldly conditions in the light of this calendar has been overwhelming. Yet the speculation that results from such an impulse has always been fraught with problems. When has the level of wars, rumors of wars, and earthquakes escalated enough to provide premillennialists with certain knowledge that Christ is about to return? Or, for postmillennialists, when have the moral, social, political, and spiritual conditions been seasoned enough to provide any assurance that the worldly process has run its course? The enigmatic character of these calculations has not, however, prevented speculators from offering a certainty that the New Testament, with better wisdom, chose not to provide. Unfortunately, this kind of speculation diverts eschatology from its divinely intended function in Christian life. Eschatology is diverted in such a way as to jeopardize faith. The chief purpose of New Testament eschatology is not to encourage speculative fascination with world politics but, rather, to compel a deep and unremitting commitment to ethical action in the world.

If there are two aspects to the announcement of the kingdom, namely, salvation and judgment, then there are two emphases in the ethical demands that it entails. If the announcement of the kingdom is also an announcement of salvation, then the ethical implication is a summons to repentance and to identification with the life and values of the "age to come." Inasmuch as the kingdom is also a declaration of judgment—because the "present age" is dying, its god is defeated, and God is approaching for a final reckoning with all evil—two important consequences follow. First, there is a moral accountability even if, in the "present age," unbelievers claim that there are neither absolutes nor durable moral standards. Whatever the denizens of "this world" suppose, it does stand accountable before God, who is its creator and judge. Second, if the "age to come" is above, and not merely in continuity with this "present age," then everything in this life has a relative value. There is no person, no race, no political system or program, no ideals that can claim anyone's absolute allegiance, except God alone. Those who belong to God live within the worldly system, but they also live apart from it. They understand themselves to be in a "temporary ensconcement" within it, for the present life of this world is but provisional and interim.

There are, then, elements of both continuity and discontinuity in the believer's relationship to the "present age." Eschatology makes the believer an alien in this world, and eschatology makes the same believer a ruler, in the name of Christ, over the world, since that world belongs to the Lord. The Christian ethic, therefore, must contain elements of paradox, of transformation, of antithesis, and of identity.

CONCLUSION

The actual ways in which ethics should be realized in the modern world would take us far beyond the parameters of this discussion. It is sufficient to note that this view of the two ages demands a different role for eschatology in theology and a different role for eschatology in Christian proclamation.

In traditional systematic theologies, eschatology is commonly treated in a final section. The reasons for this are both logical and chronological. Logically, there is something to be said for considering God, creation, revelation, human nature, the person and work of Christ, sanctification, and the church before eschatology because they are all logical antecedents to it. After all, can one understand the new heavens and the new earth before one has understood the significance of the first heavens and earth? Can one grasp the meaning of the coming cosmic renovation if one knows nothing of Christ's cross? Would the judgment make any sense if one knew nothing of the fall or of God's character? What would it mean to speak of Christ's heavenly bride if one were ignorant about the church purchased by his blood? There is, too, a chronological logic to this order. It begins with what came before our birth—God, creation, revelation, the person and work of Christ. It moves on to what is contemporary to us—the work of the Spirit, sanctification, and the church. And it concludes with what lies ahead—death, resurrection, the return of Christ, judgment. What has logical merit and what fits into a chronological sequence is not, however, identical with the demands of a *theological* point of view.

If we are to define eschatology as the intrusion of the divine rule, the inbreaking in space and time of the "age to come," then it is clearly foundational to many of the theological *loci*. The incarnation, therefore, may be seen as the establishment and beginning of eschatology because the age of the future arrived in and with the Word incarnate. The death of Christ, likewise, is eschatological inasmuch as the judgment at the end of time was brought forward chronologically and enacted upon Christ, who stood in the place of those whom he represented. In addition, the Christian life possesses a central and critical eschatological dimension. The Holy Spirit, the sign of the presence of the messianic age, now provides a taste of the age to come, infuses hope, and gives certainty that believers have been transferred from the kingdom of darkness to the kingdom of light. Christian faith, therefore, is not simply living out a behavioral code but living by the power and in conformity with the values of the "age to come." There is, finally, an eschatological dimension to the church's life. In its preaching and hearing of the word of God, in its exercise of spiritual gifts, in its service and witness in the world, it should be experiencing and should be pointing to realities that are, in the eschatological sense, otherworldly.

Second, this view suggests a different role for eschatology in Christian proclamation. It has been customary to suppose that secular people could take little interest in eschatology until they had come to believe in the veracity of the Bible and therefore were willing to accept its predictions about the future. This assumption, however, misunderstands the secular mind and, as I have suggested, also misunderstands the role of eschatology.

Jacques Ellul is correct in observing that although secularism has no interest in God and his revelation it does preserve the major motifs of the Judeo-Christian worldview; it is the content that has been changed. Secularists believe in salvation, damnation, providence, and eschatology, but these themes are now worked out with reference not to God but to human potential. Salvation is self-realization and self-fulfillment; providence is exercising control over the future by planning; eschatology is mapping out scenarios for the future quarried from human resources and worked out through technological domination. Secularists, on their own terms, work all the time with a distinction between "this age" and the "age to come."

What biblical eschatology asserts, and what unbelievers need to hear, is that "this age" and the "age to come" are not in continuity with one another. Were that the case, the "age to come" could be quarried from or, in the case of B. F. Skinner, manipulated out of present human resources. The fact is that the "age to come" cannot be humanly constructed. This is what is so offensive and threatening about it to secularists. Such a proclamation judges all human life because it is not part of this age.

Will modern people therefore heed the biblical, eschatological message? At a rational level they may not, but powerful psychological forces flow in the opposite direction. The modern experience, shaped by a secularity that powerfully shifts our attention to the future, to a vision of humanity poised on the brink of a terrifying abyss, means that few of our contemporaries can ignore the future. And biblical faith, above all else, wants them to consider it.

Notes

1. Introduction: Modern Evangelicalism

1. For fuller consideration of the vitality of religion in the supposedly secular world, see David Martin, *A General Theory of Secularization* (New York: Harper & Row, 1978); Peter L. Berger, *A Rumor of Angels: Modern Society and the Rediscovery of the Supernatural* (Garden City, N.Y.: Doubleday, 1969); Hugh McLeod, *Religion and the People of Western Europe 1789–1970* (New York: Oxford Univ. Press, 1981); Jeffrey Cox, *The English Churches in a Secular Society: Lambeth, 1870–1930* (New York: Oxford Univ. Press, 1982); and Theodore Caplow, *Middletown Families: Fifty Years of Change and Continuity* (Minneapolis: Univ. of Minnesota Press, 1982).

2. The stories are told with extensive documentation in David B. Barrett, *World Christian Encyclopedia* (New York: Oxford Univ. Press, 1982), and much more briefly in Robin Keeley, ed., *Christianity in Today's World: An Eerdmans Handbook* (Grand Rapids: Eerdmans, 1985).

3. The survey by Steve Bruce, *Firm in the Faith* (Aldershot, England, and Brookfield, Vt.: Gower, 1985), is a recent comparison of conservative religious practices in England, Northern Ireland, and the United States.

4. Jaroslav Pelikan, *Reformation of Church and Dogma (1300–1700)*, vol. 4 of *The Christian Tradition: A History of the Development of Doctrine* (Chicago: Univ. of Chicago Press, 1984), 128.

5. For nineteenth-century Britain, see Doreen Rosman, *Evangelicals and Culture* (Totowa, N.J.: Biblio, for Croom Helm, London, 1984), and Ian C. Bradley, *The Call to Seriousness: The Evangelical Impact on the Victorians* (New York: Macmillan, 1976). A helpful anthology for the United States is William G. McLoughlin, ed., *The American Evangelicals, 1800–1900* (New York: Harper & Row, 1968). See also the selections in Edwin S. Gaustad, ed., *A Documentary History of Religion in America*, 2 vols. (Grand Rapids: Eerdmans, 1982, 1983).

6. Smith and his students are preparing a collective historical study with the working title, "The Evangelical Mosaic."

7. George Marsden, "The Evangelical Denomination," in *Evangelicalism and Modern America*, ed. Marsden (Grand Rapids: Eerdmans, 1984), vii–xvi.

8. This process is fully described in George M. Marsden, *Fundamentalism and American Culture: The Shaping of Twentieth Century Evangelicalism, 1870–1925* (New York: Oxford Univ. Press, 1980), and idem, "The Collapse of American Evangelical Academia," in *Faith and Rationality: Reason and Belief in God,*

ed. Alvin Plantinga and Nicholas Wolterstorff (Notre Dame, Ind.: Univ. of Notre Dame Press, 1983).

9. See Joel A. Carpenter, "Fundamentalist Institutions and the Rise of Evangelical Protestantism," *Church History* 49 (March 1980): 62-75.

10. George Marsden, *Reforming Fundamentalism: Fuller Seminary and the New Evangelicalism* (Grand Rapids: Eerdmans, 1987), contains extended consideration of these developments. Also useful are Joel A. Carpenter, "From Fundamentalism to the New Evangelical Coalition," in Marsden, ed., *Evangelicalism and Modern America,* and Rudolph L. Nelson, "Fundamentalism at Harvard: The Case of Edward John Carnell," *Quarterly Review* 2 (Summer 1982): 79-98.

11. For some of the reasons behind this situation, see Mark A. Noll, "Children of the Reformation in A Brave New World: Why 'American Evangelicals' Differ from 'Lutheran Evangelicals,'" *Dialogue: A Journal of Theology* 24 (Summer 1985): 176-80.

12. A full account of the American side is James D. Bratt, *Dutch Calvinism in Modern America* (Grand Rapids: Eerdmans, 1984).

13. See Douglas Johnson, *Contending for the Faith: A History of the Evangelical Movement in the Universities and Colleges* (Leicester, England: Inter-Varsity Press, 1979).

14. Especially important was the six-volume series edited by Carl F. H. Henry under the title *Contemporary Evangelical Thought* (1957–1969), a venture that made use of five publishers (Baker, Channel, Eerdmans, Holt Rinehart and Winston, and Zondervan) and eighty-five authors (including fifty-eight Americans and thirteen Britains) from several denominations (including twenty-one Presbyterians, twenty Baptists, eleven Reformed, ten Lutherans, and six Anglicans) in the production of its 127 essays.

15. These developments have only recently begun to receive serious academic attention. Two fine examples of recent study, from a sociologist and a historian respectively, are James Davison Hunter, *American Evangelicalism: Conservative Religion and the Quandary of Modernity* (New Brunswick, N.J.: Rutgers Univ. Press, 1983), and Joel A. Carpenter, "The Renewal of American Fundamentalism, 1930–1945" (Ph.D. diss., Johns Hopkins Univ., 1984).

16. Particularly significant was his *The Uneasy Conscience of Modern Fundamentalism* (Grand Rapids: Eerdmans, 1947).

17. See Arthur F. Glasser, "The Evolution of Evangelical Missionary Theology since World War II," *International Bulletin of Missionary Research* 9 (Jan. 1985): 9-13.

18. See Carl F. H. Henry and W. Stanley Mooneyham, eds., *One Race, One Gospel, One Task; Official Reference Volumes: Papers and Reports [World Congress on Evangelism, Berlin 1966]* (Minneapolis: World Wide Publications, 1967), and J. D. Douglas, ed., *Let the Earth Hear His Voice,* International Congress on World Evangelization, Lausanne, Switzerland. Official Reference Volume: Papers and Responses (Minneapolis: World Wide Publications, 1975).

19. Prov. 11:14; 15:22; 24:6.

20. Anthony C. Thiselton, *The Two Horizons: New Testament Hermeneutics and Philosophical Description* (Grand Rapids: Eerdmans, 1980); John R. W. Stott, *Between Two Worlds: The Art of Preaching in the Twentieth Century* (Grand Rapids: Eerdmans, 1982).

2A. God the Image-Maker

1. Henry's six-volume *God, Revelation and Authority* (Waco: Word, 1974–82) covers magisterially all the arguments and debates involved in the upholding of rational theism today. Thomas F. Torrance has developed a full-scale Christ-centered epistemology and methodology for Christian encounter with the natural sciences and all forms of metaphysics. E. L. Mascall has done a parallel job, using Chalcedonian Christology and neo-Thomist ontology to establish his frame of reference.

2. See, e.g., Louis Berkhof, *Systematic Theology* (Grand Rapids: Eerdmans, 1949).

3. In fairness to Robinson, it should be said that this provocative title for his article in the *Observer* was not his, but was pressed on him by the newspaper's editors.

4. Hendrikus Berkhof writes: "With the bath water of an isolated transcendence Tillich also throws out the child, the personal I-Thou relationship. If theism is understood as including this relationship, too, the theologian, despite his dislike of isms, will have to defend the concept" (*Christian Faith* [Grand Rapids: Eerdmans, 1979], 133).

5. See, on the exegesis, W. D. Davies, *Paul and Rabbinic Judaism* (London: SPCK, 1948), 325ff.

6. Emil Brunner and Karl Barth, *Natural Theology,* trans. Peter Fraenkel (London: Geoffrey Bles, 1946).

7. Asks Geoffrey W. Bromiley: "Can one say, as Barth would say, that when describing God as love and righteousness, or as freedom and power, righteousness can be brought under love and power under freedom? Can any grouping of perfections, whether in two or more series, be finally upheld when it is seriously and properly maintained that God is and does not merely have his perfections, that he is not just this or that perfection but each and every perfection?" (*Introduction to the Theology of Karl Barth* [Grand Rapids: Eerdmans, 1979], 73-74). Otto Weber follows Barth to this conclusion: "God's righteousness is to be understood as the conformity of God's being and acting, revealed in Jesus Christ, to the covenant which he has established in love and freedom, as it is carried out as 'distributive righteousness,' as God's effective negation of sin, and as unrighteousness to Jesus Christ, and as it is authentic and authoritative reality as God's gracious Yes to the sinful and reconciled creature in the resurrected Christ" (*Foundations of Dogmatics,* vol. 1, trans. Darrell L. Guder [Grand Rapids: Eerdmans, 1981], 437). Weber then construes the wrath of God as "the manifestation of the divinity of his love toward 'the impossible possibility' of man's rejecting God" (p. 438). But is this the entire New Testament story?

8. Berkhof, *Systematic Theology,* 52-53.

9. Henry, *God, Revelation and Authority,* 3:364; 5:86.

10. Basil Mitchell, *The Justification of Religious Belief* (London: Macmillan, 1973), 19.

11. Berkhof, *Systematic Theology,* 59; italics mine.

12. Ibid. He adds: "It is important to maintain the immutability of God over against the Pelagian and Arminian doctrine that God is subject to change, not indeed in His being, but in His knowledge and will, so that his decisions are to a

great extent dependent on the actions of man [i.e., are responses to new contingencies that had no place in God's plan till man effected them—J. I. P.]; over against the pantheistic notion that God is an eternal becoming rather than an absolute Being, and that the unconscious Absolute is gradually developing into conscious personality in man; and over against the present tendency of some to speak of a finite, struggling, and gradually growing God."

13. G. L. Prestige, *God in Patristic Thought* (London: SPCK, 1952), 7. Hendrikus Berkhof writes that at Calvary God "allows himself to be made a victim. Note: he allows it to be done to him. He enters into it and at the same time stands above it; not half in it and half above it, but totally the one and totally the other. This is not self-contradictory. For the more one controls a situation, the more one can allow" (*Christian Faith*, 146). Is this acceptable as an account of impassibility in action?

14. Calvin, *Institutes of the Christian Religion*, I.vi.1; I.vii.5.

2B. Images of God

1. In the Bible revelation is a relatively marginal theme by comparison with God's speaking and acting (from both of which it ought to be distinguished) and predominantly an eschatological one. See Gerald Downing, *Has Christianity a Revelation?* (Philadelphia: Westminster, 1967); Paul Althaus, "Die Inflation des Begriffs der Offenbarung in der gegenwärtigen Theologie," *Zeitschift für Systematische Theologie* 18 (1941): 134-49; Nicholas Wolterstorff, "On God Speaking," *Reformed Journal* 19 (July-Aug. 1969): 7-11.

2. Augustine, *De trinitate* 12.5-7, rejects the popular Eastern family image of the Trinity (Adam, Eve, and Seth—with the Holy Spirit as Eve) on the grounds that (1) if one needs a whole family to reflect God then Adam was imageless until Eve was taken from his rib and a son born from their loins, and (2) *man* is in any case the image of God, woman the glory of man (from a reading of 1 Cor. 11:7; but see *De civitate Dei* 12.17 for a more inclusive view of women). Augustine thus spends most of books 9, 10, 11, and especially 14 of *De trinitate* trying out various psychological rather than family or social analogies for the Trinity.

3. Calvin's view is that what is restored in Christ—true knowledge (Col. 3:10), righteousness, and holiness (Eph. 4:24)— must be what had been originally endowed and then forfeited. These spiritual qualities thus constitute the lost "narrow" image. Calvin also holds out, however, for a so-called broad image that is retained, though impaired, through the fall. This consists in those natural faculties of reason, understanding, and will that make up the soul's faculties and distinguish humans from animals. Calvin, *Institutes of the Christian Religion*, ed. John T. McNeill, trans. Ford Lewis Battles, 2 vols. (1559; Philadelphia: Westminster, 1960), I.15.3, 4; II.12.6-7; III.3.9. For other examples of prominent use of the image of God in theological anthropology see the systematic theologies of Charles Hodge, Louis Berkhof, Francis Pieper, H. Orton Wiley, and especially G. C. Berkouwer, *Man: The Image of God*, trans. Dirk W. Jellema (Grand Rapids: Eerdmans, 1962).

4. For the connection between social ethics and image in Calvin see *Institutes* III.7.6 and *Commentary on Gen. 9:6*, both cited in Brian A. Gerrish, "The Mirror of God's Goodness: A Key Metaphor in Calvin's View of Man," in *Read-*

ings in Calvin's Theology, ed. Donald K. McKim (Grand Rapids: Baker, 1984), 110. Two modern statements of the same connection are Paul Ramsey, *Basic Christian Ethics* (New York: Charles Scribner's Sons, 1950), esp. 249-84, and George F. Thomas, *Christian Ethics and Moral Philosophy* (New York: Charles Scribner's Sons, 1955), esp. 156-62.

5. 1 Cor. 11:7 argues obscurely against male headcovering on the ground that a man is the image and glory of God. James 3:9 argues like Gen. 9:6 against violating another human on the ground that such violence shatters the precious image. None of these texts, nor Gen. 5:1, states the content of the image. The James and Corinthians references are casual. I will use "image of God" throughout as roughly synonymous with "likeness of God" (Gen. 1:26), following the tradition since the Renaissance, even though biblical scholars often think of image (*ṣelem*) as the more concrete term (perhaps connoting a statue) and likeness (*dᵉmût*) as a more abstract term.

6. Phyllis A. Bird, "Male and Female He Created Them," *Harvard Theological Review* 74 (1981): 130.

7. Hendrikus Berkhof, *Christian Faith: An Introduction to the Study of the Faith,* trans. Sierd Woudstra (Grand Rapids: Eerdmans, 1979), 179. A standard catalog of theological interpretations of the image of God is Emil Brunner, *Man in Revolt,* trans. Olive Wyon (New York: Charles Scribner's Sons, 1939), Appendix I (pp. 498-515).

8. In some key places "image of God" or "likeness of God" *does* mean general God-resemblance. See n. 5 above on *dᵉmût* and, on Gen. 1:26-27 and 5:1-2, Meredith Kline, "Creation in the Image of the Glory-Spirit," *Westminster Theological Journal* 39 (1977): 261.

9. As maintained, e.g., by Berkouwer, *Man,* 73-74.

10. Kline, "Creation in the Image," 264, and Calvin, *Institutes* I.15.3.

11. Not merely a correspondence, or a "correspondence of unlikes," as sometimes suggested by Barthian-inclined theologians.

12. Rationality, will, and freedom are commonly and rightly mentioned— i.e., essential attributes of personhood. In "Christian Philosophy and the Heritage of Descartes" (mimeographed), Nicholas Wolterstorff calls attention to responsibility (or accountability) and action as main items in the essence of humanity. No doubt at least the latter figures as an image of God as well. For a survey of possibilities for inclusion in the broad image, see Berkouwer, *Man,* 38-41, 51-53, 61-63, 74.

13. Scripture does, of course, present God as thinking, willing, feeling, making moral judgments, etc., but the interest is focused on *what* God thinks, wills, feels, and judges. So for humans.

14. Bird, "Male and Female," 144.

15. Ulrich Mauser, "Image of God and Incarnation," *Interpretation* 24 (1970): 341, points out that the text also implies, naturally enough, that God is like human beings—a relative novelty among Israel's neighbors, who tended to conceive God in the likeness of plants or animals. "In Israel alone the representation of Yahweh as a man holds sway to such an extent as to command a virtual monopoly."

16. As suggested by Claus Westermann, *Genesis 1–11: A Commentary,* trans. John J. Scullion (Minneapolis: Augsburg, 1984), 155.

17. See, e.g., Kline, "Creation in the Image," 264-65; Bird, "Male and Female," 139-40, and the vast literature (Hehn, von Rad, Schmidt, etc.) she cites. Much depends on seeing Gen. 1:26 in the light of its oldest commentary, Ps. 8, where kingly "honor and glory" come to the fore for the humanity that is adorned with this crown in order to rule.

18. Some commentators think that is *all* that can be said about 1:26. See, e.g., Gerhard von Rad, "eikōn," *Theological Dictionary of the New Testament,* ed. Gerhard Kittel, trans. Geoffrey Bromiley, 10 vols. (Grand Rapids: Eerdmans, 1964–75), 2:392.

19. Gerhard von Rad, *Genesis: A Commentary,* rev. ed. (Philadelphia: Westminster, 1971), 60.

20. Bird, "Male and Female," 138.

21. I owe this suggestion and general enlightenment on Genesis 1 to my colleague John Stek.

22. Karl Heinrich Rengstorff, "Apostellō, apostolos," *Theological Dictionary of the New Testament,* 1:415, 421. John's Gospel follows this tradition for the Son, who represents the Father, and for the Paraclete, who represents the Son, and for the church, which represents all three. See below on the church as Trinitarian likeness.

23. This is a natural place to see that the broad image is a condition for expressing or exercising the narrow: one needs to be able to think, for instance, in order to rule.

24. The fact that humans have a patent on the image may be connected to the second commandment prohibition against *other* graven images.

25. Karl Barth, *Church Dogmatics,* ed. and trans. Geoffrey W. Bromiley and Thomas F. Torrance, 4 vols. (Edinburgh: T. & T. Clark, 1936–69), III/1, 196; III/2, 323-24.

26. For a range of views of Adam as bisexual, God as female as well as male, procreative couples as sole image-bearers, Renaissance conclusions on the nobility of women, Thomistic double concepts of the image—one to fit Gen. 1:27, one to fit the exclusivist 1 Cor. 11:7-9—and much else of interest, see Maryanne Cline Horowitz, "The Image of God in Man—Is Woman Included?" *Harvard Theological Review* 72 (1979): 175-206.

27. Bird, "Male and Female," 147. For a fascinating comparison with the Babylonian Epic of Atrahasis on this point (humankind's multiplying capacity is a sore topic among the gods, who must suffer insomnia on account of all the uproar) see Tivka Frymer-Kensky, "The Atrahasis Epic and Its Significance for Our Understanding of Genesis 1–9," *Biblical Archaeologist* 40 (1977): 149.

28. I.e., mirror or reflection; Calvin, *Institutes* I.14.21.

29. I.e., there is no analogy in Genesis 1 and 2 of the following sort: just as Adam was incomplete until complemented by Eve, so with God until the creation of humanity. Nor in these chapters can one find other obvious links between divine/human fellowship and intrahuman fellowship.

30. Berkouwer, *Man,* 112.

31. Rom. 8:18-23, 29, 32; 2 Cor. 3:18; 4:10-11.

32. Abraham Heschel, *The Prophets* (New York: Harper & Row, 1962).

33. Phil. 3:10; 1 Cor. 15:48; Rom. 6:1-11. In the Romans passage dying and

rising with Christ seems to include baptism, mortification/vivification, and physical death/resurrection.

34. Besides Heschel, *Prophets*, and Mauser, "Image of God," see also Jürgen Moltmann, *The Crucified God: The Cross of Christ as the Foundation and Criticism of Christian Theology*, trans. R. A. Wilson and John Bowden (New York: Harper & Row, 1974), and idem, *The Trinity and the Kingdom*, trans. Margaret Kohl (San Francisco: Harper & Row, 1981).

35. As in Moltmann's theology, above, and in other Hegelian-influenced liberation theology. See, e.g., Juan Luis Segundo, *Our Idea of God*, trans. John Drury, vol. 3 of A Theology for Artisans of a New Humanity (Maryknoll, N.Y.: Orbis Books, 1974).

36. This is especially so in process thought, where God is *eminently* related to us. See, e.g., Charles Hartshorne, *The Divine Relativity: A Social Conception of God* (New Haven: Yale Univ. Press, 1948), esp. 26-27, 34-36, 77-82.

37. Paul Althaus, *The Theology of Martin Luther*, trans. Robert Schultz (Philadelphia: Fortress, 1966), 26-27.

38. See Calvin, *Comm. on 1 Cor. 15:44-50*, for a Scotist strain that implies the need for Christ even if Adam had stood. What we are restored to is the image of the *second* Adam, who does not just duplicate, but vastly improves upon, the first. Richard Prins, "The Image of God in Adam and the Restoration of Man in Jesus Christ," *Scottish Journal of Theology* 25 (1972): 32-44, has an illuminating discussion of Calvin's double "restoration" theology: it sometimes means recovery of Adam's status; elsewhere it means transformation according to the higher image of Christ.

39. For hesitant images of God in Hosea see Mauser, "Image of God." For a general discussion of God's purposely self-limiting power see Daniel L. Migliore, *The Power of God* (Philadelphia: Westminster, 1983).

40. I owe this observation to Jack Roeda.

41. By "person" I mean a distinct center of love, will, knowledge, and action.

42. First, a level at which triadic references sometimes appear, but only incidentally. There is no emphasis on them and no probing of relationships: 1 Pet. 1:2; Tit. 3:4-6; Heb. 10:29; Jude 20-21. Second, in a number of places there is structural or other stress on the formula and some account of the activity of Father, Son, and Spirit, but still little or no attempt to work out some solution to the relational problems (chiefly, the relation of the divinity of Christ to the unity of God): Mark 1:10-11 and parallels; Matt. 1:20; 12:28; 28:19; Luke 24:49; Acts 2:38-39. Third, especially in John, there is stress on the mutual, yet distinct, activity of the three persons and some attempt to work out a solution to the problem of their relation. See Arthur Wainwright, *The Trinity in the New Testament* (London: SPCK, 1962), 248-59.

43. Ibid., 260. According to C. K. Barrett, "More than any other New Testament writer [John] lays the foundation for a doctrine of a co-equal Trinity" (*The Gospel According to St. John: An Introduction with Commentary and Notes on the Greek Text* [London: SPCK, 1955], 78). For similar statements, see W. F. Howard, *Christianity According to St. John* (Philadelphia: Westminster, 1946), 36, and T. Evan Pollard, *Johannine Christology and the Early Church* (Cambridge: Cambridge Univ. Press, 1970), chap. 3. Pollard's study demonstrates the

extent to which early Trinitarian controversies centered around Fourth Gospel interpretation—esp. 10:30 and 14:28.

44. Indeed, the plainness of John's syntactical style itself presents a major problem for the interpreter; viz., how all the central soteriological/Christological concepts (light, life, truth, grace, love, glory, word, etc.) are *related*. The absence of very many clarifying subordinating clauses often prevents a good view of the author's conceptual map. The text seems to present a high plateau without many valleys.

45. Rudolf Bultmann, *Theology of the New Testament,* trans. Kendrick Grobel (2 vols. in 1), 2:50-52. Many students of John notice this inescapable Christological feature. David L. Mealand, e.g., states: "The paradoxical blending of distinction and unity, and of subordination and equality, ensured the complexity of subsequent theological debate" ("The Christology of the Fourth Gospel," *Scottish Journal of Theology* 31 [1978]: 461).

46. Rudolf Schnackenburg, *Das Johannesevangelium,* Neutestamentliche Abhandlungen no. 21 (3 vols.), 3:216-21 (see the *Beziehung* diagrams, p. 219); Ernst Käsemann, *The Testament of Jesus,* tr. Gerhard Krodel (Philadelphia: Fortress, 1968), 29.

47. Mark L. Appold, *The Oneness Motif in the Fourth Gospel,* Wissenschaftliche Untersuchungen zum Neuen Testament, no. 2 (Tübingen: J. C. B. Mohr, 1976), 18.

48. Ibid., 282.

49. Barth's *Church Dogmatics* contains a famous architectonic scheme of correspondences and dependencies that derives from the Trinitarian relations. Hence the God who exists "in relationship and fellowship" within his own Triune being creates man as male and female to be in covenant partnership with him and, simultaneously, to live in cooperation, encounter, and fellow humanity with each other. Though all this sounds promisingly Johannine, Barth's own statement of the Trinity doctrine emerges as disappointingly monist—hardly more than an I/I relation, a fellowship of a single person with himself; *Church Dogmatics* III/1, 196. Moltmann, *Trinity and the Kingdom,* rightly scores Barth on this point but seems relatively unconcerned about the linkage of his own Trinity view with the biblical materials.

50. Ernst Haenchen, "'Der Vater, Der Mich Gesandt Hat,'" *New Testament Studies* 9 (1963): 208-16.

51. Schnackenburg, *Johannesevangelium,* 3:403-4.

52. The former reciprocal relation is constitutive for the latter.

53. For a "mutual knowledge" table, see C. H. Dodd, *The Interpretation of the Fourth Gospel* (Cambridge: Cambridge Univ. Press, 1953), 187. Dodd also relates knowledge to "inness."

54. Käsemann, *Testament,* 50, believes that such Johannnine categories as glory, love, knowledge, truth, light, etc., are really almost interchangeable. See n. 44 above.

55. C. K. Barrett, *Gospel According to St. John,* 21.

56. Raymond Brown, *The Gospel According to John,* The Anchor Bible, vols. 29, 29A (Garden City, N.Y.: Doubleday & Co., 1966), 29A:661.

57. "Integrity" as an image of God is Calvin's word, *Institutes* I.15.3.

58. Sidney Greidanus, "Human Rights in Biblical Perspective," *Calvin Theological Journal* 19 (1984): 13-31.

59. As John Baillie puts it, "There are some things you can't comfortably do with a crown upon your head" (*A Reasoned Faith*, 98, quoted in Carl F. H. Henry, *God Who Speaks and Shows*, vol. 4 of *God, Revelation and Authority* [Waco: Word, 1979], 12).

60. C. S. Lewis, *The Weight of Glory and Other Addresses*, ed. Walter Hooper (New York: Macmillan, 1980), 18.

61. Neal Punt, *Unconditional Good News* (Grand Rapids: Eerdmans, 1980), 7.

62. E.g., Sartre: "Even if one does not believe in God, there are elements of the idea of God that remain in us and that cause us to see the world with some divine aspects. . . . As for me, I don't see myself as so much dust that has appeared in the world, but as a being that was expected, prefigured, called forth. In short, as a being that could, it seems, come only from a creator. . . . I often think in this way for want of being able to think otherwise" ("Conversation about Death and God with Sartre," *Harper's*, Feb. 1984, 39).

63. M. Scott Peck, *People of the Lie* (New York: Simon and Schuster, 1983), 75. In a remark on the present essay, psychologist Mary Stewart Van Leeuwen observed that Christianly based counseling often helps unbelievers precisely because they may possess what look like Christian virtues and fruit of the Spirit. Further, believers are themselves varyingly endowed with such virtues, the less sanctified among them often put in the shade by the more sanctified. In such gift-bestowing God is the supreme relativist. See also Mary Stewart Van Leeuwen, *The Person in Psychology: A Contemporary Christian Appraisal* (Grand Rapids: Eerdmans, 1985).

64. C. S. Lewis (N. W. Clerk), *A Grief Observed* (Greenwich, Conn.: Seabury, 1963), 9.

65. I owe this point to Alvin Plantinga.

66. Cf. Robert T. Sears, "Trinitarian Love as the Ground of the Church," *Theological Studies* 37 (1976): 676. In continuing her comment noted in n. 63, Van Leeuwen cautions against simple equation of church communal conformity with sanctification, and recommends balance between corporate and individual theories of the image of God. Certain studies, in fact, associate schizophrenia with isolation or undersocialization and depression with forced conformity and over-socialization.

67. Augustine, *Epistles* 98.9, cited in Taymans d'Eypernon, *The Blessed Trinity and the Sacraments* (Westminster, Md.: Newman, 1961), 8.

68. "L'enfer, c'est les autres" (Jean-Paul Sartre, *Huit Clos,* quoted in Paul Henry, *Saint Augustine on Personality: The Saint Augustine Lecture, 1959,* the Saint Augustine Lecture Series [New York: Macmillan, 1960], 23). See also Moltmann, *Trinity and the Kingdom,* 199.

2C. A Christian View of the Person for Today

1. Richard Dawkins, *The Selfish Gene* (New York: Oxford Univ. Press, 1976), ix.

2. Donald M. MacKay, *Human Science and Human Dignity* (Downers Grove, Ill.: InterVarsity Press, 1979), 114-15.

3. Ibid., 115.

4. Karl Barth, *Nein!* 25, 27, quoted in Emil Brunner, *Man in Revolt* (Philadelphia: Westminster, 1939), 95.

5. Stephen Neill, *What Is Man?* (London: United Society for Christian Literature, 1968), 16.

6. Brunner, *Man in Revolt.*

7. *The Sickness unto Death,* trans. Howard V. Hong and Edna H. Hong (Princeton, N.J.: Princeton Univ. Press, 1980), 13-14.

8. See Brunner's historical account of the Reformers' views here in Appendix I to *Man in Revolt.*

9. See Philip Schaff, *The Creeds of Christendom* (New York: Harper and Brothers, 1877), 325-26.

10. Article vii, in ibid., 434.

11. Chapter IV, 2, in ibid., 611.

12. "For God not only created the body and soul of Adam and Eve before the fall, but has also created our bodies and souls since the fall . . ." (Article I, in ibid., 998).

13. I made a struggling attempt to do this in my article "Separable Souls: A Defense of 'Minimal Dualism,'" *The Southern Journal of Philosophy* 19 (1981): 313-31. A different effort I see as achieving the same goal is found in Chapter 3 of William Hasker, *Metaphysics: Constructing a World View* (Downers Grove, Ill.: InterVarsity Press, 1983). Hasker calls his view "emergentism," but it can be seen as a new form of dualism.

14. John Cooper has argued this very well in his fine two-part article "Body and Soul" in the *Reformed Journal* (Sept. and Oct. 1982).

15. Chapter XXXII, I, in *Creeds of Christendom,* 670.

16. Murray Harris, *Raised Immortal* (London: Marshall Morgan & Scott, 1983; Grand Rapids: Eerdmans, 1985).

3A. God the Discloser

1. Karl Menninger, *Whatever Became of Sin?* (New York: Hawthorn Books, 1973).

2. As in William Wolf, *No Cross, No Crown* (Garden City, N.Y.: Doubleday, 1957), 27-30.

3. I have sought to identify the Manichean and Zoroastrian tendencies in the religious right in *The Religious Right and Christian Faith* (Grand Rapids: Eerdmans, 1982), 47-52, 84, and *passim.*

4. For an analysis of narrative theology and a typology of current expressions of it, see my "Narrative Theology: An Overview," *Interpretation* 37 (Oct. 1983): 340-52.

5. As in Heinrich Heppe, *Reformed Dogmatics,* ed. Ernst Bizer, trans. G. T. Thomson (Grand Rapids: Baker, 1978), on the one hand, and Carl Braaten and Robert Jenson, eds., *Christian Dogmatics,* vols. 1 and 2 (Philadelphia: Fortress, 1984), on the other.

6. James Orr went a step further and argued that the narrative of faith as

found in Scripture and in books on systematic theology is reflected in the history of dogma, as each chapter in succession became the occasion for the notable controversies; Orr, *Progress of Dogma* (London: Hodder & Stoughton, 1901). For Peter Toon's illuminating commentary on this, see his *The Development of Doctrine in the Church* (Grand Rapids: Eerdmans, 1979), 62-70.

7. A passage of Scripture, John 1:1-18, that in short compass indicates this larger biblical arc, will provide the framework for the following section.

8. For an exposition of this and other deeds/doctrines in the narrative, see my *The Christian Story*, rev. ed. (Grand Rapids: Eerdmans, 1984), 1:68-76. See also Robert Paul Roth, *The Theater of God: Story in Christian Doctrines* (Philadelphia: Fortress, 1985).

9. Fackre, *Christian Story*, 56-58.

10. The growing literature on religious pluralism, as well as the enlarging constituencies within both Protestant and Roman Catholic theology that question the "scandal of particularity," both raise a fundamental challenge to our deeds/disclosure narrative. A measure of how far the conversation has moved in these circles in the past few decades is found in the titles of two definitive works: W. A. Visser 't Hooft's earlier and unambiguous *No Other Name,* and Paul Knitter's *No Other Name?* (Maryknoll, N.Y.: Orbis Books, 1985). The latter traces the qualification and finally erosion of particularist views in many forms of modern theology, defending a version of the same as "theocentric universalism."

By choosing "suffering and hope" as our themes, we do not confront the issues posed by religious pluralism as directly as do other apologetic ventures. Nonetheless, the claims to particularity integral to this chapter do, of course, radically call into question the assumptions of the various current pluralist theologians (Hick, Cobb, Pannikar, Dawe, W. C. Smith, H. Smith, Knitter, etc.). For a typology and critique of such options, see my "The Scandals of Particularity and Universality," *Midstream* 22 (Jan. 1983): 32-52, and S. Mark Heim, *Is Christ the Only Way?* (Valley Forge, Pa.: Judson, 1985).

11. For a view that joins an emphasis on God's deeds with confidence in the prophetic-apostolic testimony, see William J. Abraham, *The Divine Inspiration of Holy Scripture* (London: Oxford Univ. Press, 1981).

12. On the canonical rim, see various recent writings of James Barr: *The Scope and Authority of the Bible* (Philadelphia: Westminster, 1980); *Holy Scripture, Canon, Authority, Criticism* (Philadelphia: Westminster, 1983); *Beyond Fundamentalism: Biblical Foundations for Evangelical Christianity* (Philadelphia: Westminster, 1984). Note especially the important new defense of the canon in the works of Brevard Childs, *Old Testament Theology in Canonical Context* (Philadelphia: Fortress, 1985), and *The New Testament: An Introduction* (London: SCM, 1984).

13. For a wide-ranging exposition of this view, see the two volumes of E. Schillebeeckx, *Jesus,* trans. Hubert Hoskins (New York: Seabury, 1979) and *Christ,* trans. John Bowden (New York: Seabury, 1980). For a critique of Schillebeeckx, see my "Bones Strong and Weak in the Skeletal Structure of Schillebeeckx's Christology," *Journal of Ecumenical Studies* 21 (Spring 1984): 248-77.

14. A move in this direction can be found in P. J. Achtemeier, *The Inspiration of Scripture: Problems and Proposals* (Philadelphia: Westminster, 1980).

15. For an elaboration of this point see my essay, "The Use of Scripture in

My Work in Systematics," in *The Use of the Bible in Theology: Evangelical Options,* ed. Robert Johnston (Richmond: John Knox, 1985).

16. Austin Farrer, *The Glass of Vision* (Westminster, Md..: Dacre, 1948), 43-57.

17. Carl F. H. Henry, *God, Revelation and Authority,* 6 vols. (Waco: Word, 1974–82), 4:467-69.

18. In the United Church of Christ with which I am associated the commitment to "relevance" regularly imperils theological identity. Hence, the concerned efforts in the UCC to get its doctrinal bearings. See, e.g., "Letter to Our Brothers and Sisters in Christ" from the 1984 Craigville Colloquy, *Keeping You Posted,* June 15, 1984.

19. I have argued this point relative to political fundamentalism in *Religious Right and Christian Faith.*

20. For a discussion of these issues see D. A. Carson, ed., *Biblical Interpretation and the Church* (Exeter: Paternoster, 1984).

21. For the employment of this kind of sociology of knowledge in criticizing the aforementioned Craigville Letter, see Alfred Krass, "Evangelism, Social Action and the Craigville Colloquy," in *Seventh Angel* (Sept. 1984): 22-23.

22. A refrain in Carl Henry. See, e.g., *God, Revelation and Authority,* 1:96-111.

23. See Fackre, *Christian Story,* 248-49.

24. The previous four paragraphs are, in substance, from my *Christian Story,* 248-49.

3B. Rationality and the Christian Revelation

1. Following what they take to be the lead of Kierkegaard, and influenced heavily by Kant, numerous existentialist and neoorthodox theologians seem to have held this view.

2. John Wisdom, *Paradox and Discovery* (Oxford: Basil Blackwell, 1965), 19-20.

3. See, e.g., Don Cupitt, "The Finality of Christ," *Theology* 78 (Dec. 1975): 625, and John Hick, "Jesus and the World Religions," in *The Myth of God Incarnate,* ed. John Hick (London: SCM, 1977).

4. For some of the conceptual apparatus of such an argument, see the opening pages of Alvin Plantinga, *The Nature of Necessity* (Oxford: Clarendon, 1974).

5. Grace Jantzen, "Incarnation and Epistemology," *Theology* 83 (May 1983): 171.

6. See my *Understanding Identity Statements* (Aberdeen: Aberdeen Univ. Press and Humanities Press, 1984), chap. 9; "Divinity, Humanity, and Death," *Religious Studies* 19 (Dec. 1983): 451-58; and "Incarnational Anthropology," *Theology* 87 (Sept. 1984): 344-50. I have explored the challenge in greater detail in chaps. 1-6 of a recently completed study entitled *The Logic of God Incarnate* (Ithaca, N.Y.: Cornell Univ. Press, 1986).

7. One contemporary theologian who has hinted repeatedly at the importance of this view is Brian Hebblethwaite. See, e.g., his article "The Propriety of the Doctrine of the Incarnation as a Way of Interpreting Christ," *Scottish Journal of Theology* 33 (1980): 201-22.

8. Francis Young, "Can There Be Any Evidence?" in *Incarnation and Myth: The Debate Continued*, ed. Michael Goulder (Grand Rapids: Eerdmans, 1979), 62.

9. Brian Hebblethwaite, "Incarnation—The Essence of Christianity?" *Theology* 80 (1977).

10. Keith Ward, "Incarnation or Inspiration—A False Dichotomy?" *Theology* 80 (1977).

11. Jantzen, "Incarnation and Epistemology," 173-74.

12. See Richard Creel, "Can God Know That He Is God?" *Religious Studies* 16 (June 1980): 195-201.

3C. Speaking and Hearing

1. Willard Swartley, *Slavery, Sabbath, War and Women: Case Issues in Biblical Interpretation* (Scottdale, Pa.: Herald Press, 1983), 31.

2. Paul Ricoeur, *Freud and Philosophy* (New Haven: Yale Univ. Press, 1970), 20-56. Cf. also *The Conflict of Interpretation: Essays on Hermeneutics* (Evanston, Ill.: Northwestern Univ. Press, 1974), 99-210.

3. Ricoeur, *Freud and Philosophy,* 18-28, 88-102, 186-211, 494-506.

4. Jürgen Habermas, *Knowledge and Human Interests,* 2d ed. (London: Heinemann, 1978); idem, *Theory and Practice* (London: Heinemann, 1974); and (as joint editor) *Hermeneutik und Ideologiekritik* (Frankfurt: Suhrkamp, 1971). Cf. more broadly the survey of Zygmunt Bauman, *Hermeneutics and Social Science: Approaches to Understanding* (London: Hutchison, 1978).

5. Gerd Theissen, *On Having a Critical Faith* (London: SCM, 1979), 10-11.

6. Ellen Flesseman-van Leer, ed., *The Bible: Its Authority and Interpretation in the Ecumenical Movement* (Geneva: World Council of Churches, 1981), 31, 40.

7. Ibid., 32.

8. Brevard S. Childs, *Introduction to the Old Testament as Scripture* (London: SCM, 1979), and *The New Testament as Canon: An Introduction* (London: SCM, 1984).

9. See further James D. G. Dunn, "Levels of Canonical Authority," *Horizons in Biblical Theology* 4 (1982): 13-60.

10. Childs, *New Testament as Canon,* 280.

11. Cf. D. A. Carson, ed., *Biblical Interpretation and the Church: The Problem of Contextualization* (Nashville: Nelson, 1984), esp. Carson's own essay, 20-24.

12. F. D. E. Schleiermacher, *Hermeneutik,* ed. H. Kimmerle (Heidelberg: Winter, 1959), 40; there are numerous examples in Wittgenstein.

13. A. C. Thiselton, *The Two Horizons* (Grand Rapids: Eerdmans, 1980), esp. 3-23, 103-14, 300-385.

14. Robert Alter, *The Art of Biblical Narrative* (New York: Basic Books, 1981), 63-87 and *passim*.

15. Roman Jakobson, "Closing Statement: Linguistics and Poetics," in *Style and Language,* ed. T. A. Sebeok (Cambridge: MIT Press, 1960), esp. 353-57; cf. *Selected Writings,* 4 vols. (The Hague: Mouton, 1962).

16. A. C. Thiselton, "Knowledge, Myth and Corporate Memory," in *Believing in the Church: The Corporate Nature of Faith,* Report of the Doctrine Commission of the Church of England (London: SPCK, 1981), 45-78. Cf. also *Two Horizons,* 300-326, 379-85.

3D. The Finality of Jesus Christ

1. E. C. Dewick gives us a historical overview of the question in *The Christian Attitude to Other Religions* (Cambridge: Cambridge Univ. Press, 1953). Some of the recent discussion appears in these three books: Donald G. Dawe and John B. Carman, eds., *Christian Faith in a Religiously Plural World* (Maryknoll, N.Y.: Orbis Books, 1978); Gerald H. Anderson and Thomas F. Stransky, eds., *Mission Trends No. 5: Faith Meets Faith* (Grand Rapids: Eerdmans; New York: Paulist, 1981); and idem, *Christ's Lordship and Religious Pluralism* (Maryknoll, N.Y.: Orbis Books, 1981).

2. The issues are ably presented in two recent Catholic works: Alan Race, *Christians and Religious Pluralism: Patterns in the Christian Theology of Religions* (Maryknoll, N.Y.: Orbis Books, 1982), and Paul F. Knitter, *No Other Name? A Critical Survey of Christian Attitudes toward the World Religions* (Maryknoll, N.Y.: Orbis Books, 1985).

3. See Harold Coward, *Pluralism: Challenge to World Religions* (Maryknoll, N.Y.: Orbis Books, 1985).

4. Evangelicals tend to neglect the subject of hermeneutics, but it forces itself upon us anyway in connection with such issues as this one. David Tracy has a profound discussion in *The Analogical Imagination: Christian Theology and the Culture of Pluralism* (New York: Crossroad, 1981), chap. 3.

5. On the universalism of St. Luke, see N. Q. King, "The Universalism of the Third Gospel," in *Studia Evangelica,* ed. Kurt Aland et al. (Berlin: Akademie Verlag, 1959), 199-205; Joseph A. Fitzmyer, *Gospel according to St. Luke I-IX* (Garden City, N.Y.: Doubleday, 1981), 187-92; Stephen G. Wilson, *The Gentiles and the Gentile Mission in Luke-Acts* (Cambridge: Cambridge Univ. Press, 1973).

6. My earlier essays were "Why Is Jesus the Only Way?" *Eternity,* Dec. 1976, and "Can the Unevangelised Be Saved?" *The Canadian Baptist,* Nov. 1981. I received a quantity of letters in the wake of both these articles indicating, in addition to some support, that my ideas here were dangerously neoliberal.

7. James D. Hunter, *American Evangelicalism: Conservative Religion and the Quandary of Modernity* (New Brunswick, N.J.: Rutgers Univ. Press, 1983), 84-91.

8. See Robert E. Speer, *The Finality of Jesus Christ* (Westwood, N.J.: Revell, 1933), and Russell F. Aldwinckle, *Jesus—A Savior or The Savior?* (Macon, Ga.: Mercer Univ. Press, 1982).

9. See George A. Lindbeck's discussion of the cultural-linguistic view of dogma in *The Nature of Dogma, Religion and Theology in a Post-Liberal Age* (Philadelphia: Westminster, 1984).

10. I rest my view on the work of scholars like Moule, Hengel, Jeremias, Marshall, and Pohlmann. See the summary of their contentions in William L. Craig, *Apologetics: An Introduction* (Chicago: Moody, 1984), 159-66.

11. I agree with Macquarrie, who contends that lesser views of the Christ

tend to lead to a full doctrine of incarnation when more thought is given to them. See his book *In Search of Deity* (London: SCM, 1984), 232-33.

12. See David F. Wells, *The Person of Christ: A Biblical and Historical Analysis of the Incarnation* (Westchester, Ill.: Crossway, 1984), 145-47.

13. I appreciate Rahner, who for all his liberality on this subject still maintains that we cannot surrender our belief in the incarnate One as our only Savior. Karl Rahner, *Foundations of Christian Faith: An Introduction to the Idea of Christianity* (New York: Seabury, 1978), chap. 6.

14. Two of Hick's books that detail his plans are *God and the Universe of Faiths* (New York: St. Martin's, 1973), and *God Has Many Names* (London: Macmillan, 1980).

15. Knitter, *No Other Name?* 171-204.

16. I still admire Kenneth Hamilton's protest, inspired no doubt by Barth, that we have no business creating earth-bound gods. See *Revolt against Heaven* (Grand Rapids: Eerdmans, 1965).

17. The missionary writer Don Richardson has done a lot to open up evangelicals to this truth. See *Eternity in Their Hearts* (Ventura, Calif.: Regal, 1981).

18. Bruce Demarest has written a fine book on this subject, *General Revelation, Historical Views and Contemporary Issues* (Grand Rapids: Zondervan, 1982). It is especially useful in that the author sees religious pluralism as the pressing issue today in regard to the topic.

19. Jack Cottrell, *What the Bible Says about God the Creator* (Joplin, Mo.: College Press, 1983), 352.

20. Millard Erickson, *Christian Theology,* vol. 1 (Grand Rapids: Baker, 1983), 172-73; Demarest, *General Revelation,* 253-62.

21. See Knitter, *No Other Name?* chap. 6, where he discusses Pannenberg, Althaus, Tillich, Braaten, and others.

22. See the new edition of his older book: J. N. D. Anderson, *Christianity and World Religions: The Challenge of Pluralism* (Leicester: Inter-Varsity Press, 1984). Anderson states that he rejects the notion that those who do not hear the gospel are inevitably lost; see esp. chap. 5.

23. On the "extra ecclesiam" slogan, see Hans Küng, *The Church* (New York: Sheed and Ward, 1967), 313-19.

24. See Joachim Jeremias, *Jesus' Promise to the Nations* (London: SCM, 1958), and *New Testament Theology: The Proclamation of Jesus* (New York: Scribner's, 1971), 103-8.

25. Pinchas Lapide and Jürgen Moltmann, *Jewish Monotheism and Christian Trinitarian Doctrine* (Philadelphia: Fortress, 1981), 72.

26. Carl E. Braaten, *The Flaming Center: A Theology of the Christian Mission* (Philadelphia: Fortress, 1971), 109.

27. The reader will notice that I take for granted the truth of the universal salvific will of God (1 Tim. 2:4). The problem arises from making that assumption.

28. Even Robert H. Gundry shut the door firmly to all but explicit believers in Jesus at least since A.D. 32. See "Salvation according to Scripture: No Middle Ground," *Christianity Today,* Dec. 9, 1977.

29. Anderson, *Christianity and World Religions,* 148-49. See also Charles Kraft, *Christianity in Culture* (Maryknoll, N.Y.: Orbis Books, 1979), 253-57.

30. Stuart C. Hackett, *The Reconstruction of the Christian Revelation Claim* (Grand Rapids: Baker, 1984), 244-46.

31. J. I. Packer, *God's Words: Studies of Key Bible Themes* (Downers Grove, Ill.: InterVarsity Press, 1981), 210.

32. Dale Moody, *The Word of Truth* (Grand Rapids: Eerdmans, 1981), 57-62.

33. See the discussion of Rahner in Knitter, *No Other Name?* chap. 7, and in Race, *Christians and Religious Pluralism,* chap. 3. Worth attention also is Aldwinckle's critique in *Jesus—A Savior or The Savior?* chap. 8.

34. Aldwinckle, *Jesus—A Savior or The Savior?* 214.

35. Ladislaus Boros, *The Mystery of Death* (New York: Seabury, n.d.), chap. 3.

36. It is well known that Luke shows a special concern in his writings for the poor and the oppressed. If so, are not the unevangelized the neediest of all? For they are not only marginalized by society, but in relation to the grace of God. See Allen Verhey, *The Great Reversal: Ethics and the New Testament* (Grand Rapids: Eerdmans, 1984), 92.

37. See C. E. B. Cranfield's two commentaries on 1 Peter.

38. Wolfhart Pannenberg, *The Apostles' Creed in the Light of Today's Questions* (Philadelphia: Westminster, 1972), 95.

39. G. R. Beasley-Murray, *Baptism in the New Testament* (Grand Rapids: Eerdmans, 1962), 258.

40. E.g., Packer, *God's Words,* 210, and Millard Erickson, *Christian Theology,* vol. 2 (Grand Rapids: Baker, 1985), 776.

41. Further research into historical theology would, I am sure, bring to light dozens of examples where people have argued exactly as I have here: e.g., the Andover liberals, P. T. Forsyth, Charles Briggs, et al.

42. See William Barclay, *William Barclay: A Spiritual Autobiography* (Grand Rapids: Eerdmans, 1975), 58-61; also J. A. T. Robinson, *In the End God* (London: James Clarke, 1950), and E. Stauffer, *New Testament Theology* (London: SCM, 1955), chap. 57.

43. Edward W. Fudge, *The Fire That Consumes* (Houston: Providential Press, 1982).

44. Lewis is surely a wise man in the context of twentieth-century theology. See his *The Problem of Pain,* chap. 8, and *Mere Christianity.*

45. Braaten, *Flaming Center,* 15-17.

46. Hackett, *Reconstruction of the Christian Revelation Claim,* 246.

4A. God the Civilizer

1. For the integral relation between culture and worldviews see Max L. Stackhouse, *Creeds, Society, and Human Rights: A Study in Three Cultures* (Grand Rapids: Eerdmans, 1984).

2. *American Heritage Dictionary* (Boston: Houghton Mifflin, 1982), 277.

3. H. Richard Niebuhr, *Christ and Culture* (New York: Harper & Bros., 1951).

4. Karl Barth, *The Humanity of God,* trans. Thomas Wieser and John Newton Thomas (Richmond: John Knox, 1960).

5. Karl Barth, "Church and Culture," in *Theology and Church,* trans. Louise Pettibone Smith (New York: Harper & Row, 1962), 343.

6. Stanley Hauerwas, *Vision and Virtue* (Notre Dame, Ind.: Fides, 1974), 206. Hauerwas is here purportedly describing John Howard Yoder's position.

In a recently published study on the early Anabaptist leader, Michael Sattler, historian C. Arnold Snyder makes a convincing case that Sattler's spirituality is much closer to the tradition of Benedictine monasticism than to the mainline Protestant Reformation. C. Arnold Snyder, *The Life and Thought of Michael Sattler* (Scottdale, Pa.: Herald Press, 1984).

7. Niebuhr's typology should be treated as a heuristic tool and not as a definitive judgment on the landscape of theology. I am well aware of the criticisms of this typology, but I have not found the suggested alternatives any more enlightening. Fundamentalists have faulted Niebuhr for placing them in the Christ-of-culture camp (though their disclaimers are not convincing), and some Anabaptists have been uncomfortable with Niebuhr's conviction that they deserve the "Christ-against-culture" label. For my part, I have difficulty with Niebuhr's contention that the consistent transformationist will be a universalist. Yet granting certain limitations in the way Niebuhr develops his typology, it is nevertheless exceedingly helpful for the kind of analysis that I am undertaking here.

8. While liberationists and feminists in particular are intent on reforming society, they identify with particular cultural ideologies that claim to speak for the oppressed and thereby end up in a Christ-of-culture position.

9. One can discern both conversionist and separatist motifs in Eberhard Arnold, founder of the communalistic Society of Brothers. Arnold says that Christians should not expend their energies in trying to convert the old order into the service of the new. Instead, we should labor in the hope of the dawning of an entirely new kingdom that stands in contrast to "the crumbling world-city which we must now finally leave." At the same time, he insists that "the garden must be won back for God," though "God himself will conquer and rule it." Our task is to accept and rejoice in his rule. See Emmy Arnold, ed., *Inner Words* (Rifton, N.Y.: Plough, 1975), 57, 48.

10. Although there are conversionist and dualistic strands in Tillich as well, he is a theologian of synthesis par excellence. His typology of autonomy, heteronomy, and theonomy cannot be understood except in this light.

11. It was only in his early, liberal phase and in his last phase that Barth sought to ascertain a correspondence between a socialist society and the kingdom of God. In his second phase, that of dialectical theology, he was adamant that the kingdom of God stands in judgment over all cultural and political activity. He remained convinced, even in his later years, that socialism as an ideology contradicted the kingdom of God, but he was sympathetic to socialism as a concerted attempt to fashion a more humane society.

12. Barth writes that in their zeal for the honor of God, Christians will always find themselves in conflict with the principalities and powers of the age. Karl Barth, *The Christian Life,* trans. G. W. Bromiley (Grand Rapids: Eerdmans, 1981), 206-7.

13. Barth would not speak of Christianizing social structures, since they already belong to Christ by virtue of his victory over the principalities and powers

of the culture. Yet they need to be humanized so that they can reflect and bear witness to the cosmic victory of Christ.

14. See Paul Tillich, *Theology of Culture,* ed. Robert C. Kimball (New York: Oxford Univ. Press, 1972); *The Protestant Era,* trans. James Luther Adams (Chicago: Univ. of Chicago Press, 1948), 55-65; *Political Expectation,* ed. James Luther Adams (Macon, Ga.: Mercer Univ. Press, 1981), 1-39; and James Luther Adams, *Paul Tillich's Philosophy of Culture, Science, and Religion* (New York: Harper & Row, 1965).

15. Tillich, *Theology of Culture,* 51.

16. See Reinhold Niebuhr, *Moral Man and Immoral Society* (New York: Charles Scribner's Sons, 1932), 256, and *Beyond Tragedy* (New York: Charles Scribner's Sons, 1937), 186, 193, 224. See also John D. Barbour, "Niebuhr versus Niebuhr: The Tragic Nature of History," *Christian Century,* Nov. 21, 1984, 1096-99.

17. Tillich, *Theology of Culture,* 26.

18. According to Ernst Troeltsch, "The ethic of civilization of St. Thomas according to the principle: *'Gratia praesupponit et perficit naturam,'* contains all the principles of modern Catholicism" (*The Social Teaching of the Christian Churches,* vol. 1, trans. Olive Wyon [New York: Macmillan, 1950], 420).

19. Schleiermacher, who exemplifies this position, differed from Aquinas in that he regarded redemption as basically the maturation of creation, whereas Thomas contended that there is a yawning gap between the two that can be bridged only by divine grace bestowed sacramentally from above. While Schleiermacher saw religion ennobling everything that is, Thomas saw religion as perfecting and purifying human cultural endeavor. For Thomas culture is ultimately transcended in the contemplation of God.

20. Friedrich Schleiermacher, *The Christian Faith,* vol. 2, ed. H. R. Mackintosh and J. S. Stewart (New York: Harper & Row, 1963), 368.

21. Jürgen Moltmann, *The Trinity and the Kingdom,* trans. Margaret Kohl (San Francisco: Harper & Row, 1981), 118.

22. See Kurt Rudolph, *Gnosis,* ed. Robert McLachlan Wilson (San Francisco: Harper & Row, 1983).

23. While Walter Kasper also speaks in this fashion and claims that this is the position of the classical theologians of the church, including Augustine and Aquinas, he means a nature that is deficient apart from the perfecting grace of redemption. The emphasis is quite different in Barth, who contends that creation is complete in itself but needs to be restored because of human sin. Kasper takes issue with Barth's condemnation of natural theology and the *analogia entis.* See Walter Kasper, *The God of Jesus Christ,* trans. Matthew J. O'Connell (New York: Crossroad, 1984), 74-75.

24. Barth, "Church and Culture," 347.

25. Emil Brunner, *The Divine Imperative,* trans. Olive Wyon (Philadelphia: Westminster, 1974), 214.

26. Barth, "Church and Culture," 344.

27. Tillich, *Theology and Culture,* 143-44.

28. See Robert J. Palma, *Karl Barth's Theology of Culture* (Allison Park, Pa.: Pickwick, 1983).

29. Barth, *Christian Life,* 266.

30. Jesus Christ is Lord of this world *de facto* and Redeemer of the world *de jure*. He does not become Redeemer in fact until he is accepted in faith as Savior and Lord. Yet he rules in such a way as to direct people to his redemption, which becomes concrete and tangible in the community of faith and love.

31. Augustine, *The City of God*, vol. 2 of *The Basic Writings of Saint Augustine*, ed. Whitney J. Oates (New York: Random House, 1948).

32. See Jürgen Moltmann, "Luther's Doctrine of the Two Kingdoms and Its Use Today," in his *On Human Dignity*, trans. M. Douglas Meeks (Philadelphia: Fortress, 1984), 61-77; and Paul Althaus, *The Ethics of Martin Luther*, trans. Robert C. Schultz (Philadelphia: Fortress, 1972), 50-53.

33. For Ernst Troeltsch's brilliant exposition of Calvin's concept of the holy community, see his *The Social Teaching of the Christian Churches*, vol. 2, trans. Olive Wyon (New York: Macmillan, 1950), 590-602.

34. See Reinhold Niebuhr, *An Interpretaton of Christian Ethics* (New York: Seabury, 1979); *Reflections on the End of an Era* (New York: Charles Scribner's Sons, 1934); *The Nature and Destiny of Man*, 2 vols. (New York: Charles Scribner's Sons, 1951); and *Christian Realism and Political Problems* (New York: Charles Scribner's Sons, 1953).

35. Niebuhr describes the pure sacrificial love, which is the essence of the kingdom of God, as an "impossible possibility" in that it cannot be deliberately willed by individuals, but it can take place in human life and experience when we are opened to the grace of God by faith. It can never be a political strategy, but it can be an object of hope that lends meaning to human existence and history. See Niebuhr, *Interpretation of Christian Ethics*, 123-36.

36. See Paul Tillich, *Systematic Theology*, vol. 3 (Chicago: Univ. of Chicago Press, 1963), 297-423.

37. See Moltmann, *On Human Dignity*, 79-96. According to Moltmann, Christ now reigns not as triumphal king but as the crucified one. His power is that of vicarious or suffering love.

38. See Jürgen Moltmann, *Theology of Hope*, trans. James W. Leitch (New York: Harper & Row, 1965); *The Church in the Power of the Spirit*, trans. Margaret Kohl (New York: Harper & Row, 1977); *The Trinity and the Kingdom* (New York: Harper & Row, 1981); *The Crucified God*, trans. R. A. Wilson and John Bowden (New York: Harper & Row, 1974); *Religion, Revolution and the Future*, trans. M. Douglas Meeks (New York: Charles Scribner's Sons, 1969); *Hope and Planning* (New York: Harper & Row, 1971); and *On Human Dignity* (Philadelphia: Fortress,1984).

39. Moltmann, *Church in the Power of the Spirit*, 163.

40. Moltmann, *On Human Dignity*, 113-31.

41. Moltmann, *Crucified God*, 317-40.

42. Moltmann views transcendence in terms of the future into which we are raised; see *Church in the Power of the Spirit*, 287.

43. Ibid., 164.

44. Barth, *Christian Life*, 197-201.

45. H. Richard Niebuhr, Wilhelm Pauck, and Francis P. Miller, *The Church Against the World* (Chicago: Willett, Clark & Co., 1935), 126.

46. Ibid.

47. Barth, *Christian Life*, 129.

48. Lynn Harold Hough, *The Civilized Mind* (New York: Abingdon, 1937), 58.

49. See H. Richard Niebuhr et al., *Church Against the World,* 138-39.

50. Richard John Neuhaus, *The Naked Public Square* (Grand Rapids: Eerdmans, 1984).

51. For a brilliant study of the loss of this transcendent vision in American culture, see John Patrick Diggins, *The Lost Soul of American Politics* (New York: Basic Books, 1984).

52. H. Richard Niebuhr, *The Kingdom of God in America* (Chicago: Willett, Clark & Co., 1937), 179.

4B. Calling, Work, and Rest

1. *Oeconomicus* IV:2, 3; Claud Mossé, *The Ancient World at Work* (London: Chatto and Windus, 1969), 25. See also Pierre Jacard, *Histoire sociale du travail* (Paris: Payot, 1960), 66, 75. On the attitudes of those who actually did the work, see A. T. Geoghegan, *The Attitude toward Labour in Early Christianity and Ancient Culture* (Washington: Catholic Univ. of America Press, 1945), 47-54. In these historical sections I have borrowed from my "Vocation, Work and Jobs," in P. Marshall et al., *Labour of Love: Essays on Work* (Toronto: Wedge, 1980), 1-19, and my "The Shape of the Modern Work Ethic," in *Work in Canada,* ed. J. Peters, J. Redekup, and J. Jenkins (Waterloo, Ont.: Wilfrid Laurier Univ. Interdisciplinary Research Seminar, 1986).

2. *Politics* 1329a, 1-2. *De officiis* I:42, 150; Mossé, *Ancient World at Work,* 25. See also Alison Burford, *Craftsmen in Greek and Roman Society* (London: Thames and Hudson, 1972), esp. 29-30 on Cicero's attitude toward farmers; Geoghegan, *Attitude toward Labour,* 37-38.

3. Hannah Arendt, *The Human Condition* (New York: Doubleday, 1959), 324.

4. W. Westerman, "Between Slavery and Freedom," *American Historical Review* 50 (1945): 213-27. See also E. G. Kaiser, *Theology of Work* (Westminster, Md.: Newman, 1966), 32ff.

5. *Nichomachaean Ethics* I:5; *Eudaemonian Ethics* 1215a, 35-36; *Politics* 1337b, 5; Arendt, *Human Condition,* 302; R. Schlaifer, "Greek Theories of Slavery from Homer to Aristotle," *Harvard Studies in Classical Philology* 47 (1936): 165-204.

6. See Josef Pieper, *Leisure: The Basis of Culture* (New York: Random House, 1963), 20-21. Aristotle equated *skole* and *aergia,* leisure and laziness; cf. Arendt, *Human Condition,* 323-24.

7. Stoicism forms a partial exception to this trend; cf. Ludwig Edelstein, *The Meaning of Stoicism* (Cambridge: Cambridge Univ. Press, 1966), 74-78. But this should not be exaggerated; see, e.g., the comments of Seneca, *Epistolae* 31, 4-5; 44, 1-4; *De brevitate vitae* 15, 3. See also *Epistolae* 13, 20, 28, 88, 89; J. N. Sevenster, *Paul and Seneca* (Leiden: E. J. Brill, 1961), 215.

8. Dom Cuthbert Butler, *Western Mysticism* (New York: Barnes and Noble, 1968), 157-65; Arendt, *Human Condition,* 13, 15, 304, 376-77; "Sermon" CLXIX, 17; *De civitate dei* XI, 16; XIX, 1, 2, 19; *In Ioann. Evangel,* 6, 25-26;

Tract. in Ioann. CXXIV, 5. See also Herbert A. Deane, *The Political and Social Ideas of St. Augustine* (New York: Columbia Univ. Press, 1963), 44, 108ff.

9. *Summa theologiae* ii.2.179, 181, 182; *Expositio in Psalmos* 45.3; *Summa contra gentiles* iii.135; Arendt, *Human Condition,* 290, 303-4, 377. See also S. M. Killeen, *The Philosophy of Labour according to Thomas Aquinas* (Washington: Catholic Univ. of America Press, 1939).

10. Cf. Barth: "According to the view prevalent at the height of the high Middle ages [secular work] only existed to free for the work of their professions those who were totally and exclusively occupied in rendering true obedience for the salvation of each and all. There could be no question of calling for Christians in other professions" (from "Vocation," in *Church Dogmatics* [Edinburgh: T. & T. Clark, 1961], III/4, 602). See also Th. Scharmann, G. Mensching, F. Lau, W. Freytag, W. Nordmann, and J. Fichtner, "Beruf," in *Die Religion in Geschichte und Gegenwart,* ed. J. C. B. Mohr (Tübingen: J. C. B. Mohr, 1957), 1078; K. Holl, "Die Geschichte des Worts 'Beruf,'" in *Gesammelte Aufsätze zur Kirchengeschichte,* vol. 3 (Tübingen: J. C. B. Mohr, 1931), 199ff.

The most notable exceptions to this trend are the German mystics Meister Eckhart and Johann Tauler, and the English John Wyclif. But each of these figures was regarded as mildly or even outrightly heretical. Their unorthodox stance merely serves to bring into sharper focus the prevailing ethos of medieval Christianity. For Eckhart, see R. C. Petry, *Late Medieval Mysticism* (Philadelphia: Westminster, 1957), 193-99; for Tauler, see *Oeuvre complètes,* 9 vols. (Paris: Tralin, 1911), 3:454-64; 4:126-47. For Wyclif, see *Select English Works,* 3 vols. (Oxford: Oxford Univ. Press, 1871), 3:130-34, 142-43, 148ff.

11. William Tyndale, "A Parable of the Wicked Mammon" (1527), in *Doctrinal Treatises and Portions of Holy Scripture* (Cambridge: Parker Society, 1848), 98, 104.

12. Quoted in Gustav Wingren, *Luther on Vocation* (Philadelphia: Muhlenberg, 1957), 70-72; Paul Althaus, *The Ethics of Martin Luther* (Philadelphia: Muhlenberg, 1972), 40, 101.

13. *Institutes* I.16.3; Mario Miegge, *I Talenti Messi a Profitto* (Urbino: Argalia, 1969), 7, 112-13; André Biéler, *La pensée économique et sociale de Calvin* (Geneva: Librairie de l'Université, 1961), 321.

14. Max Weber, *The Sociology of Religion* (Boston: Beacon, 1964), 187.

15. Weber, *The Protestant Ethic and the Spirit of Capitalism* (New York: Scribner's, 1958), 183. Weber has frequently been criticized on the grounds that Protestant theology did not stress a relation between calling, work, and assurance of salvation. This is a misplaced criticism because Weber maintained that, regardless of official doctrine, Protestants had a *psychological* compulsion to demonstrate their election through their labors. This is why the major source for Weber's "Protestant ethic" is Richard Baxter's *Christian Directory,* a casuistic work that gives insight into the actual problems for which parishioners sought counsel.

16. See B. Nelson, "Weber's Protestant Ethic: Its Origins, Wanderings, and Forseeable Future," in *Beyond the Classics?* ed. C. Y. Glock and P. E. Hammond (New York: Harper & Row, 1973), 75.

17. Weber, *Sociology of Religion,* 220. I have traced the post-Reformation evolution of calling as job in "The Calling: Secularization and Economics in the Seventeenth Century," paper presented at the Annual Meeting of the Canadian

Political Science Association, London, Ontario, 1978, and in "John Locke: Between God and Mammon," *Canadian Journal of Political Science* 12 (1979): 73-96.

18. William Leiss describes this well in *The Domination of Nature* (Boston: Beacon, 1974).

19. See P. D. Anthony, *The Ideology of Work* (London: Tavistock, 1977), 83-112.

20. Karl Marx, "Private Property and Communism," in *Karl Marx: Early Writings,* ed. T. B. Bottomore (New York: McGraw-Hill, 1964), 166; italics in original.

21. Marx, "Wages of Labour," in ibid., 76.

22. *Capital,* 3 vols. (New York: International Publishers, 1967), 1:592.

23. Ibid., 3:820.

24. J. M. Keynes, *Essays in Persuasion* (London: Macmillan, 1972), 331. Cf. also the findings of P. J. D. Drenth, "World View and Meaning of Working," in *World View and Social Science,* ed. P. Marshall, S. Griffioen, and R. Mouw (Lanham, Md.: Univ. Press of America, forthcoming).

25. On the cultural mandate see Claus Westermann, "Work, Civilization and Culture in the Bible," in *Work and Religion,* ed. Gregory Baum (New York: Seabury, 1980), 81-91; A. Wolters, "The Foundational Command: Subdue the Earth" (Toronto: Institute for Christian Studies, 1973).

26. Cf. Isa. 58:6-12; Second Vatican Ecumenical Council, *Pastoral Constitution on the Church in the Modern World (Gaudium et Spes),* 7 Dec. 1965, in *Documents of Vatican II,* ed. Austin P. Flannery (Grand Rapids: Eerdmans, 1975), 934; Dorothee Soelle with Shirley A. Cloyes, *To Work and to Love* (Philadelphia: Fortress, 1984), 39-40.

27. On this theme see Richard Mouw, *When the Kings Go Marching In* (Grand Rapids: Eerdmans, 1983); P. Marshall, *Thine Is the Kingdom* (Grand Rapids: Eerdmans, 1986), chaps. 2-3.

28. See also Matt. 9:34; 10:10; Luke 10:7. On the theology of work, see Westermann, "Work, Civilization and Culture"; Alan Richardson, *The Biblical Doctrine of Work* (London: SCM, 1958); E. Borne and F. Henry, *A Philosophy of Work* (London: Sheed and Ward, 1938); Geoghegan, *Attitude toward Labour,* 47-64; J. O. Nelson, ed., *Work and Vocation* (New York: Harper, 1954); David Attwood, *The Spade and the Thistle* (Bramcote: Grove Books, 1980); W. R. Forrester, *Christian Vocation: Studies in Faith and Work* (London: Lutterworth, 1951); F. R. McCurley and John H. Reumann, "Work in the Providence of God," in *Work as Praise,* ed. G. W. Forell and W. H. Lazareth (Philadelphia: Fortress, 1979), 26-42; H. Rondet, "Elements pour une theologie du travail," *Nouvelle Revue Theologique* 77 (1955): 27-48, 123-43; M. Moser and P. G. Schervish, "Theology of Work: A Liberation Perspective," *Radical Religion* 3 (1978): 30-36; and the essays in Baum, *Work and Religion.*

29. Cf. 2 Thess. 3:6; Richardson, *Biblical Doctrine of Work,* 57ff.; E. Gryglewicz, "La valeur du travail manuel dans la terminologie grecque de la bible," *Biblica* 7 (1965): 314-37; J. N. Sevenster, *Paul and Seneca,* 211ff.

30. Cf. Arendt, *Human Condition,* 289. Also note that Paul's sweeping portrayal of the centrality and significance of the resurrection seems to have the aim of showing "that in the Lord your labor is not in vain" (1 Cor. 15:58).

31. See also Isa. 11:1-7; Hos. 2:18-23.

32. This is in contrast to Jacques Ellul's correlation of work and necessity and his consequent claim that work cannot be a calling. See his "Work and Calling," in *Callings!* ed. J. Y. Holloway and W. D. Campbell (New York: Paulist, 1974). Barth makes some similar points in "Vocation."

33. Sander Griffioen, "The Challenge of Marxist and Neo-Marxist Ideologies for Christian Scholarship," in *The Challenge of Marxists and Neo-Marxist Ideologies for Christian Scholarship,* ed. John C. Vanderstelt (Sioux Center, Iowa: Dordt College, 1982), 13.

34. Marx, *Capital,* loc. cit.

35. Second Vatican Ecumenical Council, *Pastoral Constitution on the Church in the Modern World,* quoted in John Paul II, *On Human Work (Laborem Exercens)* (Boston: St. Paul Editions, 1981), 61.

36. R. H. Tawney, *Religion and the Rise of Capitalism* (New York: Mentor, 1954), 233.

37. For examples of developing such responsibility in work see Bob Goudzwaard, *Capitalism and Progress* (Grand Rapids: Eerdmans, 1979), part 4; E. F. Schumacher, *Good Work* (New York: Harper, 1979); George Goyder, *The Responsible Company* (Oxford: Blackwell, 1961), and the essays in P. Marshall et al., *Labour of Love.*

38. See Barth, "Vocation"; William W. Klein, "Paul's Use of *Kalein:* A Proposal," *Journal of the Evangelical Theological Society* 27 (March 1984): 53-64.

39. On the theme of idolatry see Bob Goudzwaard, *Idols of Our Time* (Downers Grove, Ill.: InterVarsity Press, 1984).

40. J. K. Galbraith, *The New Industrial State* (Boston: Houghton Mifflin, 1967), 398. Cf. R. H. Tawney, *The Acquisitive Society* (London: Collins, 1961), 190; Weber, *Protestant Ethic,* 181-83.

41. Cf. Acts 17:24-25, which may be a paraphrase of Ps. 50.

42. One of the major tendencies of the modern age is to treat all limits as limits imposed by other people. The tendency of the left is to treat all limits as political and to refuse to address the theme of personal and state self-limitation. Conversely, the right tends to confuse current limits with the nature of reality and, hence, with the will of God.

43. *Summa theologia* ii.2.9,7.

44. Pieper, *Leisure: The Basis of Culture,* 40. See also W. Still, *Rhythms of Rest and Word* (n.p.; n.d.).

45. This is not, of course, a criticism of the idea of shortening the work day. There is per se no virtue in working longer hours and, in our time of increasing structural unemployment, sharing of work may be a good step. See the remarks of Ed Vanderkloet, "Will There Be Work for Our Children?" in E. VanderKloet and D. De Vos, *Will There Be Work For Our Children?* (Toronto: C.L.A.C., 1984), 6.

46. Arendt, *Human Condition,* 115. Cf. Charles Taylor: "The drive to consumption is therefore no adventitious fad, no product of clever manipulation. It will not be easy to contain. It is tied up with the economic self-image of modern society, and this in turn is linked to a set of powerfully entrenched conceptions of what the value of human life consists in" ("The Agony of Economic Man," in

Essays on the Left: In Honour of T. C. Douglas, ed. Laurier LaPierre et al. [Toronto: McClelland and Stewart, 1971], 232-33).

4C. An Evangelical Theology of Poverty

1. "First Draft of the U.S. Bishops' Pastoral Letter on Catholic Social Teaching and the U.S. Economy," *Origins: NC Documentary Service,* Nov. 15, 1984.

2. See, e.g., the discussion by José Míguez-Bonino, *Christians and Marxists: The Mutual Challenge to Revolution* (Grand Rapids: Eerdmans, 1976), 29-31.

3. Ronald Sider, "An Evangelical Theology of Liberation," in *Perspectives on Evangelical Theology,* ed. Kenneth Kantzer and Stanley Gundry (Grand Rapids: Baker, 1979), 119.

4. Thomas D. Hanks, *God So Loved the Third World: The Biblical Vocabulary of Oppression* (Maryknoll, N.Y.: Orbis Books, 1983), chap. 5.

5. John Calvin, *Institutes of the Christian Religion* (Philadelphia: Westminster, 1960), IV.iv.8

6. See F. Ernest Stoeffler, *The Rise of Evangelical Pietism* (Leiden: E. J. Brill, 1965), and Dale Brown, *Understanding Pietism* (Grand Rapids: Eerdmans, 1978).

7. Ronald H. Nash, *Social Justice and the Christian Church* (Milford, Mich.: Mott Media, 1983), 167.

8. L. John Van Til, "Latin America and Liberation Theology," *Special Report no. 28* (Grove City, Pa.: Public Policy Education Fund, 1985), 4.

9. Clark Pinnock, "A Pilgrimage in Political Theology," in *Liberation Theology,* ed. Ronald Nash (Milford, Mich.: Mott Media, 1984), 118.

10. See my "Jesus and the Poor: Unity in Christ in an Unjust World," *Reformed Journal,* May 1980.

11. Julio de Santa Ana, *Good News to the Poor: The Challenge of the Poor in the History of the Church* (Maryknoll, N.Y.: Orbis Books, 1979), 14-18.

12. Sider, "Evangelical Theology of Liberation," 120-21.

13. Nash, *Social Justice,* 164.

14. Cf. de Santa Ana, *Good News to the Poor,* chap. 6.

15. Jacques Ellul, *The Betrayal of the West* (New York: Seabury, 1978), chap. 11.

16. Quoted by Rius, *Marx for Beginners* (New York: Pantheon, 1976), 120.

17. Richard J. Neuhaus, *Freedom for Ministry* (New York: Harper & Row, 1979), 6.

18. Stanley Hauerwas and William H. Willimon, "Embarrassed by God's Presence," *Christian Century,* Jan. 30, 1985, 100.

19. John Howard Yoder, "Exodus and Exile: The Two Faces of Liberation," *Cross Currents* (Fall 1973): 308-9.

20. Michael Novak, *Freedom with Justice: Catholic Social Thought and Liberal Institutions* (New York: Harper & Row, 1984), xiv.

21. Gertrude Himmelfarb, *The Idea of Poverty: England in the Early Industrial Age* (New York: Knopf, 1984), 31.

4D. The Encounter between Science and Faith

1. Don Cupitt, *The Sea of Faith: Christianity in Change* (London: British Broadcasting Corporation, 1984), 79.

2. John William Draper, *History of the Conflict between Religion and Science* (London: Henry S. King & Co., 1875); Andrew Dixon White, *A History of the Warfare of Science with Theology in Christendom,* 2 vols. (London: Macmillan, 1896); James Young Simpson, *Landmarks in the Struggle between Science and Religion* (London: Hodder & Stoughton, 1925). A useful review and critique of the conflict interpretation may be found in "The 'Conflict Thesis' and Cosmology," in *Science and Belief: From Copernicus to Darwin* (Milton Keynes: Open Univ. Press, 1974), Block 1, Units 1-3.

3. For an overview see David C. Lindberg and Ronald L. Numbers, "'The Battle-fields of Science' Revisited: A Reappraisal of the Encounter between Christianity and Science," the introductory chapter to *God and Nature: A History of the Encounter between Christianity and Science,* ed. Lindberg and Numbers (Berkeley: Univ. of California Press, 1986). James R. Moore, *The Post-Darwinian Controversies: A Study of the Protestant Struggle to Come to Terms with Darwin: Great Britain and America 1870–1900* (Cambridge: Cambridge Univ. Press, 1979), 20-122, provides a full survey of the "warfare metaphor" as applied to evolution and a convincing rebuttal of its cogency.

4. See Charles Coulston Gillispie, *Genesis and Geology: A Study in the Relations of Scientific Thought, Natural Theology, and Social Opinion in Great Britain, 1790–1850* (New York: Harper & Row, 1959), and Davis A. Young, "Nineteenth Century Christian Geologists and the Doctrine of Scripture," *Christian Scholar's Review* 3 (1982): 212-28.

5. See, e.g., Robert M. Young, "Natural Theology, Victorian Periodicals and the Fragmentation of a Common Context," in *Darwin to Einstein: Historical Studies on Science and Belief,* ed. Colin Chant and John Fauvel (Harlow: Longman, 1980), 69-107; John Hedley Brooke, "The Natural Theology of the Geologists: Some Theological Strata," in *Images of the Earth: Essays in the History of the Environmental Sciences,* ed. L. J. Jordanova and Roy Porter (Chalfont St. Giles: British Society for the History of Science, 1979), 39-64; Dov Ospovat, "Perfect Adaptation and Teleological Explanation: Approaches to the Problem of the History of Life in the Mid-Nineteenth Century," *Studies in the History of Biology* 14 (1981): 193-230; idem, *The Development of Darwin's Theory: Natural History, Natural Theology, and Natural Selection, 1838–1859* (Cambridge: Cambridge Univ. Press, 1981); Richard Yeo, "William Whewell, Natural Theology and the Philosophy of Science in Mid-Nineteenth Century Britain," *Annals of Science* 36 (1979): 493-516; David N. Livingstone, "Natural Theology and Neo-Lamarckism: The Changing Context of Nineteenth Century Geography in the United States and Great Britain," *Annals of the Association of American Geographers* 74 (1984): 9-28; idem, "The History of Science and the History of Geography: Interactions and Implications," *History of Science* 22 (1984): 271-302.

6. Moore, *Post-Darwinian Controversies.* See also my book *Darwin's Forgotten Defenders: The Encounter between Evangelical Theology and Evolutionary Thought* (Grand Rapids: Eerdmans, 1987).

7. J. R. Lucas, "Wilberforce and Huxley: A Legendary Encounter," *Histori-*

cal Journal 22 (1979): 313-30; Sheridan Gilley, "The Huxley-Wilberforce Debate: A Reconsideration," in *Religion and Humanism,* ed. Keith Robbins, Studies in Church History 17 (Oxford: Basil Blackwell, 1981), 325-40; Sheridan Gilley and Ann Loades, "Thomas Henry Huxley: The War between Science and Religion," *Journal of Religion* 61 (1981): 285-308. The traditional story is told in William Irvine, *Apes, Angels and Victorians: A Joint Biography of Darwin and Huxley* (London: Weidenfeld and Nicholson, 1956).

8. See H. R. Murphy, "The Ethical Revolt against Christian Orthodoxy in Early Victorian England," *American Historical Review* 60 (1955): 800-817; Owen Chadwick, *The Victorian Church,* 2 vols. (London: Adam & Charles Black, 1970); James R. Moore, "1859 and All That: Remaking the Story of Evolution-and-Religion," in *Charles Darwin, 1809–1882: A Centennial Commemorative,* ed. Roger G. Chapman and Cleveland T. Duval (Wellington, N.Z.: Nova Pacifica, 1982), 167-94.

9. Alexander Winchell, *Reconciliation of Science and Religion* (New York: Harper and Brothers, 1877).

10. See discussions in Moore, *Post-Darwinian Controversies;* Milton Berman, *John Fiske: The Evolution of a Popularizer* (Cambridge: Harvard Univ. Press, 1961); Frank Miller Turner, *Between Science and Religion: The Reaction to Scientific Naturalism in Late Victorian England* (New Haven: Yale Univ. Press, 1974).

11. E.g., Kenneth M. Pierce, "Putting Darwin Back in the Dock," *Time,* 16 March 1981, 50-52.

12. Frank Miller Turner, "The Victorian Conflict between Science and Religion: A Professional Dimension," *Isis* 69 (1978): 356-76, and *Between Science and Religion.*

13. Frank Miller Turner, "Rainfall, Plagues, and the Prince of Wales: A Chapter in the Conflict of Religion and Science," *Journal of British Studies* 13 (1974): 46-65. Quotation on p. 65.

14. T. W. Heyck, *The Transformation of Intellectual Life in Victorian England* (London: Croom Helm, 1982), 87-88.

15. See David N. Livingstone, "The Idea of Design: The Vicissitudes of a Key Concept in the Princeton Response to Darwin," *Scottish Journal of Theology* 37 (1984): 329-57.

16. Gilley and Loades, "Huxley," 290; Francis Galton, *English Men of Science: Their Nature and Nurture* (London: Macmillan, 1874), 193; Patrick Geddes, "Biology," *Chambers's Encyclopaedia,* vol. 2 (1882; London and Edinburgh: W. and R. Chambers, 1925), 157-64.

17. See, e.g., Keith Thomas, *Religion and the Decline of Magic: Studies in Popular Belief in Sixteenth- and Seventeenth-century England* (London: Allen Lane, 1971); Frances Yates, *The Occult Philosophy in the Elizabethan Age* (London: Routledge & Kegan Paul, 1979).

18. Robert K. Merton, "Science and Society in the Seventeenth Century," *Osiris* 4 (1938): 360-632. It is interesting to note that Draper conceded that "modern Science is the legitimate sister—indeed, it is the twin-sister—of the Reformation" (*Conflict,* 353).

19. R. Hooykaas, *Religion and the Rise of Modern Science* (Edinburgh: Scottish Academic Press, 1972).

20. See R. Hooykaas, "Science and Reformation," *Journal of World History* 3 (1956): 109-39, and "Puritanism and Science," in *Science and Belief: From Copernicus to Darwin,* Block 3: *Scientific Progress and Religious Dissent* (Milton Keynes: Open Univ. Press, 1974), 7-32.

21. R. Hooykaas, *Philosophia Libera: Christian Faith and the Freedom of Science* (London: Tyndale, 1957).

22. M. B. Foster, "The Christian Doctrine of Creation and the Rise of Modern Natural Science," *Mind* 43 (1934): 446-68; Thomas F. Torrance, *Theological Science* (London: Oxford Univ. Press, 1969), 59-61; Christopher Hill, *Intellectual Origins of the English Revolution* (London: Oxford Univ. Press, 1965); and Alfred North Whitehead, *Science and the Modern World* (Cambridge: Cambridge Univ. Press, 1926), 13-14.

23. The following are some of the major items: Ian G. Barbour, *Issues in Science and Religion* (New York: Harper & Row, 1971); John Dillenberger, *Protestant Thought and Natural Science: A Historical Interpretation* (London: Collins, 1961); Eugene M. Klaaren, *Religious Origins of Modern Science: Belief in Creation in Seventeenth-Century Thought* (Grand Rapids: Eerdmans, 1977); Peter Hodgson, "The Judaeo-Christian Origin of Science," *The Ampleforth Journal* 79 (1974): 39-44; Richard Westfall, *Science and Religion in Seventeenth-Century England* (New Haven: Yale Univ. Press, 1958); Charles Webster, ed., *The Intellectual Revolution of the Seventeenth Century* (London: Routledge & Kegan Paul, 1974); idem, *The Great Instauration: Science, Medicine and Reform 1626-60* (London: Duckworth, 1975).

24. See E. G. R. Taylor, *The Mathematical Practitioners of Tudor and Stuart England* (Cambridge: Cambridge Univ. Press, 1954); idem, *The Haven-Finding Art: A History of Navigation from Odysseus to Captain Cook* (London: Hollis & Carter, 1956); Joan Thirsk, "Seventeenth Century Agriculture and Social Change," in *Land, Church and People,* ed. Joan Thirsk (Reading: British Agricultural History Society, 1970), 148-77; A. E. Musson and Eric Robinson, *Science and Technology in the Industrial Revolution* (Manchester: Manchester Univ. Press, 1969).

25. Michael Hunter, *Science and Society in Restoration England* (Cambridge: Cambridge Univ. Press, 1981), 114. Also D. S. Kemsley, "Religious Influences in the Rise of Modern Science: A Review and Criticism, Particularly of the 'Protestant-Puritan Ethic' Theory," *Annals of Science* 24 (1968): 199-216; John Morgan, "Puritanism and Science: A Reinterpretation," *Historical Journal* 22 (1979): 535-60.

26. Robert E. Schofield, "John Wesley and Science in 18th Century England," *Isis* 44 (1953): 331-40; Frederick Dreyer, "Faith and Experience in the Thought of John Wesley," *American Historical Review* 88 (1983): 12-30.

27. I.e., Stanley L. Jaki, "Science and Christian Theism: A Mutual Witness," *Scottish Journal of Theology* 32 (1979): 563-70; idem, *The Road of Science and the Ways to God* (Edinburgh: Scottish Academic Press, 1978); Thomas Forsyth Torrance, *The Ground and Grammar of Theology* (Belfast: Christian Journals Ltd., 1979); John C. Polkinghorne, *The Way the World Is: The Christian Perspective of a Scientist* (Grand Rapids: Eerdmans, 1984).

28. Robert Young, "Natural Theology"; also "The Impact of Darwin on Conventional Thought," in *The Victorian Crisis of Faith,* ed. John Symondson (Lon-

don: SPCK, 1970), 13-35; "The Historiographic and Ideological Contexts of the Nineteenth-Century Debate on Man's Place in Nature," in *Changing Perspectives in the History of Science: Essays in Honour of Joseph Needham*, ed. Mikulás Teich and Robert Young (London: Heinemann, 1973), 344-438; and "The Naturalization of Value Systems in the Human Sciences," in *Science and Belief: From Darwin to Einstein*, Block VI: *Problems in the Biological and Human Sciences* (Milton Keynes: Open Univ. Press, 1981), 63-110.

29. Moore, "1859 and All That," 194.

30. See John S. Haller, Jr., *Outcasts from Evolution: Scientific Attitudes of Racial Inferiority, 1859–1900* (Chicago and London: Univ. of Illinois Press, 1971); Thomas F. Gossett, *Race: The History of an Idea in America* (Dallas: Southern Methodist Univ. Press, 1963); Stephen Jay Gould, *The Mismeasure of Man* (New York: W. W. Norton, 1981).

31. Robert M. Young, "Evolutionary Biology and Ideology: Then and Now," *Science Studies* 1 (1971): 177-206. Reference on p. 177.

32. Arnold Guyot, *The Earth and Man: Lectures on Comparative Physical Geography in Its Relation to the History of Mankind* (1849; New York: Scribner's, 1897), 251. Guyot, it may be noted, addressed the New York meeting of the Evangelical Alliance in 1873 on the subject "Cosmogony and the Bible; or, The Biblical Account of Creation in the Light of Modern Science."

33. Alexander Winchell, *Preadamites; or, A Demonstration of the Existence of Men before Adam; together with a Study of Their Condition, Antiquity, Racial Affinities, and Progressive Dispersion over the Earth* (Chicago: S. C. Griggs and Company, 1880), 157.

34. In addition to the works listed in note 5 above, see John Hedley Brooke, "Natural Theology and the Plurality of Worlds: Observations on the Brewster-Whewell Debate," *Annals of Science* 34 (1977): 221-86; Robert J. Richards, "Instinct and Intelligence in British Natural Theology: Some Contributions to Darwin's Theory of the Evolution of Behavior," *Journal of the History of Biology* 14 (1981): 193-230; Peter J. Bowler, "Darwinism and the Argument from Design: Suggestions for a Re-evaluation," *Journal of the History of Biology* 10 (1977): 29-43.

35. Colin Russell, *Science and Social Change, 1700–1900* (London: Macmillan, 1983), 259.

36. A useful elementary introduction is A. F. Chalmers, *What Is This Thing Called Science?* 2d ed. (Milton Keynes: Open Univ. Press, 1982).

37. The best-known English-speaking representative was Alfred J. Ayer, author of *Language, Truth and Logic* (London: Gollancz, 1936).

38. See K. R. Popper, *The Logic of Scientific Discovery* (London: Hutchinson, 1968); see also his collections, *Objective Knowledge* (Oxford: Oxford Univ. Press, 1972) and *Conjectures and Refutations* (London: Routledge & Kegan Paul, 1969).

39. T. S. Kuhn, *The Structure of Scientific Revolutions* (Chicago: Univ. of Chicago Press, 1970).

40. His considered, programmatic statement appeared in Paul K. Feyerabend, *Against Method: Outline of an Anarchistic Theory of Knowledge* (London: New Left Books, 1975).

41. W. Newton-Smith, "In Defence of Truth," in *The Philosophy of Evolution*, ed. U. J. Jensen and R. Harré (Brighton: Harvester, 1981).

42. See Imre Lakatos, "Falsification and the Methodology of Scientific Research Programmes," in *Criticism and the Growth of Knowledge*, ed. I. Lakatos and A. Musgrave (Cambridge: Cambridge Univ. Press, 1974), 91-196.

43. Ian G. Barbour, *Myths, Models and Paradigms: The Nature of Scientific and Religious Language* (London: SCM, 1974), 114.

44. Cornelius Van Til, *A Survey of Christian Epistemology* (n.p.: Den Dulk Christian Foundation, 1969), and *The Defence of the Faith* (Philadelphia: Presbyterian and Reformed, 1972).

45. Paul Helm, "Recent Trends in the Philosophy of Science," paper presented at the Research Scientists' Christian Fellowship Annual Conference 1982 on "The Current State of the Science and Religion Discussion"; Donald MacKay, "'Value-Free Knowledge'—Myth or Norm?" *Faith and Thought* 107 (1980): 202-9.

46. See, e.g., Stephen G. Brush, "Should the History of Science be Rated X?" *Science*, 22 March 1974, 1164-72.

47. See Max Black, *Models and Metaphors: Studies in Language and Philosophy* (Ithaca, N.Y.: Cornell Univ. Press, 1962); Mary B. Hesse, *Models and Analogies in Science* (Notre Dame, Ind.: Univ. of Notre Dame Press, 1966); Andrew Ortony, ed., *Metaphor and Thought* (Cambridge: Cambridge Univ. Press, 1979).

48. Torrance, *Ground and Grammar of Theology*, 106.

49. Charles Rosenberg, "Science in American Society: A Generation of Historical Debate," *Isis* 74 (1983): 356-67. Reference on p. 367.

50. See, e.g., B. Barnes, *Scientific Knowledge and Sociological Theory* (London: Routledge & Kegan Paul, 1974); idem, *Interests and the Growth of Knowledge* (London: Routledge & Kegan Paul, 1977); David Bloor, *Knowledge and Social Imagery* (London: Routledge & Kegan Paul, 1976). For a useful general survey see Michael Mulkay, *Science and the Sociology of Knowledge* (London: George Allen & Unwin, 1979).

51. Martin Rudwick, "Senses of the Natural World and Senses of God: Another Look at the Historical Relation of Science and Religion," in *The Sciences and Theology in the Twentieth Century*, ed. A. R. Peacocke (Henley & London: Oriel, 1981), 241-61. Reference on pp. 248-49.

52. W. M. Davis, "The Faith of Reverent Science," in *The History of the Study of Landforms*, vol. 2: *The Life and Work of William Morris Davis*, ed. R. J. Chorley, R. P. Beckinsale, and A. J. Dunn (London: Wiley, 1973), 759-91. The essay was originally presented as the Second Hector Maiben Lecture to the American Association for the Advancement of Science on 28 Dec. 1933.

53. Quoted in *The Times*, 4 Sept. 1969.

54. Eileen Barker, "Thus Spake the Scientist: A Comparative Account of the New Priesthood and Its Organizational Bases," *Annual Review of the Social Sciences of Religion* 3 (1979): 79-103. Reference on p. 99.

55. Young, "Naturalization of Value Systems," 101.

56. J. R. Ravetz, *Scientific Knowledge and Its Social Problems* (Harmondsworth: Penguin, 1973), 289. See also the discussion in Stewart Richards, *Philosophy and Sociology of Science: An Introduction* (Oxford: Basil Blackwell, 1983),

135-70; Steven Rose and Hilary Rose, "The Myth of the Neutrality of Science," in *The Social Impact of Modern Biology,* ed. Watson Fuller (London: Routledge & Kegan Paul, 1971), 215-24.

57. Theodore Roszak, *The Making of a Counter Culture: Reflections on the Technocratic Society and Its Youthful Opposition* (London: Faber and Faber, 1970), 269-89.

58. See the discussion in John Passmore, *Man's Responsibility for Nature* (London: Duckworth, 1974), 43-44.

59. Rowland Moss, "God, Man and Nature: Contrasting Views in Christendom," paper presented at the Countryside Perception Conference, Peak National Park Study Centre, 27-29 Feb. 1976.

60. See Donald MacKay, *Human Science and Human Dignity* (London: Hodder & Stoughton, 1979); Rowland Moss, *The Earth in Our Hands* (London: Inter-Varsity Press, 1982); Carl F. H. Henry, ed., *Horizons of Science* (New York: Harper & Row, 1978).

61. Conrad Bonifazi, "Biblical Roots of an Ecological Conscience," in *This Little Planet,* ed. Michael Hamilton (New York: Scribner's, 1970), 226.

62. H. Paul Santmire, *Brother Earth* (New York: Nelson, 1970).

63. Thomas Z. Derr, *Ecology and Human Liberation: A Theological Critique of the Use and Abuse of Our Birthright* (Geneva: World Student Christian Federation, 1973), 34.

64. Robin W. Doughty, "Environmental Theology: Trends and Prospects in Christian Thought," *Progress in Human Geography* 5 (1981): 242. I have expressed my reservations about Doughty's proposals in "Environmental Theology: Prospect in Retrospect," *Progress in Human Geography* 7 (1983): 133-40. Chief among the advocates of process theology are J. B. Cobb and D. R. Griffin, *Process Theology: An Introductory Exposition* (Philadelphia: Westminster, 1976); W. K. Cauthen, *Science, Secularization and God: Toward a Theology of the Future* (Nashville: Abingdon, 1969); L. Charles Birch, *Nature and God* (London: SCM, 1965); idem, "Nature, Humanity and God in Ecological Perspective," in *Faith and Science in an Unjust World: Report of the World Council of Churches' Conference on Faith, Science and the Future,* vol. 1: *Plenary Presentations,* ed. Roger L. Shinn (Geneva: World Council of Churches, 1980), 62-73.

65. James Barr, "Man and Nature: The Ecological Controversy and the Old Testament," in *Ecology and Religion in History,* ed. David and Eileen Spring (New York: Harper & Row, 1974), 48-75. Reference on p. 71.

66. This is the view of such scholars as Harvey Cox, Reijer Hooykaas, and John Baillie. It has been questioned by John Macquarrie, "Creation and Environment," *Expository Times* 83 (October 1971): 4-9.

67. Quoted in Barr, "Man and Nature," 59.

68. T. F. Torrance, "Divine and Contingent Order," in Peacocke, ed., *Sciences and Theology,* 81-97. Reference on p. 84.

69. Norbert Wiener, *The Human Use of Human Beings* (Garden City, N.Y.: Doubleday Anchor Books, 1954), 193. I am grateful to Dr. Francis Sitwell for drawing my attention to this reference.

70. See, e.g., Paul Davies, *God and the New Physics* (New York: Touchstone Books, 1984); Adam Ford, "Science and Religion: Towards a Deeper Reality," *The Times,* 19 Jan. 1985.

71. John Bowker, "Did God Create This Universe?" in Peacocke, ed., *Sciences and Theology*, 98-126. Reference on p. 99.

72. Thus, e.g., Richard Swinburne, *The Existence of God* (Oxford: Clarendon, 1979).

73. See David Cairns, "Thomas Chalmers's Astronomical Discourses: A Study in Natural Theology," *Scottish Journal of Theology* 9 (1956): 410-21; Daniel F. Rice, "Natural Theology and the Scottish Philosophy in the Thought of Thomas Chalmers," *Scottish Journal of Theology* 24 (1971): 23-46.

74. Roszak, *Counter Culture*, 34, 119, 233, 246.

4E. Secularization and Secularism

1. Bryan Wilson, *Religion in Secular Society: A Sociological Comment* (Harmondsworth: Penguin, 1969), 151.

2. Karl Heim, *Der Kampf gegen den Säkularismus*, in *Säkularisierung*, ed. H. H. Schrey (Darmstadt: Wiss. Buchgesellschaft, 1981), 112ff.

3. Cf. my *Säkularismus und christlicher Glaube*, Porta-Studie 8 (Marburg: SMD, 1985), 8-9.

4. Hermann Lübbe, *Säkularisierung: Geschichte eines ideenpolitischen Begriffs*, 2d ed. (Freiburg and Munich: Alber, 1975), 23ff.

5. Franz Xaver Arnold, *Der neuzeitliche Säkularismus*, in Schrey, ed., *Säkularisierung*, 140-41.

6. C. Colpe, "Averroismus," in *Die Religion in Geschichte und Gegenwart*, 3d ed., vol. 1 (Tübingen: J. C. B. Mohr, 1957), 796ff.

7. Heim, *Der Kampf gegen den Säkularismus*, 110ff. Cf. Owen Chadwick, *The Secularization of the European Mind in the Nineteenth Century* (Cambridge: Cambridge Univ. Press, 1975), 155, 217, and Emil L. Fackenheim, *God's Presence in History: Jewish Affirmations and Philosophical Reflections* (New York: Harper Torchbooks, 1982), 36-41.

8. Chadwick, *Secularization of the European Mind*, 155.

9. Karl Marx and Frederick Engels, *Collected Works*, vol. 1 (New York: International Publishers, 1975), 102, 30-31.

10. As noted by Fackenheim, *God's Presence in History*, 57, 59, and Chadwick, *Secularization of the European Mind*, 59, 171.

11. Chadwick, *Secularization of the European Mind*, 10.

12. Ibid., 69, 79.

13. David Martin, *A General Theology of Secularization* (New York: Harper Colophon Books, 1978), 272-73.

14. Wilson, *Religion in Secular Society*, 14, 256; Martin, *General Theology of Secularization*, 288.

15. Peter L. Berger, *The Sacred Canopy* (Garden City, N.Y.: Doubleday-Anchor, 1969), 107, and *The Heretical Imperative: Contemporary Possibilities of Religious Affirmation* (Garden City, N.Y.: Doubleday-Anchor, 1979), 24.

16. Lübbe, *Säkularisierung*, 95n.11.

17. Ibid., 42, 47; Berger, *Sacred Canopy*, 125.

18. Cf., e.g., Gerhard Ritter, as cited in Schrey, ed., *Säkularisierung*, 3.

19. Martin, *General Theology of Secularization*, 63, 41.

20. Cf. J. Wesley Ariarajah's postulate, in Lesslie Newbigin, *The Other Side*

of 1984: Questions for the Churches (Geneva: World Council of Churches, 1983), 75.

21. Chadwick, *Secularization of the European Mind,* 153, 210.

22. Heim, *Der Kampf gegen den Säkularismus,* 123.

23. H. Schreiner, as cited in Lübbe, *Säkularisierung,* 89.

24. Peter L. Berger, *A Rumor of Angels: Modern Society and the Rediscovery of the Supernatural* (Garden City, N.Y.: Doubleday-Anchor, 1970), 24.

25. Manes Sperber, *Die vergebliche Warnung: All das Vergangene . . .* (Vienna: Europaverlag, 1975), 207.

26. Cf. Newbigin, *Other Side of 1984,* 1.

27. Martin, *General Theory of Secularization,* 197. This pertinent observation presents us with the opportunity to respond to the view, echoed not infrequently, that sociologists were overdoing their advertisement of secularization. Secularization was not irreversible. Did not Peter Berger himself say that people were unimprovably religious, and that there would always be the need of defining one's identity, and thus a place for religion? Also, parallel to secularization there was underway a process of resacralization in the forms; e.g., of re-Islamization in certain parts of the world or, indeed, of the influx of Eastern religions into Western civilization. Therefore, the overall development need not be understood as a change from religion to no religion but from one religion to another: the coming society would only be post-Christian, not postreligious. That is exactly David Martin's point. But surely a Christian theologian cannot feel relieved and happy at this different prospect? For him or her, the one development is as bad as the other. What we can learn from these observations is merely that Christian proclamation should not blindly treat all people simply as secular moderns and, on the basis of some theory of secularization, ignore their quest for the transcendent and the proclivity to religion that will always resurface.

28. Newbigin, *Other Side of 1984,* 18.

29. Martin, *General Theory of Secularization,* 77, 83, 88, 108, 205.

30. Newbigin, *Other Side of 1984,* 11, 22.

31. Lübbe, *Säkularisierung,* 77; Chadwick, *Secularization of the European Mind,* 131.

32. Chadwick, *Secularization of the European Mind,* 28ff., 232.

33. Friedrich Nietzsche, *Werke,* vol. 2, ed. K. Schlechta (Darmstadt: Wiss. Buchgesellschaft, 1966), 960.

34. James Hitchcock, "Self, Jesus, and God: The Roots of Religious Secularization," in *Summons to Faith and Renewal: Christian Renewal in a Post-Christian World,* ed. P. Williamson and K. Perrotta (Ann Arbor: Servant Books, 1983), 29, 35.

35. Lübbe, *Säkularisierung,* 70.

36. O. H. von der Gablentz, as cited in ibid., 123-24.

37. Wilson, *Religion in Secular Society,* 254, 261ff. It is very doubtful whether the "influx of Eastern religions" will provide social bonding through "impersonal goodwill," a sense of civil vocation, and concern for the public square with which Christianity originally endowed Western civilization.

38. Martin, *General Theory of Secularization,* 164, 89; cf. 46, 90, 188.

39. Frederick Copleston, S.J., *A History of Philosophy,* vol. 6: *Modern Philosophy,* pt. 2, *Kant* (Garden City, N.Y.: Doubleday Image Books, 1964), 135.

40. Chadwick, *Secularization of the European Mind*, 243.

41. Cf. Schrey, ed., *Säkularisierung*, 130.

42. Heim, *Der Kampf gegen den Säkularismus*, 110, 112, 130. However, Heim felt in 1930 that Christians were approaching a final battle of the spirits; see p. 127.

43. Tatjana Goritschewa, *Von Gott zu reden ist gefährlich: Meine Erfahrungen im Osten und im Westen* (Freiburg: Herder, 1985).

44. Berger, *Sacred Canopy*, 167; Hitchcock, "Self, Jesus, and God," 28-29.

45. Hitchcock, "Self, Jesus, and God," 24.

46. Berger, *Rumor of Angels*, 19ff.

47. Berger, *Heretical Imperative*, 92, 102, 99, 111; cf. *Rumor of Angels*, 11.

48. Lübbe, *Säkularisierung*, 120-21; Berger on Gogarten: *Sacred Canopy*, 151, 165; cf. *Rumor of Angels*, 9ff.

49. For H. Thielicke, see his *Theologische Ethik*, vol. 2, pt. 2 (Tübingen: J. C. B. Mohr, 1958), 244, 733-34; for J. B. Metz, see Schrey, ed., *Säkularisierung*, 30, 32.

50. At this point we may perhaps comment on the exaggerated claims of some sociologists (especially among those representing the "sociology of knowledge") to trace theological developments back to certain underlying socioeconomic processes, as, e.g., Peter Berger: "One may say, with only some exaggeration, that economic data on industrial productivity or capital expansion can predict the religious crisis or credibility in a particular society more easily than the data derived from the 'history of ideas' of that society" (*Sacred Canopy*, 151). This claim covers not only general associations, as between industrialization and urbanization on the one hand, and secularization on the other, but also Berger's ability to date "with embarrassing clarity" (*Sacred Canopy*, 164; cf. *Rumor of Angels*, 11) particular theological events like Bultmann's program of demythologization and Gogarten's "new attitude to the secular world" of 1953 as consequences of the West German currency reform of 1948 and the ensuing recovery of the economy. Also, Berger regards Barth's attitude in 1934 as expressed in his pamphlet "No! Response to Emil Brunner" as "appropriate" to a sociopolitical situation where the monolithic ideology of un-Christian National Socialism prevailed.

However, Barth proclaimed his antithetical stance to culture not after 1933, when it would seem "plausible," but in 1922, during the heyday of cultural pluralism. Rudolf Bultmann wrote his essay on "New Testament and Mythology" in 1940, under the economic restrictions of the early war years. Friedrich Gogarten developed his understanding of the reformational two-kingdom doctrine as the autonomy of the secular around 1930 before he applied it, as he did, to the events of 1933. If there is one thing "embarrassingly clear," it is the *lack* of detailed coincidence between major theological advances and socioeconomic factors determining them. Indeed, those advances may, as antitheses or as continuations, perhaps yet be better understood in the context of the history of theology. Also, the study of Kant seems to remain just as important as the perception of socioeconomic milieux.

In addition, one should be hesitant to look at the general history of secularization solely in terms of a one-directional determination of the (religious) superstructure by the (socioeconomic) basis, or else one might be led to a vulgar historical materialism Karl Marx himself did not espouse. There are facts that do not fit the sociological theory; for instance, that the rural provinces of northern Germany seem to be far more "secular" in terms of low figures of church attendance than the higly industrialized and urbanized land of Württemberg in the South where pietism traditionally has a strong presence. Moreover, in the United States the nineteenth century, the century of industrialization, was certainly not at the same time the century of secularization. By the middle of the twentieth century Christianity seems to be no less accepted than a hundred years earlier. Of course some sociologists might marshal the facts in order to uphold their general findings, and denounce North American Christianity as superficial, to make it as secular as the European situation. I reject that facile solution on the basis of my own observation and comparison of both continents. There are considerable quantitative and qualitative differences. This does not, of course, exclude the possibility that those differences might disappear over time.

51. Berger, *Sacred Canopy,* 159, 167; also *Rumor of Angels,* 9.

52. Berger, *Heretical Imperative,* 59.

53. Ibid., x.

54. Hitchcock, *Self, Jesus, and God,* 28-29.

55. Ernst Jünger, *Strahlungen III* (Munich: dtv, 1966), 14, cf. 27-28.

56. Os Guinness, *The Gravedigger File: Papers on the Subversion of the Church* (Downers Grove, Ill.: InterVarsity Press, 1983), 233.

57. Martin, *General Theory of Secularization,* 34, 69.

58. Newbigin, *Other Side of 1984,* 31-32. To be sure, Newbigin introduces a note of confusion by calling for a dialogue that can lead to conversion either way.

4F. The Future

1. Peter Berger, *Facing Up to Modernity: Excursions in Society, Politics and Religion* (New York: Basic Books, 1977), 162-81.

2. Jacques Ellul has rightly argued that our secular society still thinks in terms of Christian concepts but radically changes their substance: "Post-Christian society has been deeply affected by Christianity, and bears the latter's mark: the mark of original sin, of the desire for salvation, hope, and a kingdom of God, of the conviction that a Saviour is needed, of the anxiety of those who are aware of radical guilt yet know that they cannot pardon themselves. We have not ceased to be products of the Christian era, but we have managed to reject what is specifically Christian in this product and retain only its psychic aspect. Thus, post-Christian society is a society of men who are at the point to which Christianity brought them but who no longer believe in the specific truth of the Christian revelation" (*The New Demons,* trans. C. Edward Hopkin [New York: Seabury, 1973], 24).

3. Herman Kahn proposes four groups. What he classifies as the "convinced Neo-Malthusian" and the "guarded pessimist" I have bracketed together in one group. Likewise, his "guarded optimist" and "technology-and-growth enthusiast" I have bracketed in the other group. Herman Kahn, William Brown, and Leon Martel, *The Next 200 Years: A Scenario for America and the World* (New York: Morrow, 1976), 10-16. See also Herman Kahn and B. Bruce-Briggs, *Things to Come: Thinking about the Seventies and Eighties* (New York: Macmillan, 1972).

4. Harrison Brown, *The Human Future Revisited: The World Predicament and Possible Solution* (New York: Norton, 1978), 221.

5. Danella H. Meadows, Dennis L. Meadows, Jorgen Randers, and William Behrens, *The Limits to Growth: A Report for the Club of Rome's Project on the Predicament of Mankind* (New York: Universe Books, 1972).

6. Mihajlo Mesarovic and Edvard Pestel, *Mankind at the Turning Point: The Second Report to the Club of Rome* (New York: Dulton, 1974).

7. Jan Tinbergen, *Reshaping the International Order* (New York: Dulton, 1976).

8. It is, naturally, more than technology that is eroding our humanness. The impact of modern forms of social organization, especially around large cities, has also taken its toll. And the same tendencies were long ago observed in education by C. S. Lewis in *The Abolition of Man* (London: Macmillan, 1943).

9. In America this proposition has been argued by B. F. Skinner in *Beyond Freedom and Dignity* (New York: Knopf, 1971). In his novel, *Walden Two,* Skinner has sketched the utopian community he believes could result from the kind of conditioning that proper control would bring.

10. Augustine, *City of God,* 14.28.

11. *Luther: Letters of Spiritual Counsel,* ed. Theodore Tappert, Library of Christian Classics, 26 vols. (Philadelphia: Westminster, 1953–66), 18:170.

12. John Calvin, *Institutes of the Christian Religion,* trans. Ford Battles, ed. John McNeill, Library of Christian Classics, vols. 20-21 (Philadelphia: Westminster, 1953–66), III.20.42.

13. Martin Chemnitz, *Examination of the Council of Trent,* trans. Fred Kramer (St. Louis: Concordia, 1971), 164. See also Philip Hughes, *Theology of the English Reformers* (Grand Rapids: Eerdmans, 1966), 225-31.

14. Jürgen Moltmann, *Religion, Revolution and the Future,* trans. M. Douglas Meeks (New York: Scribner, 1969), 182.

15. This is a point made generally by Ernst Käsemann, *New Testament Questions for Today* (London: Fortress, 1969), 82-107. The role eschatology and apocalyptic elements played in New Testament thought has received an increasing amount of attention in recent years. Although Oscar Cullmann has some typical neoorthodox disjunctures between faith and reason, revelation and history, the essential position for which he argues in terms of the realization of eschatology is accepted here; see his *Salvation in History,* trans. Sidney Sowers (London: SCM, 1967). This view, however was earlier adumbrated by Geerhardus Vos, *Pauline Eschatology* (Grand Rapids: Baker, 1982), and *The Kingdom and the Church* (Grand Rapids: Eerdmans, 1951), to whom I am especially indebted. See also G. R. Beasley-Murray, "A Century of Eschatological Discussion," *Expository Times* 64 (July 1953): 312-16; John Bourman, "From Schweitzer to Bultmann," *Theology Today* 11 (July 1954): 160-78; C. K. Barrett, "New Testament Eschatology," *Scottish Journal of Theology* 6 (June 1953): 136-55, and 6 (Sept. 1953): 225-43; G. E. Ladd, "Apocalyptic and the New Testament Theology," in *Reconciliation and Hope,* ed. R. Banks (Grand Rapids: Eerdmans, 1974), 285-96.

16. J. Guhrt, "aiōn," *The New International Dictionary of New Testament Theology,* 3 vols., ed. Colin Brown (Grand Rapids: Zondervan, 1979), 3:826-33. See also James Barr, *Biblical Words for Time* (Naperville, Ill.: Allenson, 1969).

17. See the development of this antithesis in Andrew Lincoln, *Paradise Now and Not Yet: Studies in the Heavenly Dimension in Paul's Thought with Special Reference to His Eschatology* (Cambridge: Cambridge Univ. Press, 1981).

18. Seyoon Kim, *The Origin of Paul's Gospel* (Grand Rapids: Eerdmans, 1981), 233-68.

19. Barrett, "New Testament Eschatology," 148.

20. See Richard Gaffin, *The Centrality of the Resurrection: A Study in Paul's Soteriology* (Grand Rapids: Eerdmans, 1978), 90-119.

21. George Eldon Ladd, *Jesus and the Kingdom: The Eschatology of Biblical Realism* (Waco, Tex.: Word, 1964), 189. In the biblical material that follows I am summarizing the evidence and the argument that I have put forth in my book *The Person of Christ: A Biblical and Historical Analysis of the Incarnation* (Westchester, Ill.: Crossway, 1984), 21-66.

22. See Vos, *The Kingdom and the Church*, 61: "The end is placed in the light of the beginning, and all intermediate developments are construed with reference to the purpose *a quo* and the terminus *ad quem*. Eschatology, in other words, even that of the most primitive kind, yields *ipso facto* a philosophy of history. . . . And every philosophy of history bears in itself the seed of a theology."

23. See, e.g., John Murray, *The Imputation of Adam's Sin* (Grand Rapids: Eerdmans, 1959).

24. See Leon Morris, *The Apostolic Preaching of the Cross* (Grand Rapids: Eerdmans, 1955).

25. This doctrine of the Spirit is carefully and incisively developed by James Packer, *Keep in Step with the Spirit* (Old Tappan, N.J.: Revell, 1984).

26. Leonard Sweet, "Theology à la Mode," *Reformed Journal* 34 (Oct. 1984): 16.

27. Hebert Roux, "Note Marginale sur le Fondement Théologique de 'Gaudium et Spes,'" in *L'Eglise dans Le Monde de ce Temps: Constitution Pastorale "Gaudium et Spes,"* 3 vols., ed. Y. M. J. Congar and M. Peuchmaurd (Paris: Les Editions du Cerf, 1967), 3:112-13.

28. *Con. Gaudium et Spes*, 2.

29. Ibid., 1.

30. Ibid., 22.

31. Congar and Peuchmaurd, *L'Eglise dans Le Monde*, 2:167.

32. M. E. P. Dournes, "Lecture de la Déclaration par un Missionaries d'Asie," in *Les Relations de l'Eglise avec les Religions non-Chrétiennes*, ed. A. M. Henry (Paris: Les Editions du Cerf, 1966), 90-93.

33. Karl Rahner, *Theological Investigation*, vol. 1: *God, Christ, Mary and Grace*, trans. Cornelius Ernst (London: Darton, Longman, and Todd, 1961), 297-368. See also David F. Wells, *The Search for Salvation* (Downers Grove, Ill.: InterVarsity Press, 1978), 142-58.

34. *Con. Gaudium et Spes*, 16.

35. James Cone, *God of the Oppressed* (New York: Seabury, 1975); idem, *A Black Theology of Liberation* (Philadelphia: Lippincott, 1970); Carl E. Braaten, *The Future of God: The Revolutionary Dynamics of Hope* (New York: Harper & Row, 1969); idem, *Christ and Counter-Christ: Apocalyptic Themes in Theology and Culture* (Philadelphia: Fortress, 1972); Carl E. Braaten and Robert E. Jenson, *The Futuristic Option* (New York: Newman, 1978).

36. See James Yerkes, "Hegel and the End of Days: Philosophy, Theology and Hope," *Thought* 56 (Sept. 1981): 352-66.

37. See F. Kerr, "Eschatology as Politics," *New Blackfriar* 49 (April 1968): 343-51; David Tracy, "Horizon Analysis and Eschatology," *Continuum* 6 (Summer 1968): 166-79.

38. Norman Pittenger, *"The Last Things" in a Process Perspective* (London: Epworth, 1970). A valuable and incisive analysis of process thought as a whole is provided by Royce Gruenler, *The Inexhaustible God: Biblical Faith and the Challenge of Process Theism* (Grand Rapids: Baker, 1983).

39. See, e.g., the parallels that emerge in the discussion of apocalyptic in H. H. Rowley, *Jewish Apocalyptic and the Dead Sea Scrolls* (London: University Press, 1957). Rowley makes certain critical assumptions about the nature of Scripture, so a useful counterweight at this point is Leon Morris, *Apocalyptic* (Grand Rapids: Eerdmans, 1972). Substantial work has been done in recent years on the role that apocalyptic and millennial ideas have played in American religious history and, even more broadly, in the shaping of the American soul. For an excellent survey, see Leonard Sweet, "Millennialism in America: Recent Studies," *Theological Studies* 40 (Sept. 1979): 510-31. Note also Sacvan Bercovitch, *The American Jeremiah* (Madison: Univ. of Wisconsin Press, 1978); James West Davidson, *The Logic of Millennial Thought: Eighteenth Century New England* (New Haven: Yale Univ. Press, 1977); James C. Whorton, *Crusades for Fitness: The History of American Health Reformers* (Princeton, N.J.: Princeton Univ. Press, 1982); Jack A. Maddex, "Proslavery Millennialism: Social Eschatology in Antebellum Southern Calvinism," *American Quarterly* 31 (Spring 1979): 46-62; Nathan Hatch, *The Sacred Cause of Liberty: Republican Thought and the Millennium in Revolutionary New England* (New Haven: Yale Univ. Press, 1977). These works and their significance are discussed in Leonard Sweet, "The Evangelical Tradition in America," *The Evangelical Tradition in America,* ed. Leonard Sweet (Macon, Ga.: Mercer Univ. Press, 1984), 22-25.

40. See the fine essay by Carl Raschke, "Human Potential Movement," *Theology Today* 33 (Oct. 1976): 253-62. See also James Wiggins, "Eschatological Consciousness: Response to Temporality," *Journal of American Academy of Religion* 43 (March 1975): 27-38; John T. Watts, "Robert N. Bellah's Theory of Eschatology Hope," *Journal of Church and State* 22 (Winter 1980): 5-22; Hugh A. Koops, "Secular Eschatology," *Reformed World* 35 (Summer 1978): 119-25; Thomas Loren, "Death and Dying (Modern Thanatology Movement)," *Update* 7 (June 1983): 48-57; Barbara Hargrove, "New Religious Movements and the End of the Age," *Iliff Review* 30 (Spring 1982): 41-52; Richard D. Kahoe and Rebecca Dunn, "Fear of Death and Religious Attitudes and Behavior," *Journal for the Scientific Study of Religion* 14 (Dec. 1975): 379-82.

41. Helmut Thielicke, *Theological Ethics,* 2 vols., ed. William Lazareth (Philadelphia: Fortress, 1966–69), 1:43.

42. Karl Barth, *The Word of God and the Word of Man,* trans. Douglas Horton (Boston: Pilgrim, 1928), 157-58.

43. To say that the *telos* of life is not within the earthly process but above it could be misunderstood. Both premillennialists and postmillennialists argue that there is a goal to history that will be realized within space and time. Both positions are genuinely seeking the meaning of biblical faith and I am here criticiz-

ing neither position. The point being made, with which evangelical premillennialists and postmillennialists should agree, is that the city of God in its genesis, its nature, and its life, is fundamentally different from the city of man in its genesis, nature, and life, however the former may overlap with and affect the latter.

44. According to the New Testament, Jesus has been elevated above every name and given authority over all realms of existence, even over the "rulers," the "authorities," and the "powers of this dark world" (Eph. 6:12; cf. 1:21; 2:2; 3:10; 4:27; 6:11, 16). The traditional exegesis has concluded that these powers are spiritual and demonic. Markus Barth, however, has proposed that they refer just to institutions. He has in mind the state (Rom. 13:1-5), Jewish religious rulers, or ecclesiastical authorities (1 Cor. 2:8). These terms also refer to death and life (Rom. 8:38; 1 Cor. 15:24-7), to ritual law and religious principles (Gal. 3:23; 4:3, 8; cf. Col. 2:8), and to certain social positions (Eph. 6:5-9; 1:21). "We conclude," he says, "that by principalities and powers, Paul means the world of axioms and principles of politics and religion, of economics and society, of morals and biology, of history and culture" (*The Broken Wall: A Study of the Epistle to the Ephesians* [Philadelphia: Judson, 1959], 90). Hendrikus Berkhof, in his *Christ and the Powers,* trans. John H. Yoder (Scottdale, Pa.: Mennonite Publishing House, 1962), argues similarly for a cultural and political interpretation. This, in turn, has stimulated sharp critiques of present power structures by William Stringfellow, *An Ethic for Christians and Other Aliens in a Stange Land* (Waco, Tex.: Word, 1973), and John Howard Yoder, *The Politics of Jesus* (Grand Rapids: Eerdmans, 1972), from a traditionally Anabaptist perspective. The modern distaste for the so-called mythological world of organized evil is not, however, a distaste shared by the New Testament in general, and if this is the motive for attempting to reconstruct Paul's language it is less than commendable. On the other hand, it is equally doubtful that the New Testament advocates opposition to institutions and political structures per se. The state exists to establish justice, and its existence in this capacity is an expression of God's will (Rom. 13:1-7; cf. 1 Pet. 2:13-14). To Caesar we are obliged to render an appropriate due. To oppose the state in its proper function is, in fact, to set oneself against God's will. Thus it is appropriate to pay taxes (Rom. 13:6-7) and pray for those in power (1 Tim. 2:2), and even to use our citizenship as a safeguard to our circumstances (Acts 22:28). It is true that the state can itself extend the interests of evil, rather than oppose them, in which case a Christian's compliance with the state must cease (cf. Acts 4:5-7; 5:21, 19). Nevertheless, the objective in this is to oppose the evil and not the structure per se.

Index

Aldwinckle, Russell, 165
Alter, Robert, 147
Althaus, Paul, 58
Anabaptism, 16, 179, 278-79
Anderson, J. N. D., 160, 163, 319
Anglican theology, 16
anomie, 272-76
Apostles' Creed, 5, 96
Appold, Mark, 60
Aquinas, Thomas, 33, 183, 322; on human nature, 76, 79; on natural theology, 32, 41, 184; on work, 201, 214
Arendt, Hannah, 216
Aristotle, 32-33, 200-201
Arnold, Eberhard, 321
Arnold, F. X., 265
Augustine, 66, 201, 205; on the trinity, 47, 51, 96, 308; on the two kingdoms, 188, 268, 289

Baillie, John, 313
Barclay, William, 166
Barker, Eileen, 254
Barmen Declaration, 38
Barr, James, 258-59, 315
Barrett, C. K., 61, 293, 311
Barth, Karl, 7, 37, 43, 55, 56, 60, 64, 72, 73, 159, 281-82, 300, 337; on Christ as revelation, 38-39; on culture, 177-78, 180-81, 182-84, 187, 190, 193, 194, 321, 322, 325; on the trinity, 48, 312
Barth, Markus, 342
Beasley-Murray, G. R., 166
Belgic Confession, 79

Berdyaev, Nicholas, 186
Berger, Peter, 271, 278-81, 285, 336, 337-38
Berkhof, Hendrikus, 51, 307, 308, 342
Berkhof, Louis, 40, 42, 43-44, 308
Berkouwer, G. C., 57
Berlin Congress on World Evangelization, 14
Bible: as authority for evangelicals, 5, 17, 18, 28, 31-32, 100-101, 142; diversity within, 143-45; evangelical views concerning, 101-4; and human nature, 78-83; illumination of, 104-11; interpretation of, 107-11, 139-51; and tradition, 150-51
Bible passages discussed or cited at length: Gen. 1:26-28, 51-56, 75, 206-7; Exod. 35:30-32, 208; Deut. 15:12-15, 230; Job 28:12-28, 23-26; Ps. 8, 130; Ps. 135:15-18, 213; Isa. 2:15-21, 212; Isa. 65:21-22, 209; Jer. 22:15-16, 225-26; Matt. 6:25-30, 212; Matt. 11:25-30, 89-92; John (and the social image of the trinity), 59-63; John 1:1-18, 97-100; John 3:1-21, 135-36; Acts, 111-12, 153-55, 158-60; Phil. 2:3-7, 66; Rev. 4:1-11, 171-75
Biéler, André, 202
Bonhoeffer, Dietrich, 186
Bonifazi, Conrad, 258
Boros, Ladislaus, 165
Bowker, John, 260
Braaten, Carl, 162
Bromiley, Geoffrey, 307

343